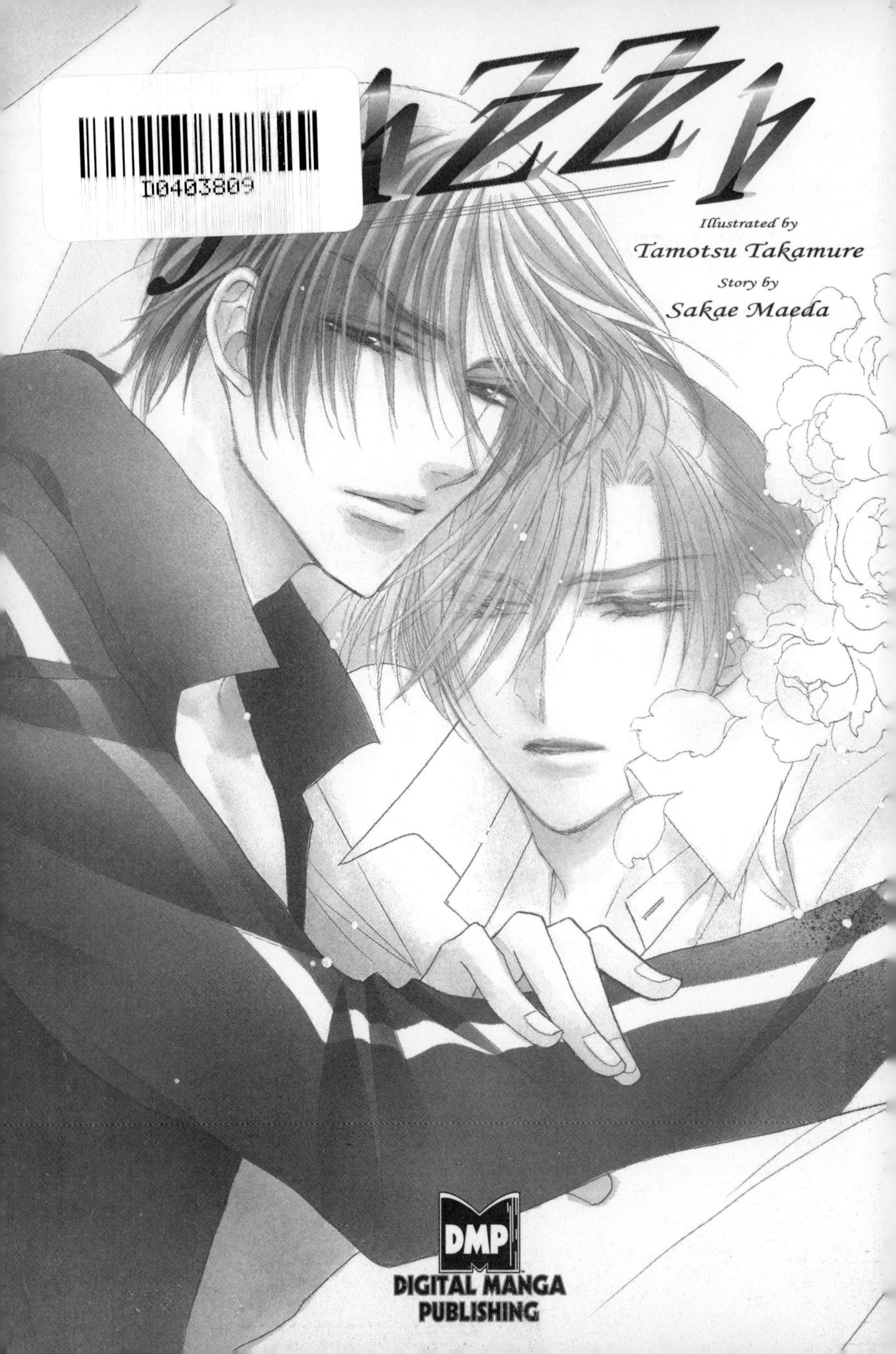
Illustrated by
Tamotsu Takamure
Story by
Sakae Maeda
DMP
DIGITAL MANGA
PUBLISHING

Translation	G. Genki
Lettering	Studio Cutie
Graphic Design	Eric Rosenberger
Editing	Stephanie Donnelly
Editor in Chief	Fred Lui
Publisher	Hikaru Sasahara

English Edition Published by
DIGITAL MANGA PUBLISHING
A division of DIGITAL MANGA, Inc.
1487 W 178th Street, Suite 300
Gardena, CA 90248

www.dmpbooks.com

First Edition: October 2005
ISBN: 1-56970-935-1

1 3 5 7 9 10 8 6 4 2

Printed in Canada

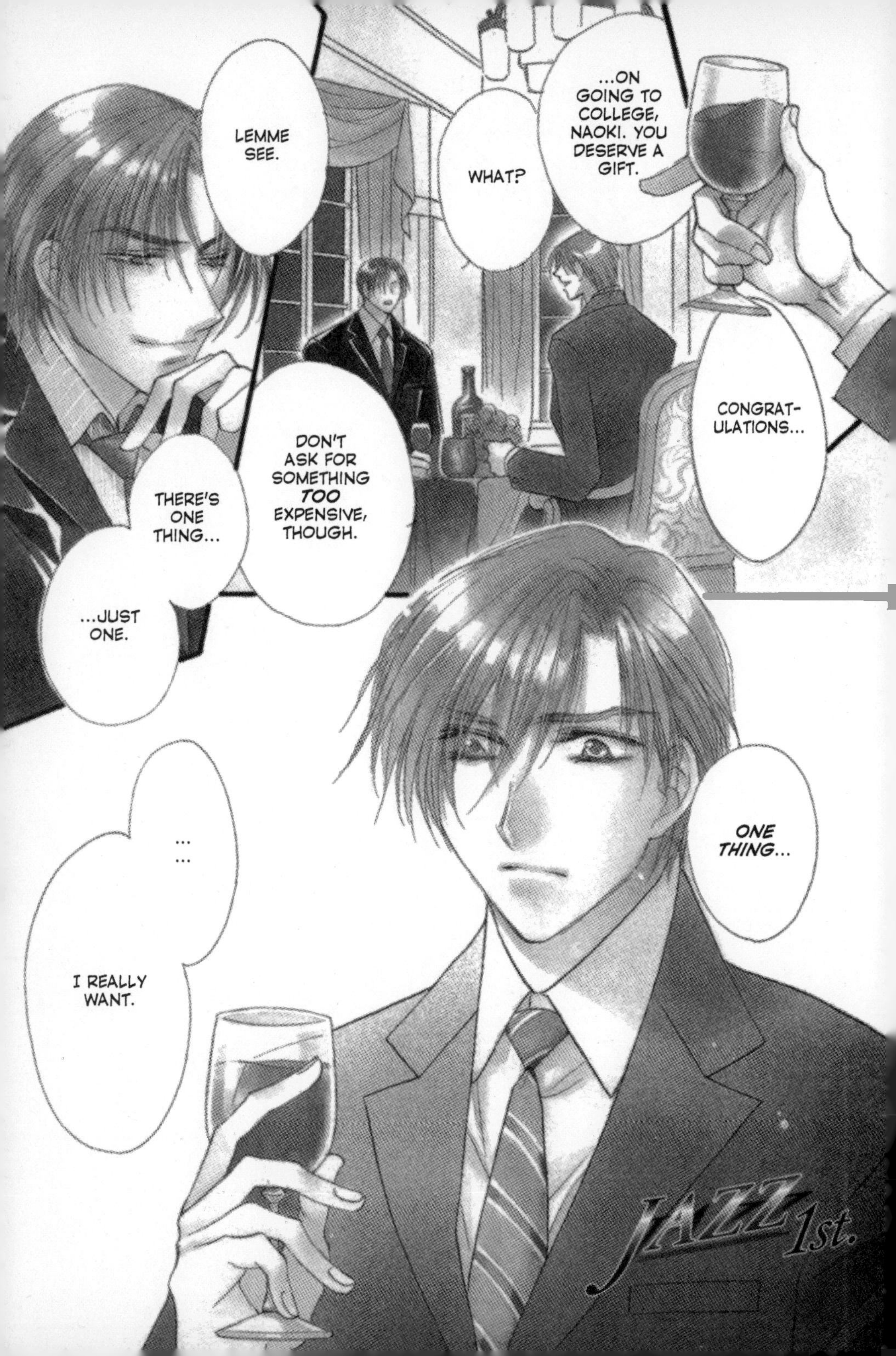
CONGRAT-ULATIONS...
...ON GOING TO COLLEGE, NAOKI. YOU DESERVE A GIFT.
WHAT?
DON'T ASK FOR SOMETHING *TOO* EXPENSIVE, THOUGH.
LEMME SEE.
THERE'S ONE THING...
...JUST ONE.
ONE THING...
... ...
I REALLY WANT.
JAZZ 1st.

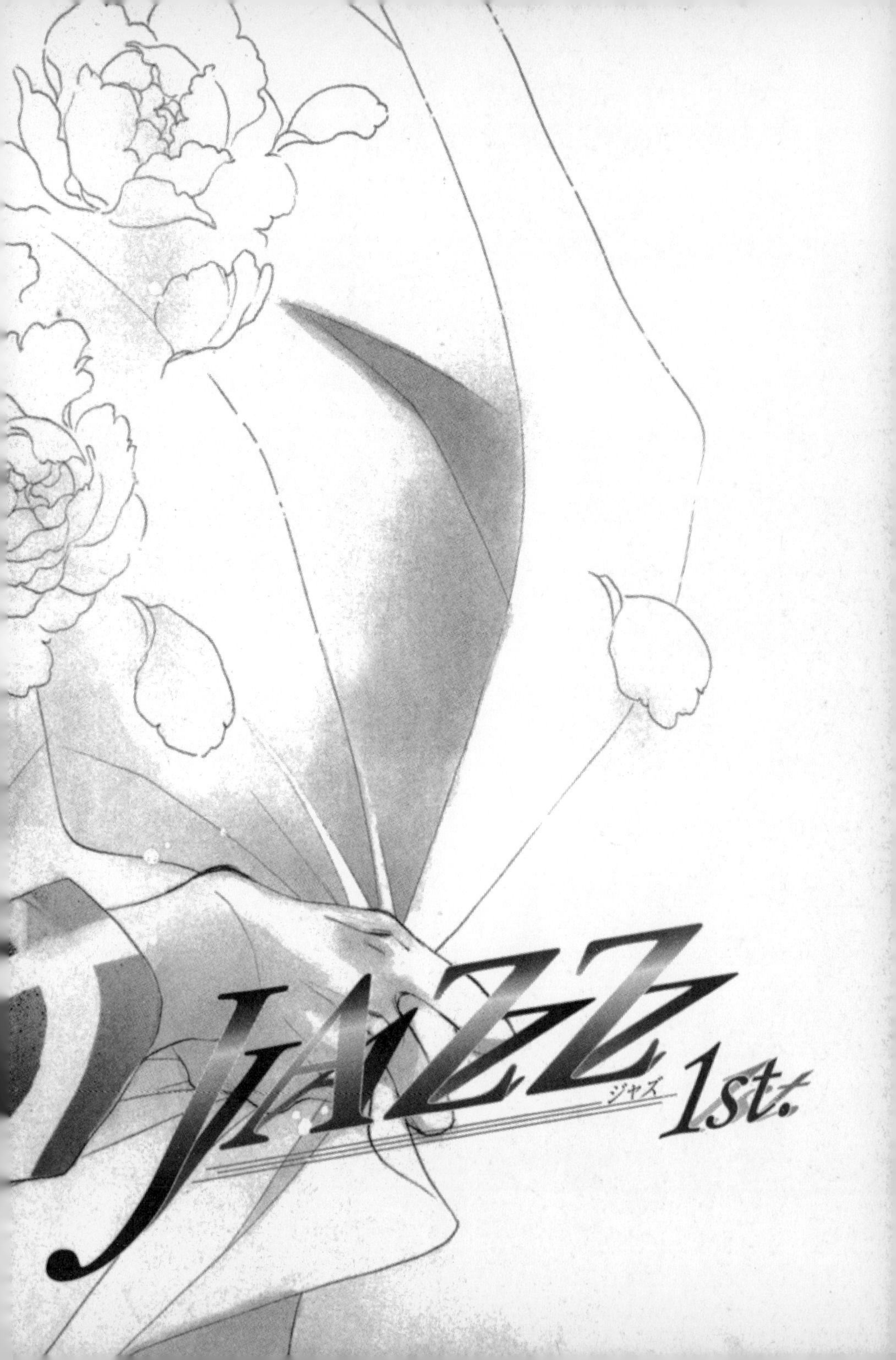
JAZZ
ジャズ
1st.

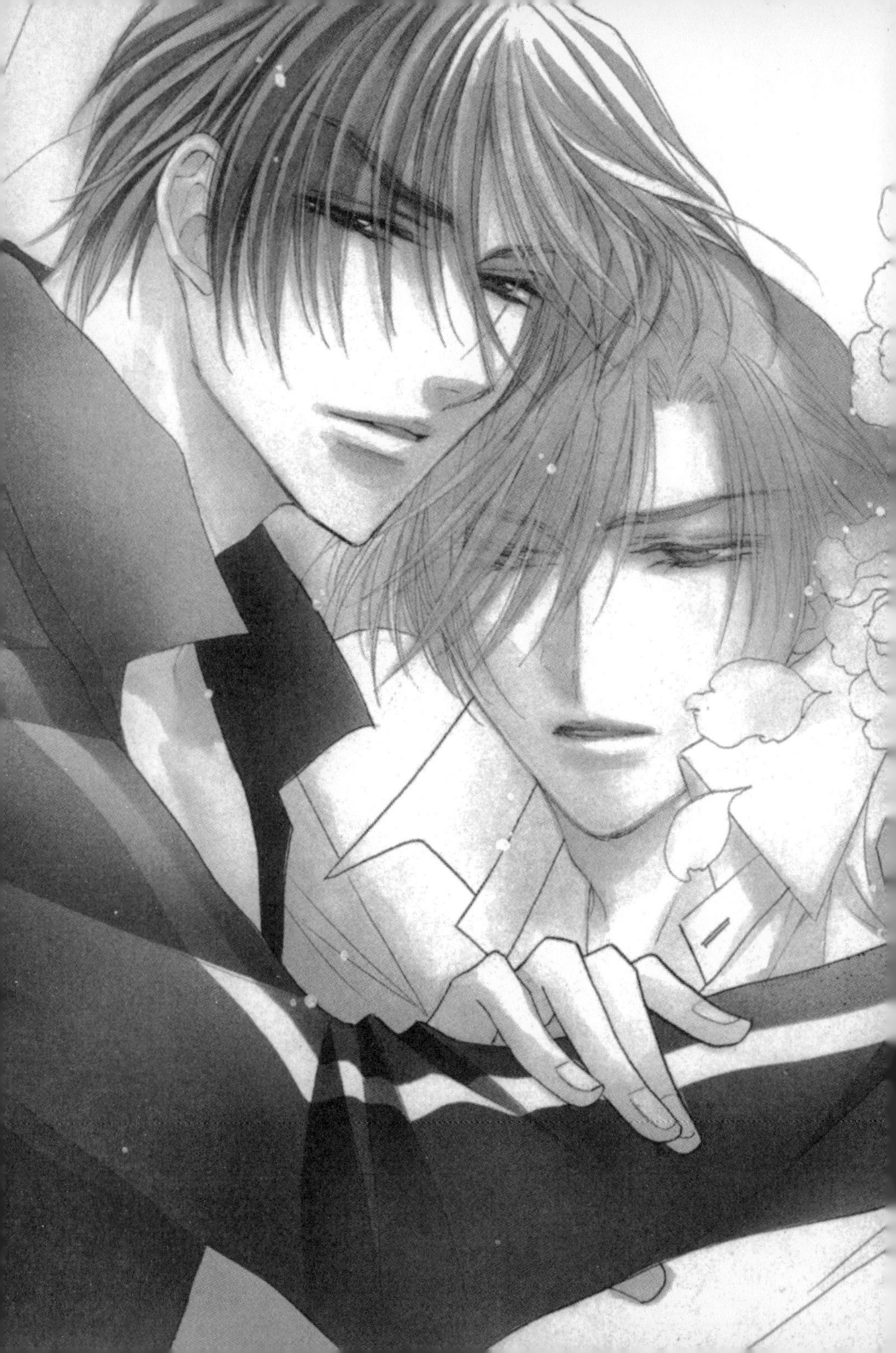

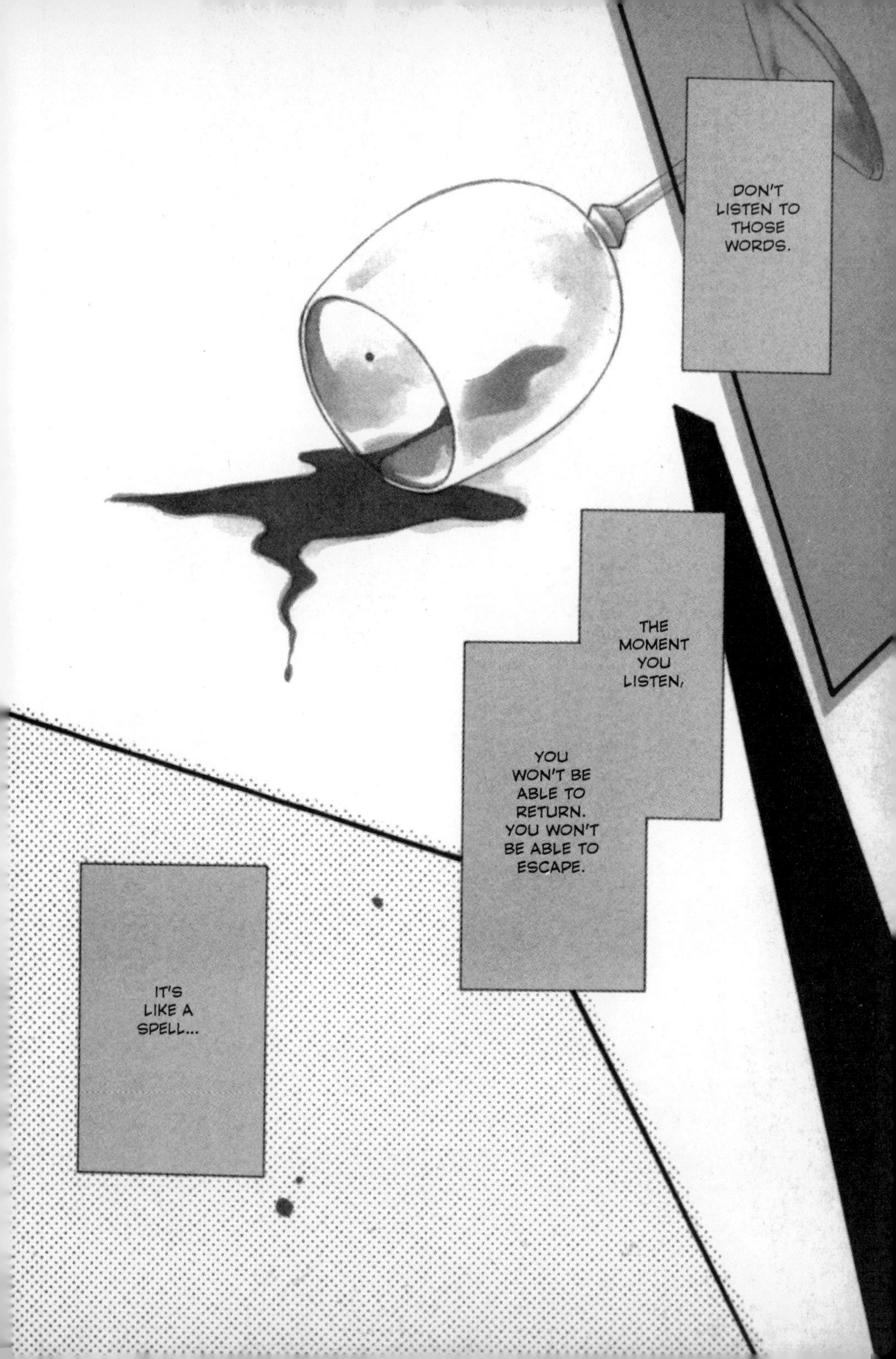
DON'T LISTEN TO THOSE WORDS.
THE MOMENT YOU LISTEN,
YOU WON'T BE ABLE TO RETURN. YOU WON'T BE ABLE TO ESCAPE.
IT'S LIKE A SPELL...

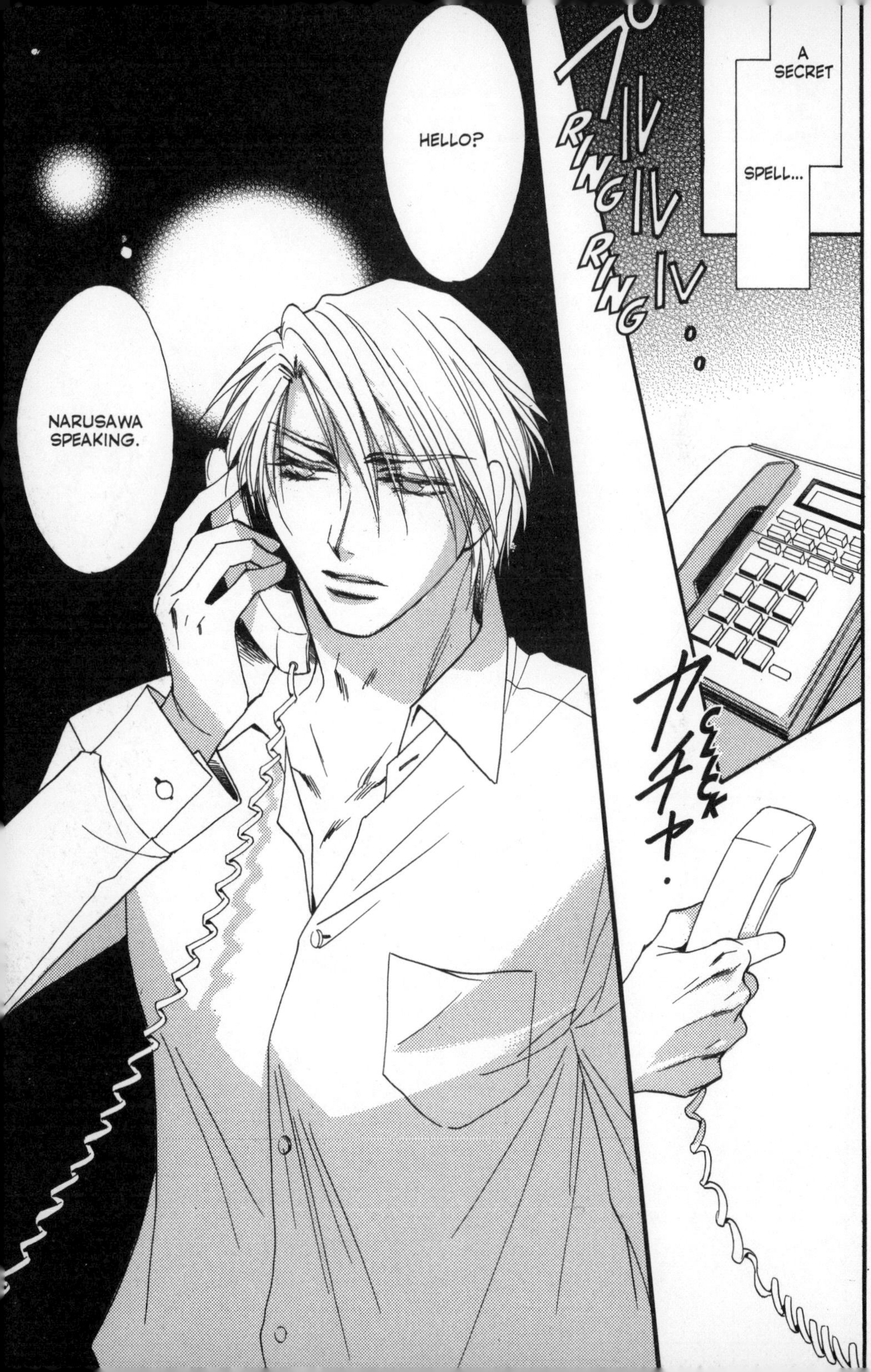
A SECRET SPELL...
RING RING
CLICK
カチャ
HELLO?
NARUSAWA SPEAKING.

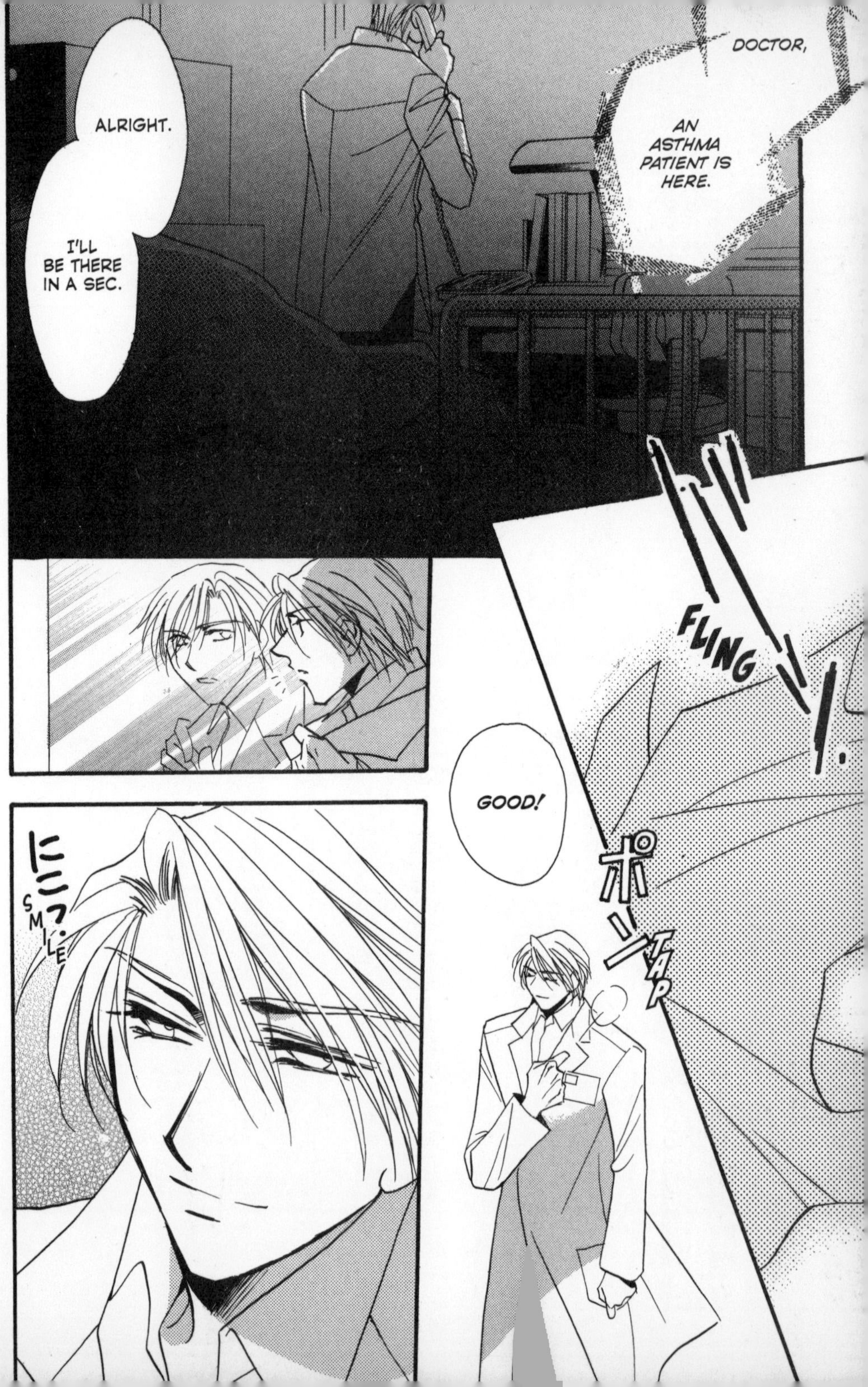
DOCTOR,
AN ASTHMA PATIENT IS HERE.
ALRIGHT.
I'LL BE THERE IN A SEC.
FLING
GOOD!
ポーン
TAP
にこっ
SMILE

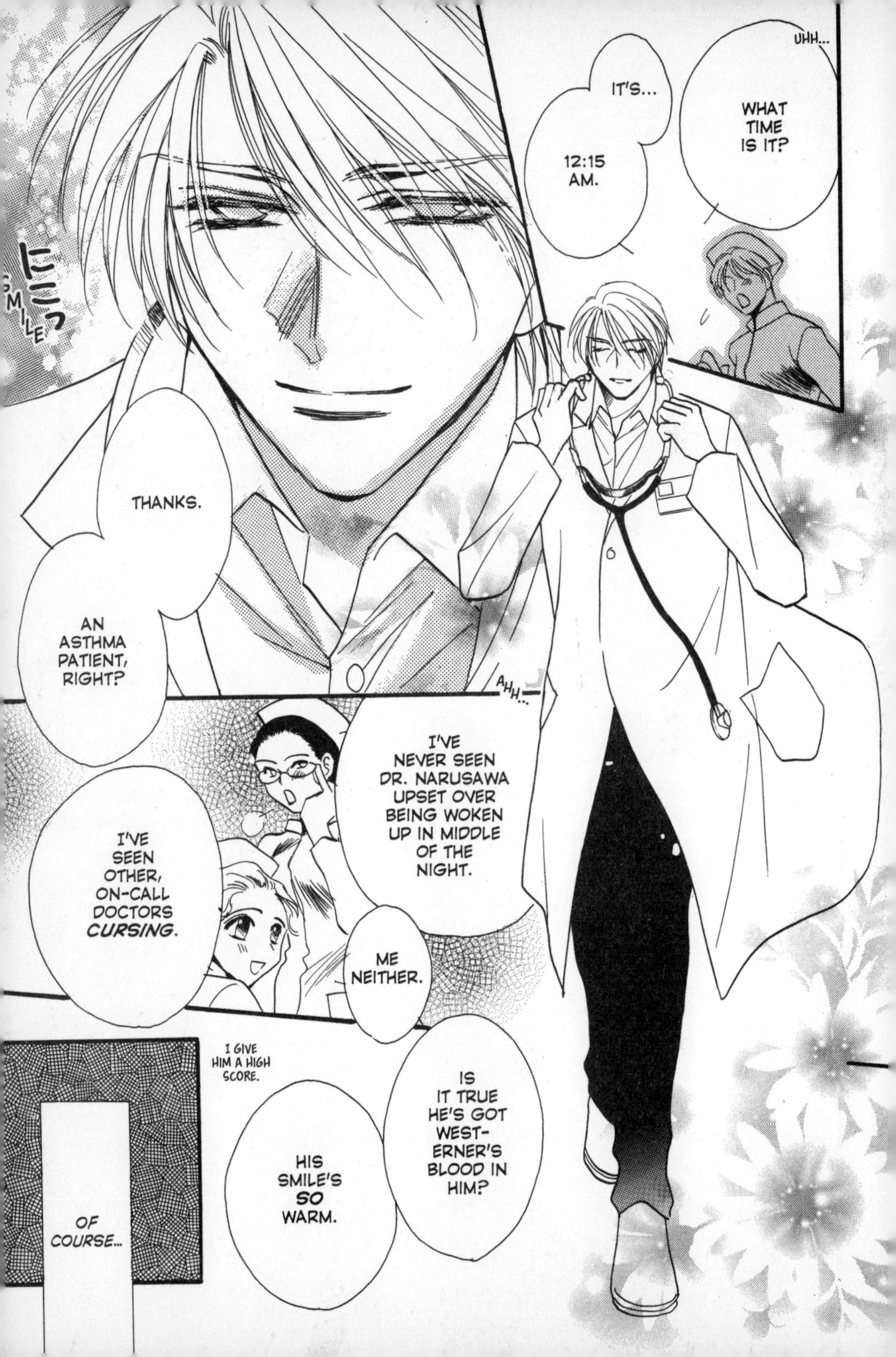
UHH...
WHAT TIME IS IT?
IT'S...
12:15 AM.
SMILE
THANKS.
AN ASTHMA PATIENT, RIGHT?
AHH...
I'VE NEVER SEEN DR. NARUSAWA UPSET OVER BEING WOKEN UP IN MIDDLE OF THE NIGHT.
I'VE SEEN OTHER, ON-CALL DOCTORS *CURSING*.
ME NEITHER.
IS IT TRUE HE'S GOT WEST-ERNER'S BLOOD IN HIM?
HIS SMILE'S **SO** WARM.
I GIVE HIM A HIGH SCORE.
OF COURSE...

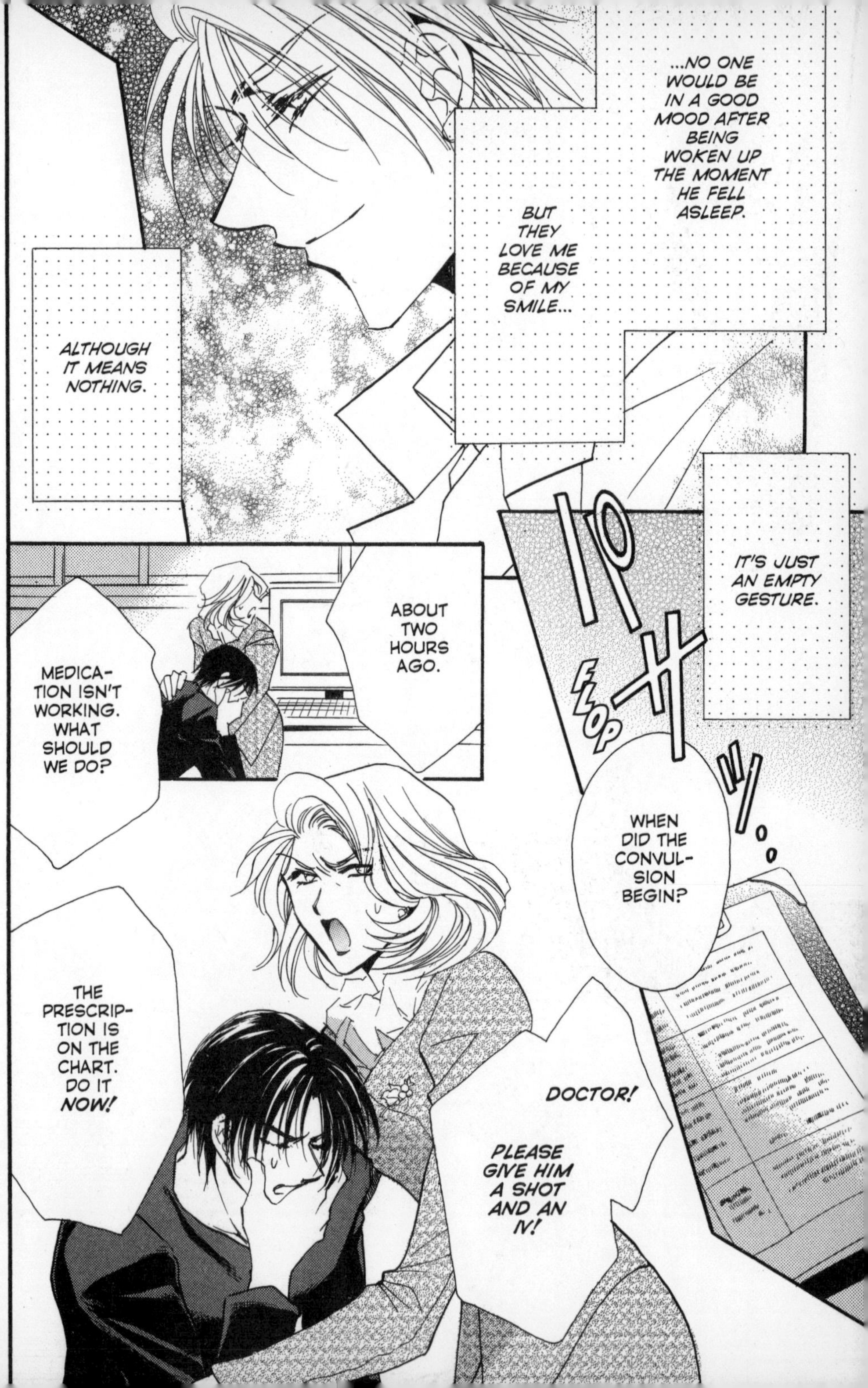
...NO ONE WOULD BE IN A GOOD MOOD AFTER BEING WOKEN UP THE MOMENT HE FELL ASLEEP.
BUT THEY LOVE ME BECAUSE OF MY SMILE...
ALTHOUGH IT MEANS NOTHING.
IT'S JUST AN EMPTY GESTURE.
FLOP
WHEN DID THE CONVUL-SION BEGIN?
ABOUT TWO HOURS AGO.
MEDICA-TION ISN'T WORKING. WHAT SHOULD WE DO?
DOCTOR!
PLEASE GIVE HIM A SHOT AND AN IV!
THE PRESCRIP-TION IS ON THE CHART. DO IT NOW!

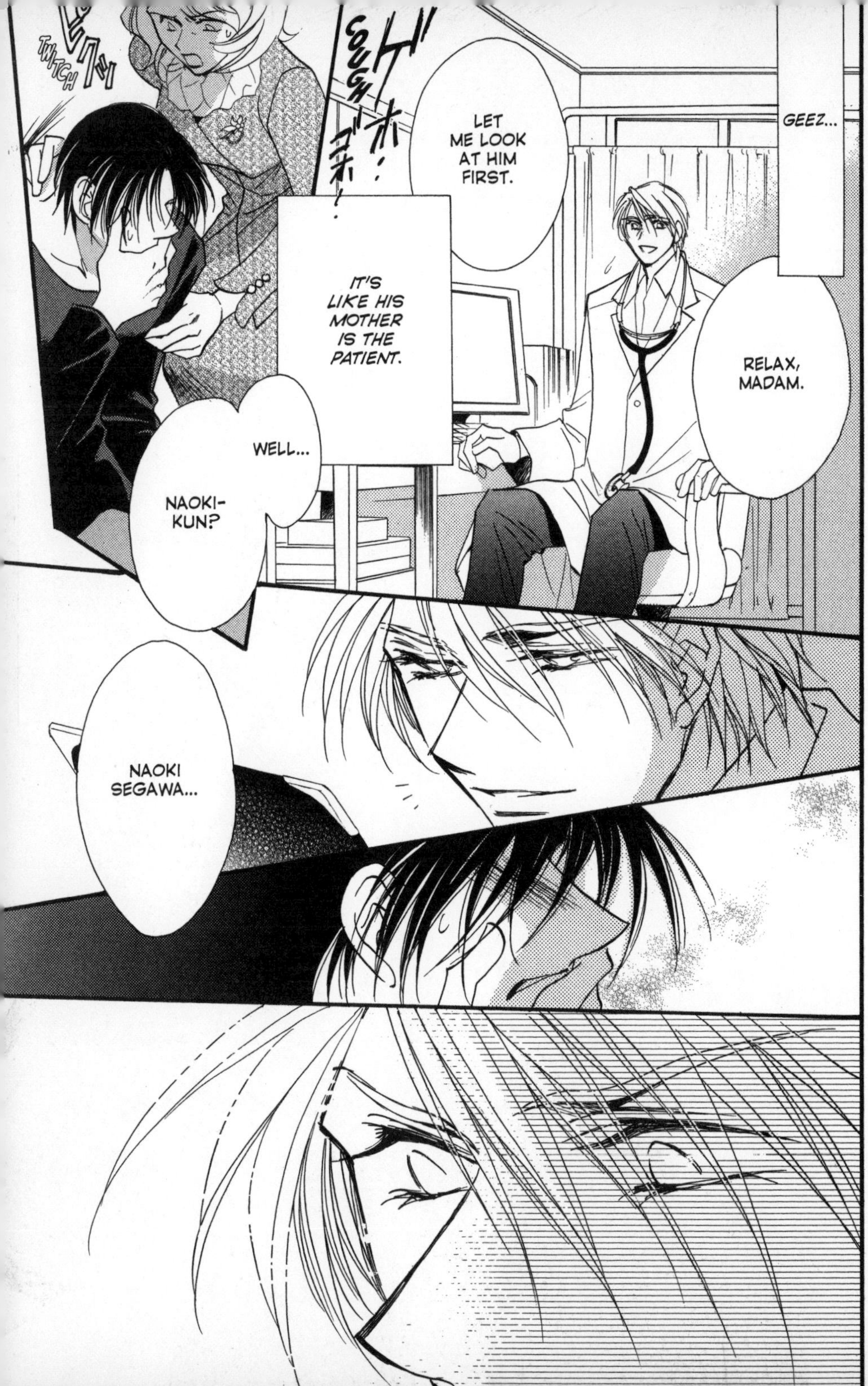
GEEZ...
LET ME LOOK AT HIM FIRST.
COUGH
TWITCH
RELAX, MADAM.
IT'S LIKE HIS MOTHER IS THE PATIENT.
WELL...
NAOKI-KUN?
NAOKI SEGAWA...

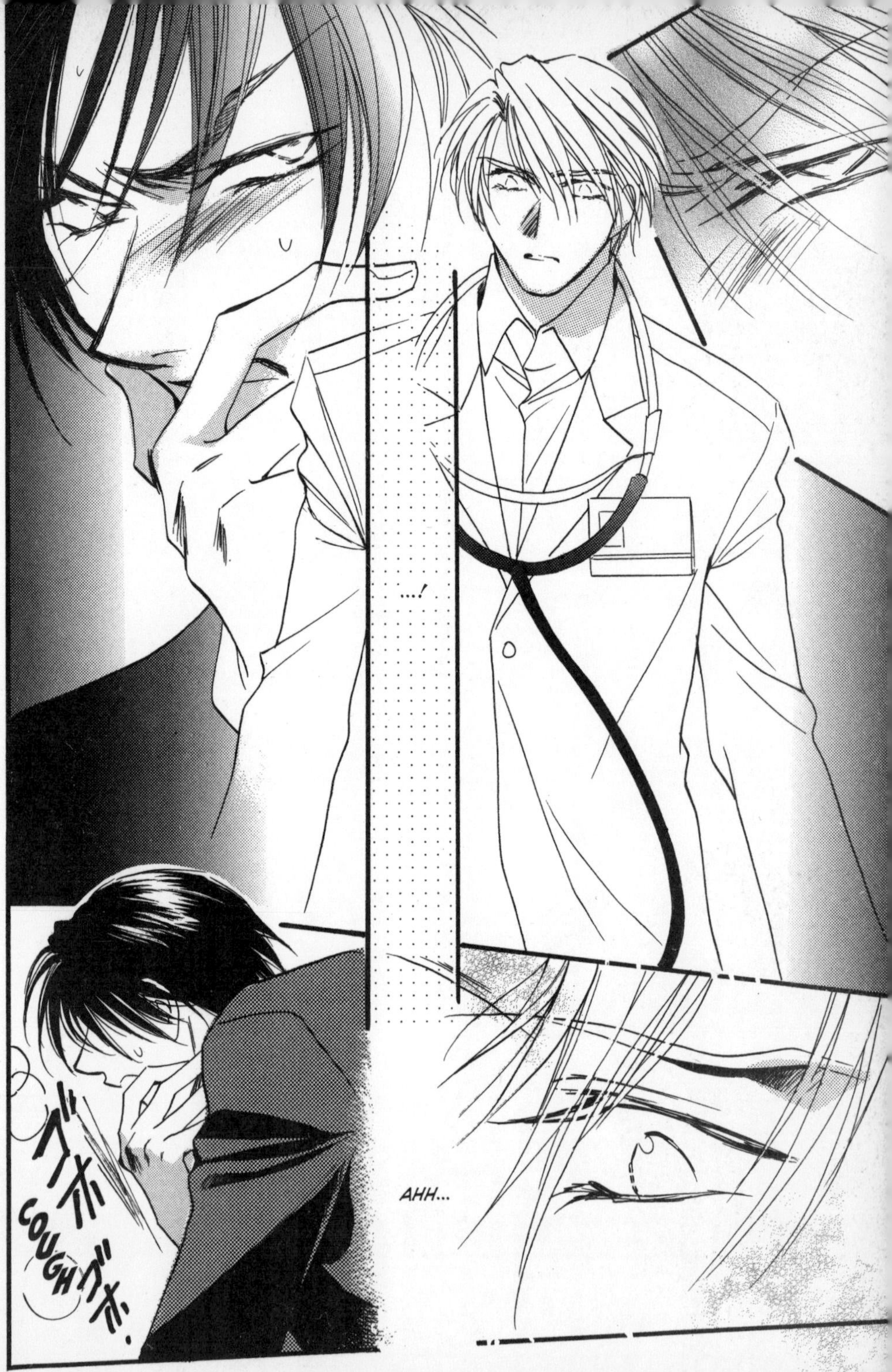
...!
AHH...
ゲホゲホ.
COUGH

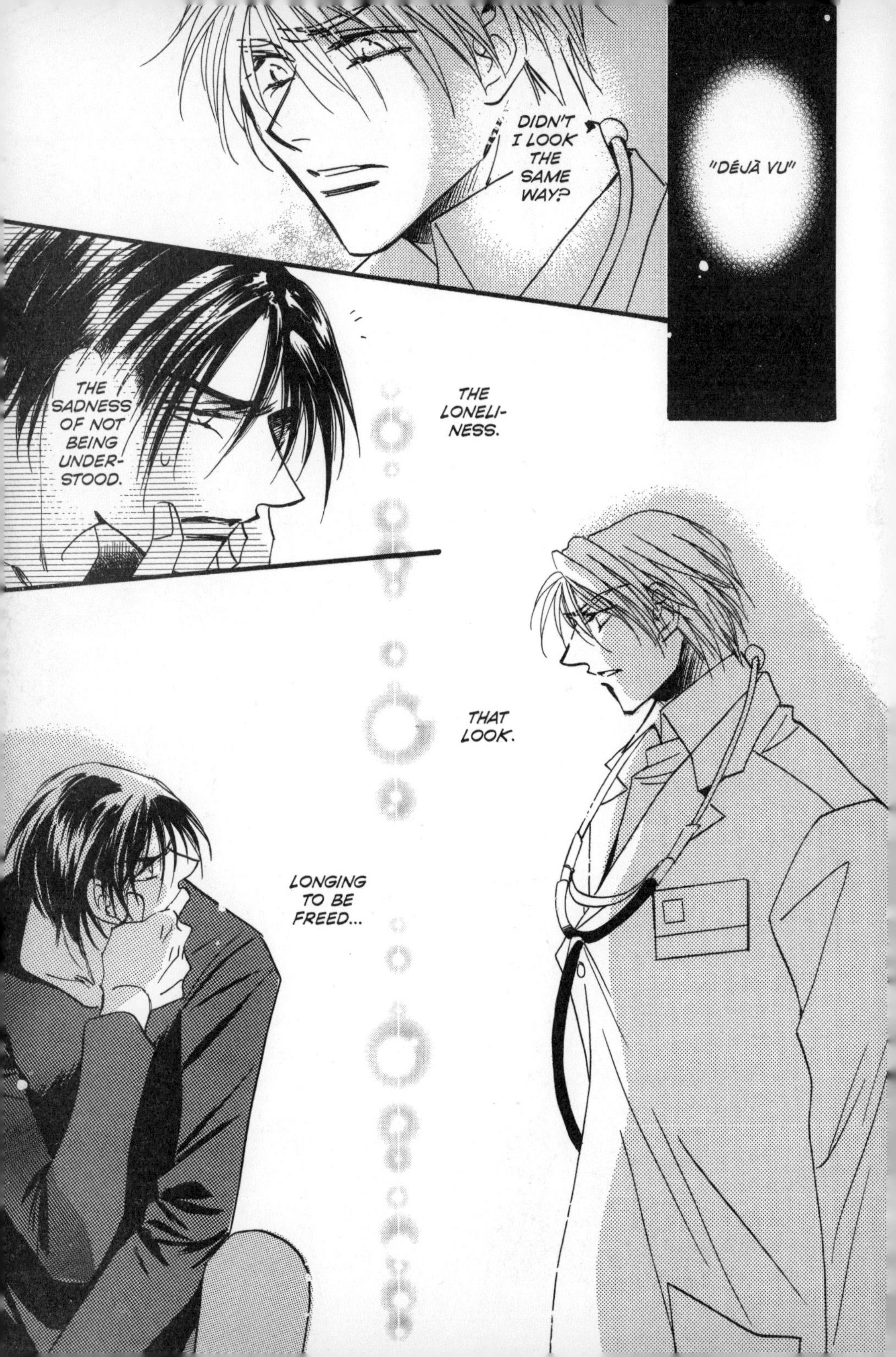
"DÉJÀ VU"
DIDN'T I LOOK THE SAME WAY?
THE LONELI-NESS.
THE SADNESS OF NOT BEING UNDER-STOOD.
THAT LOOK.
LONGING TO BE FREED...

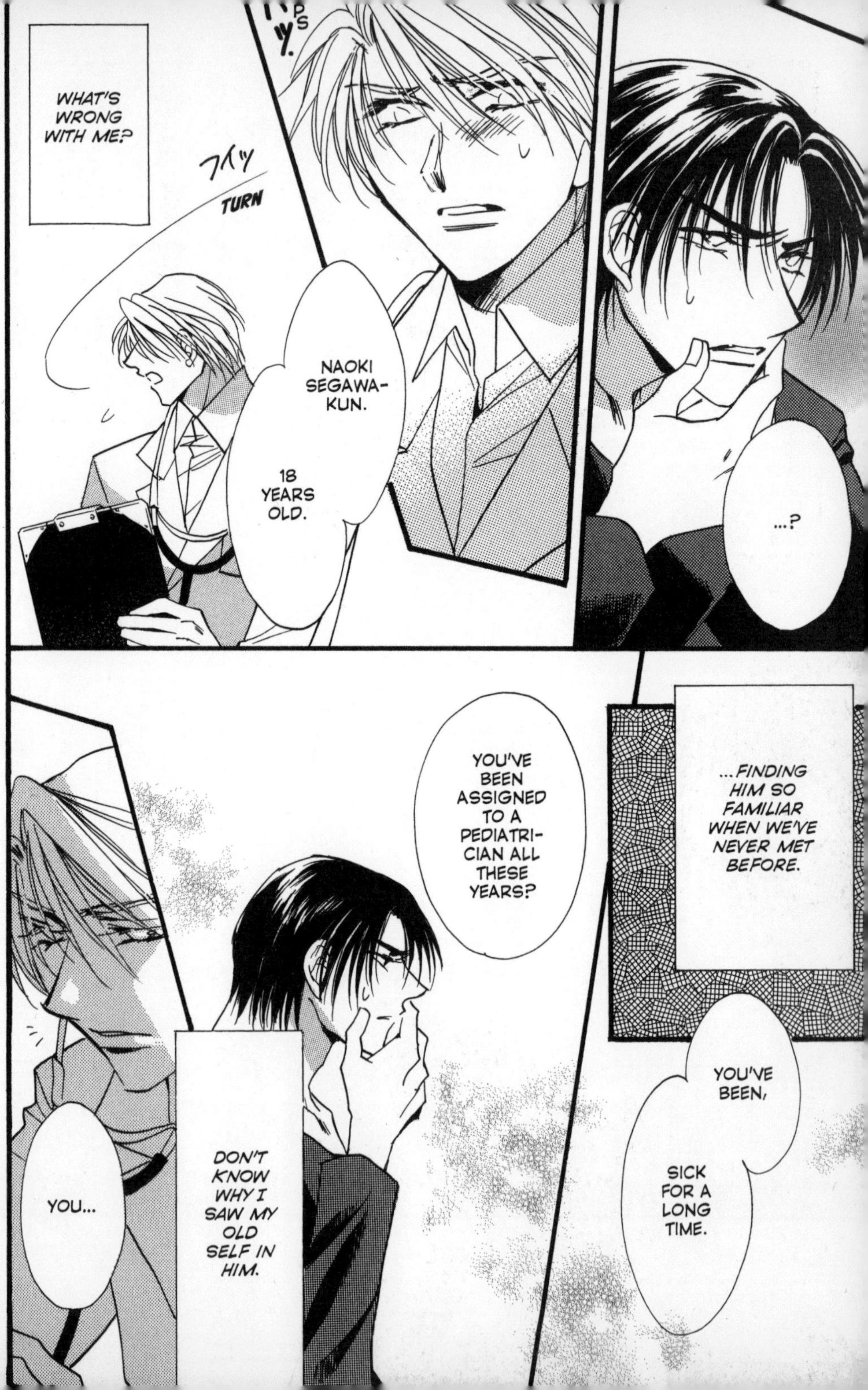
...?
ハッ
WHAT'S WRONG WITH ME?
フイッ
TURN
NAOKI SEGAWA-KUN.
18 YEARS OLD.
...FINDING HIM SO FAMILIAR WHEN WE'VE NEVER MET BEFORE.
YOU'VE BEEN,
SICK FOR A LONG TIME.
YOU'VE BEEN ASSIGNED TO A PEDIATRICIAN ALL THESE YEARS?
DON'T KNOW WHY I SAW MY OLD SELF IN HIM.
YOU...

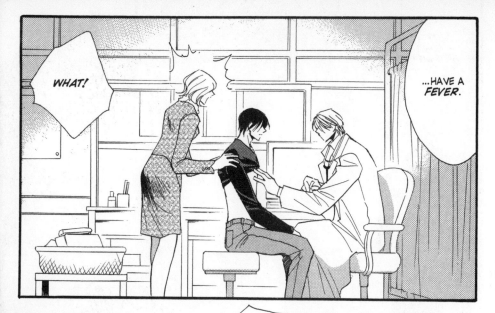

WHAT!

...HAVE A FEVER.

WHY DIDN'T YOU COME HOME EARLY?

YOU *KNOW* YOU'RE NOT STRONG...

FEVER?!

NAOKI!

SINCE *WHEN?!*

DON'T I ALWAYS REMIND YOU?!

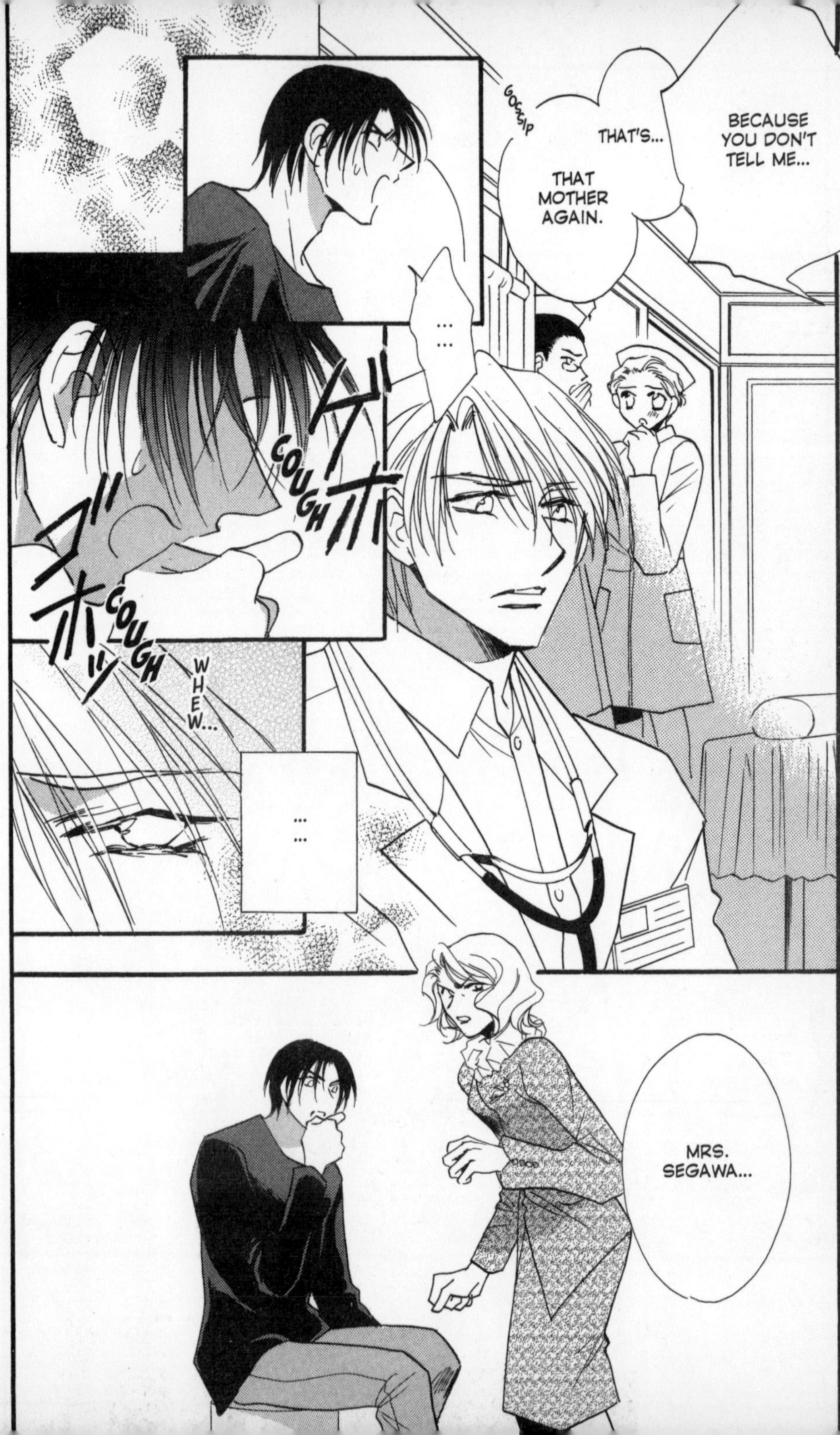
BECAUSE YOU DON'T TELL ME...
THAT'S...
GOSSIP
THAT MOTHER AGAIN.
......
ゲホ
COUGH
ゴホッ
COUGH
WHEW...
......
MRS. SEGAWA...

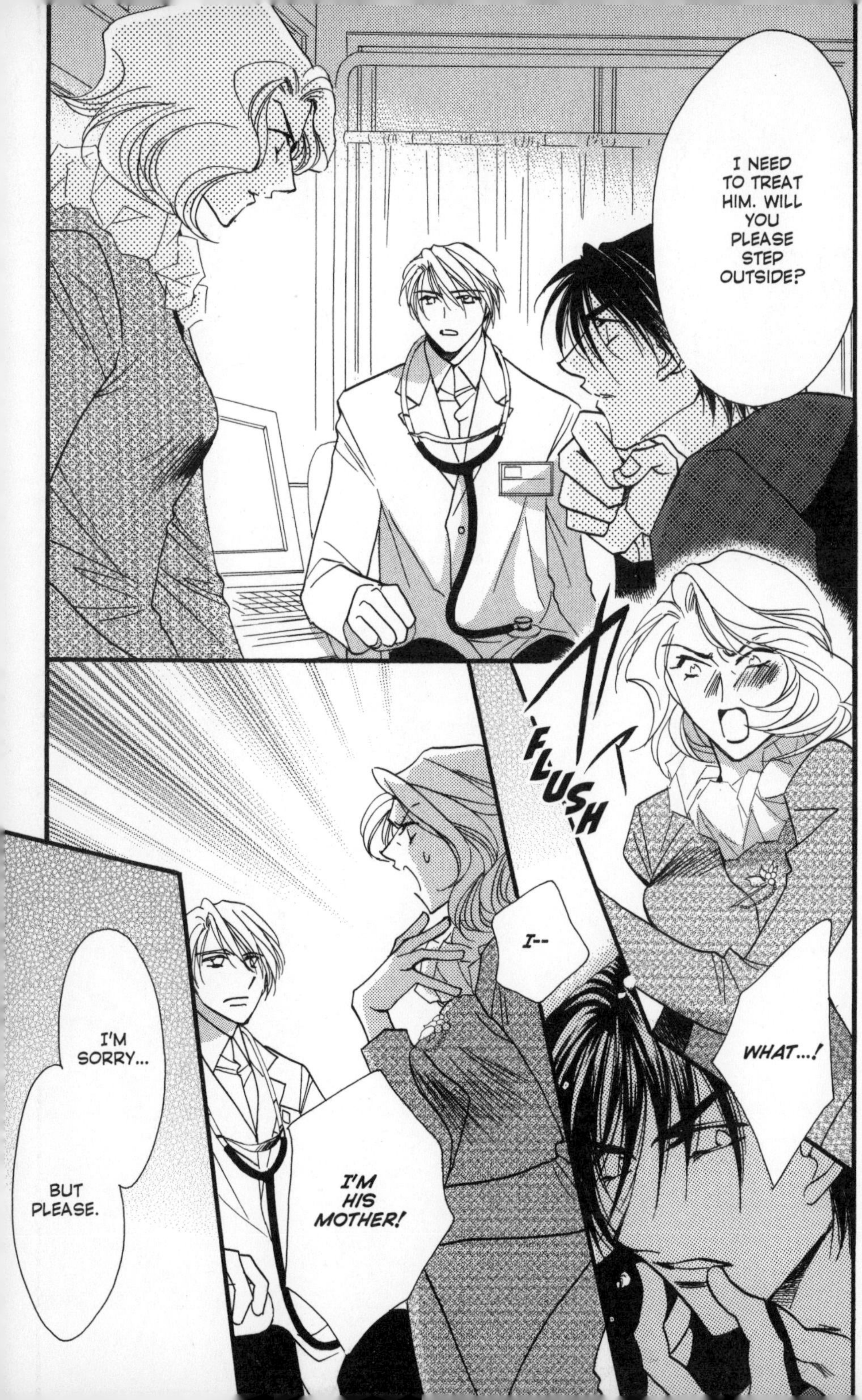
I NEED TO TREAT HIM. WILL YOU PLEASE STEP OUTSIDE?
FLUSH
WHAT...!
I--
I'M HIS MOTHER!
I'M SORRY...
BUT PLEASE.

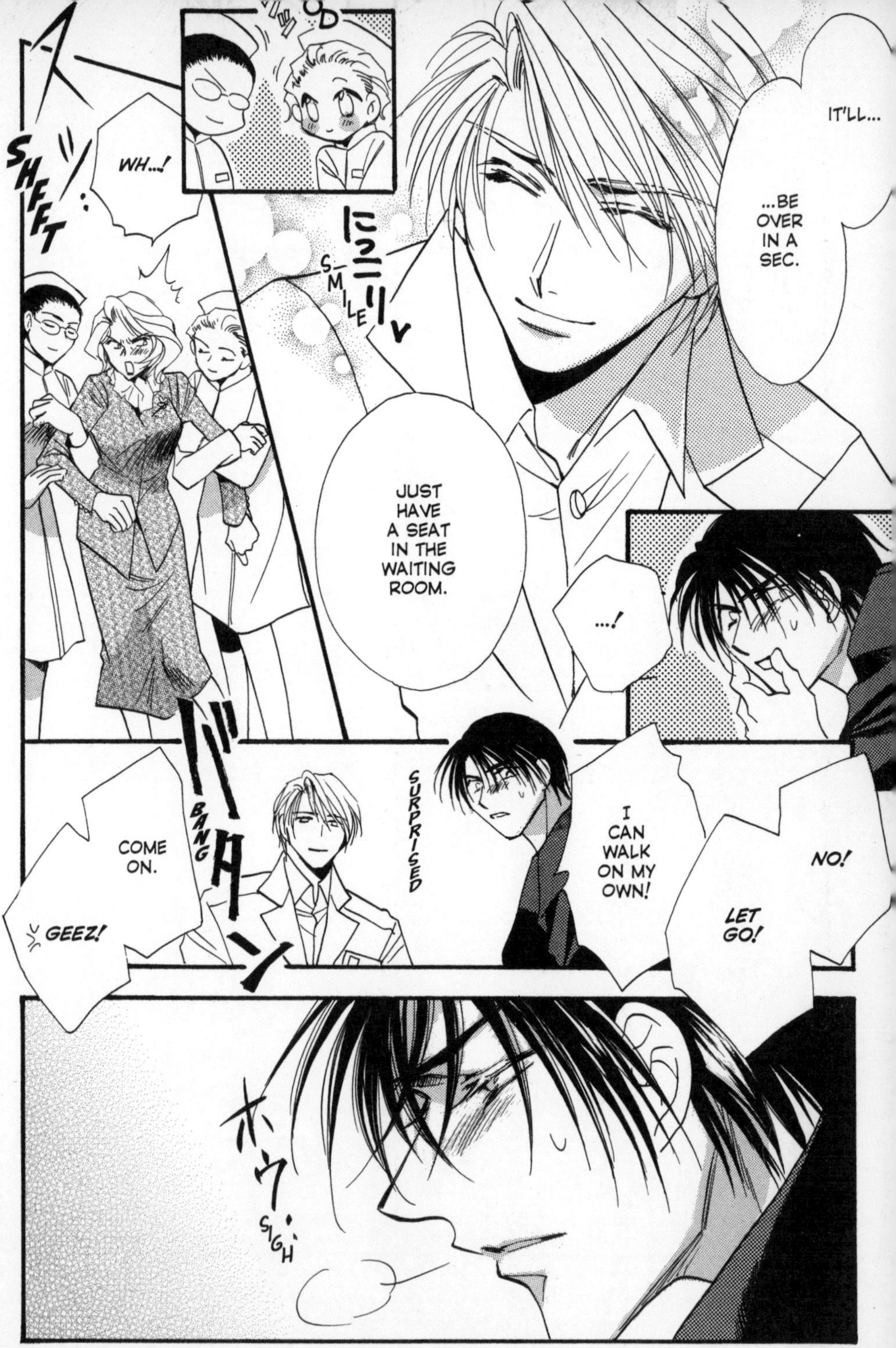
IT'LL...
...BE OVER IN A SEC.
にっこり
SMILE
JUST HAVE A SEAT IN THE WAITING ROOM.
...!
WH...!
SHFFFT
NO! LET GO!
I CAN WALK ON MY OWN!
SURPRISED
BANG
COME ON. GEEZ!
ホゥ
SIGH

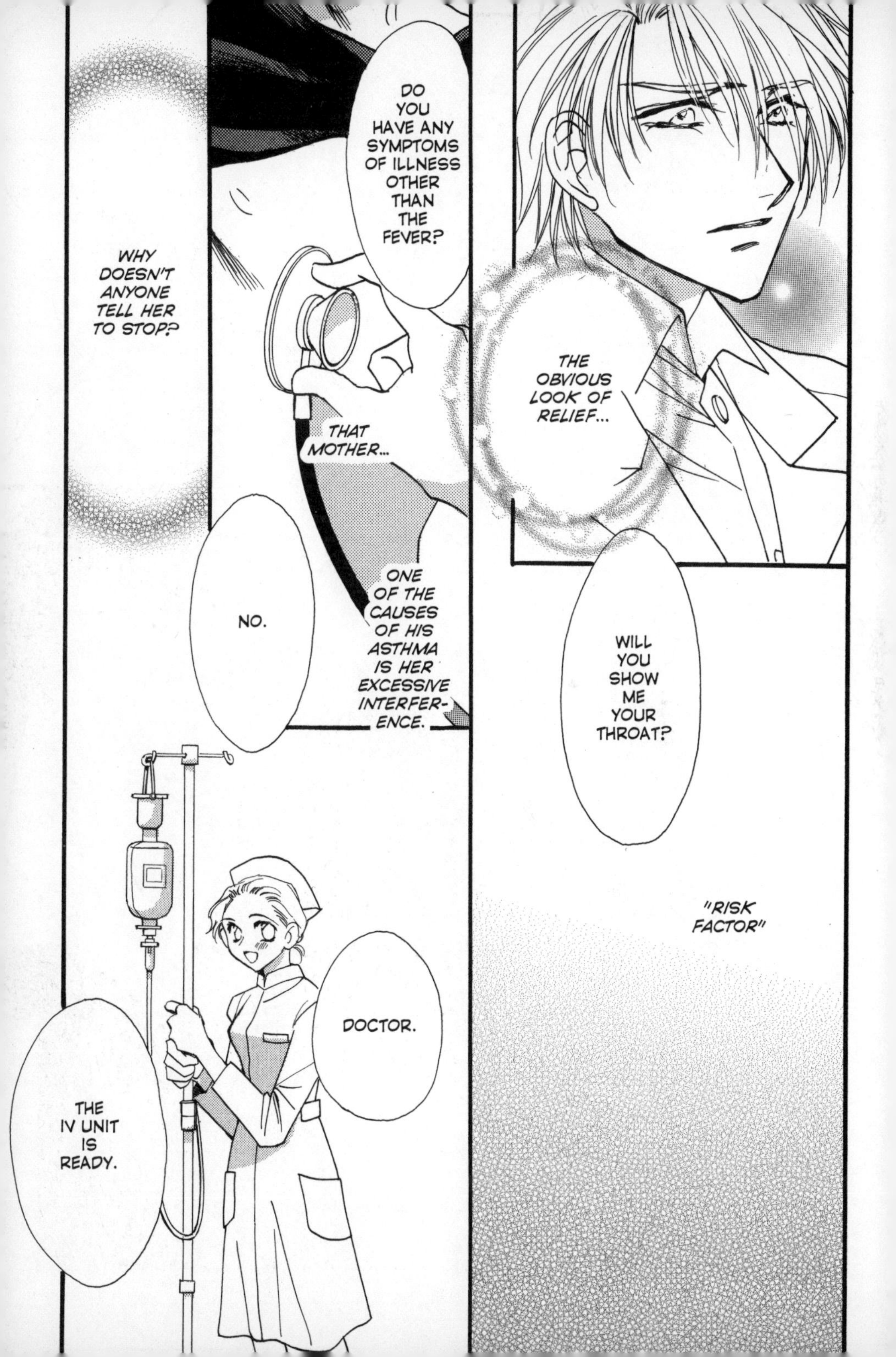
THE OBVIOUS LOOK OF RELIEF...
WILL YOU SHOW ME YOUR THROAT?
"RISK FACTOR"
DO YOU HAVE ANY SYMPTOMS OF ILLNESS OTHER THAN THE FEVER?
THAT MOTHER...
NO.
ONE OF THE CAUSES OF HIS ASTHMA IS HER EXCESSIVE INTERFERENCE.
WHY DOESN'T ANYONE TELL HER TO STOP?
DOCTOR.
THE IV UNIT IS READY.

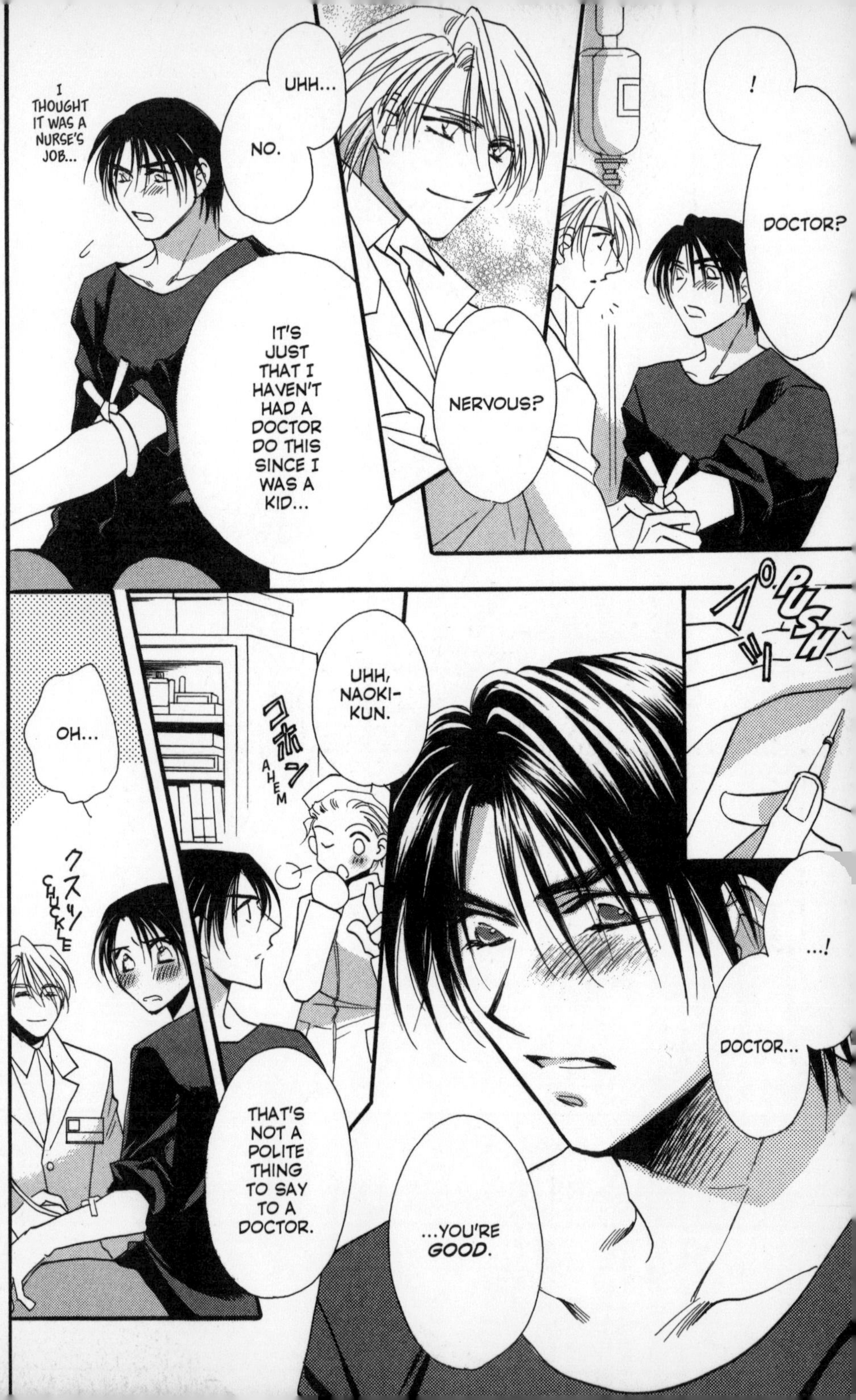
!
DOCTOR?
NERVOUS?
UHH... NO.
I THOUGHT IT WAS A NURSE'S JOB...
IT'S JUST THAT I HAVEN'T HAD A DOCTOR DO THIS SINCE I WAS A KID...
ペッ PUSH
...!
DOCTOR...
...YOU'RE *GOOD*.
UHH, NAOKI-KUN.
コホッ AHEM
THAT'S NOT A POLITE THING TO SAY TO A DOCTOR.
OH...
クスッ CHUCKLE

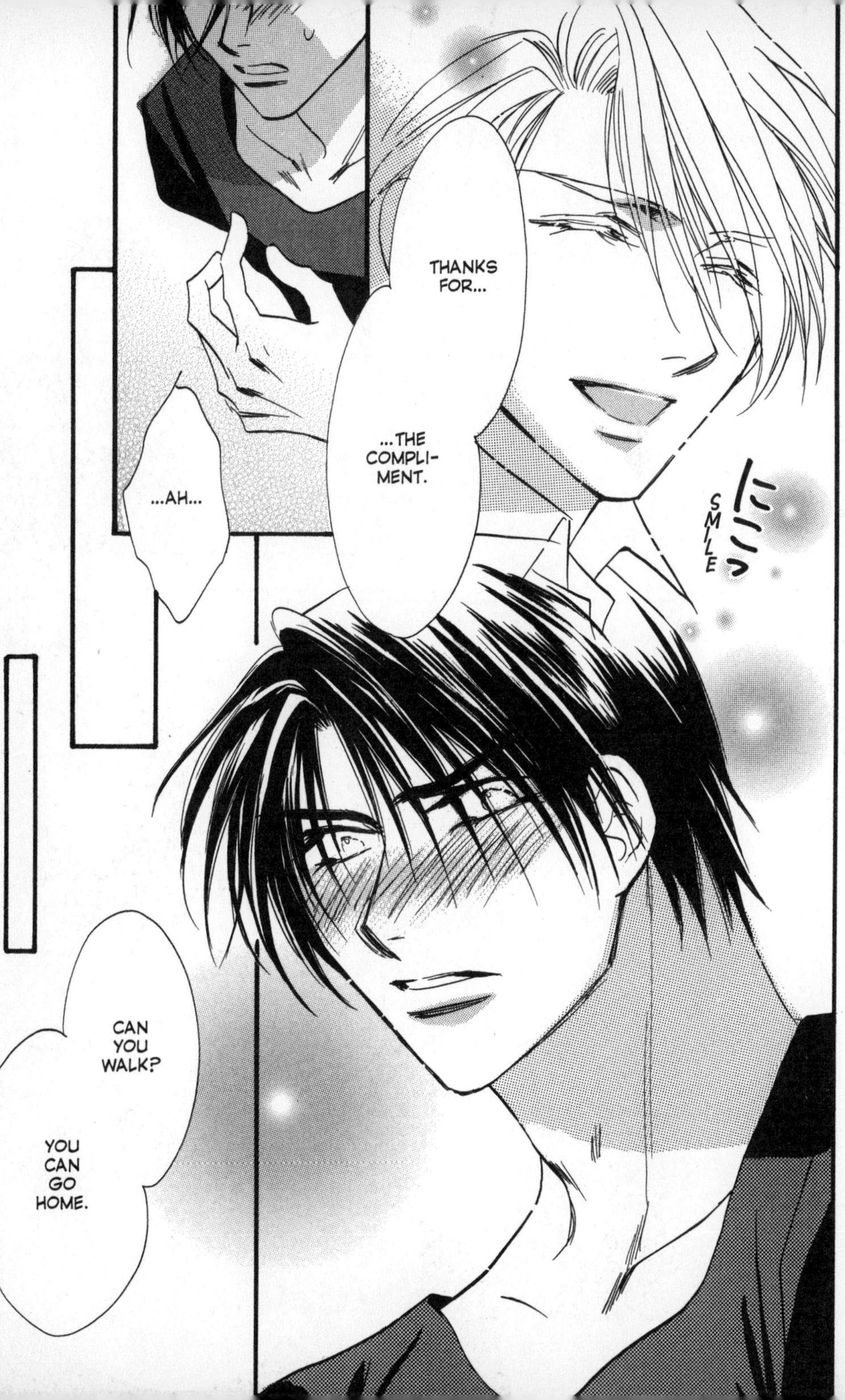
THANKS FOR...
...THE COMPLIMENT.
にこっ SMILE
...AH...
CAN YOU WALK?
YOU CAN GO HOME.

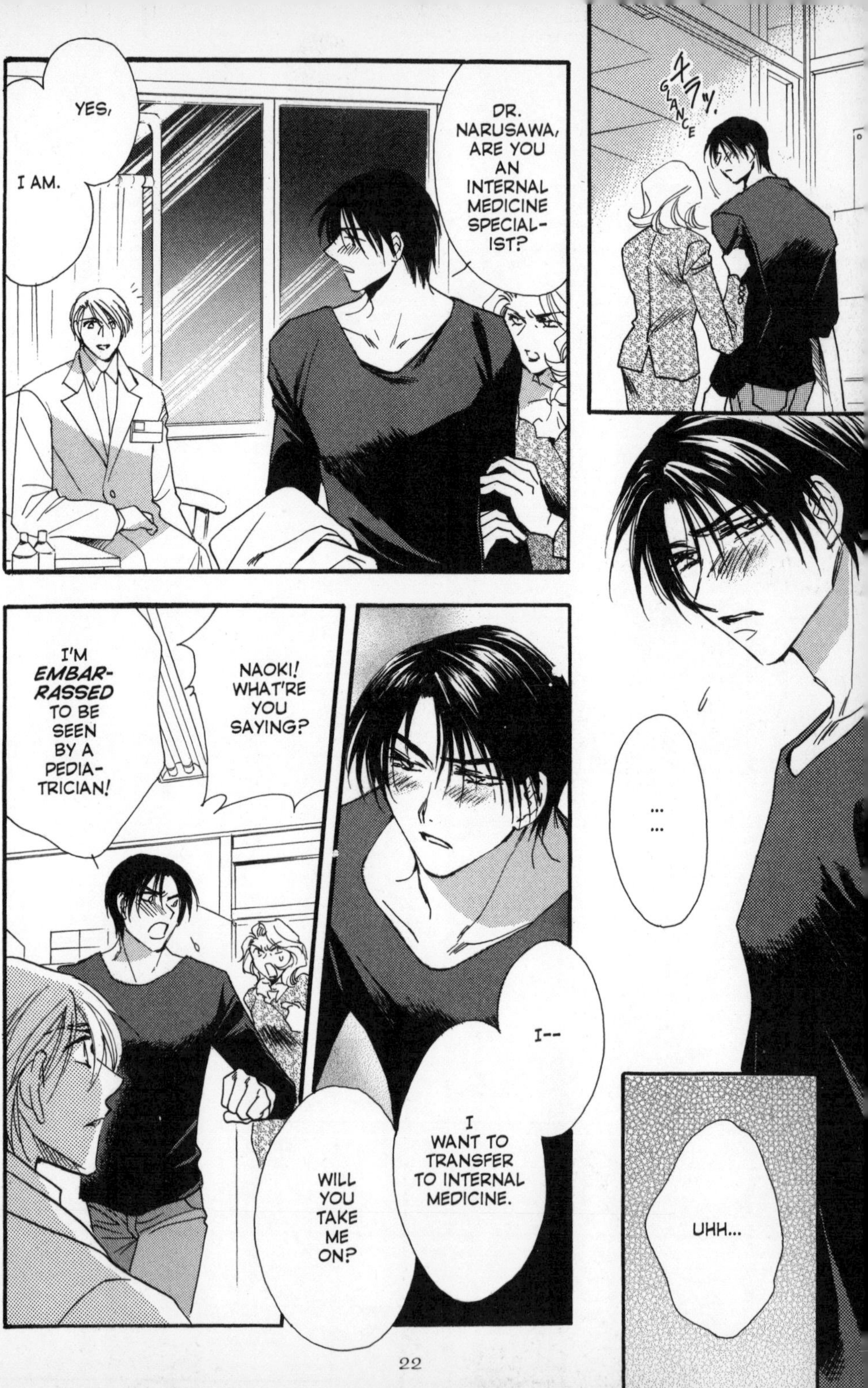

チラッ
GLANCE
DR. NARUSAWA, ARE YOU AN INTERNAL MEDICINE SPECIALIST?
YES,
I AM.
......
I--
I WANT TO TRANSFER TO INTERNAL MEDICINE.
WILL YOU TAKE ME ON?
NAOKI! WHAT'RE YOU SAYING?
I'M *EMBARRASSED* TO BE SEEN BY A PEDIATRICIAN!
UHH...

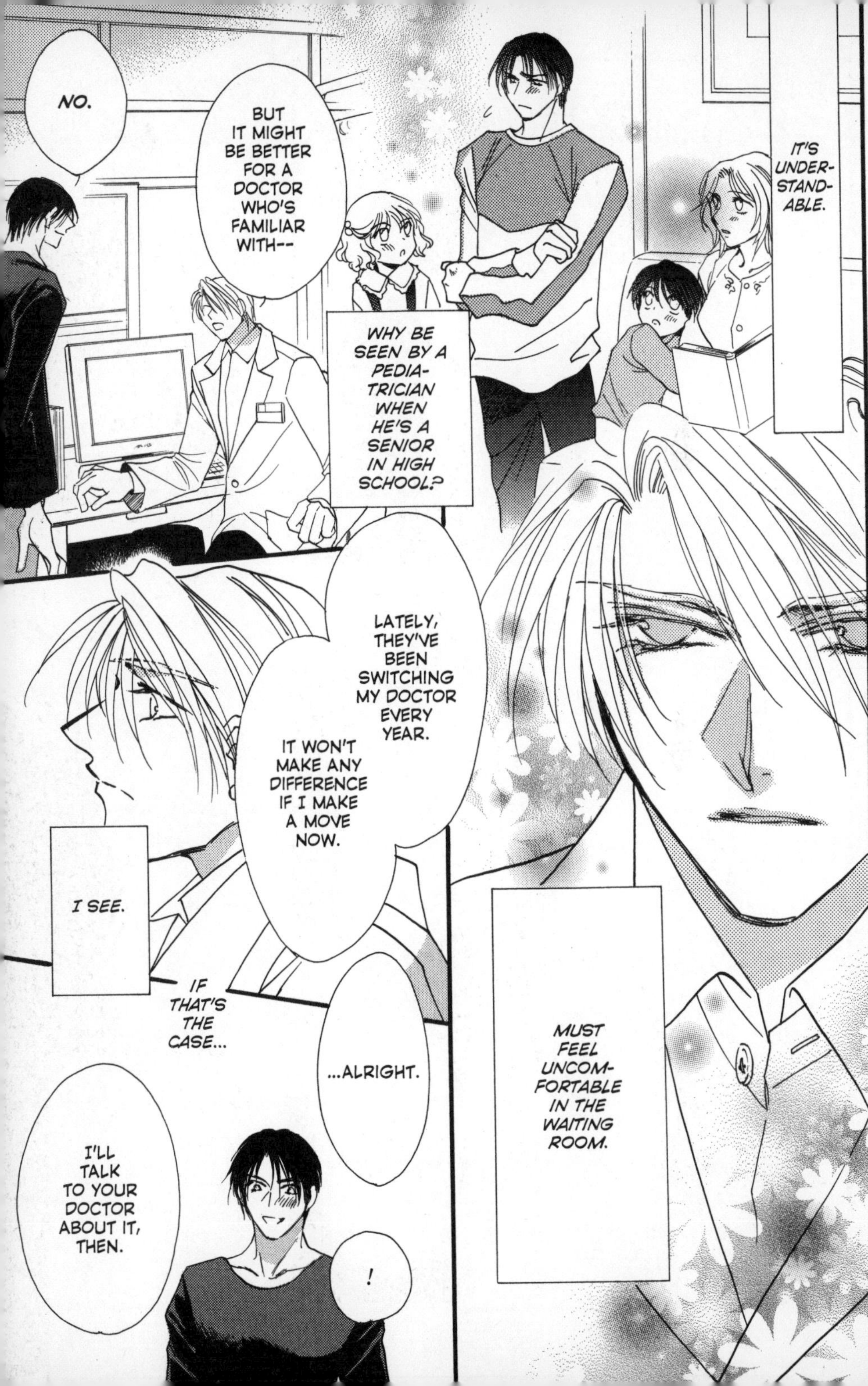
IT'S UNDER-STAND-ABLE.
WHY BE SEEN BY A PEDIA-TRICIAN WHEN HE'S A SENIOR IN HIGH SCHOOL?
BUT IT MIGHT BE BETTER FOR A DOCTOR WHO'S FAMILIAR WITH--
NO.
MUST FEEL UNCOM-FORTABLE IN THE WAITING ROOM.
LATELY, THEY'VE BEEN SWITCHING MY DOCTOR EVERY YEAR.
IT WON'T MAKE ANY DIFFERENCE IF I MAKE A MOVE NOW.
I SEE.
IF THAT'S THE CASE...
...ALRIGHT.
I'LL TALK TO YOUR DOCTOR ABOUT IT, THEN.
!

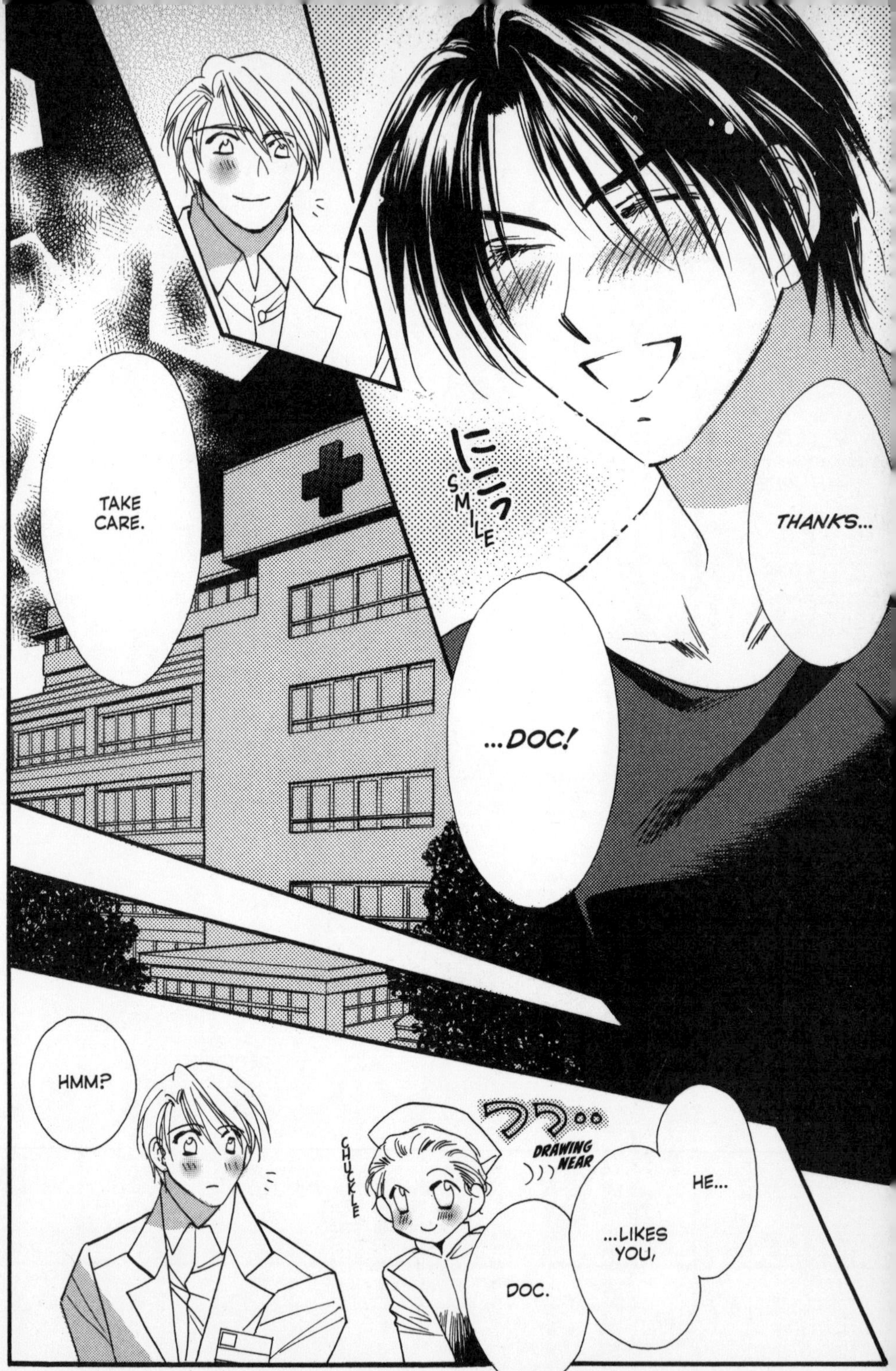
THANKS...
にこっ
SMILE
...DOC!
TAKE CARE.
つつ..
DRAWING NEAR
HE...
...LIKES YOU,
DOC.
CHUCKLE
HMM?

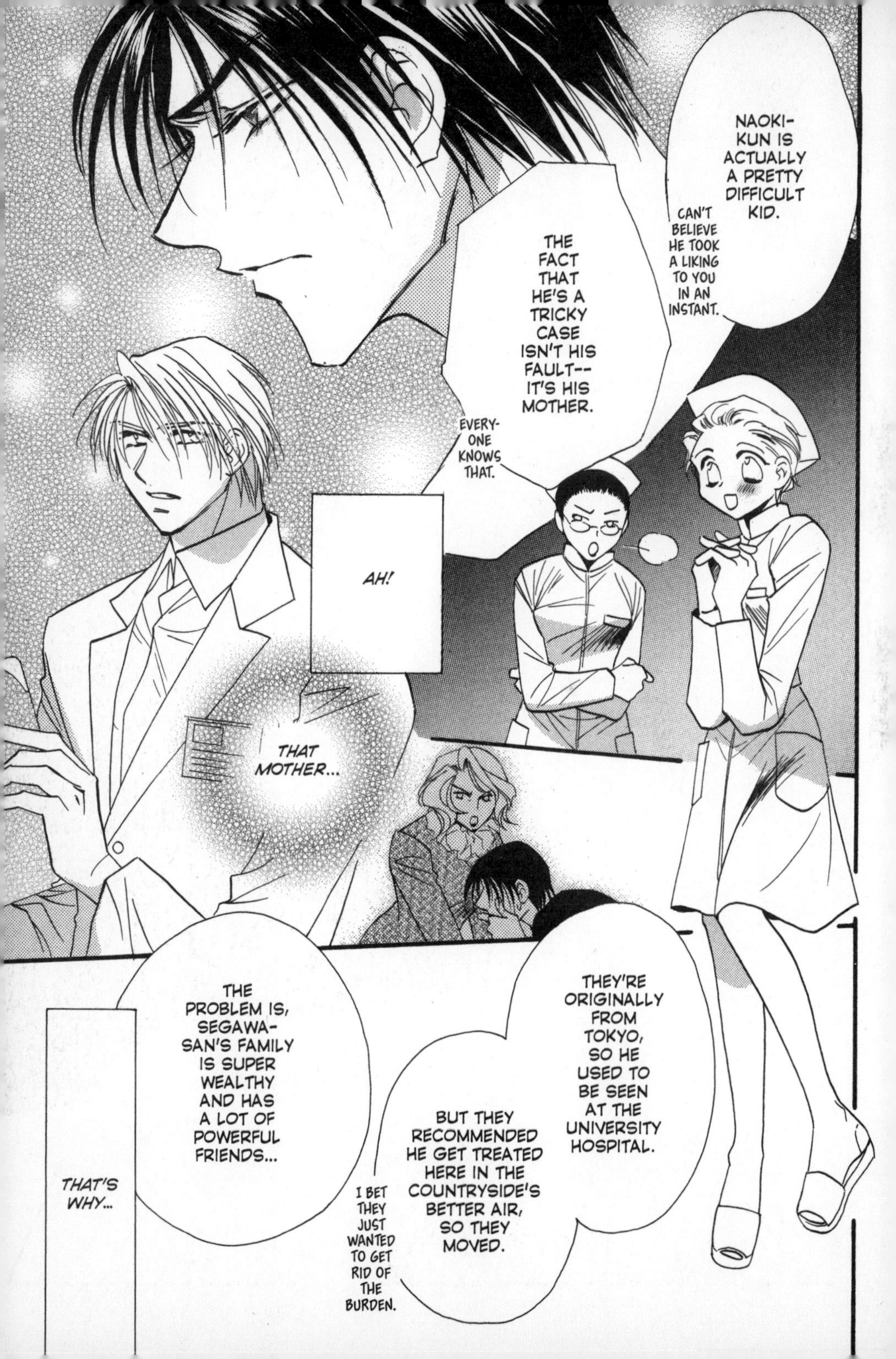
NAOKI-KUN IS ACTUALLY A PRETTY DIFFICULT KID.
CAN'T BELIEVE HE TOOK A LIKING TO YOU IN AN INSTANT.
THE FACT THAT HE'S A TRICKY CASE ISN'T HIS FAULT-- IT'S HIS MOTHER.
EVERY-ONE KNOWS THAT.
AH!
THAT MOTHER...
THEY'RE ORIGINALLY FROM TOKYO, SO HE USED TO BE SEEN AT THE UNIVERSITY HOSPITAL.
BUT THEY RECOMMENDED HE GET TREATED HERE IN THE COUNTRYSIDE'S BETTER AIR, SO THEY MOVED.
I BET THEY JUST WANTED TO GET RID OF THE BURDEN.
THE PROBLEM IS, SEGAWA-SAN'S FAMILY IS SUPER WEALTHY AND HAS A LOT OF POWERFUL FRIENDS...
THAT'S WHY...

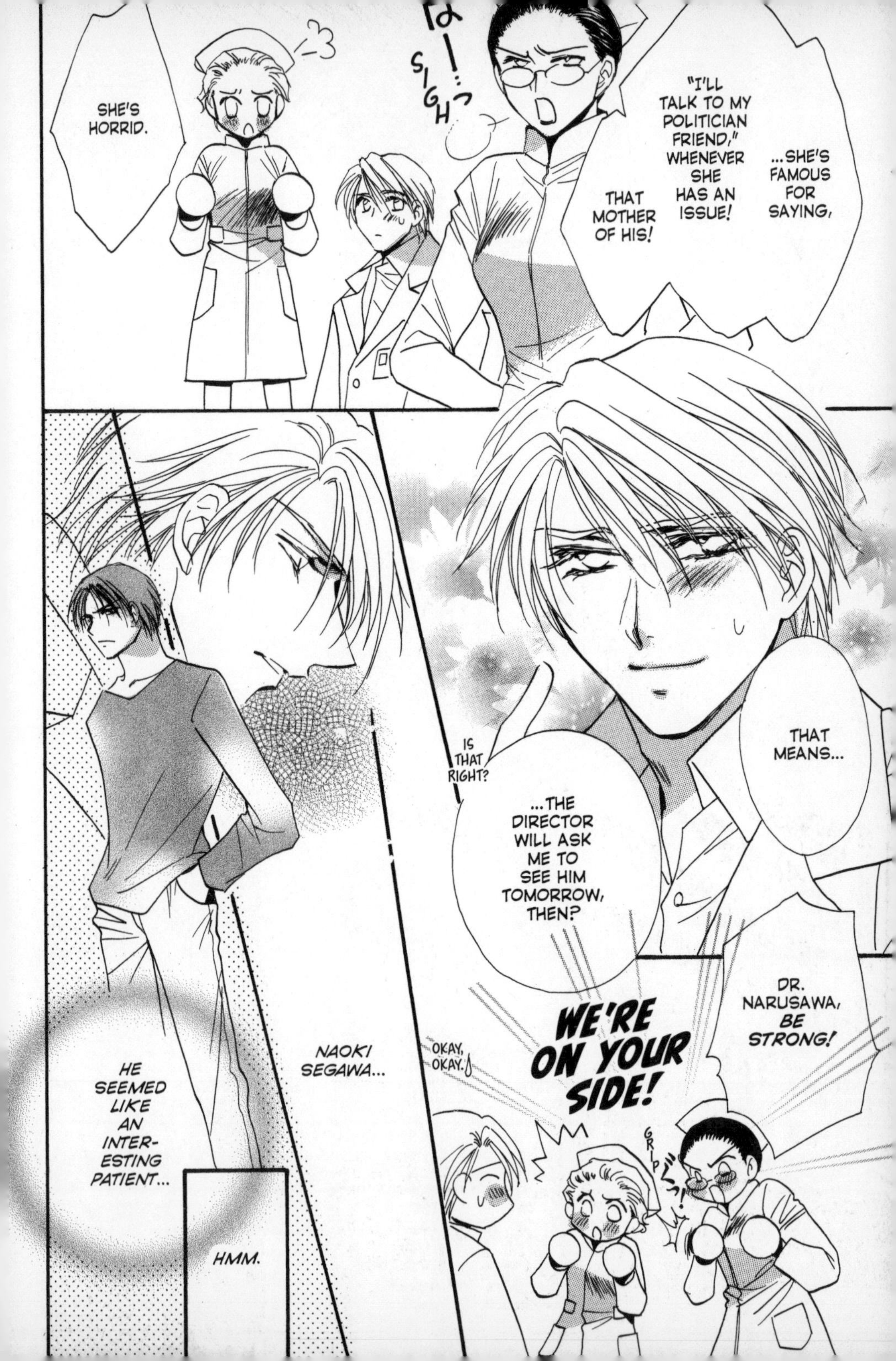
...SHE'S FAMOUS FOR SAYING,
"I'LL TALK TO MY POLITICIAN FRIEND," WHENEVER SHE HAS AN ISSUE!
THAT MOTHER OF HIS!
はー!! SIGH
SHE'S HORRID.
THAT MEANS...
...THE DIRECTOR WILL ASK ME TO SEE HIM TOMORROW, THEN?
IS THAT RIGHT?
DR. NARUSAWA, BE STRONG!
WE'RE ON YOUR SIDE!
OKAY, OKAY.
GRIP
NAOKI SEGAWA...
HE SEEMED LIKE AN INTER-ESTING PATIENT...
HMM.

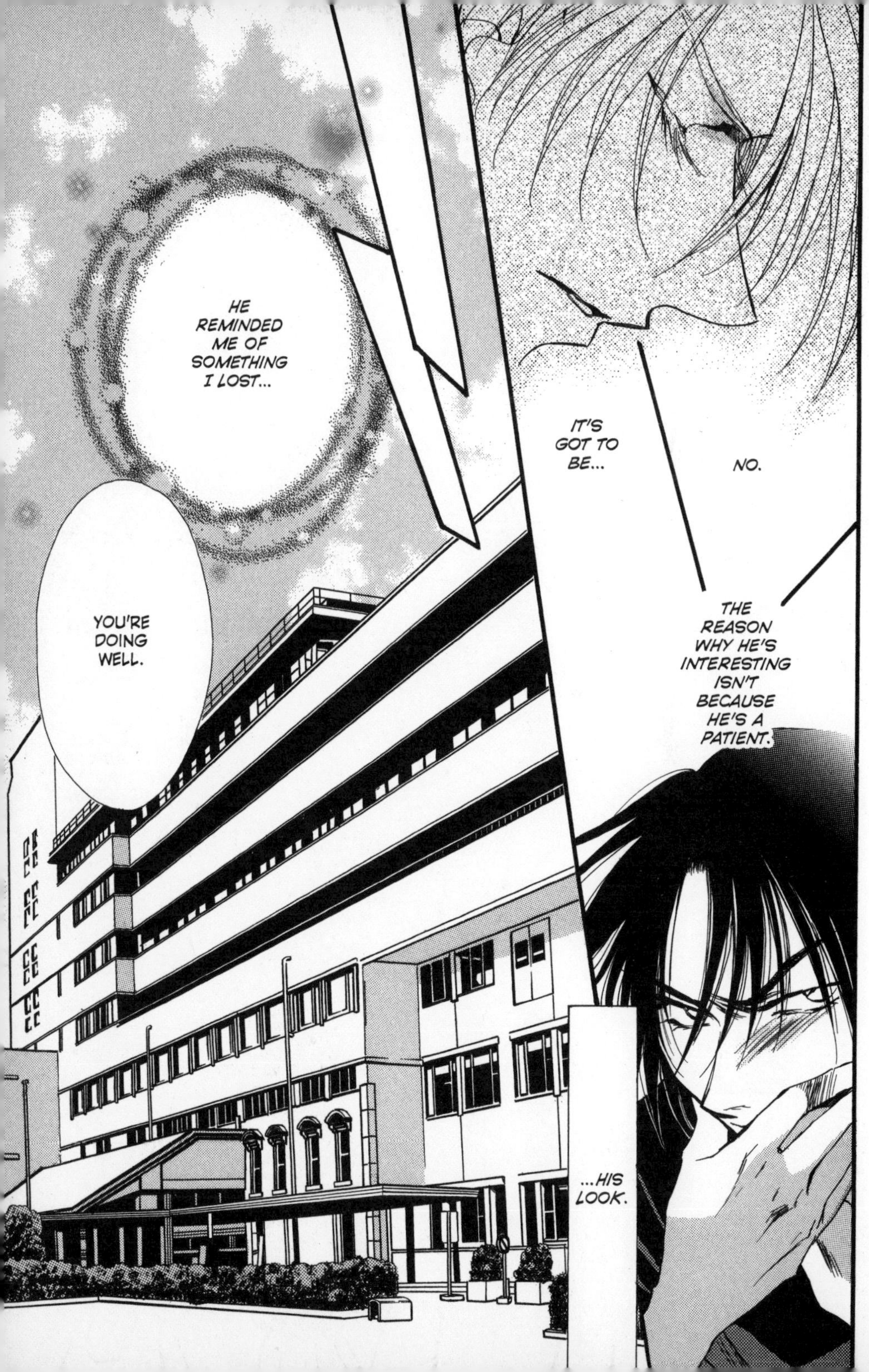
NO.
THE REASON WHY HE'S INTERESTING ISN'T BECAUSE HE'S A PATIENT.
IT'S GOT TO BE...
...HIS LOOK.
HE REMINDED ME OF SOMETHING I LOST...
YOU'RE DOING WELL.

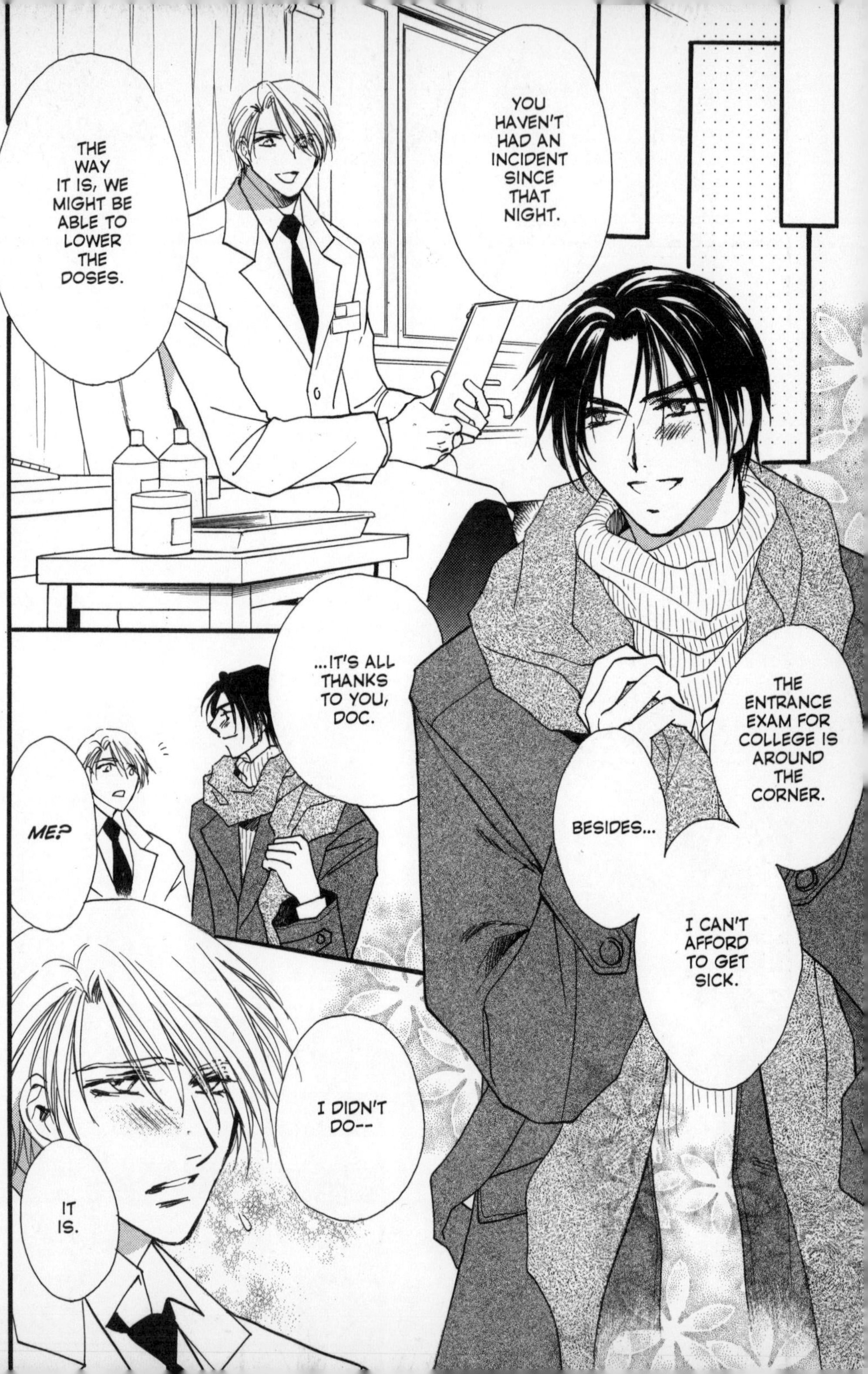
YOU HAVEN'T HAD AN INCIDENT SINCE THAT NIGHT.
THE WAY IT IS, WE MIGHT BE ABLE TO LOWER THE DOSES.
THE ENTRANCE EXAM FOR COLLEGE IS AROUND THE CORNER.
BESIDES...
I CAN'T AFFORD TO GET SICK.
...IT'S ALL THANKS TO YOU, DOC.
ME?
I DIDN'T DO--
IT IS.

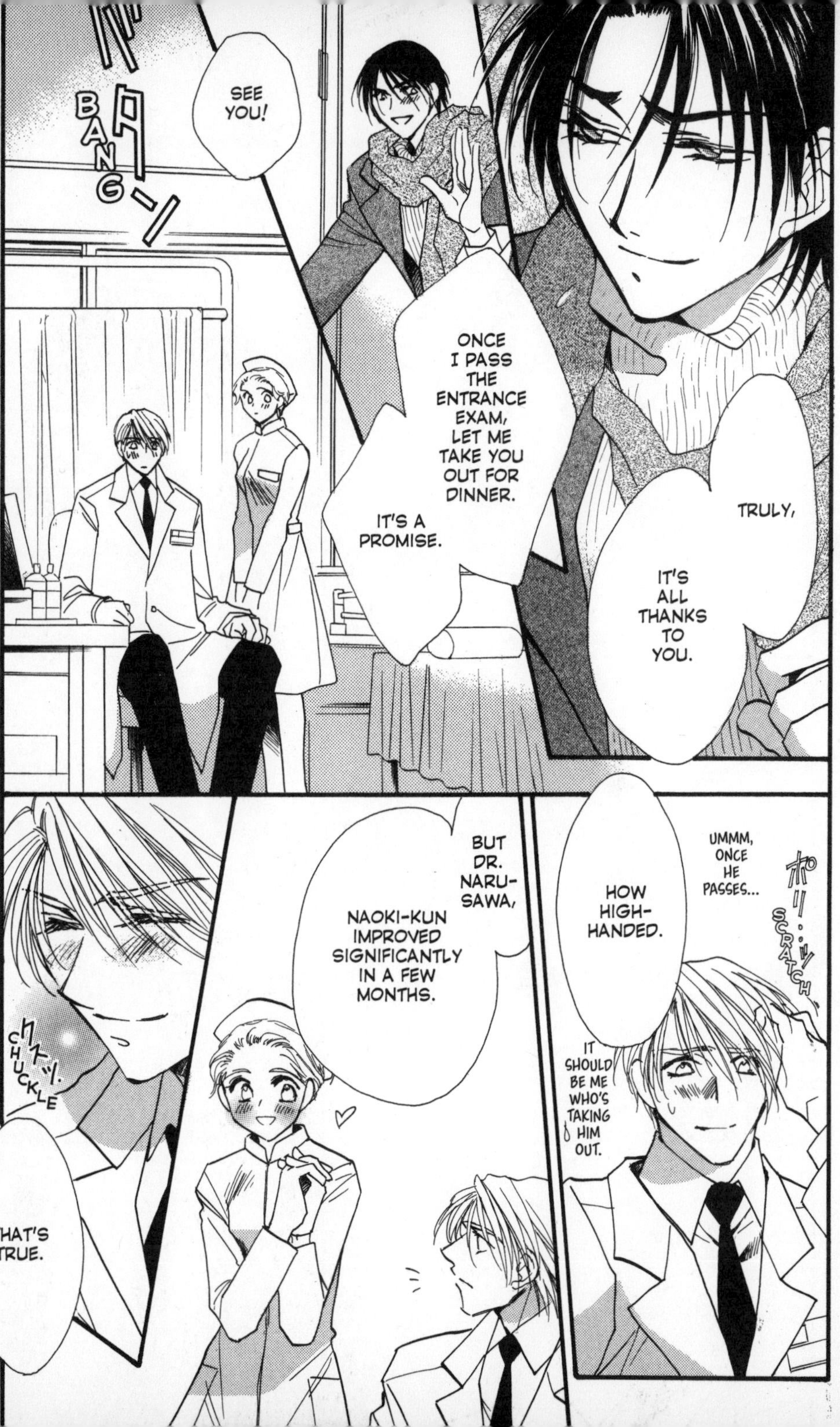

ONCE I PASS THE ENTRANCE EXAM, LET ME TAKE YOU OUT FOR DINNER.
IT'S A PROMISE.
TRULY,
IT'S ALL THANKS TO YOU.
SEE YOU!
BANG
SCRATCH
UMMM, ONCE HE PASSES...
HOW HIGH-HANDED.
IT SHOULD BE ME WHO'S TAKING HIM OUT.
BUT DR. NARU-SAWA,
NAOKI-KUN IMPROVED SIGNIFICANTLY IN A FEW MONTHS.
CHUCKLE
THAT'S TRUE.

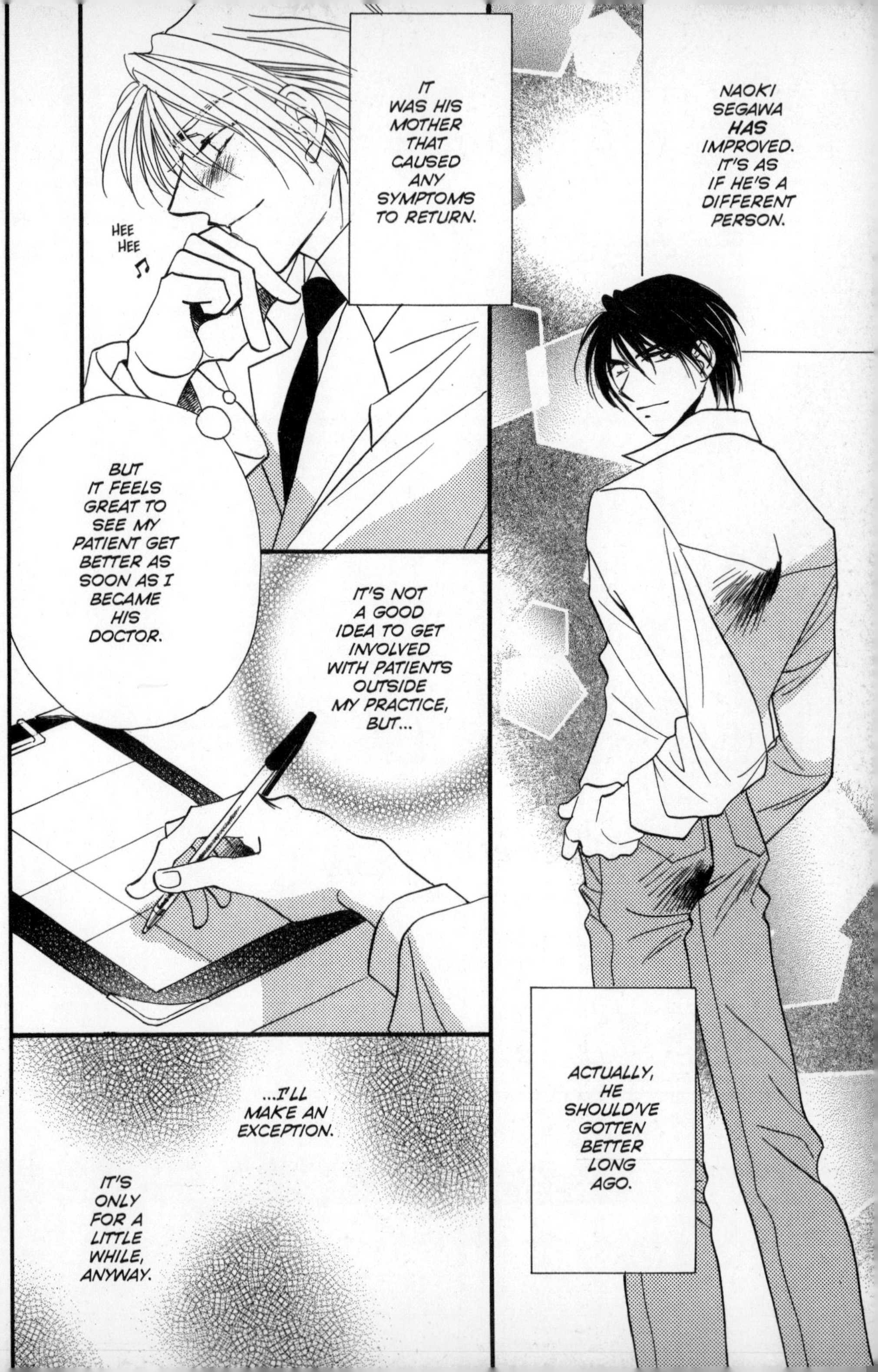
NAOKI SEGAWA HAS IMPROVED. IT'S AS IF HE'S A DIFFERENT PERSON.
ACTUALLY, HE SHOULD'VE GOTTEN BETTER LONG AGO.
IT WAS HIS MOTHER THAT CAUSED ANY SYMPTOMS TO RETURN.
HEE HEE ♪
BUT IT FEELS GREAT TO SEE MY PATIENT GET BETTER AS SOON AS I BECAME HIS DOCTOR.
IT'S NOT A GOOD IDEA TO GET INVOLVED WITH PATIENTS OUTSIDE MY PRACTICE, BUT...
...I'LL MAKE AN EXCEPTION.
IT'S ONLY FOR A LITTLE WHILE, ANYWAY.

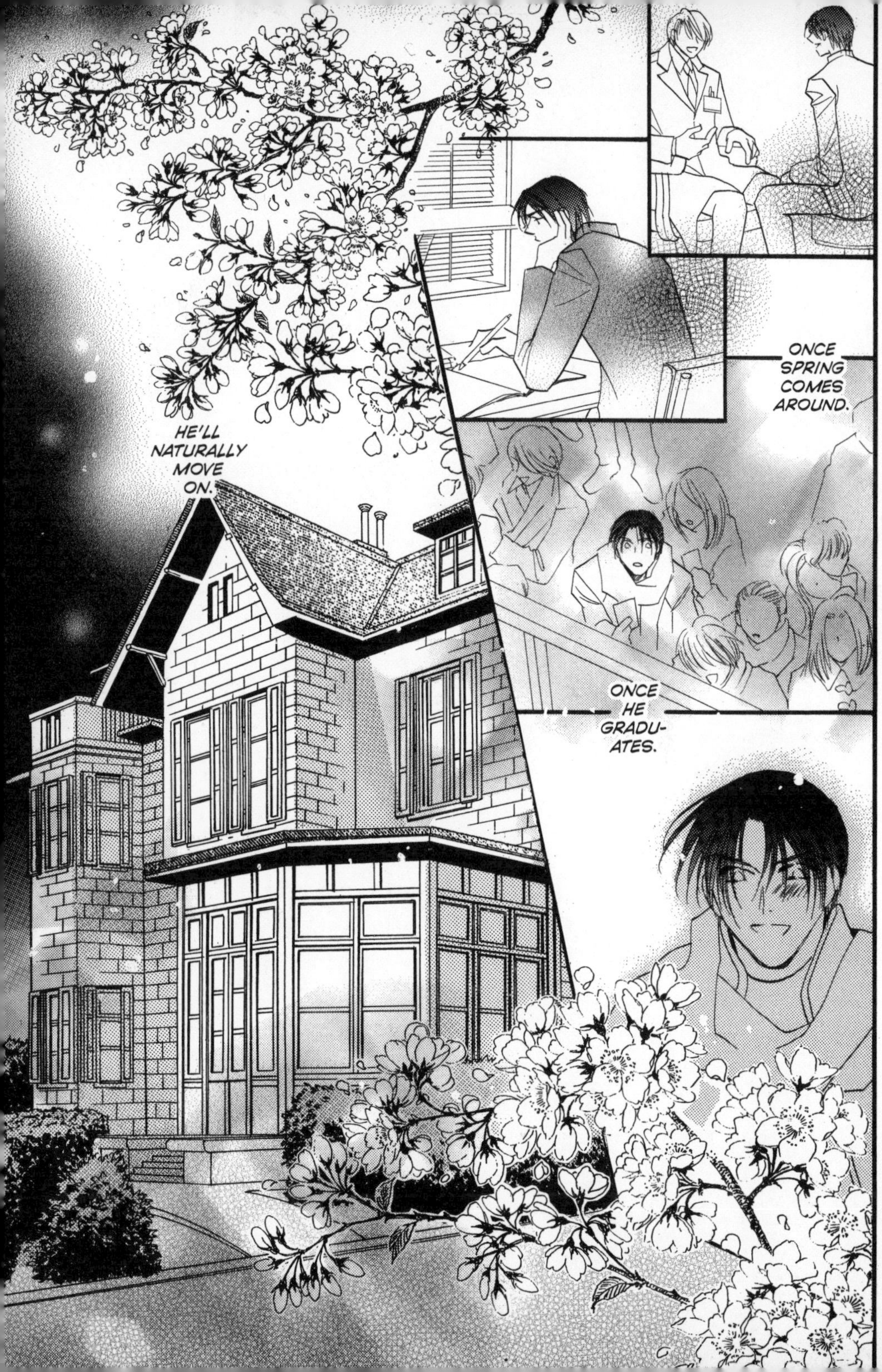
ONCE SPRING COMES AROUND.
ONCE HE GRADUATES.
HE'LL NATURALLY MOVE ON.

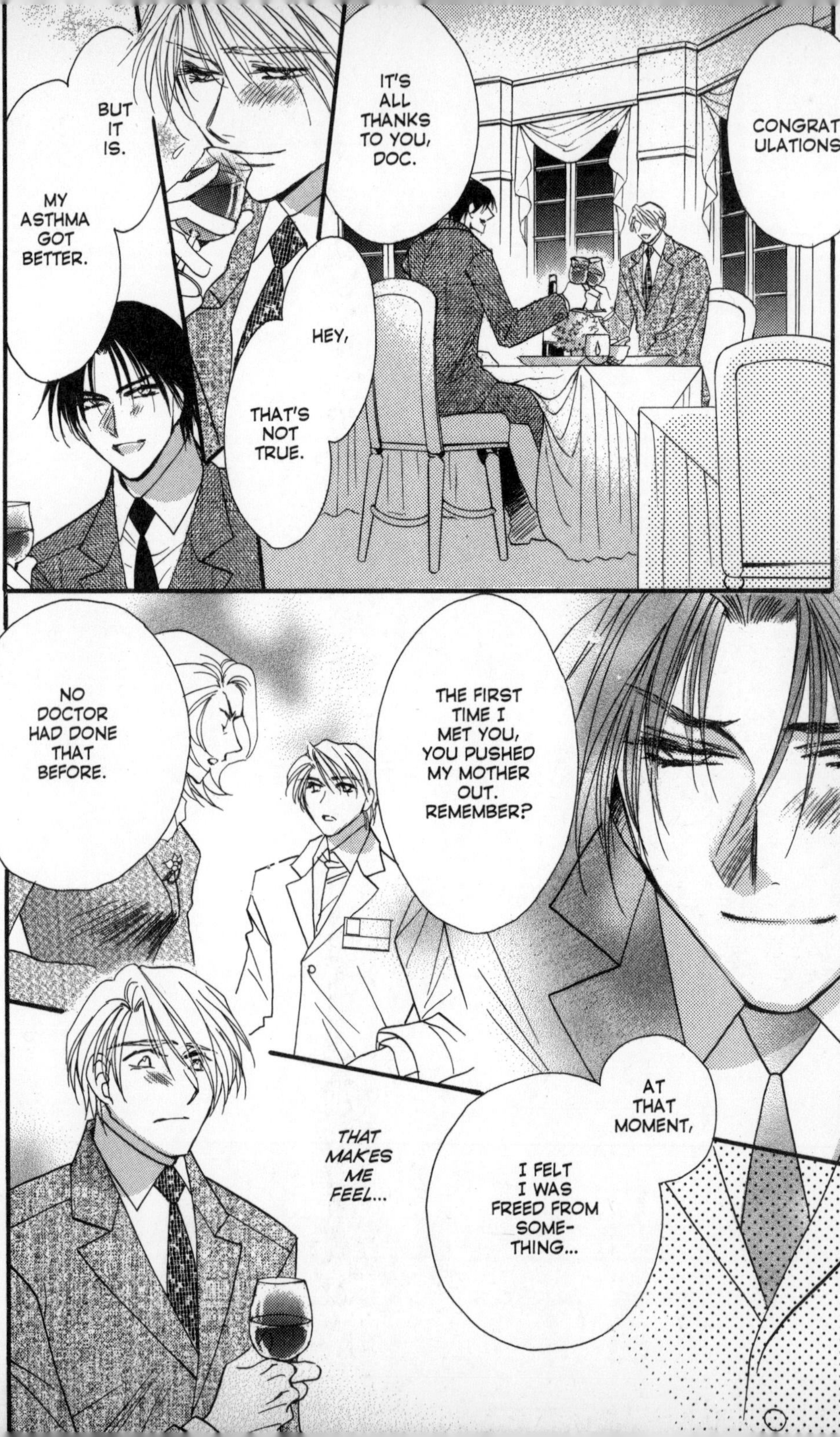
CONGRAT-ULATIONS.
IT'S ALL THANKS TO YOU, DOC.
HEY,
THAT'S NOT TRUE.
BUT IT IS.
MY ASTHMA GOT BETTER.
THE FIRST TIME I MET YOU, YOU PUSHED MY MOTHER OUT. REMEMBER?
NO DOCTOR HAD DONE THAT BEFORE.
AT THAT MOMENT,
I FELT I WAS FREED FROM SOME-THING...
THAT MAKES ME FEEL...

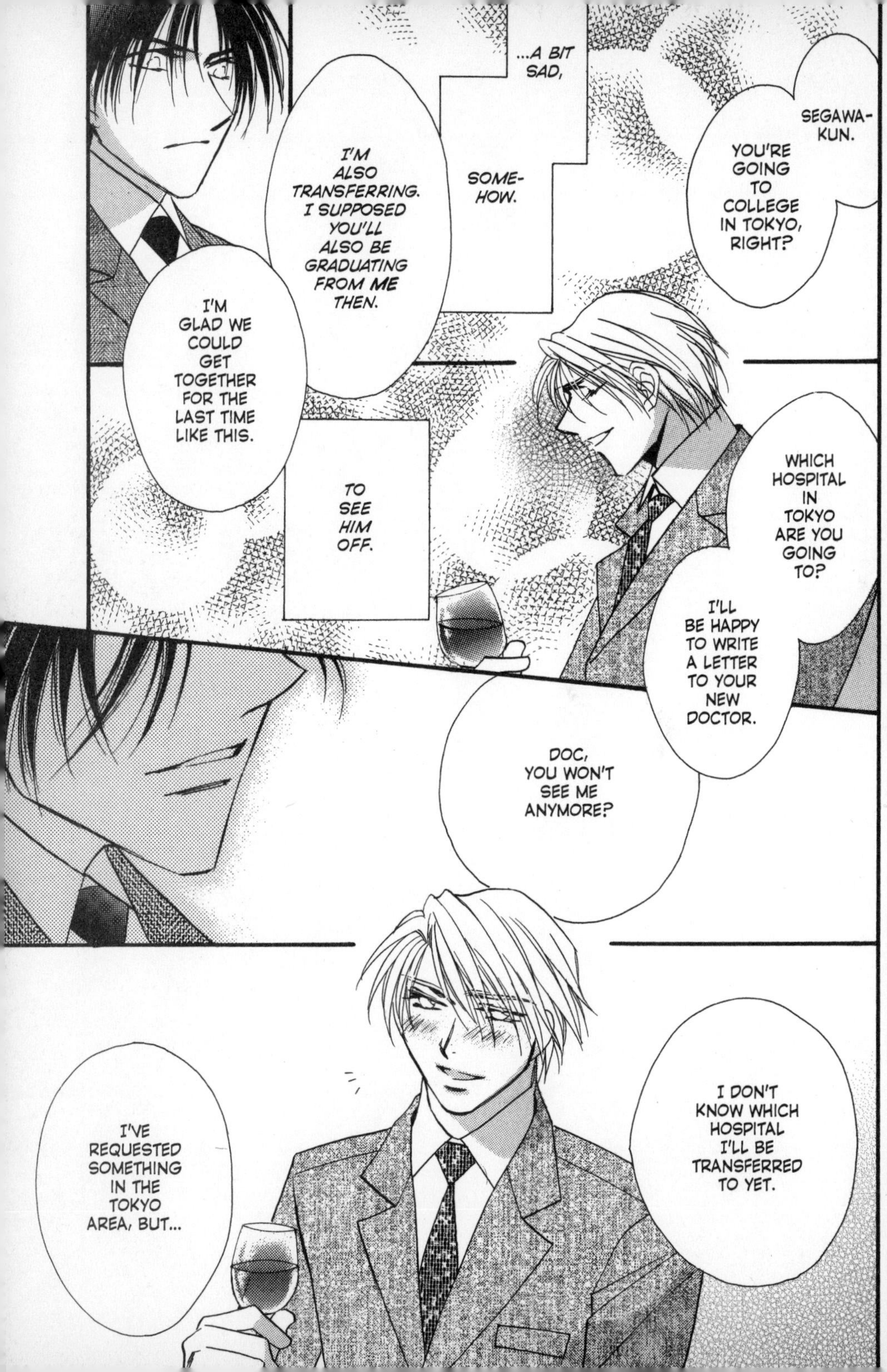
SEGAWA-KUN. YOU'RE GOING TO COLLEGE IN TOKYO, RIGHT?
...A BIT SAD,
SOME-HOW.
I'M ALSO TRANSFERRING. I SUPPOSED YOU'LL ALSO BE GRADUATING FROM ME THEN.
I'M GLAD WE COULD GET TOGETHER FOR THE LAST TIME LIKE THIS.
TO SEE HIM OFF.
WHICH HOSPITAL IN TOKYO ARE YOU GOING TO?
I'LL BE HAPPY TO WRITE A LETTER TO YOUR NEW DOCTOR.
DOC, YOU WON'T SEE ME ANYMORE?
I DON'T KNOW WHICH HOSPITAL I'LL BE TRANSFERRED TO YET.
I'VE REQUESTED SOMETHING IN THE TOKYO AREA, BUT...

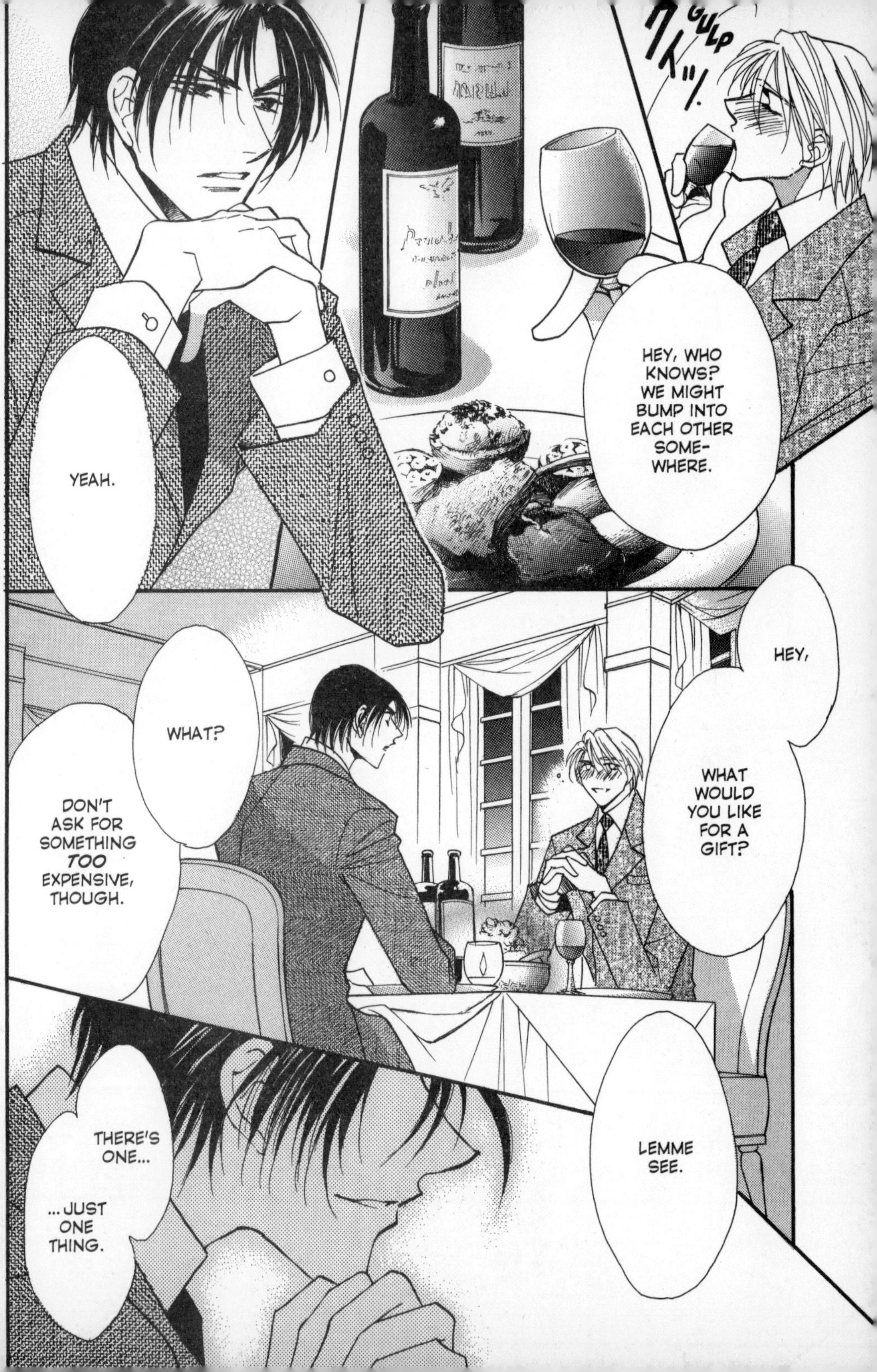
GULP
HEY, WHO KNOWS? WE MIGHT BUMP INTO EACH OTHER SOME-WHERE.
YEAH.
HEY,
WHAT WOULD YOU LIKE FOR A GIFT?
WHAT?
DON'T ASK FOR SOMETHING *TOO* EXPENSIVE, THOUGH.
LEMME SEE.
THERE'S ONE...
...JUST ONE THING.

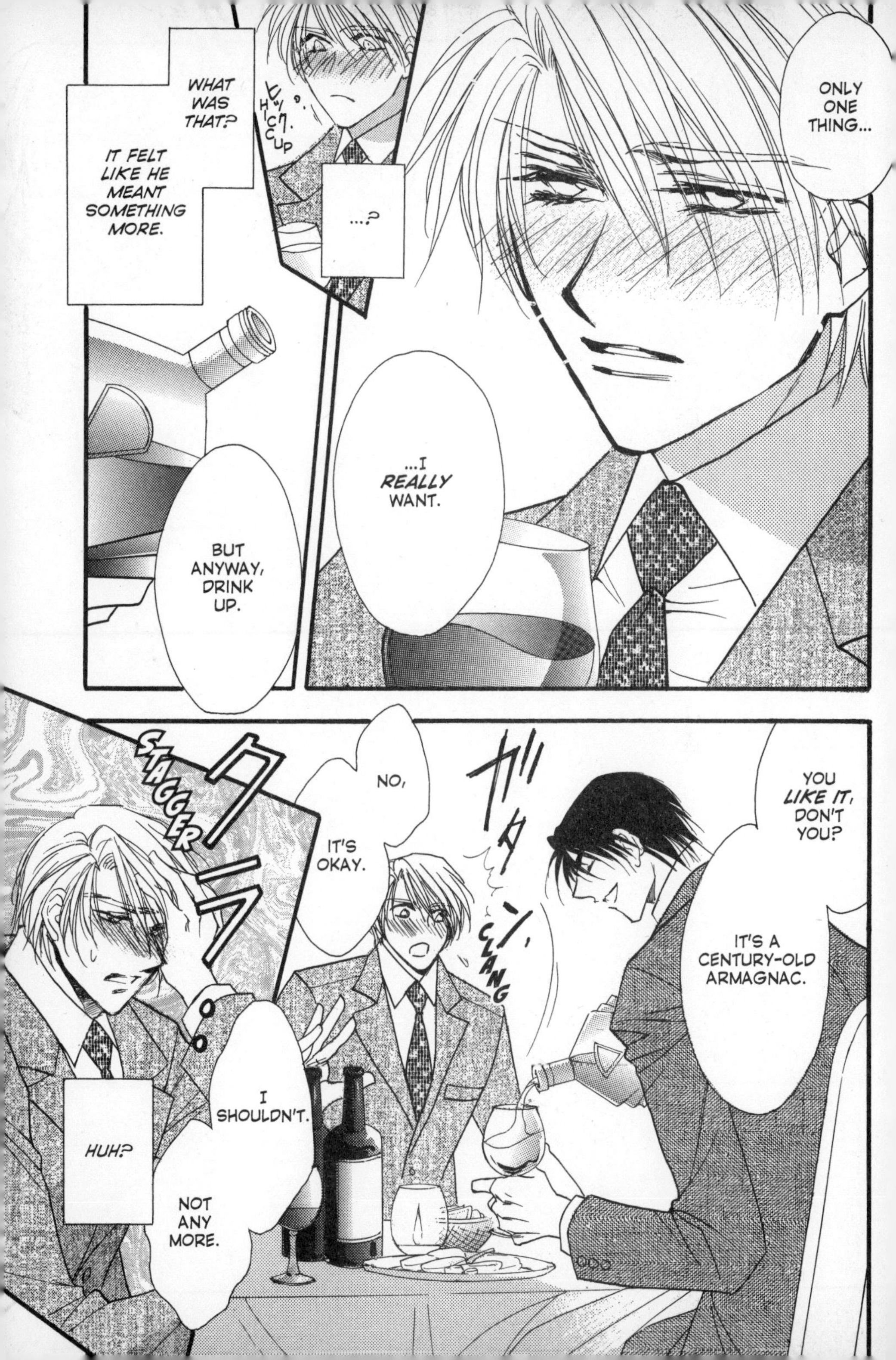
ONLY ONE THING...
...I *REALLY* WANT.
HICCUP
...?
WHAT WAS THAT?
IT FELT LIKE HE MEANT SOMETHING MORE.
BUT ANYWAY, DRINK UP.
YOU *LIKE IT*, DON'T YOU?
IT'S A CENTURY-OLD ARMAGNAC.
CLANG
NO,
IT'S OKAY.
STAGGER
I SHOULDN'T.
NOT ANY MORE.
HUH?

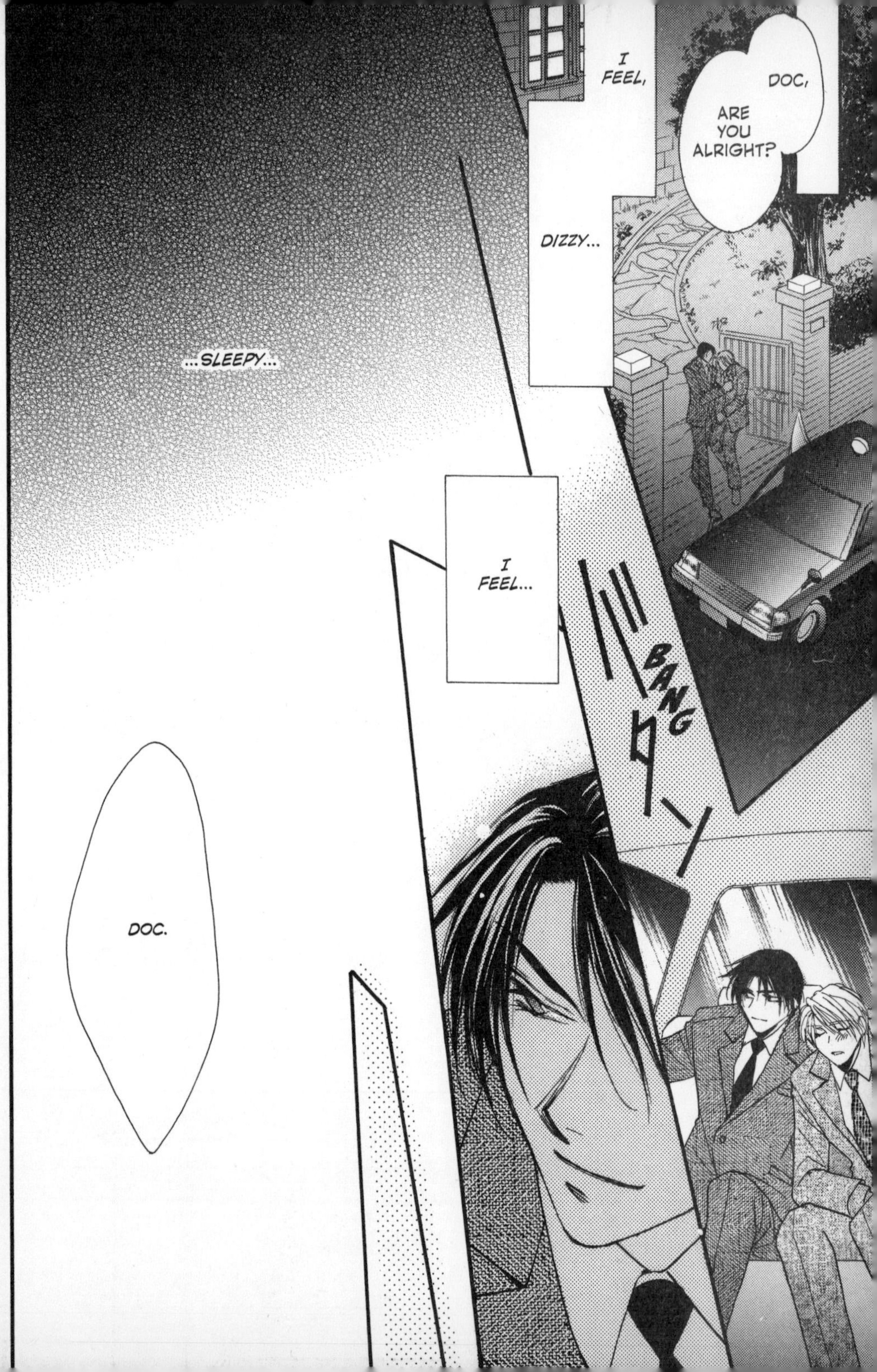
DOC, ARE YOU ALRIGHT?
I FEEL, DIZZY...
I FEEL...
BANG
...SLEEPY...
DOC.

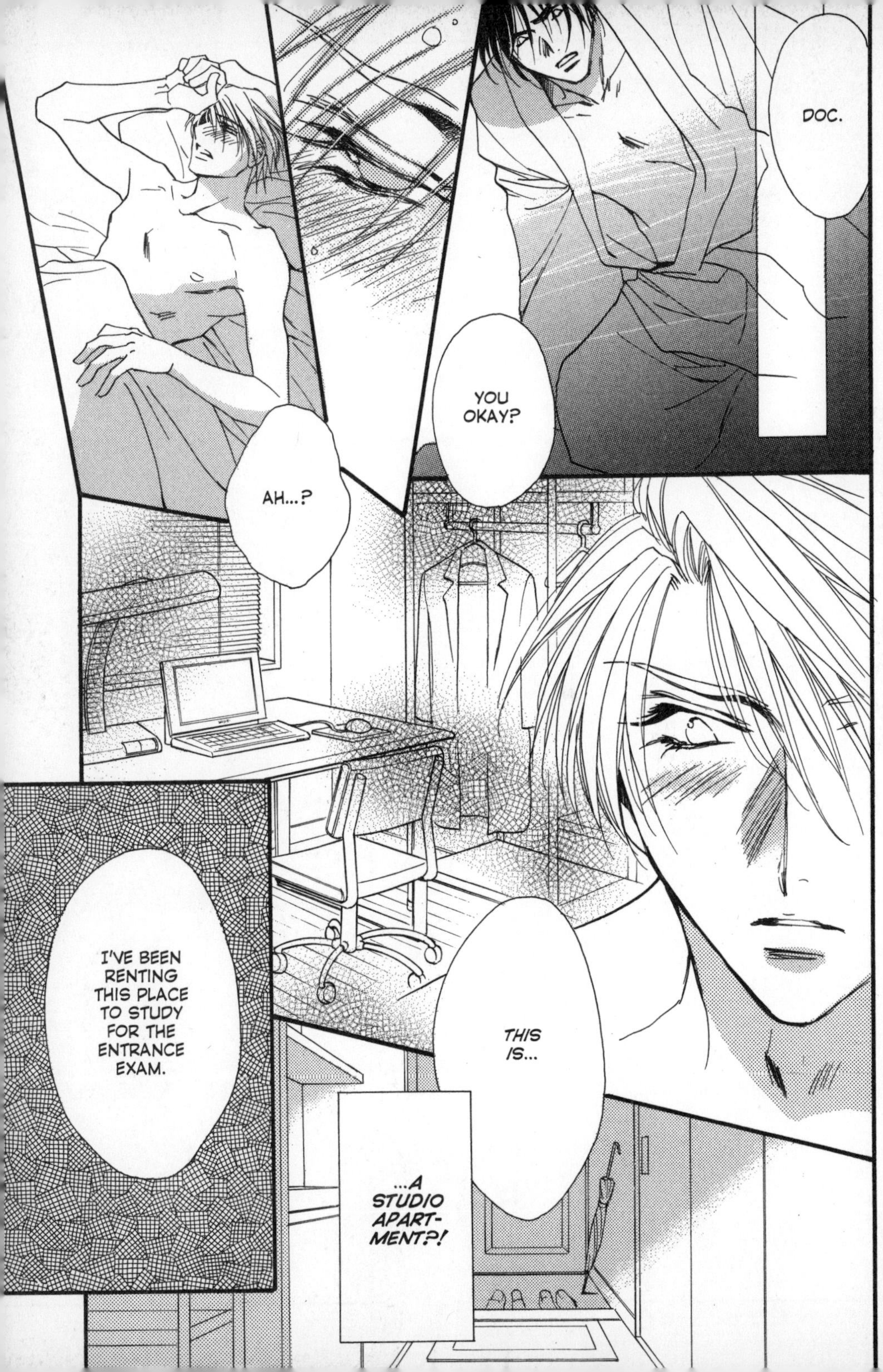
DOC.
YOU OKAY?
AH...?
THIS IS...
...A STUDIO APARTMENT?!
I'VE BEEN RENTING THIS PLACE TO STUDY FOR THE ENTRANCE EXAM.

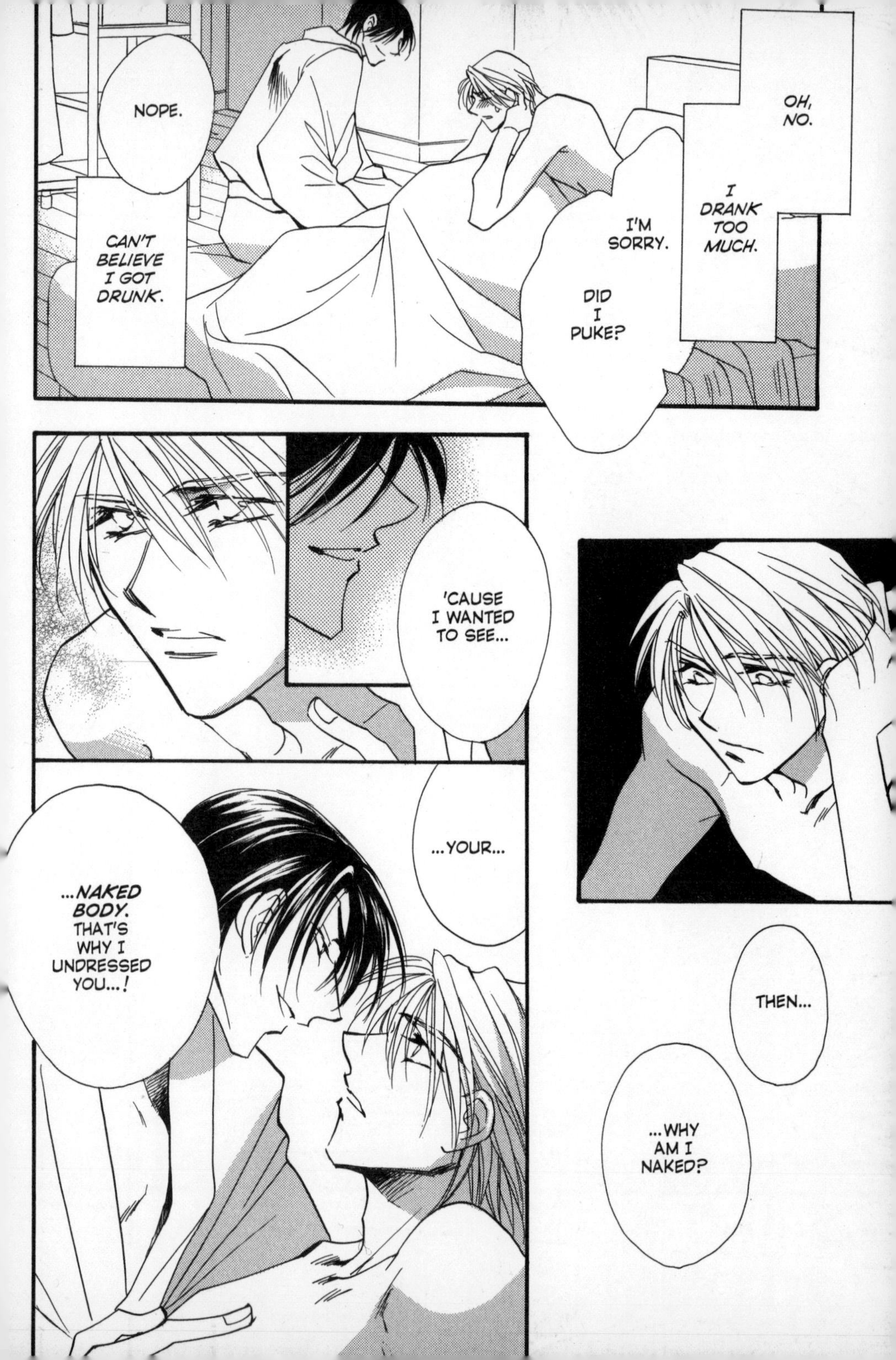
OH, NO.
I DRANK TOO MUCH.
I'M SORRY.
DID I PUKE?
NOPE.
CAN'T BELIEVE I GOT DRUNK.
THEN...
...WHY AM I NAKED?
'CAUSE I WANTED TO SEE...
...YOUR...
...NAKED BODY. THAT'S WHY I UNDRESSED YOU...!

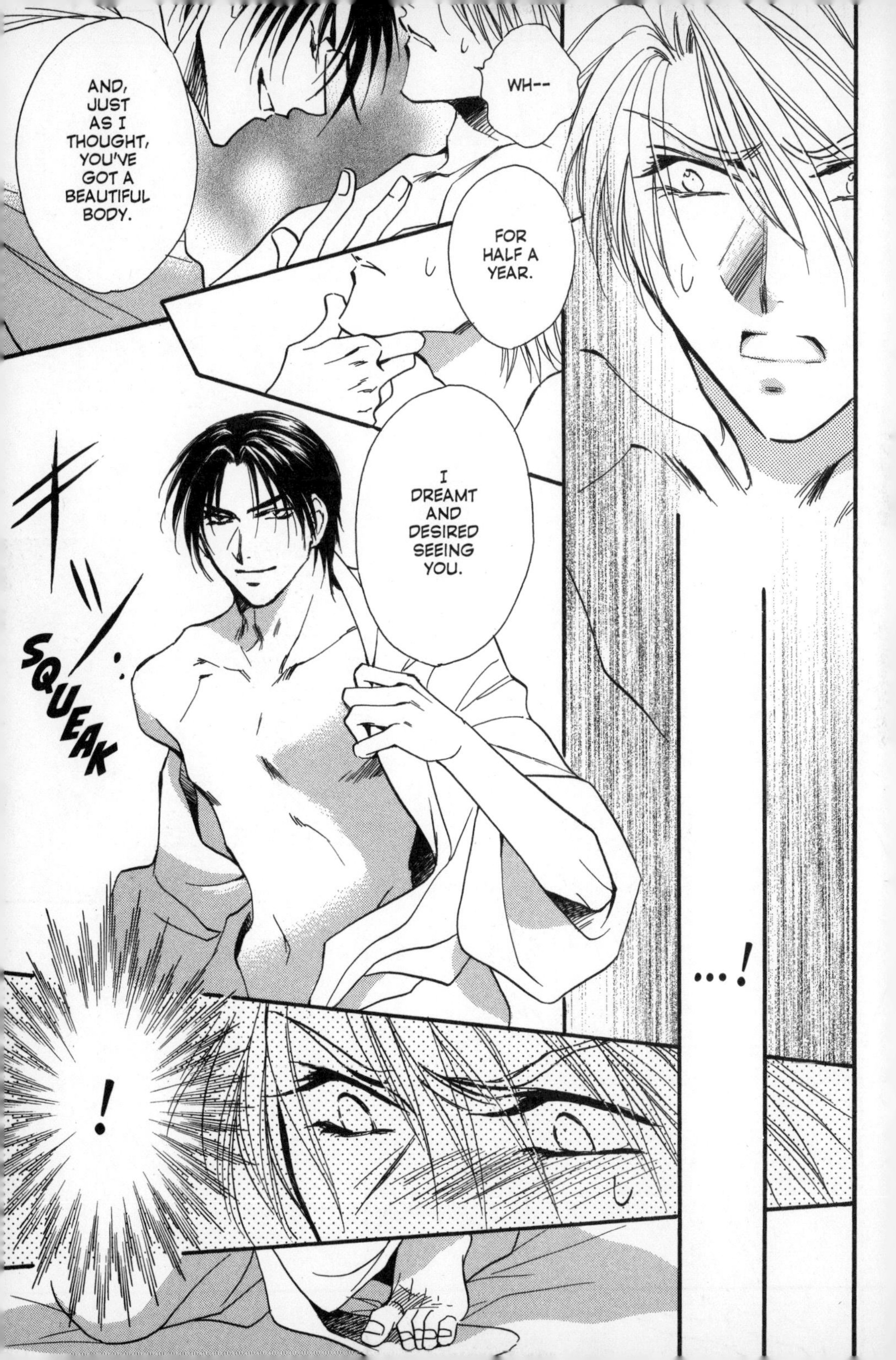

AND, JUST AS I THOUGHT, YOU'VE GOT A BEAUTIFUL BODY.
WH--
FOR HALF A YEAR.
I DREAMT AND DESIRED SEEING YOU.
SQUEAK
...!
!

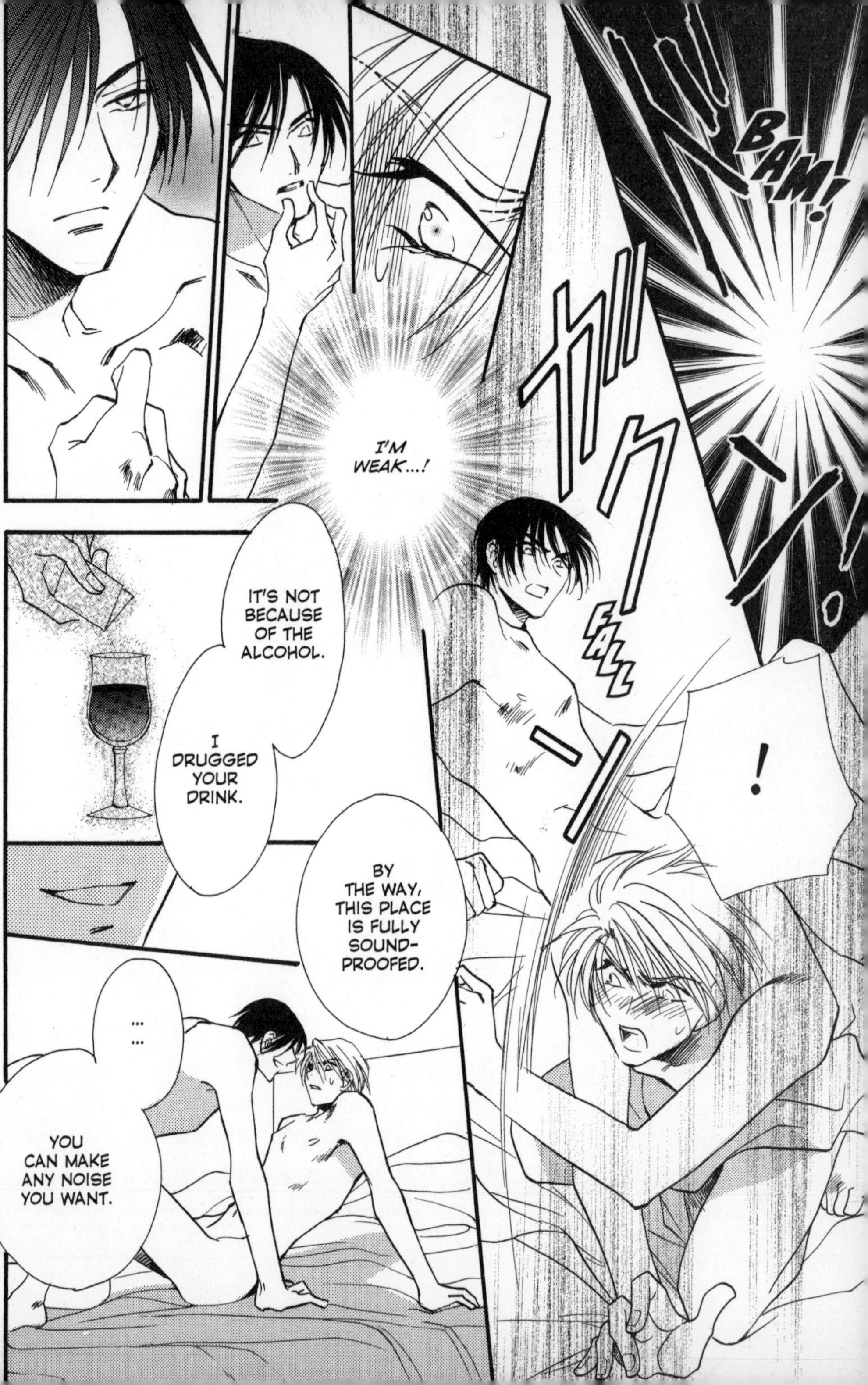

BAM!
FALL
!
I'M WEAK...!
IT'S NOT BECAUSE OF THE ALCOHOL.
I DRUGGED YOUR DRINK.
BY THE WAY, THIS PLACE IS FULLY SOUND-PROOFED.
......
YOU CAN MAKE ANY NOISE YOU WANT.

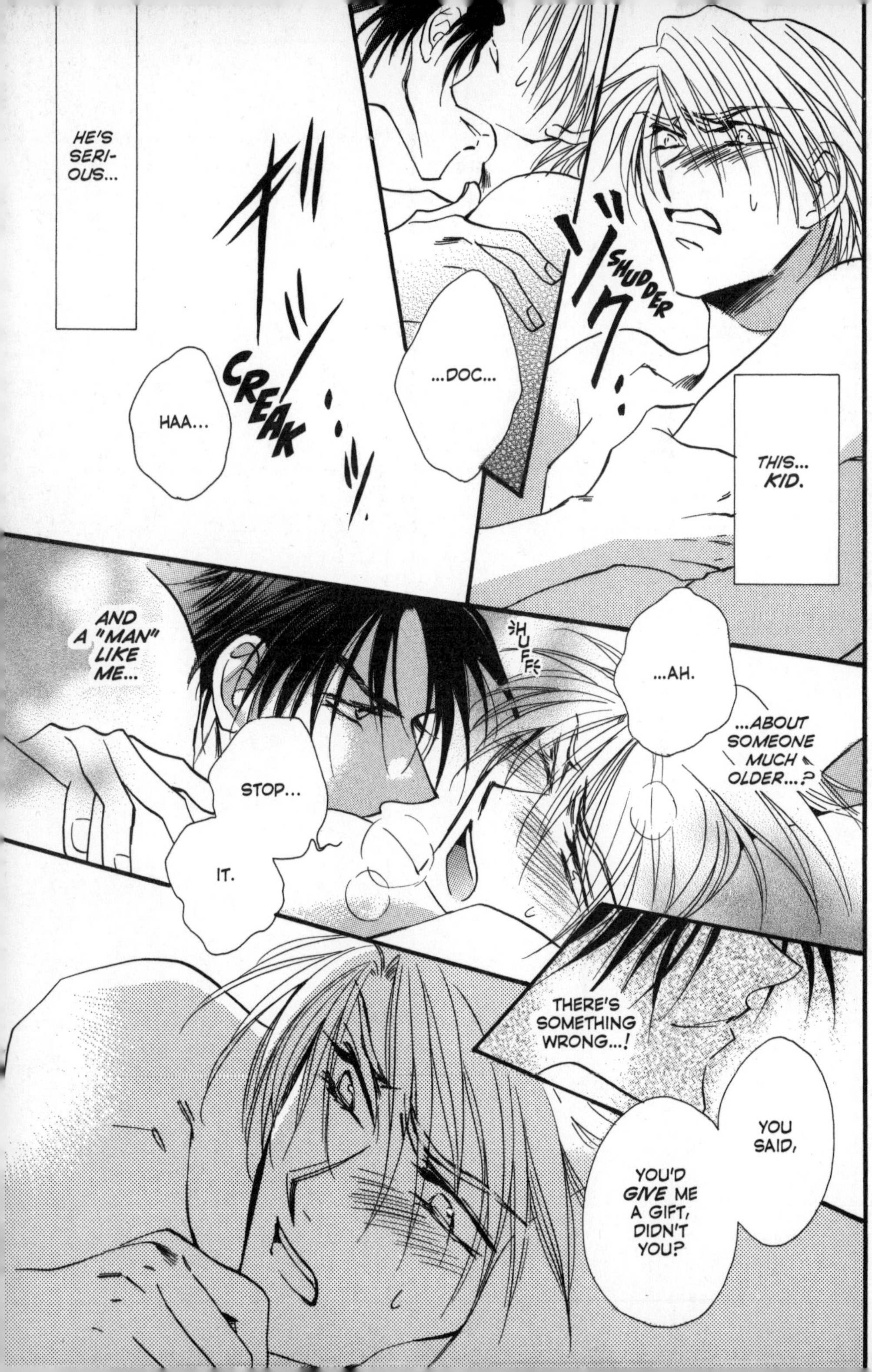
SHUDDER
THIS... KID.
...DOC...
HE'S SERI-OUS...
CREAK
HAA...
...AH.
...ABOUT SOMEONE MUCH OLDER...?
HUFF
AND A "MAN" LIKE ME...
STOP...
IT.
THERE'S SOMETHING WRONG...!
YOU SAID,
YOU'D *GIVE* ME A GIFT, DIDN'T YOU?

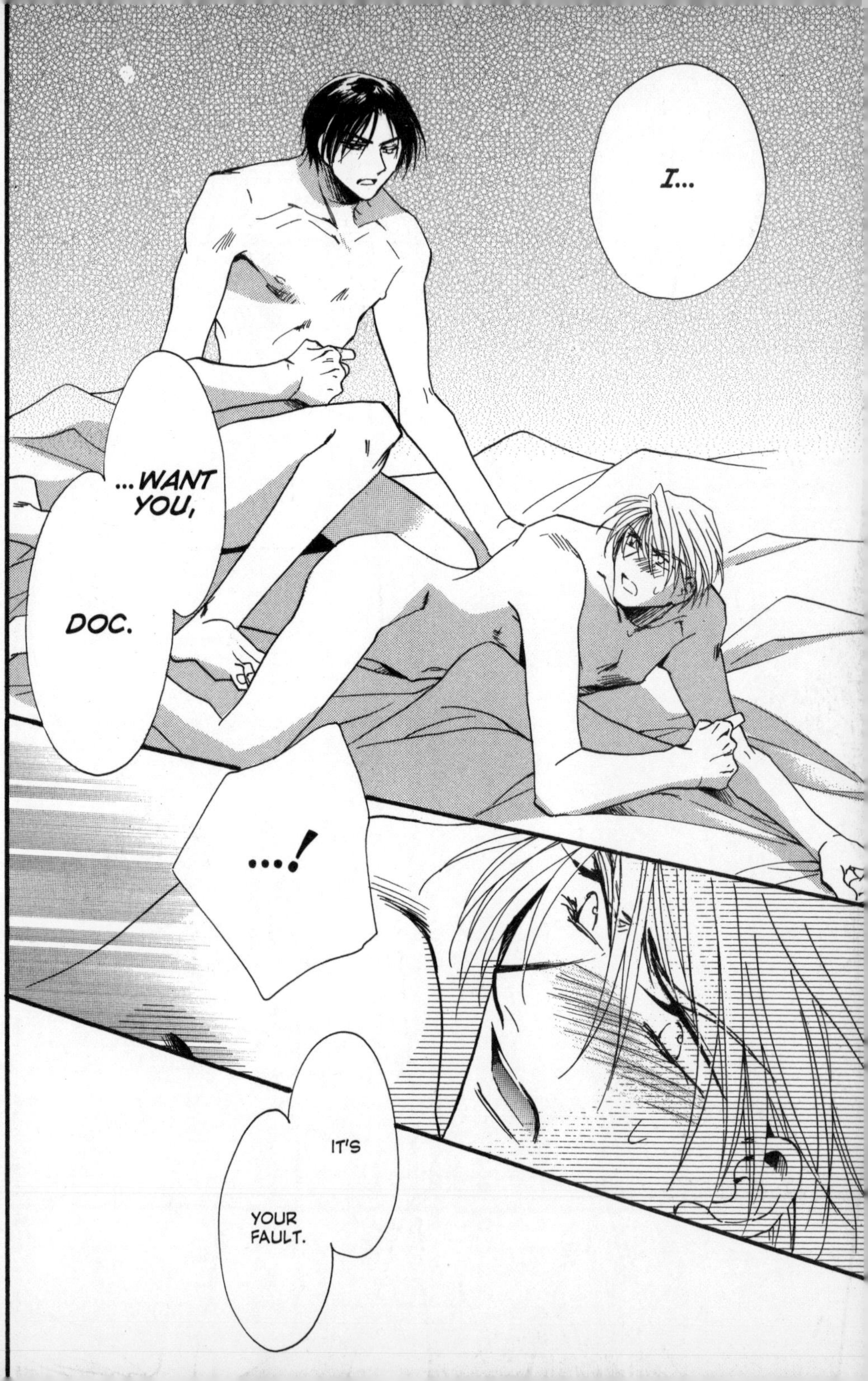
I...
...WANT YOU,
DOC.
...!
IT'S YOUR FAULT.

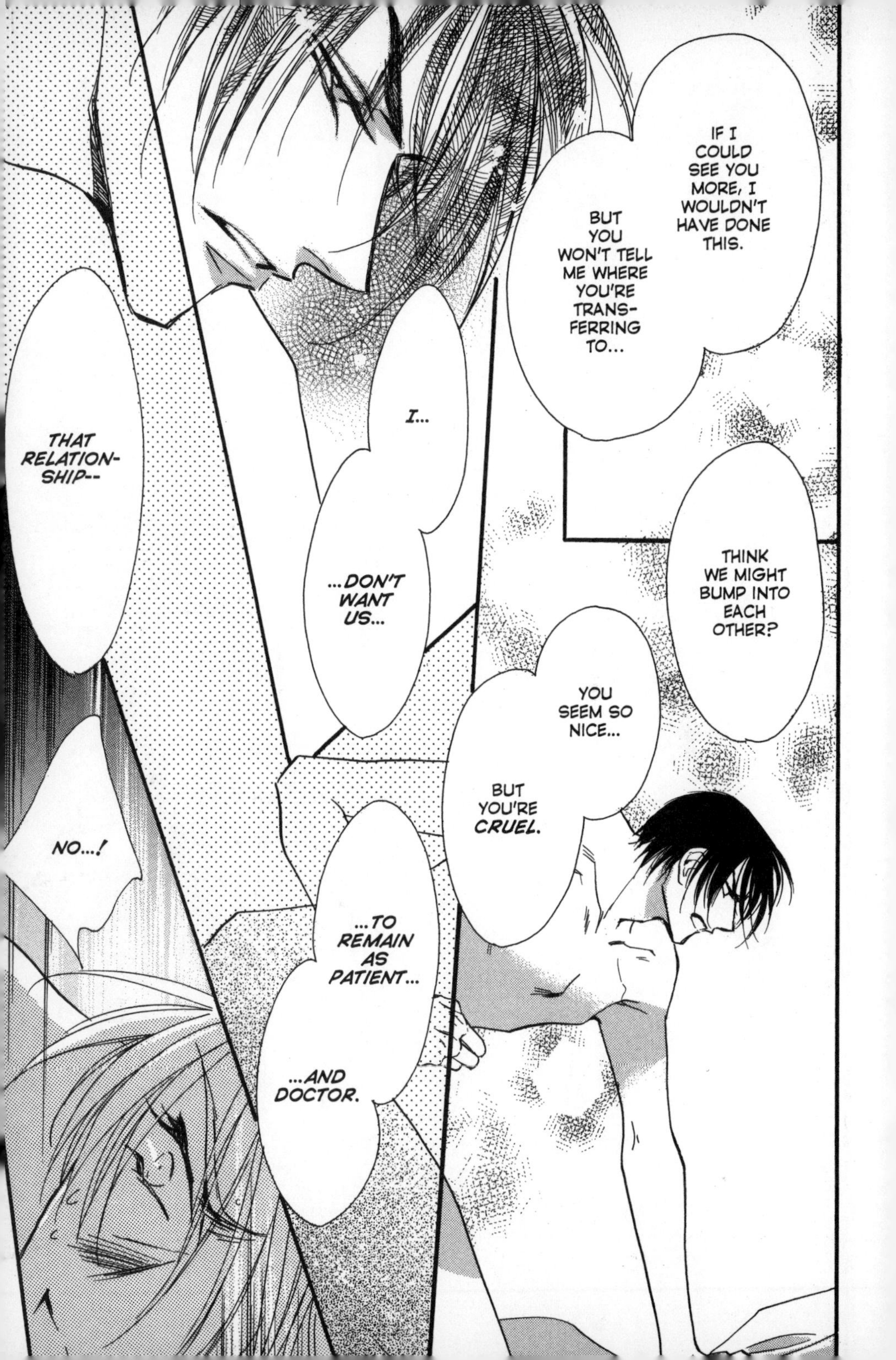
IF I COULD SEE YOU MORE, I WOULDN'T HAVE DONE THIS.
BUT YOU WON'T TELL ME WHERE YOU'RE TRANS-FERRING TO...
THINK WE MIGHT BUMP INTO EACH OTHER?
YOU SEEM SO NICE...
BUT YOU'RE *CRUEL*.
I...
...DON'T WANT US...
...TO REMAIN AS PATIENT...
...AND DOCTOR.
THAT RELATION-SHIP--
NO...!

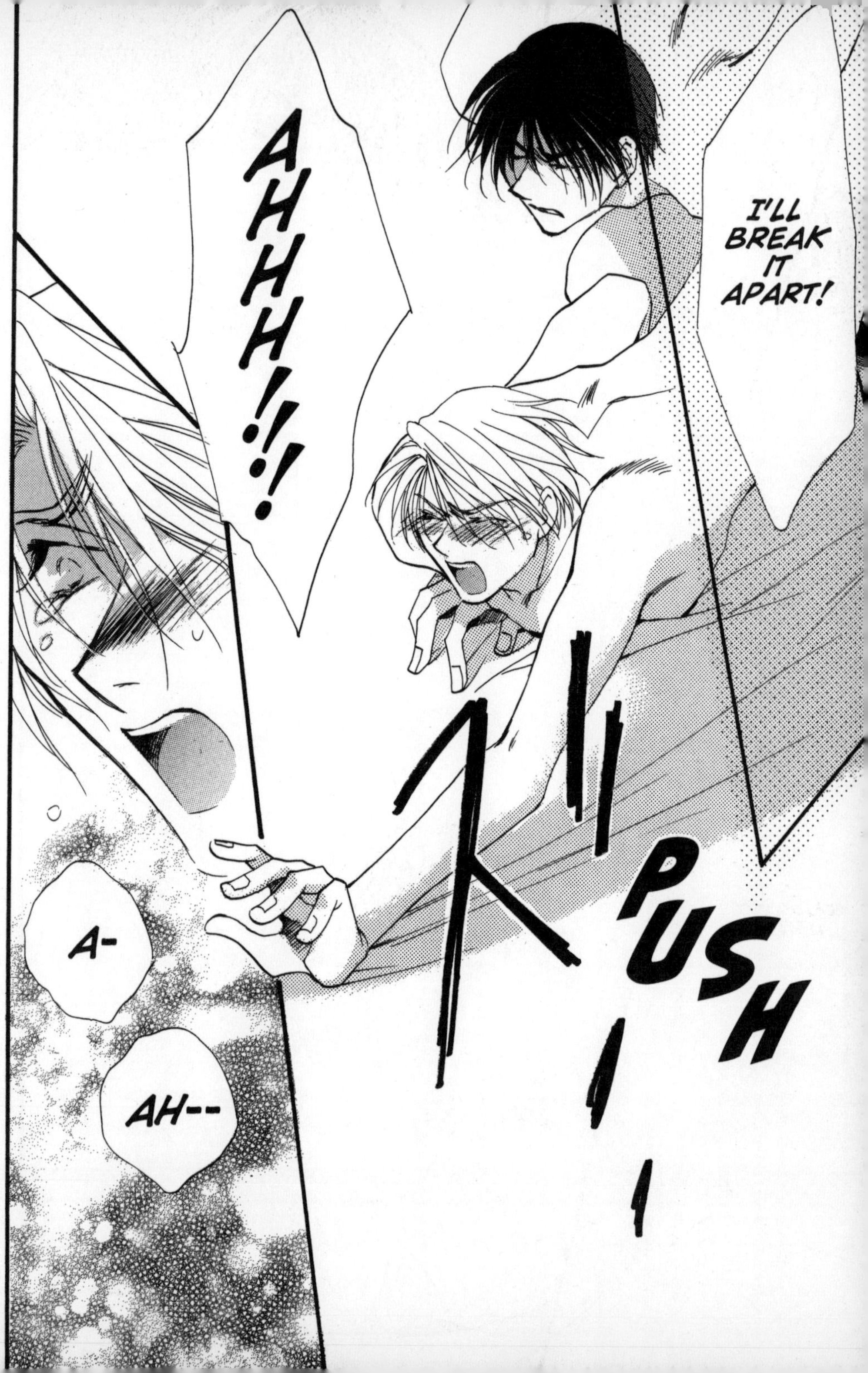
I'LL BREAK IT APART!
AHHHH!!!
PUSH
A-
AH--

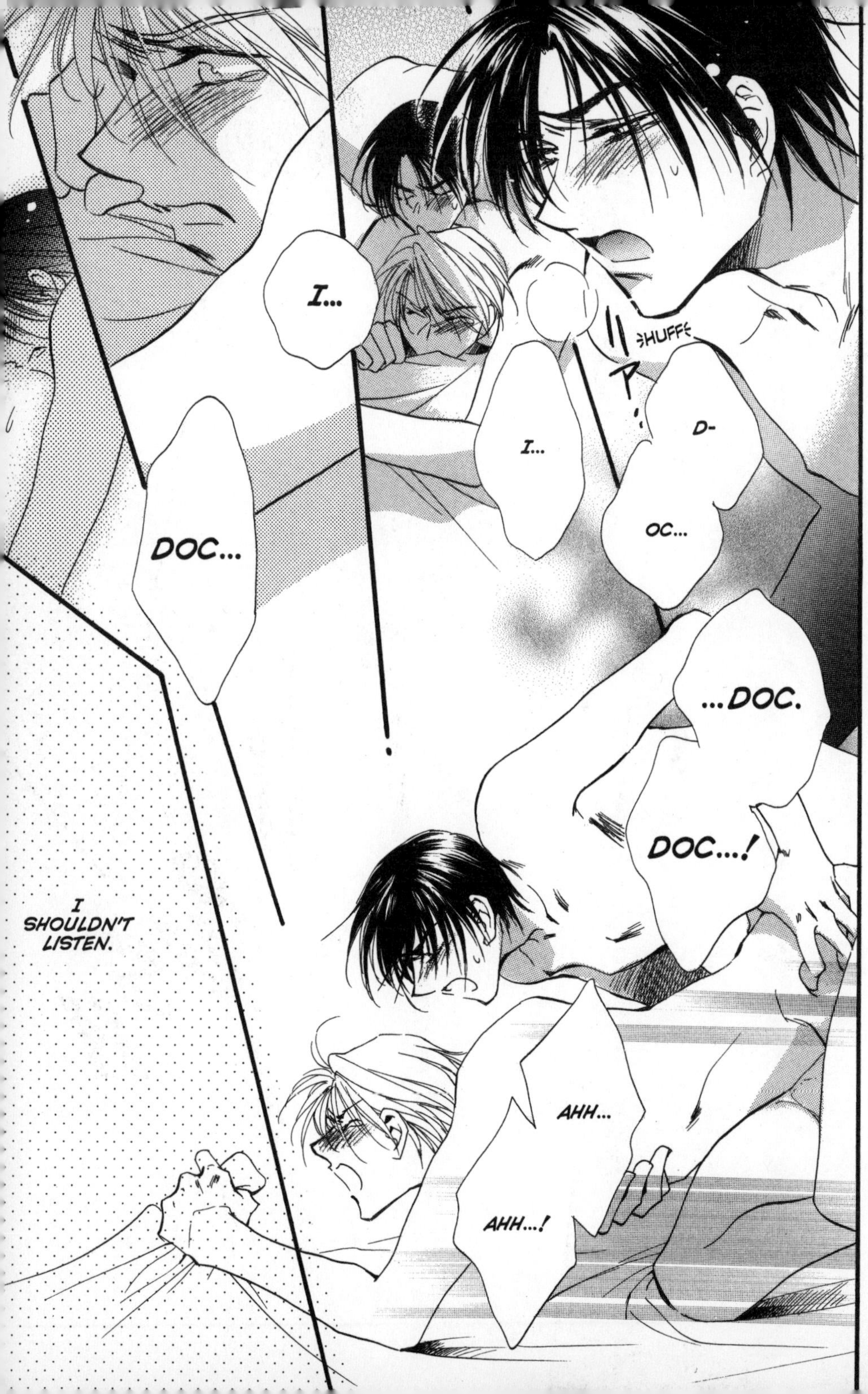

HUFF
D-
OC...
I...
I...
DOC...
...DOC.
DOC...!
AHH...
AHH...!
I SHOULDN'T LISTEN.

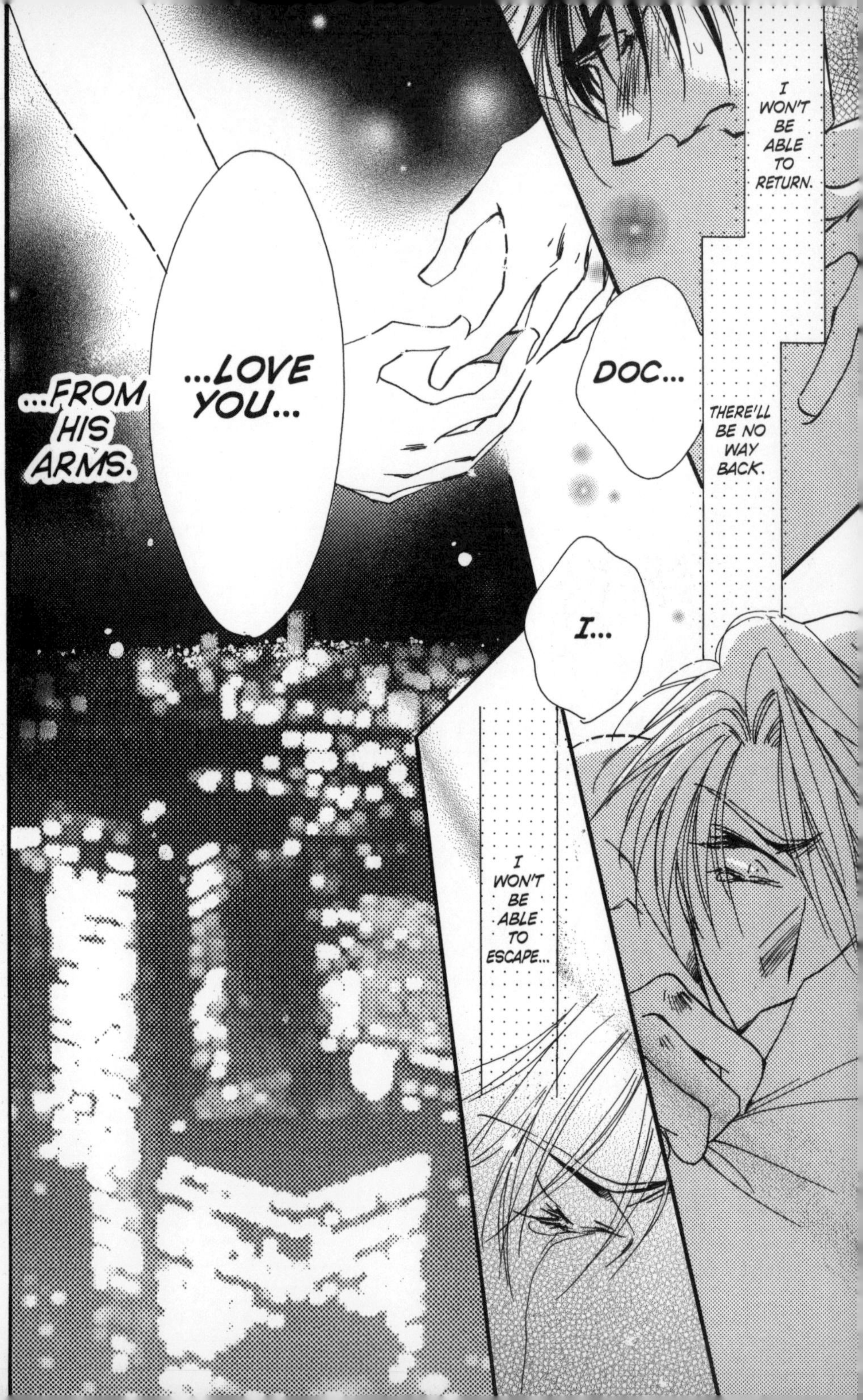
I WON'T BE ABLE TO RETURN.
DOC...
THERE'LL BE NO WAY BACK.
I...
I WON'T BE ABLE TO ESCAPE...
...LOVE YOU...
...FROM HIS ARMS.

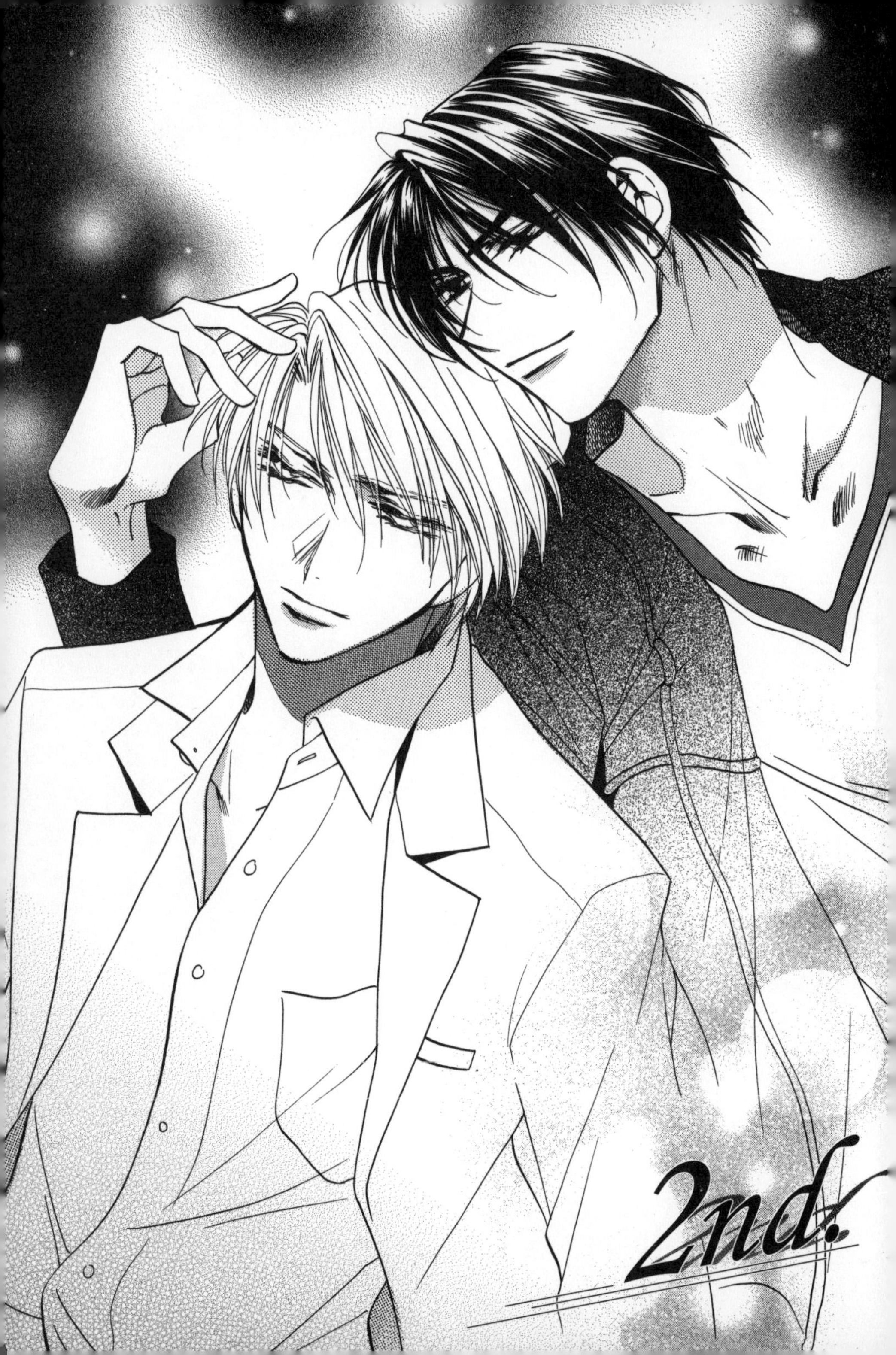
2nd.

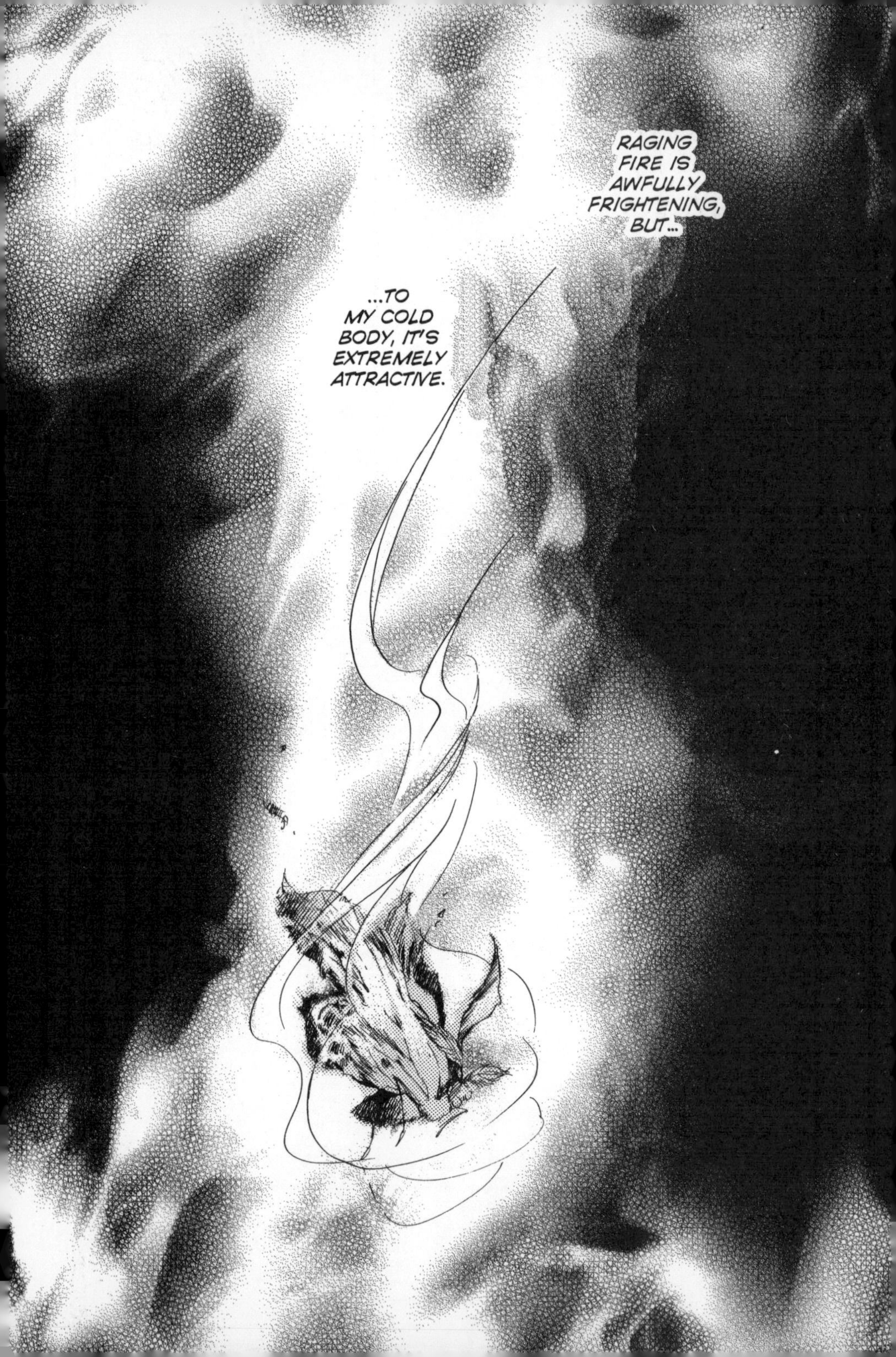
RAGING FIRE IS AWFULLY FRIGHTENING, BUT...
...TO MY COLD BODY, IT'S EXTREMELY ATTRACTIVE.

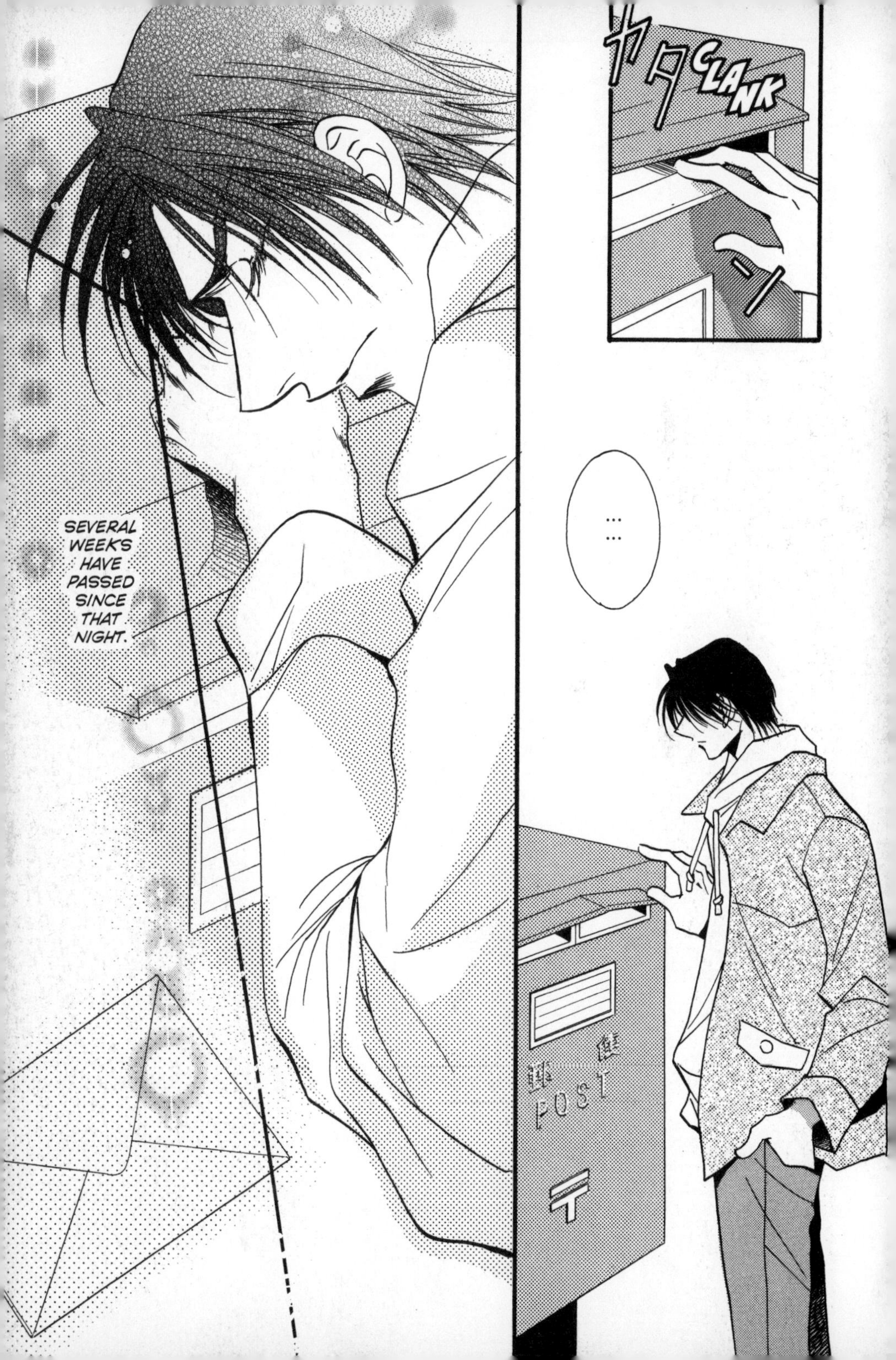
カタ CLANK
... ...
SEVERAL WEEKS HAVE PASSED SINCE THAT NIGHT.

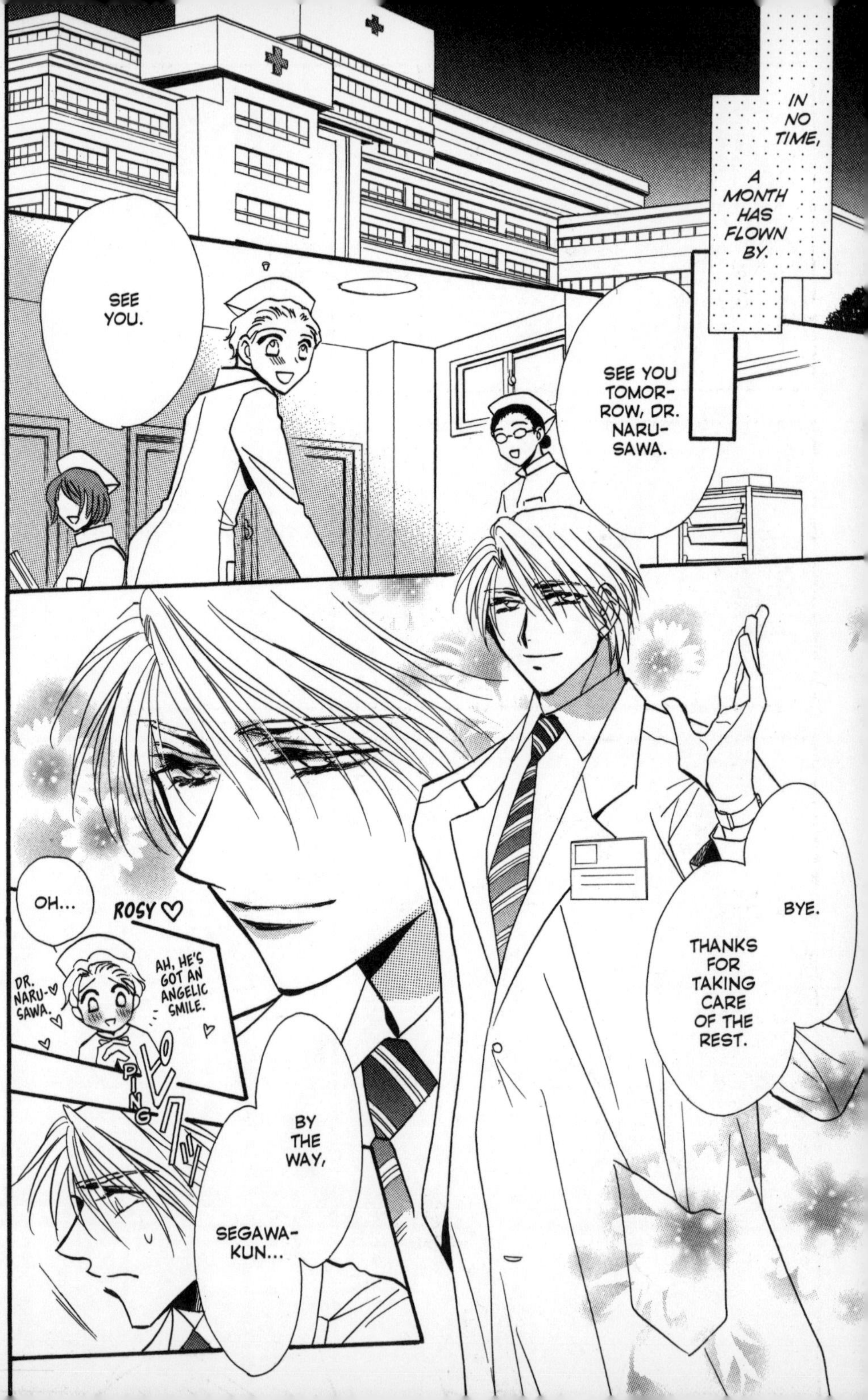

IN NO TIME, A MONTH HAS FLOWN BY.
SEE YOU TOMORROW, DR. NARUSAWA.
SEE YOU.
BYE.
THANKS FOR TAKING CARE OF THE REST.
ROSY ♡
AH, HE'S GOT AN ANGELIC SMILE.
DR. NARU-SAWA. ♡
OH...
PING
BY THE WAY,
SEGAWA-KUN...

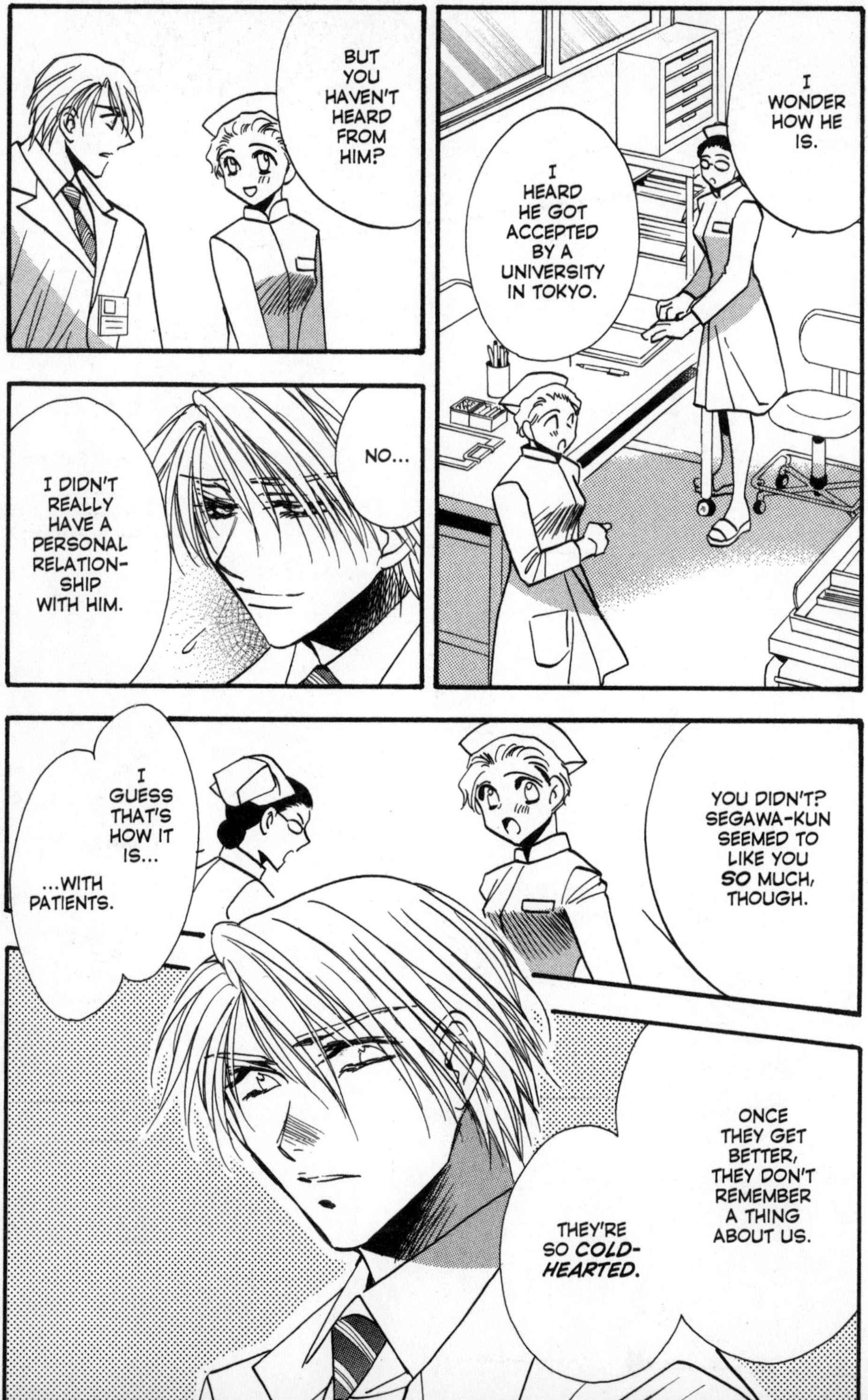
I WONDER HOW HE IS.
I HEARD HE GOT ACCEPTED BY A UNIVERSITY IN TOKYO.
BUT YOU HAVEN'T HEARD FROM HIM?
NO...
I DIDN'T REALLY HAVE A PERSONAL RELATIONSHIP WITH HIM.
YOU DIDN'T? SEGAWA-KUN SEEMED TO LIKE YOU **SO** MUCH, THOUGH.
I GUESS THAT'S HOW IT IS...
...WITH PATIENTS.
ONCE THEY GET BETTER, THEY DON'T REMEMBER A THING ABOUT US.
THEY'RE SO ***COLD-HEARTED***.

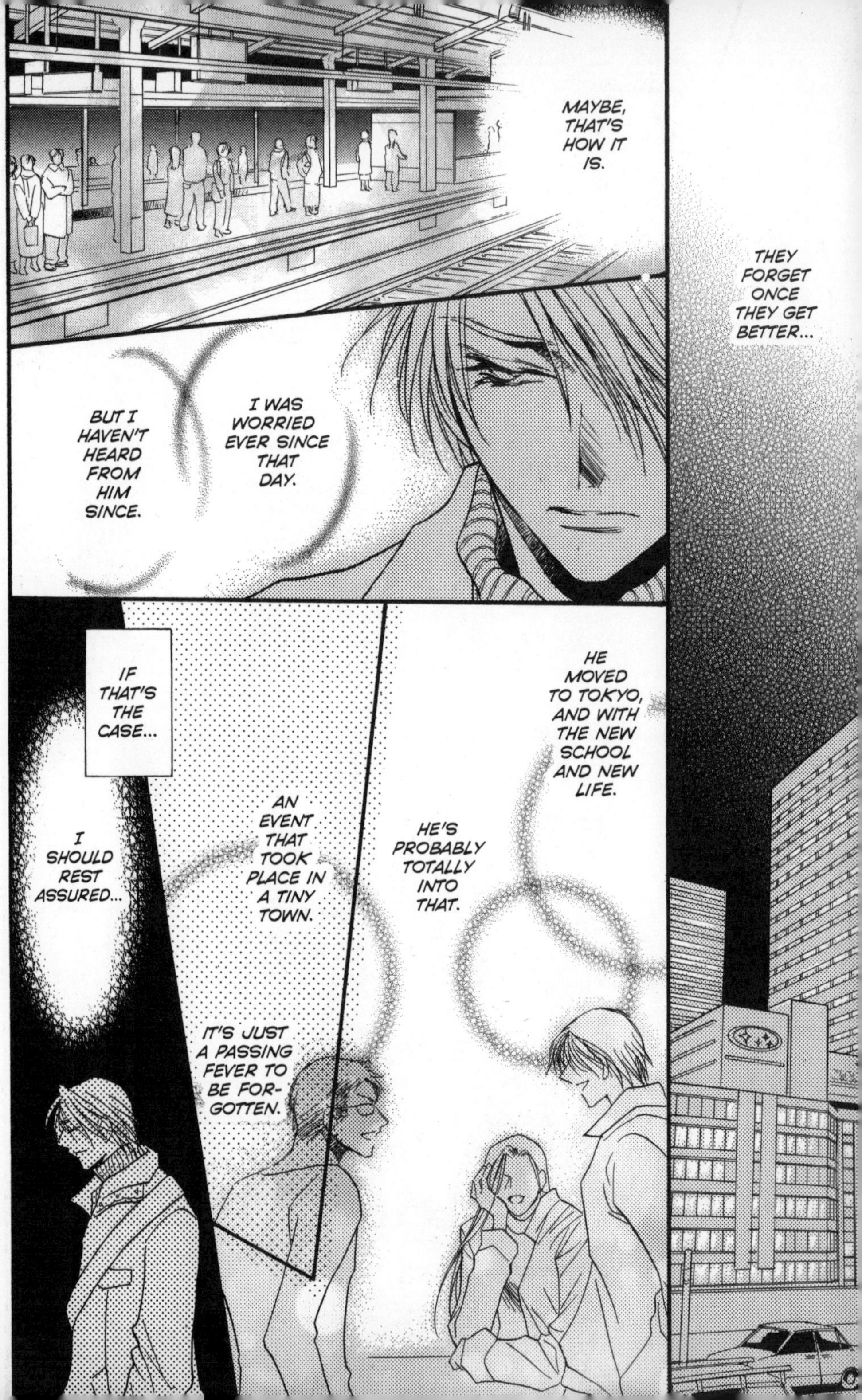

THEY FORGET ONCE THEY GET BETTER...
MAYBE, THAT'S HOW IT IS.
I WAS WORRIED EVER SINCE THAT DAY.
BUT I HAVEN'T HEARD FROM HIM SINCE.
HE MOVED TO TOKYO, AND WITH THE NEW SCHOOL AND NEW LIFE.
HE'S PROBABLY TOTALLY INTO THAT.
AN EVENT THAT TOOK PLACE IN A TINY TOWN.
IT'S JUST A PASSING FEVER TO BE FORGOTTEN.
IF THAT'S THE CASE...
I SHOULD REST ASSURED...

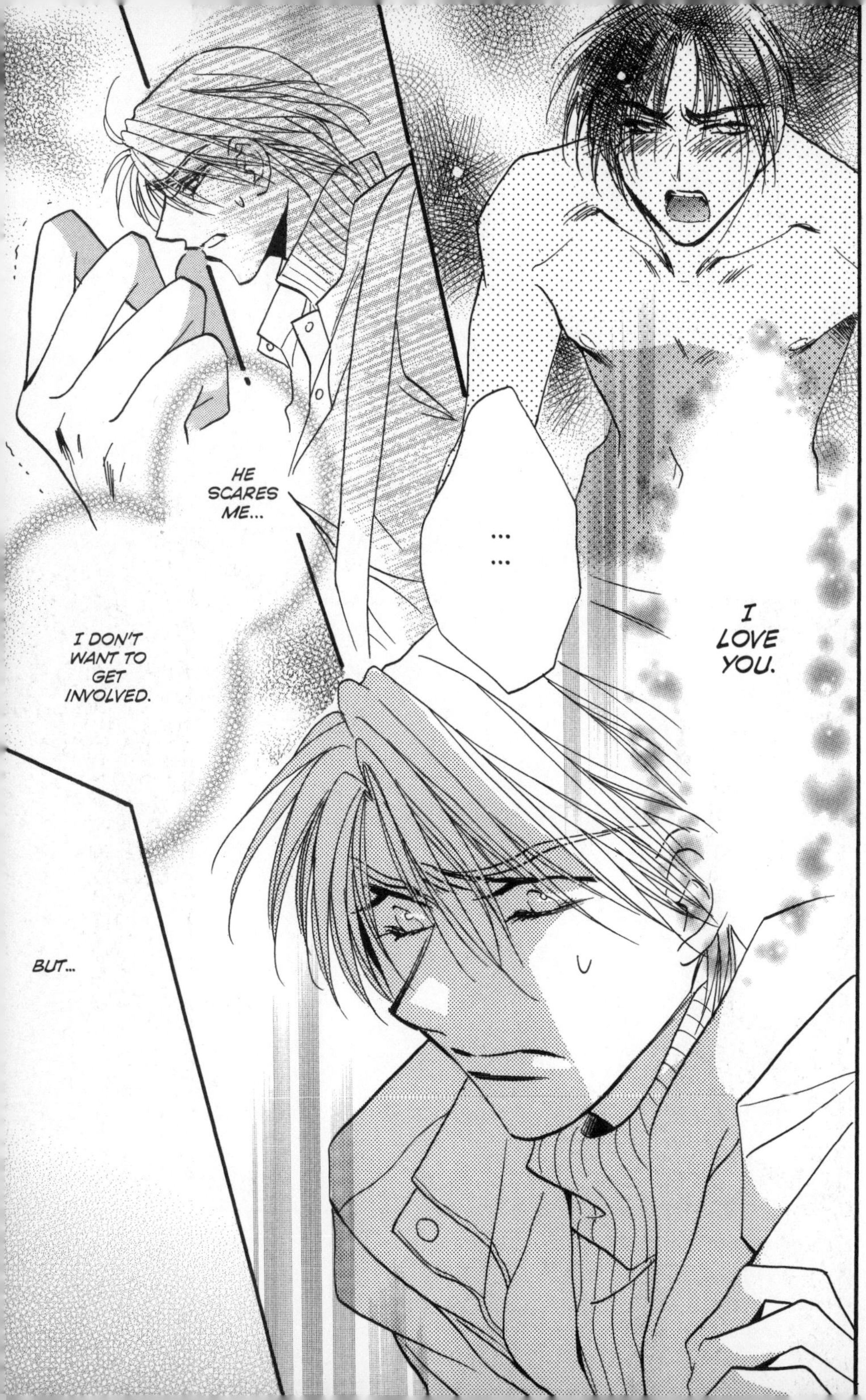
I LOVE YOU.
...
...
HE SCARES ME...
I DON'T WANT TO GET INVOLVED.
BUT...

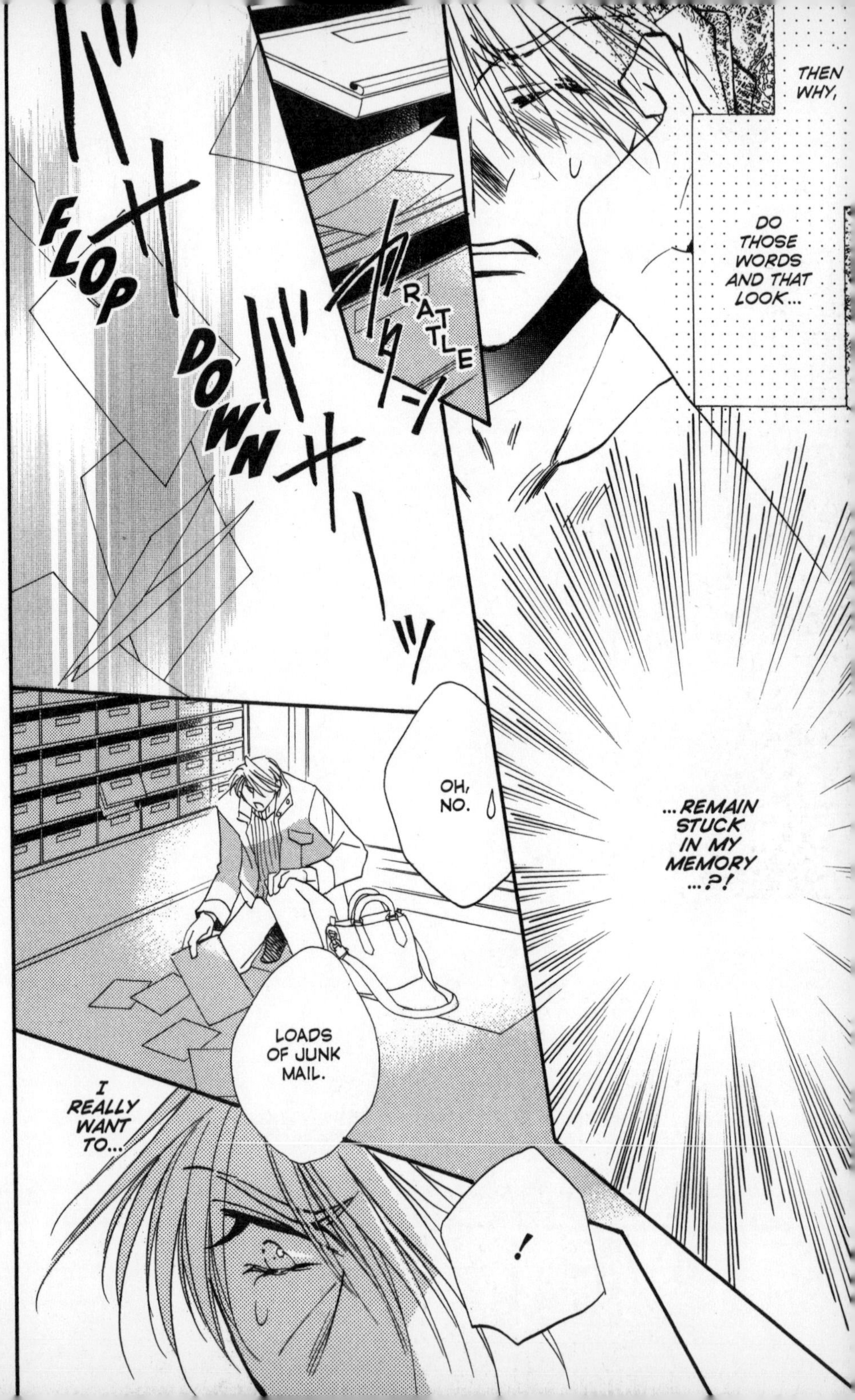
THEN WHY,
DO THOSE WORDS AND THAT LOOK...
...REMAIN STUCK IN MY MEMORY ...?!
RATTLE
FLOP DOWN
OH, NO.
LOADS OF JUNK MAIL.
I REALLY WANT TO...
!

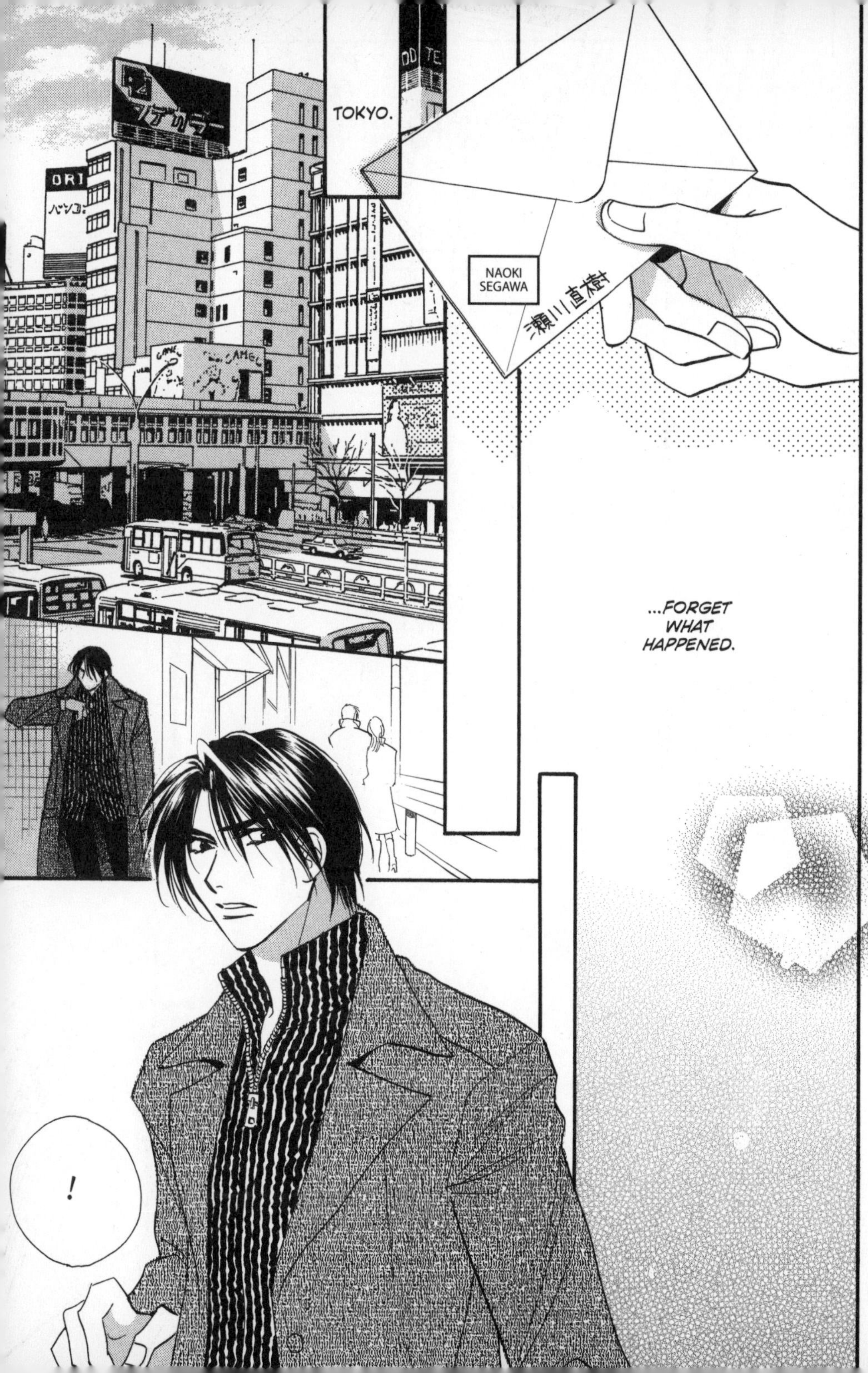
NAOKI SEGAWA
瀬川直樹
TOKYO.
...FORGET WHAT HAPPENED.
!

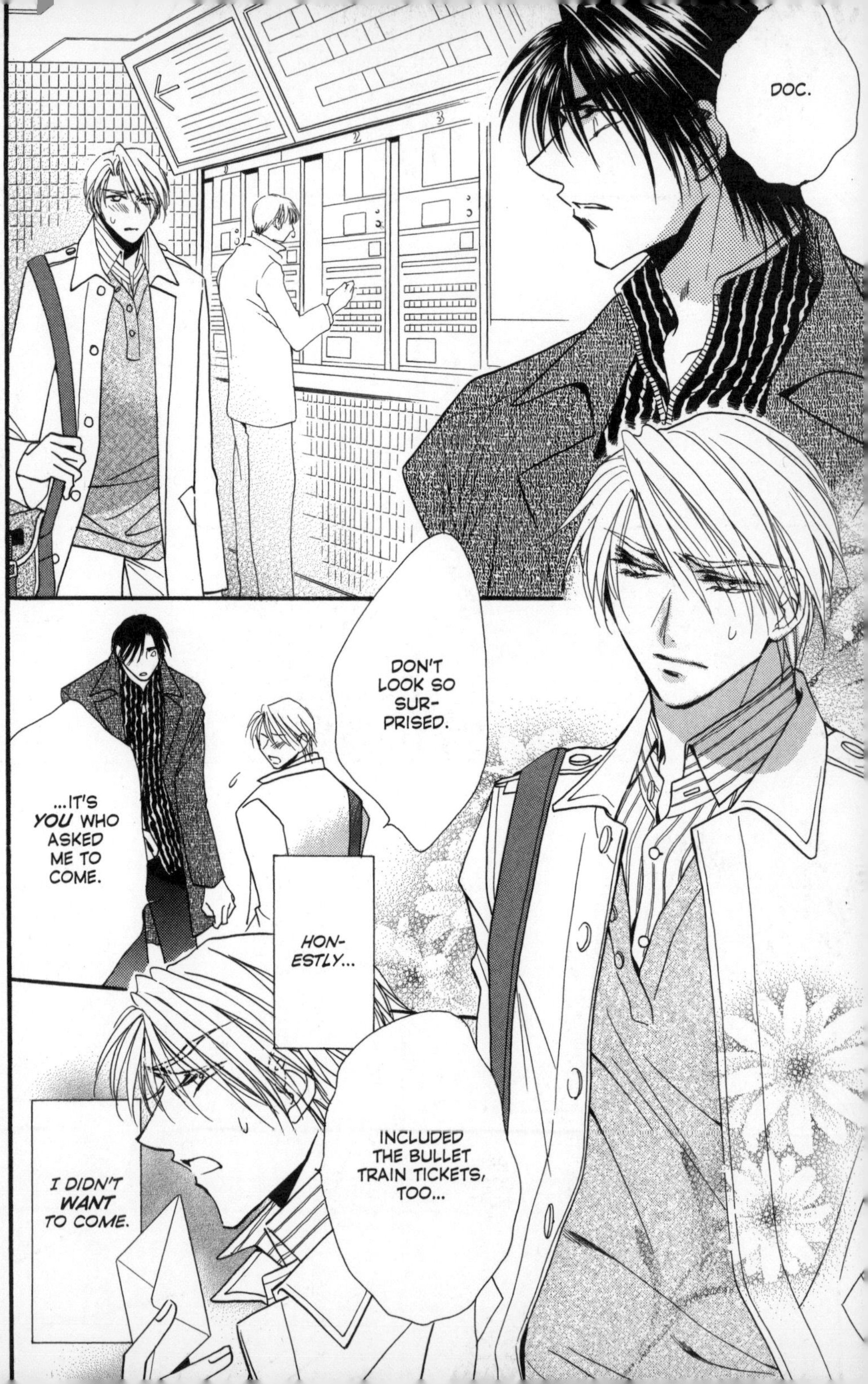
DOC.
DON'T LOOK SO SUR-PRISED.
...IT'S *YOU* WHO ASKED ME TO COME.
HON-ESTLY...
INCLUDED THE BULLET TRAIN TICKETS, TOO...
I DIDN'T WANT TO COME.

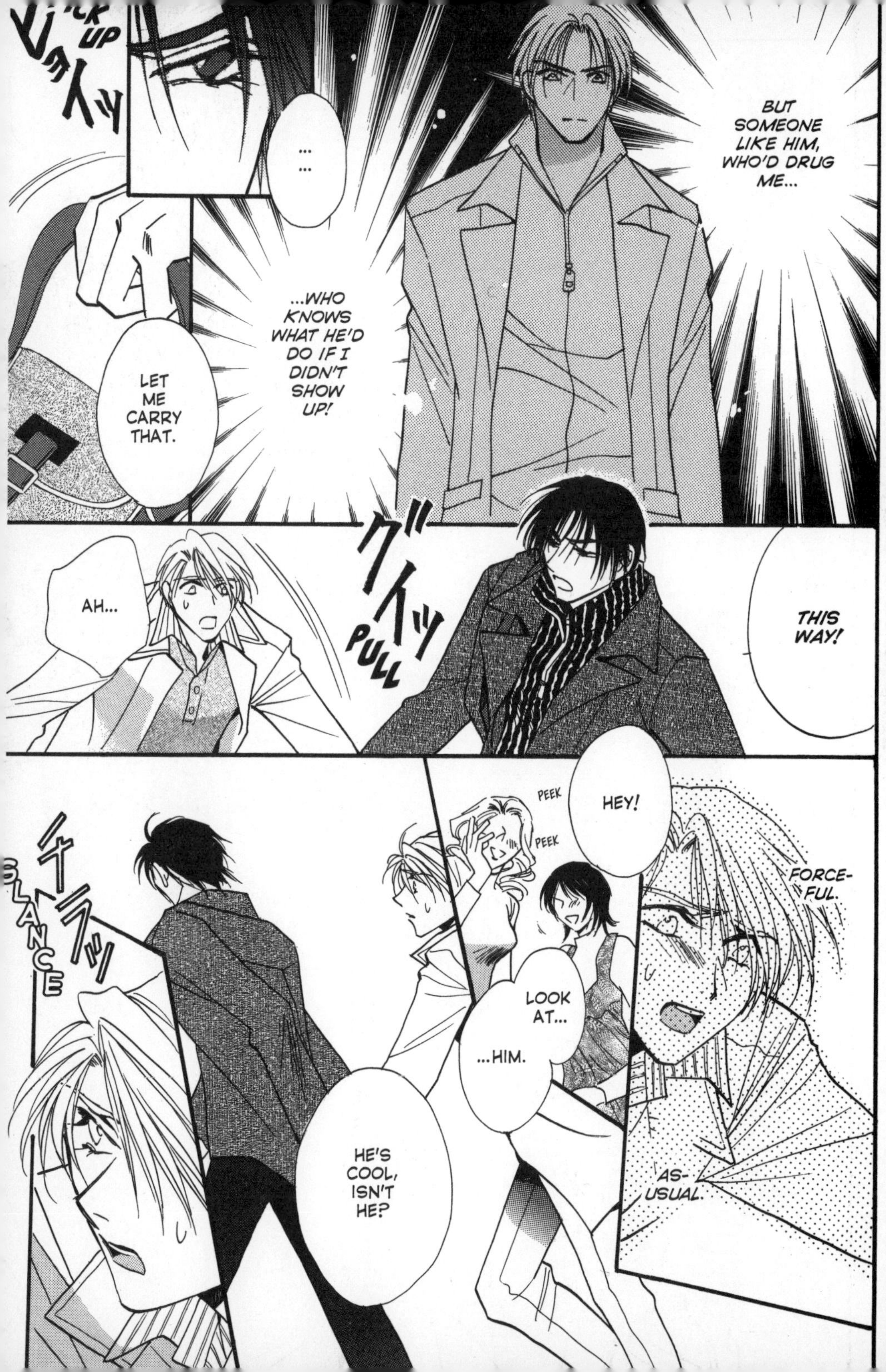
BUT SOMEONE LIKE HIM, WHO'D DRUG ME...
...WHO KNOWS WHAT HE'D DO IF I DIDN'T SHOW UP!
...
...
CK UP
LET ME CARRY THAT.
THIS WAY!
PULL
AH...
FORCE-FUL.
AS USUAL.
HEY!
PEEK
PEEK
LOOK AT...
...HIM.
HE'S COOL, ISN'T HE?
GLANCE

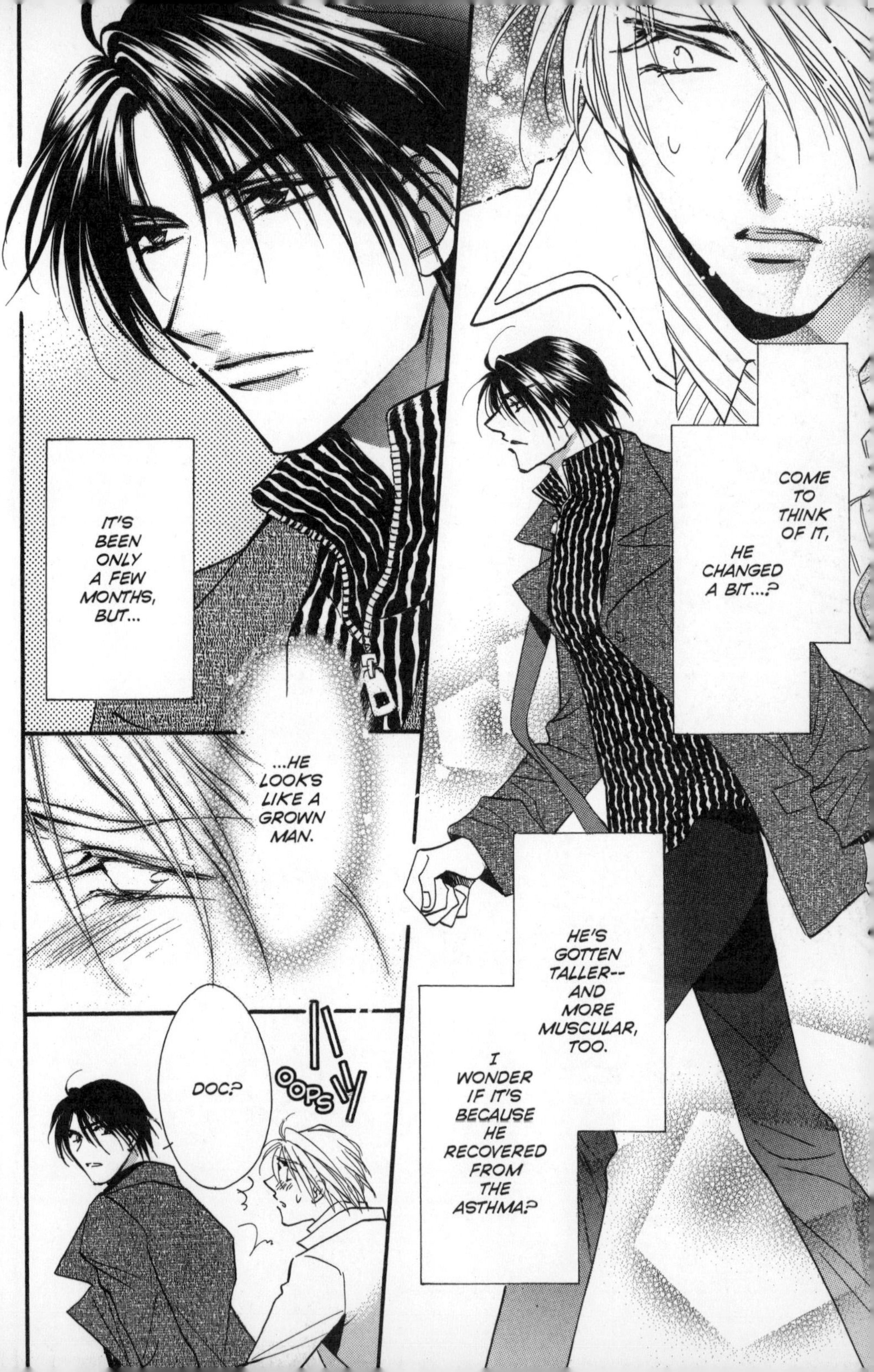
COME TO THINK OF IT, HE CHANGED A BIT...?
HE'S GOTTEN TALLER-- AND MORE MUSCULAR, TOO.
I WONDER IF IT'S BECAUSE HE RECOVERED FROM THE ASTHMA?
IT'S BEEN ONLY A FEW MONTHS, BUT...
...HE LOOKS LIKE A GROWN MAN.
DOC?
OOPS

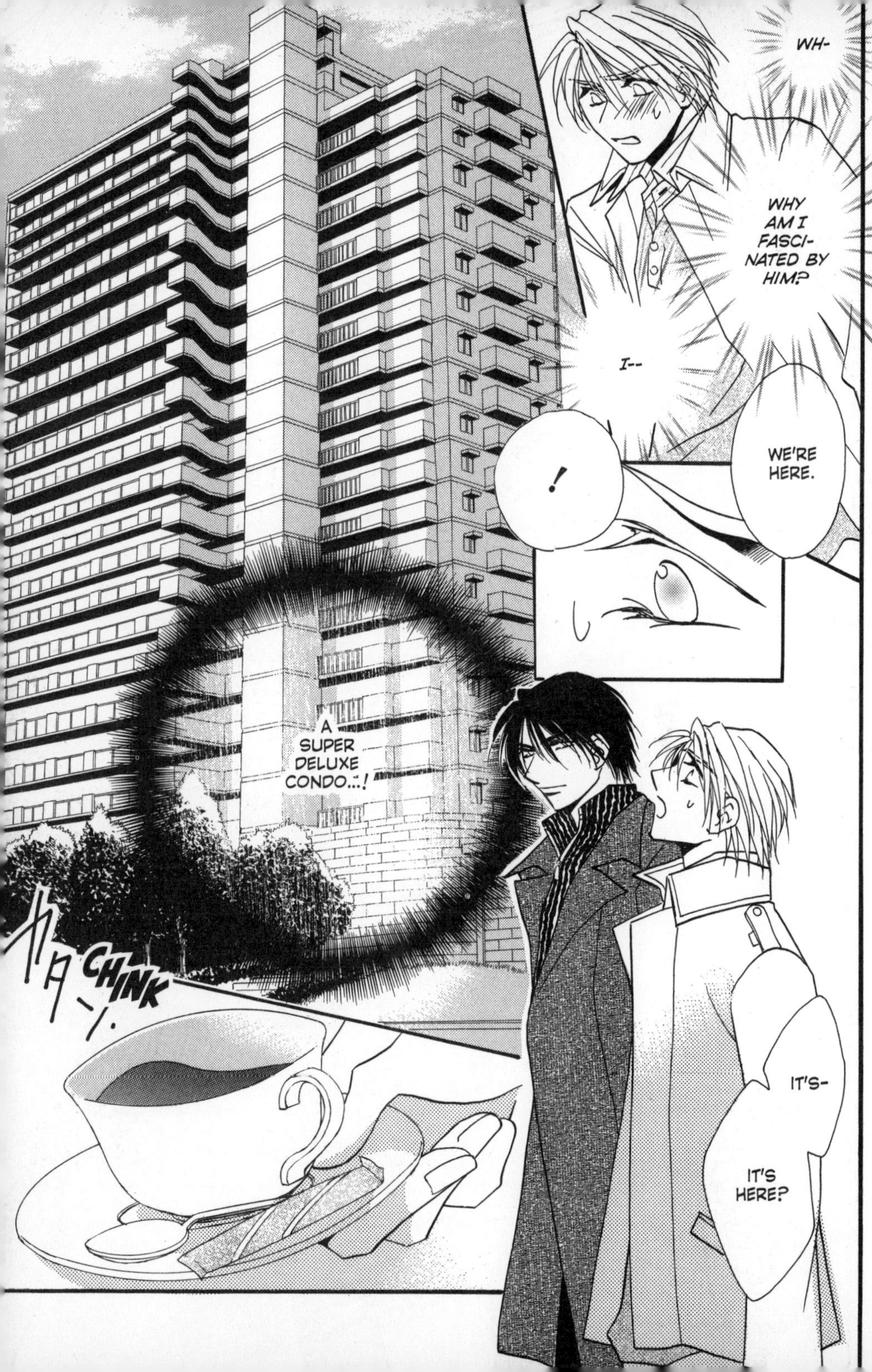
WH-
WHY AM I FASCINATED BY HIM?
I--
WE'RE HERE.
!
IT'S-
IT'S HERE?
A SUPER DELUXE CONDO...!
CHINK

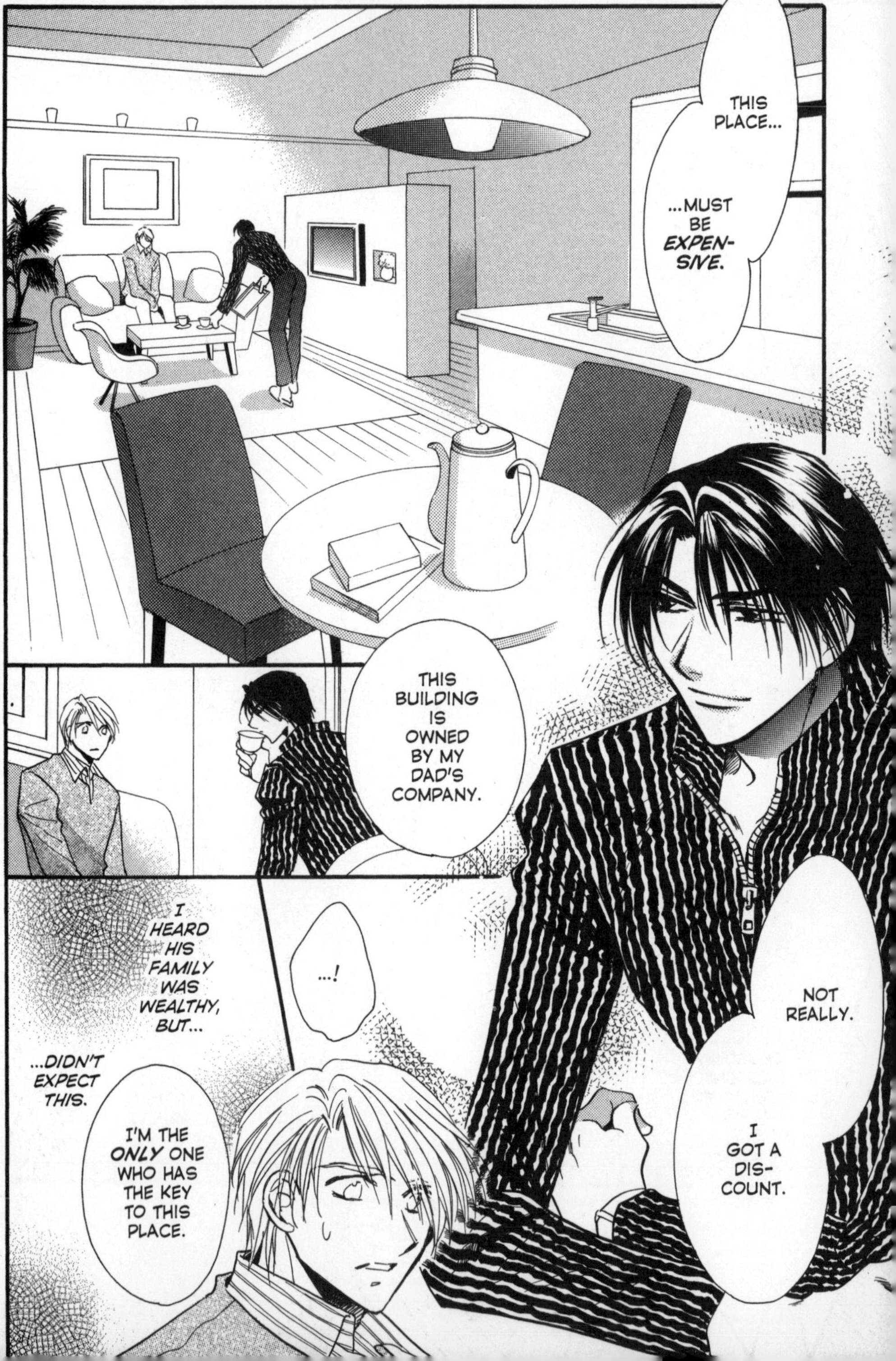
THIS PLACE...
...MUST BE EXPEN-SIVE.
NOT REALLY.
I GOT A DIS-COUNT.
THIS BUILDING IS OWNED BY MY DAD'S COMPANY.
...!
I HEARD HIS FAMILY WAS WEALTHY, BUT...
...DIDN'T EXPECT THIS.
I'M THE ONLY ONE WHO HAS THE KEY TO THIS PLACE.

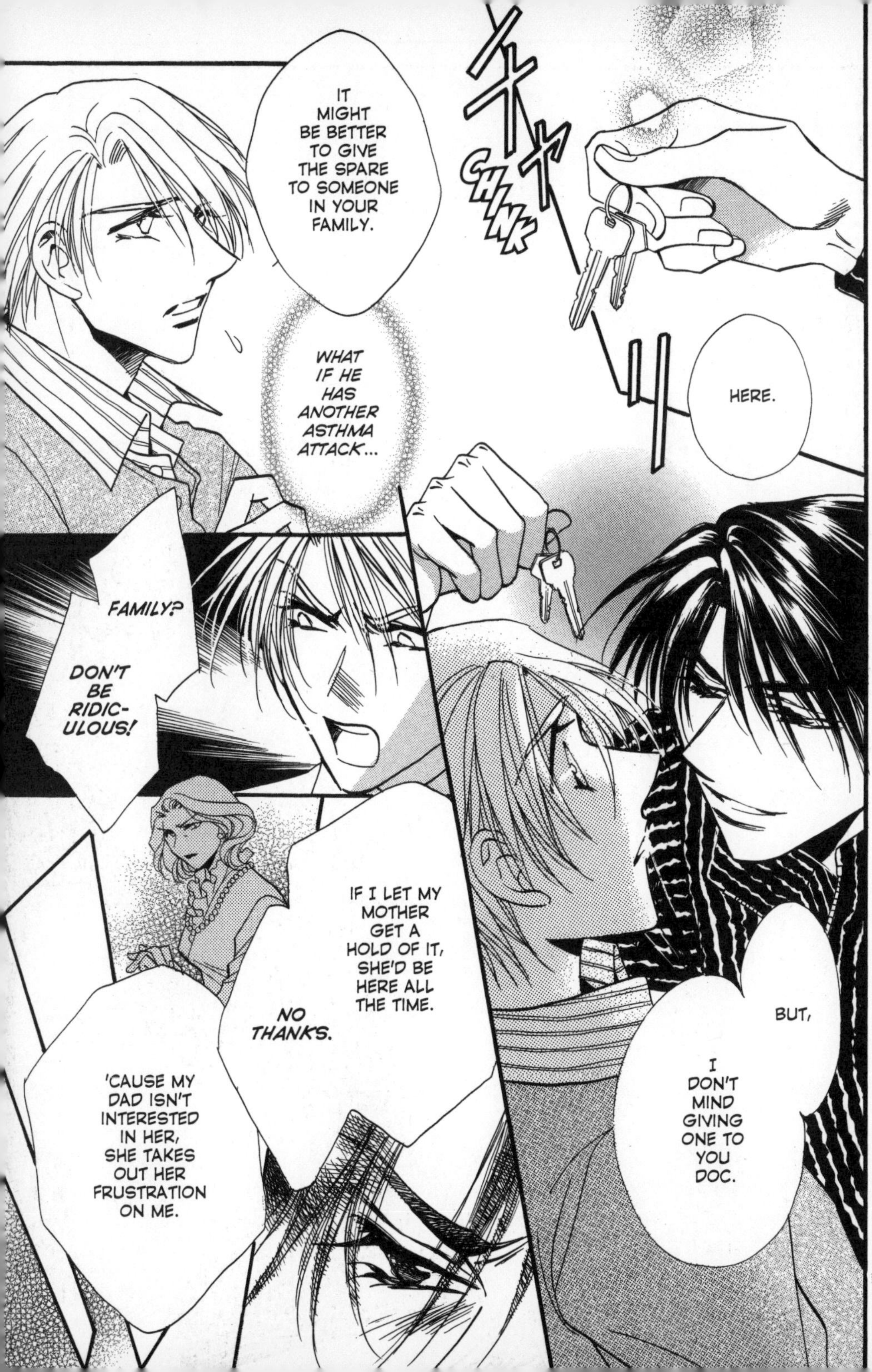
CHINK
HERE.
IT MIGHT BE BETTER TO GIVE THE SPARE TO SOMEONE IN YOUR FAMILY.
WHAT IF HE HAS ANOTHER ASTHMA ATTACK...
FAMILY?
DON'T BE RIDICULOUS!
IF I LET MY MOTHER GET A HOLD OF IT, SHE'D BE HERE ALL THE TIME.
NO THANKS.
'CAUSE MY DAD ISN'T INTERESTED IN HER, SHE TAKES OUT HER FRUSTRATION ON ME.
BUT,
I DON'T MIND GIVING ONE TO YOU DOC.

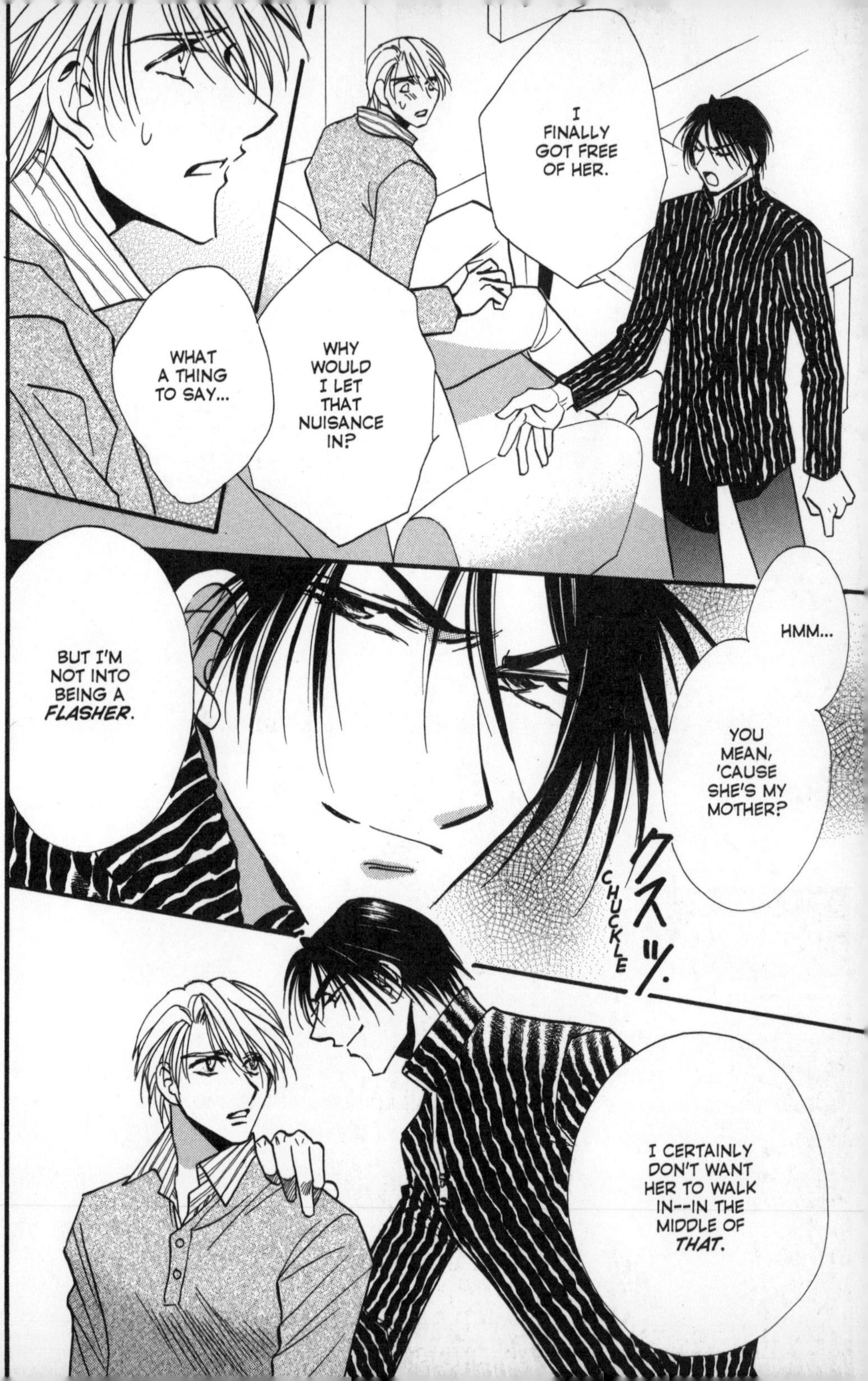
I FINALLY GOT FREE OF HER.
WHY WOULD I LET THAT NUISANCE IN?
WHAT A THING TO SAY...
HMM...
YOU MEAN, 'CAUSE SHE'S MY MOTHER?
CHUCKLE
BUT I'M NOT INTO BEING A *FLASHER*.
I CERTAINLY DON'T WANT HER TO WALK IN--IN THE MIDDLE OF *THAT*.

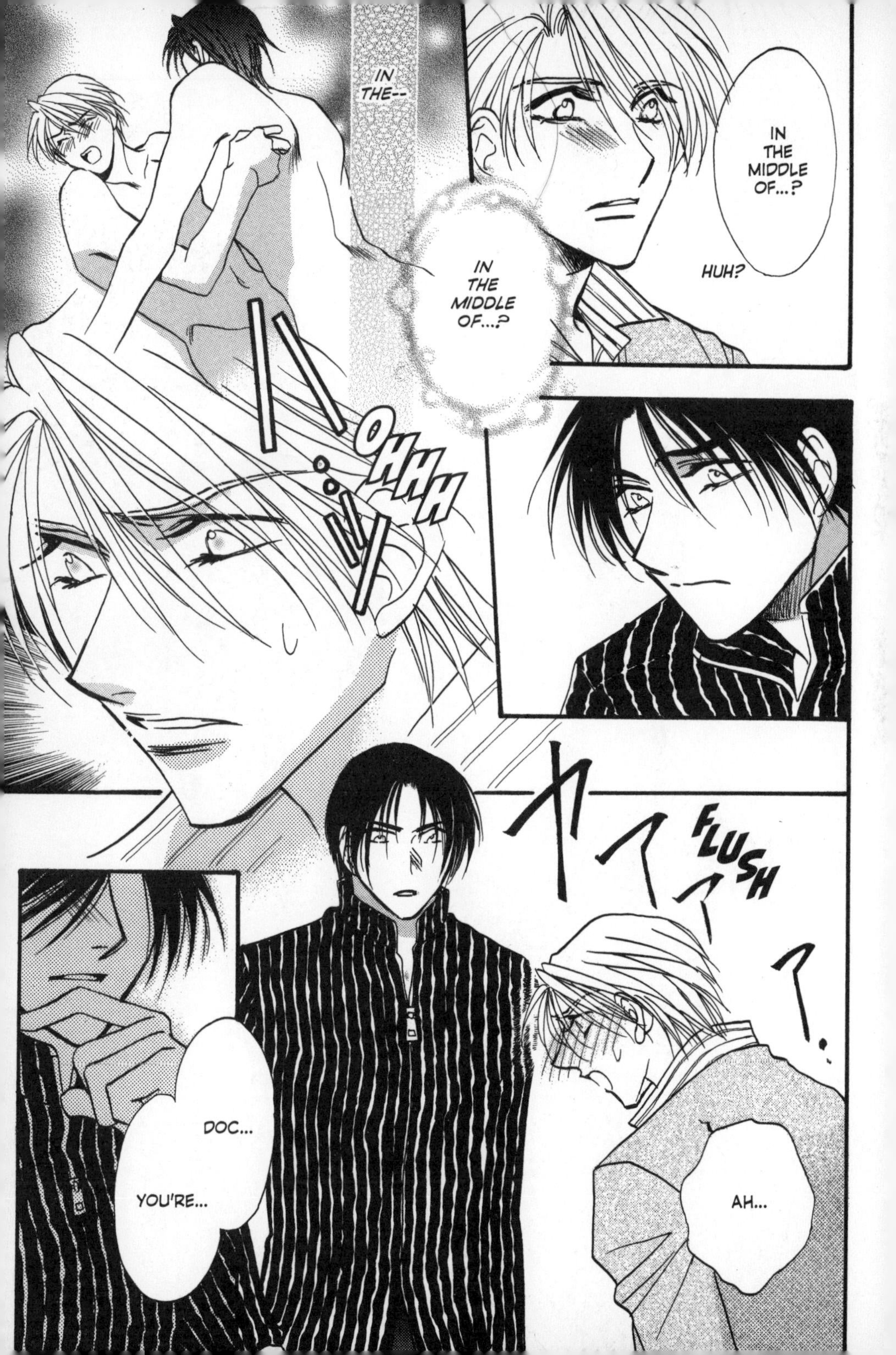
IN THE MIDDLE OF...?
HUH?
IN THE MIDDLE OF...?
IN THE--
OHHH
FLUSH
AH...
DOC...
YOU'RE...

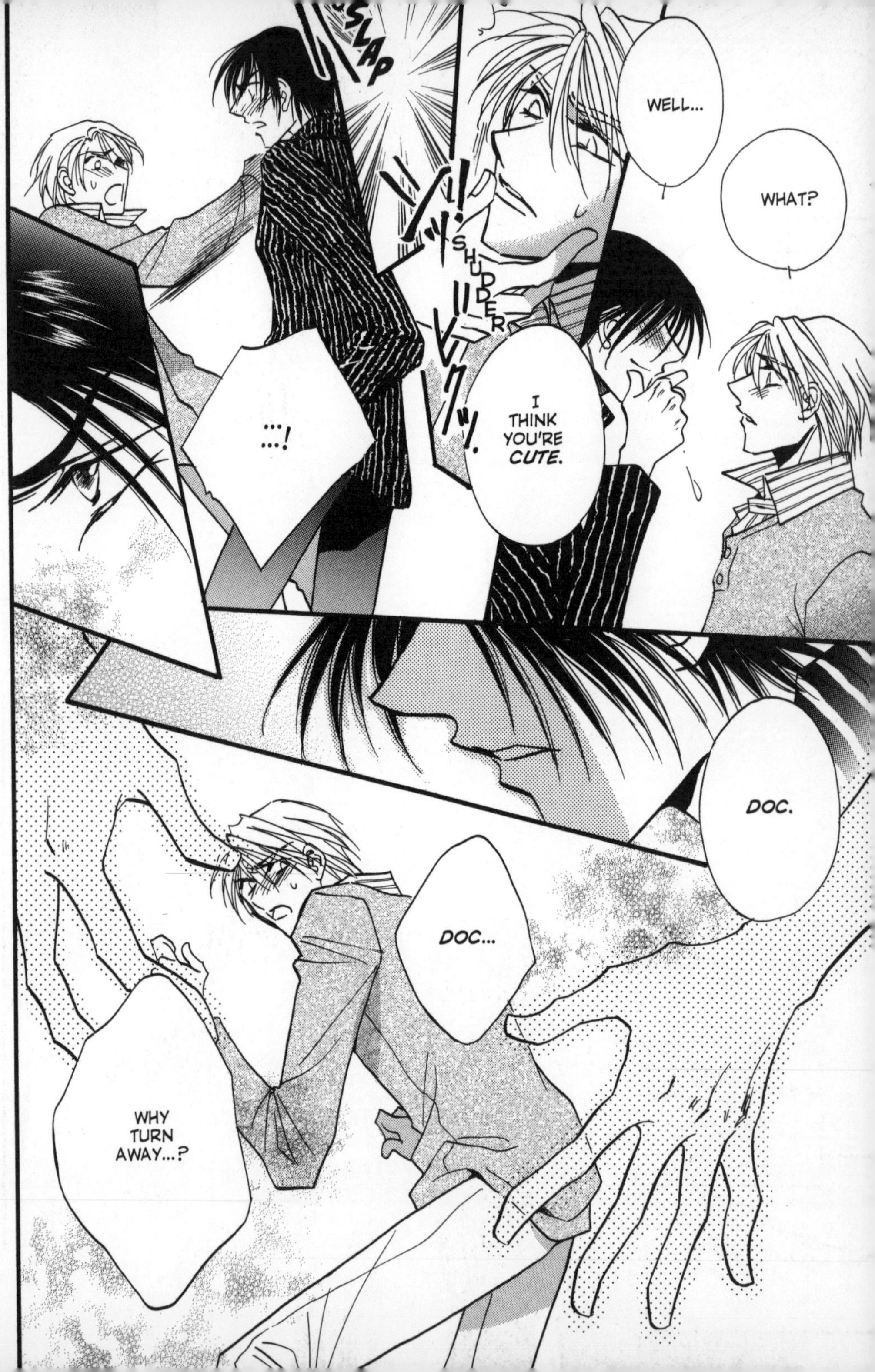
WELL...
WHAT?
I THINK YOU'RE *CUTE.*
SHUDDER
SLAP
...!
DOC.
DOC...
WHY TURN AWAY...?

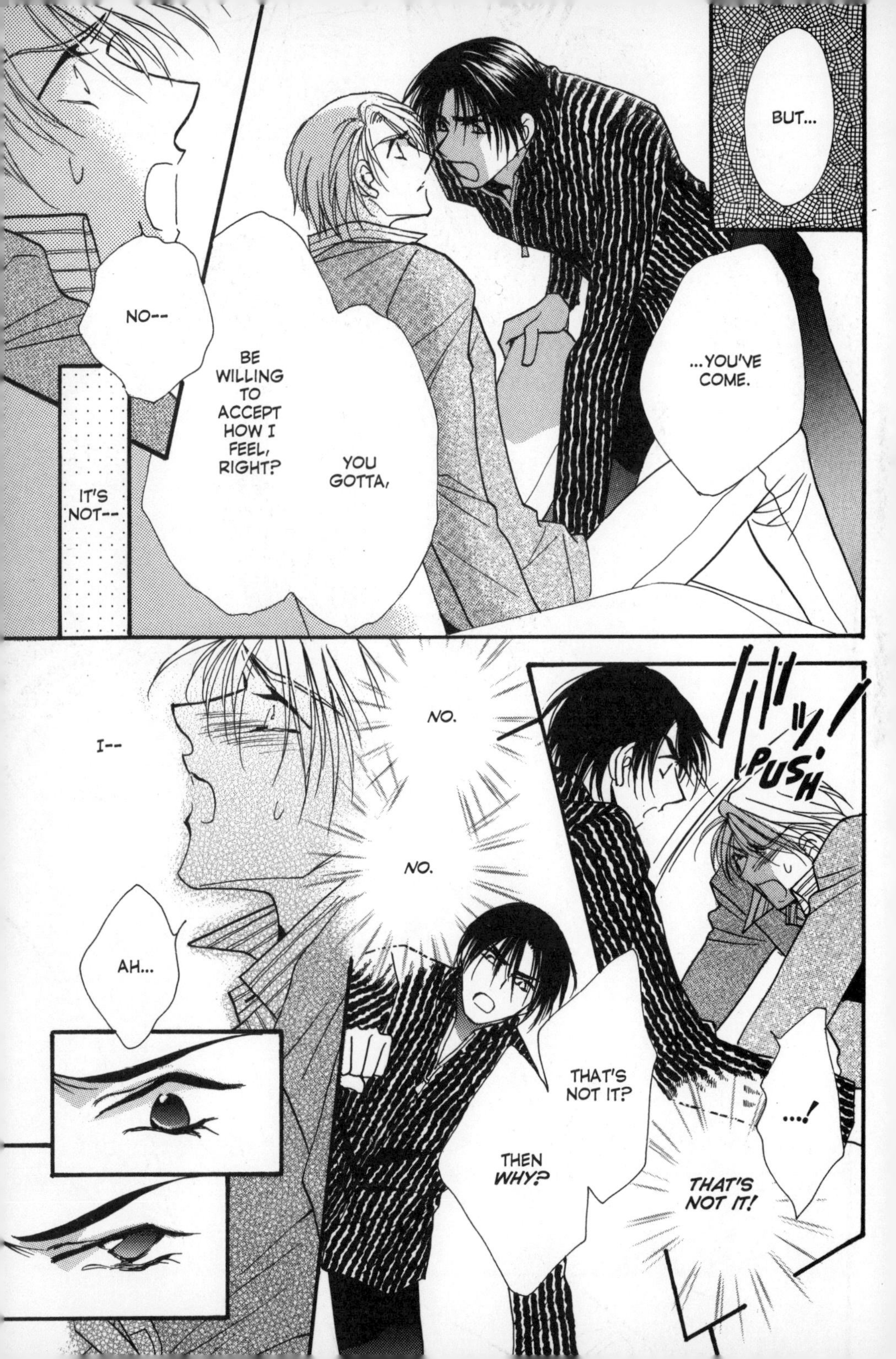
BUT...
...YOU'VE COME.
YOU GOTTA, BE WILLING TO ACCEPT HOW I FEEL, RIGHT?
NO--
IT'S NOT--
PUSH
...!
THAT'S NOT IT!
THAT'S NOT IT?
THEN WHY?
NO.
NO.
I--
AH...

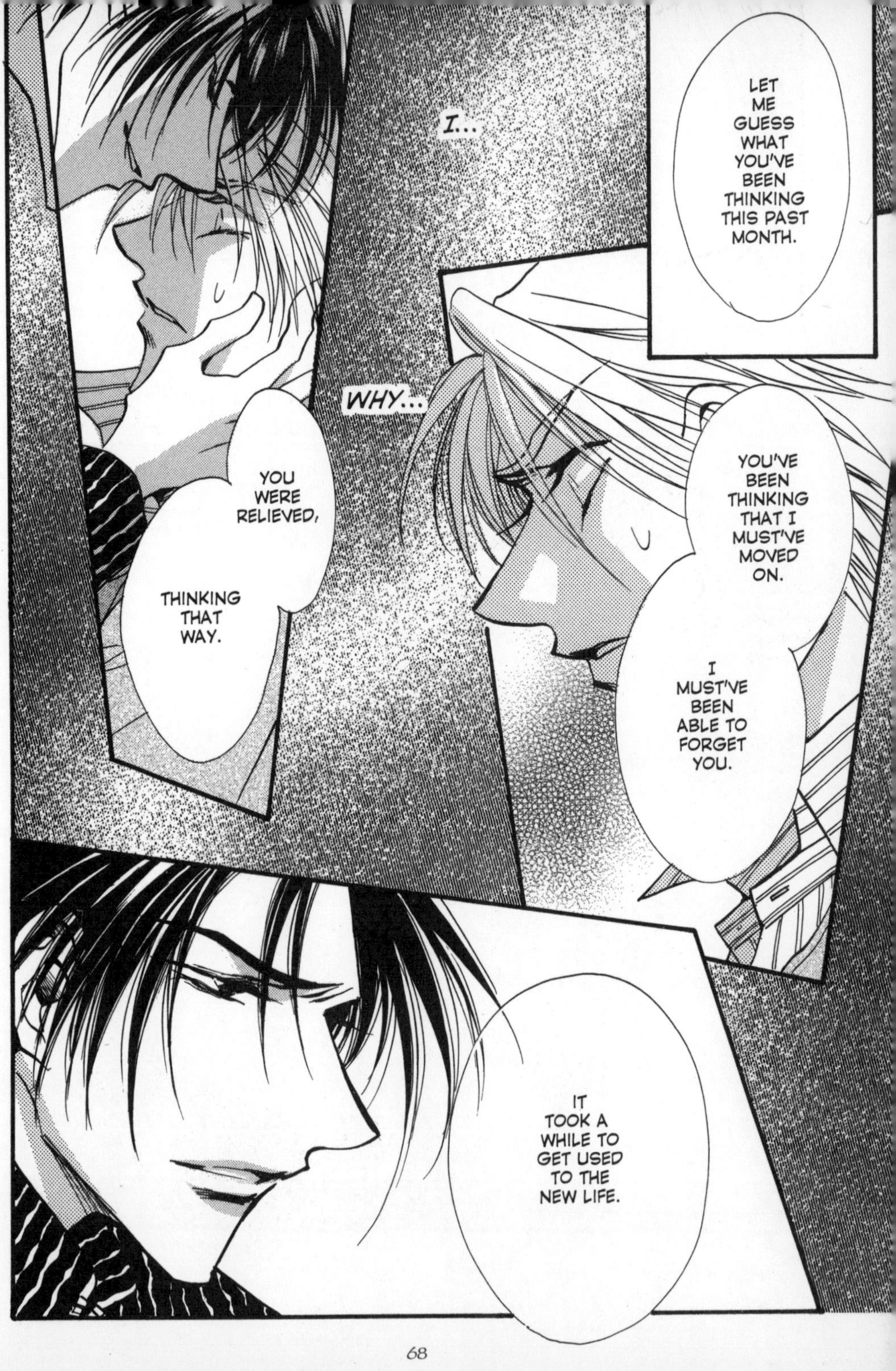
LET ME GUESS WHAT YOU'VE BEEN THINKING THIS PAST MONTH.
I...
WHY...
YOU'VE BEEN THINKING THAT I MUST'VE MOVED ON.
I MUST'VE BEEN ABLE TO FORGET YOU.
YOU WERE RELIEVED,
THINKING THAT WAY.
IT TOOK A WHILE TO GET USED TO THE NEW LIFE.

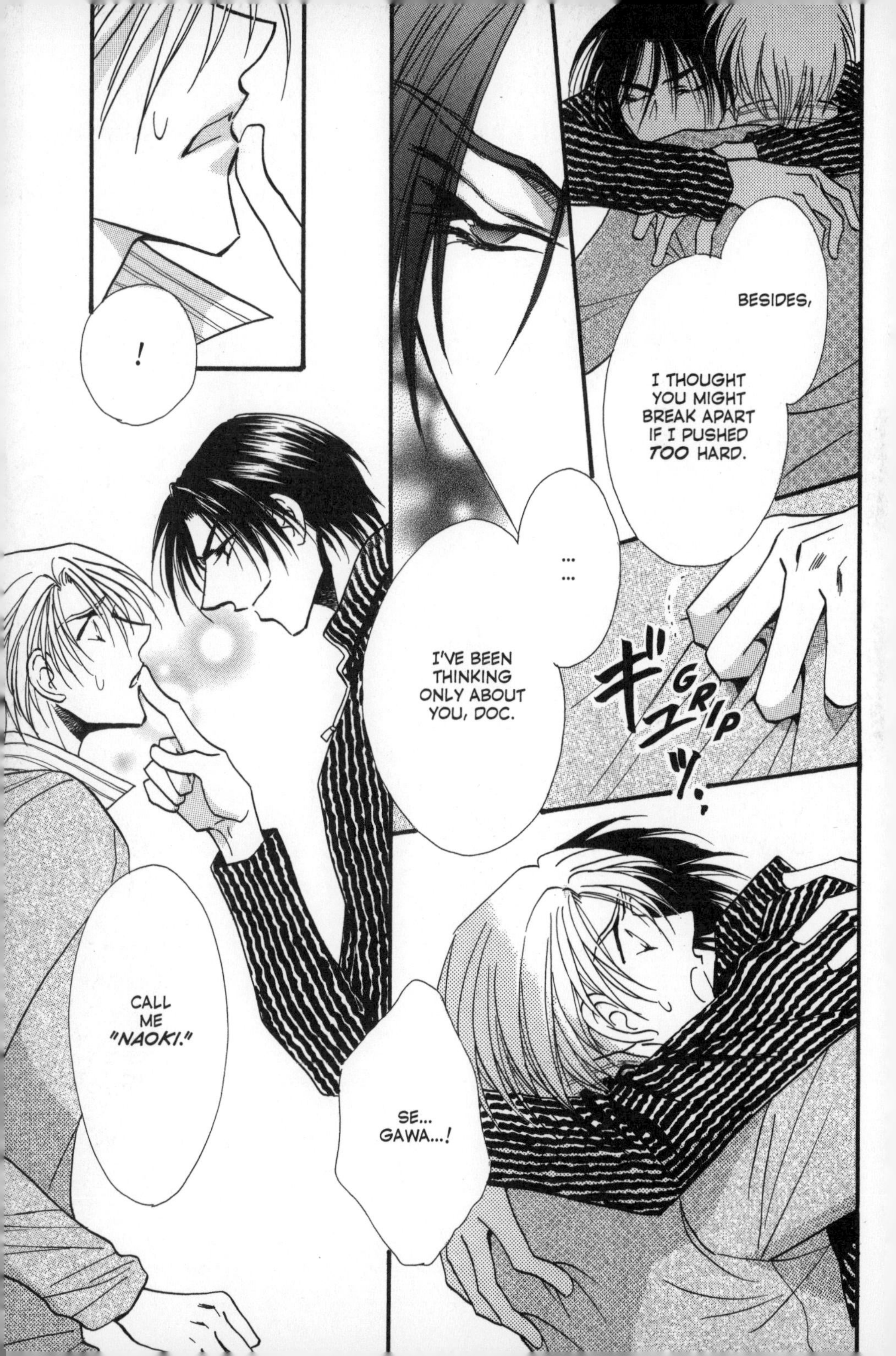
BESIDES,
I THOUGHT YOU MIGHT BREAK APART IF I PUSHED *TOO* HARD.
......
I'VE BEEN THINKING ONLY ABOUT YOU, DOC.
GRIP
!
SE... GAWA...!
CALL ME *"NAOKI."*

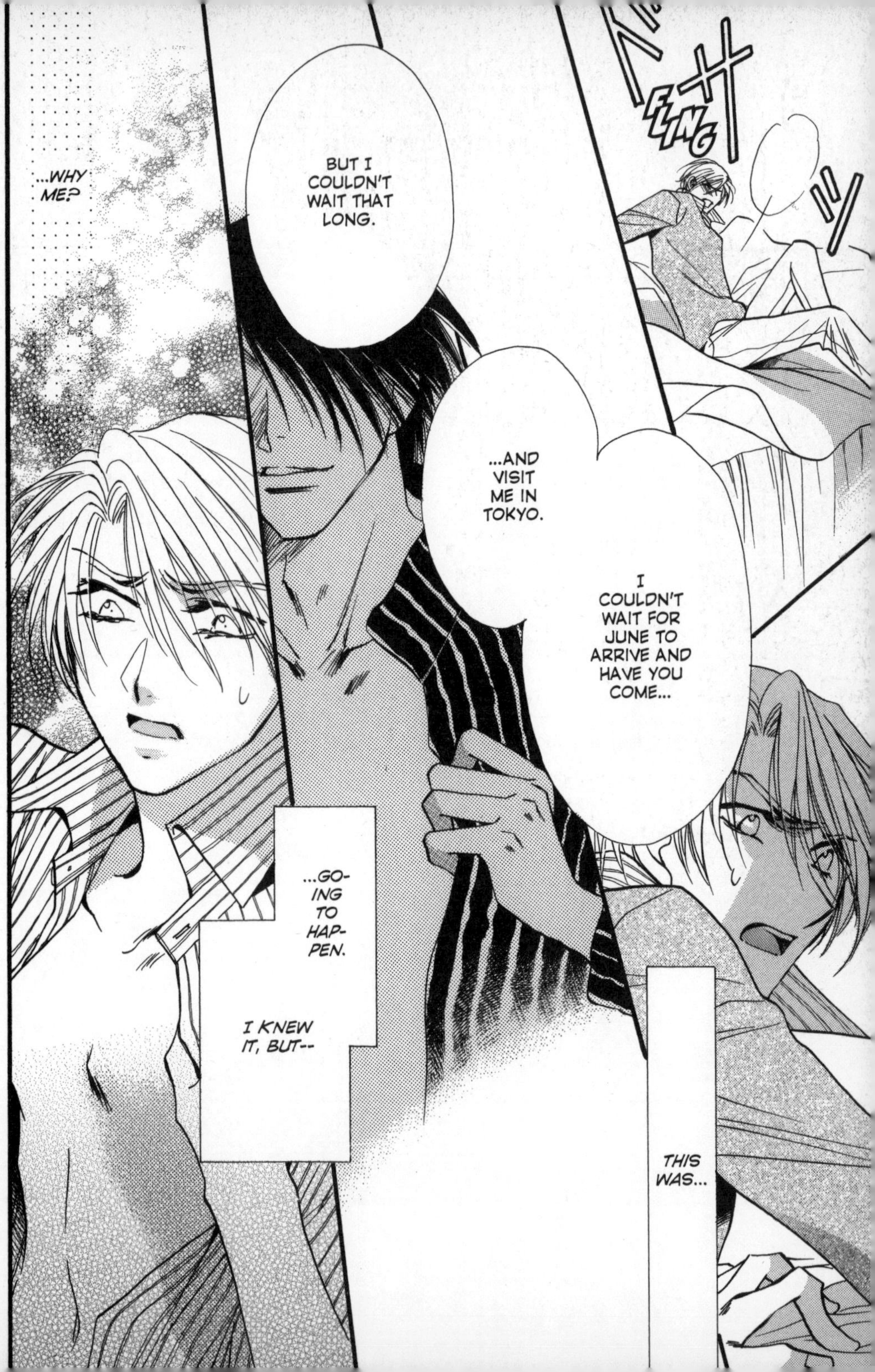
FLING
I COULDN'T WAIT FOR JUNE TO ARRIVE AND HAVE YOU COME...
...AND VISIT ME IN TOKYO.
BUT I COULDN'T WAIT THAT LONG.
THIS WAS...
...GO-ING TO HAP-PEN.
I KNEW IT, BUT--
...WHY ME?

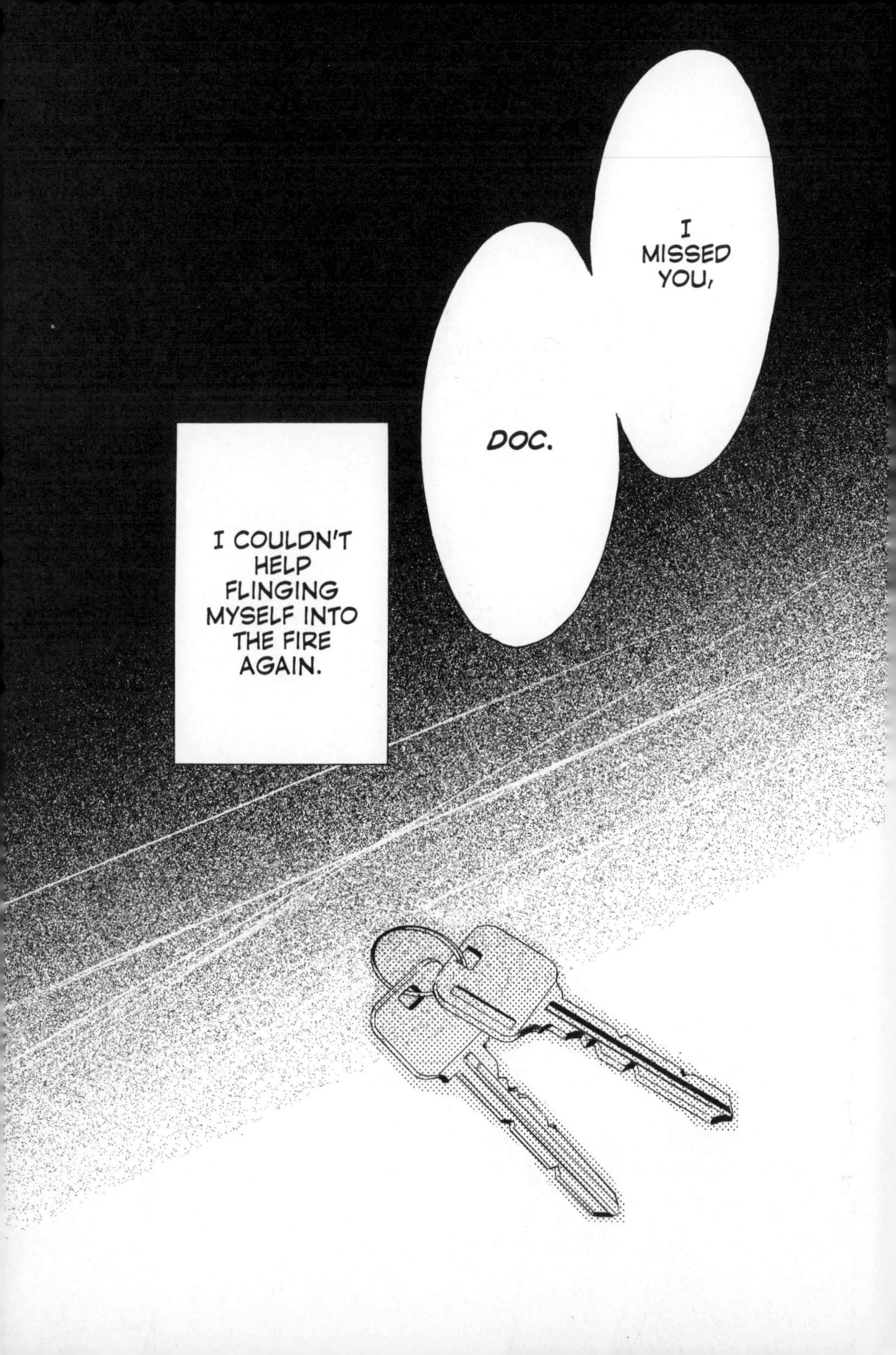
I MISSED YOU,
DOC.
I COULDN'T HELP FLINGING MYSELF INTO THE FIRE AGAIN.

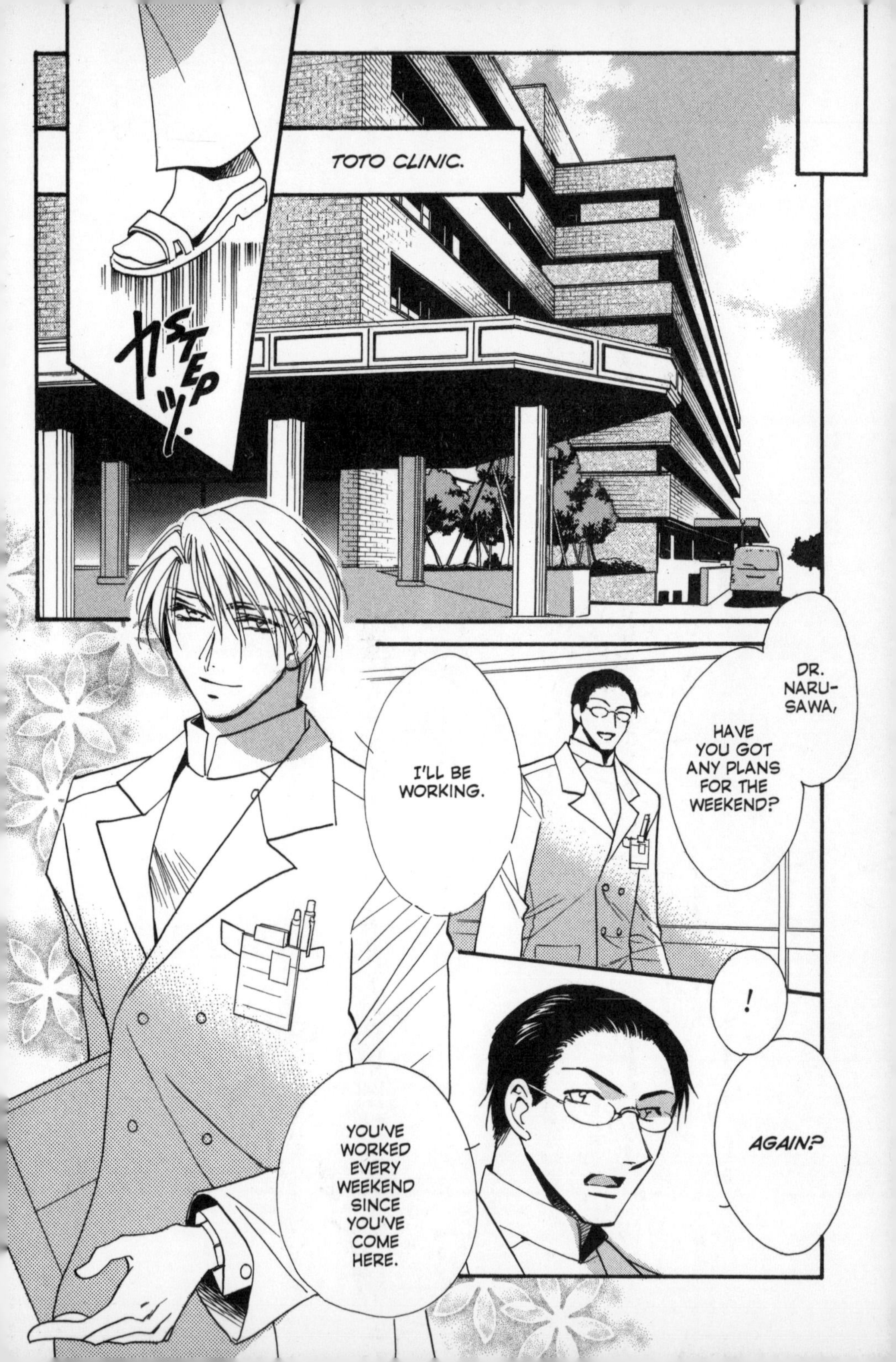
TOTO CLINIC.
STEP
カツッ
DR. NARUSAWA, HAVE YOU GOT ANY PLANS FOR THE WEEKEND?
I'LL BE WORKING.
!
AGAIN?
YOU'VE WORKED EVERY WEEKEND SINCE YOU'VE COME HERE.

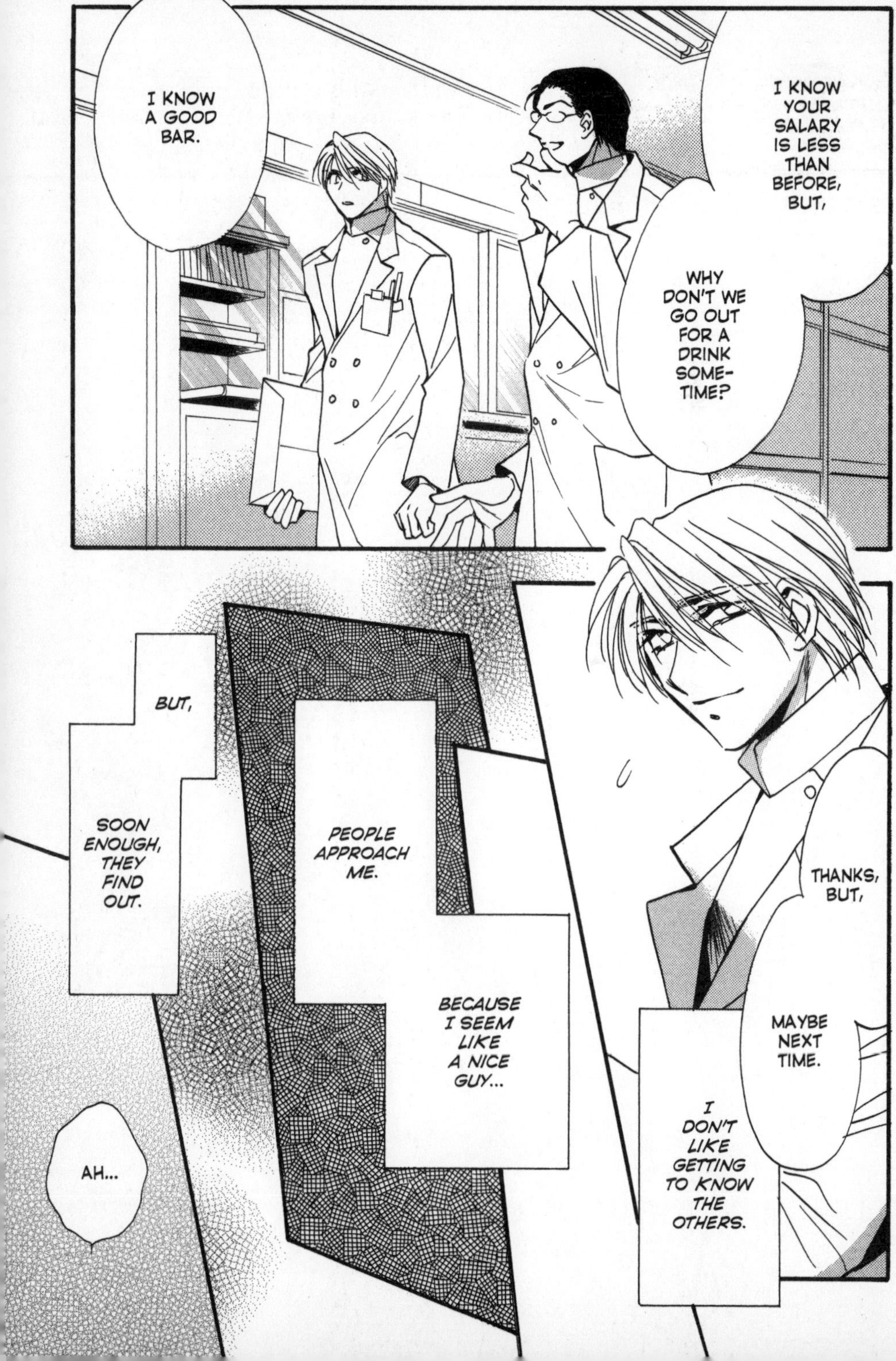
I KNOW YOUR SALARY IS LESS THAN BEFORE, BUT,
WHY DON'T WE GO OUT FOR A DRINK SOMETIME?
I KNOW A GOOD BAR.
THANKS, BUT,
MAYBE NEXT TIME.
I DON'T LIKE GETTING TO KNOW THE OTHERS.
BECAUSE I SEEM LIKE A NICE GUY...
PEOPLE APPROACH ME.
BUT,
SOON ENOUGH, THEY FIND OUT.
AH...

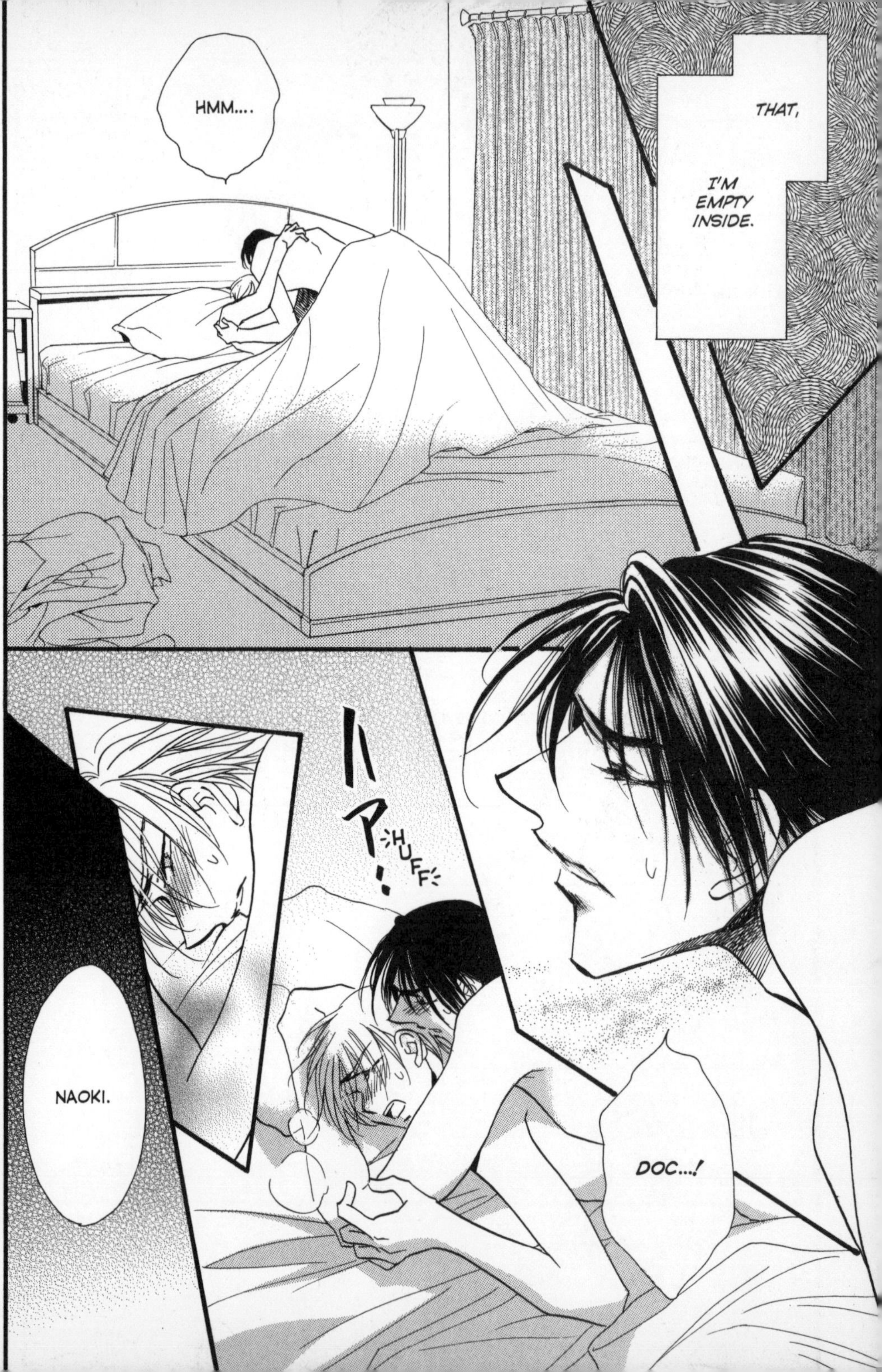
THAT,
I'M EMPTY INSIDE.
HMM....
DOC...!
HUFF
NAOKI.

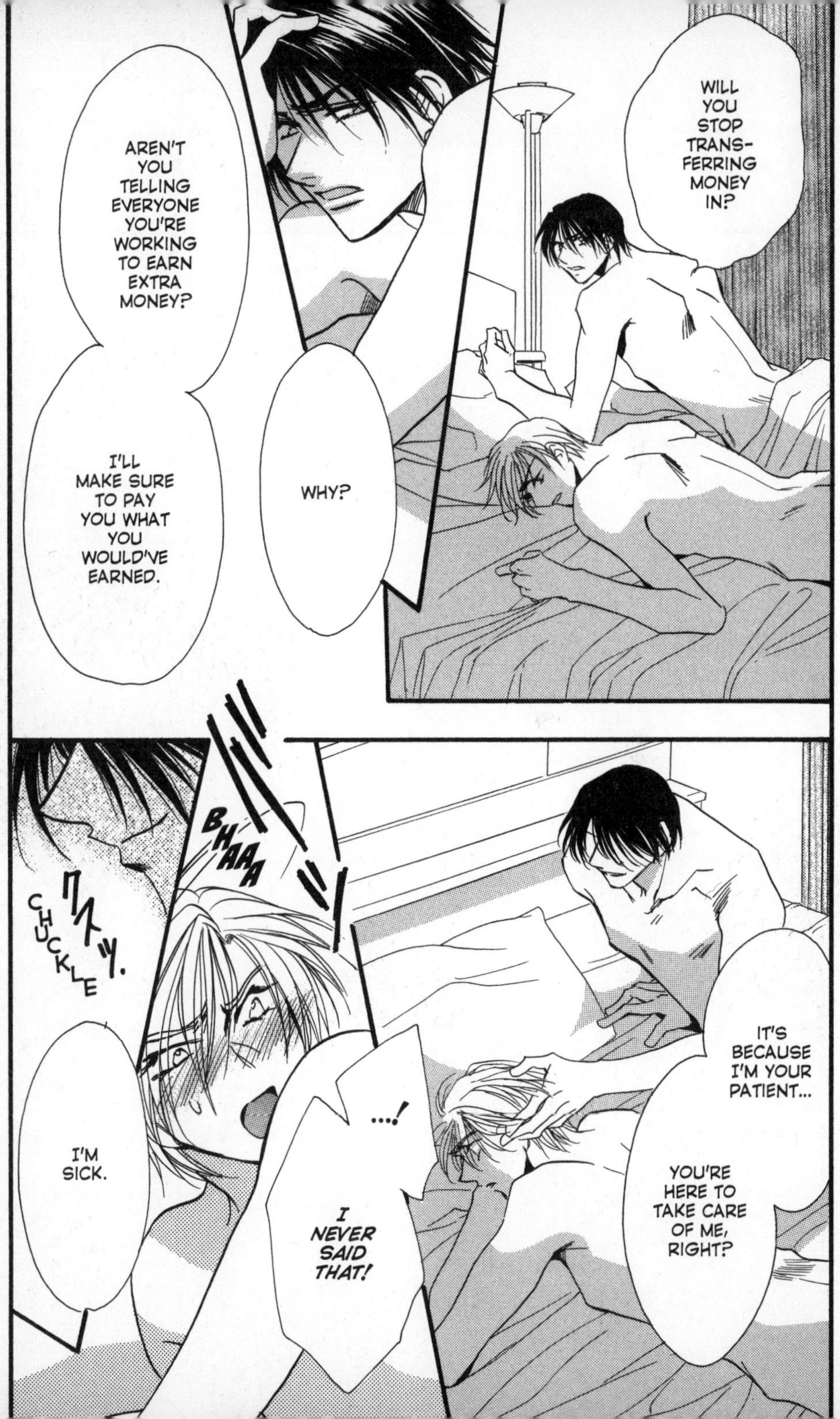
WILL YOU STOP TRANS-FERRING MONEY IN?
WHY?
AREN'T YOU TELLING EVERYONE YOU'RE WORKING TO EARN EXTRA MONEY?
I'LL MAKE SURE TO PAY YOU WHAT YOU WOULD'VE EARNED.
IT'S BECAUSE I'M YOUR PATIENT...
YOU'RE HERE TO TAKE CARE OF ME, RIGHT?
...!
I NEVER SAID THAT!
BHAAA
クスッ.
CHUCKLE
I'M SICK.

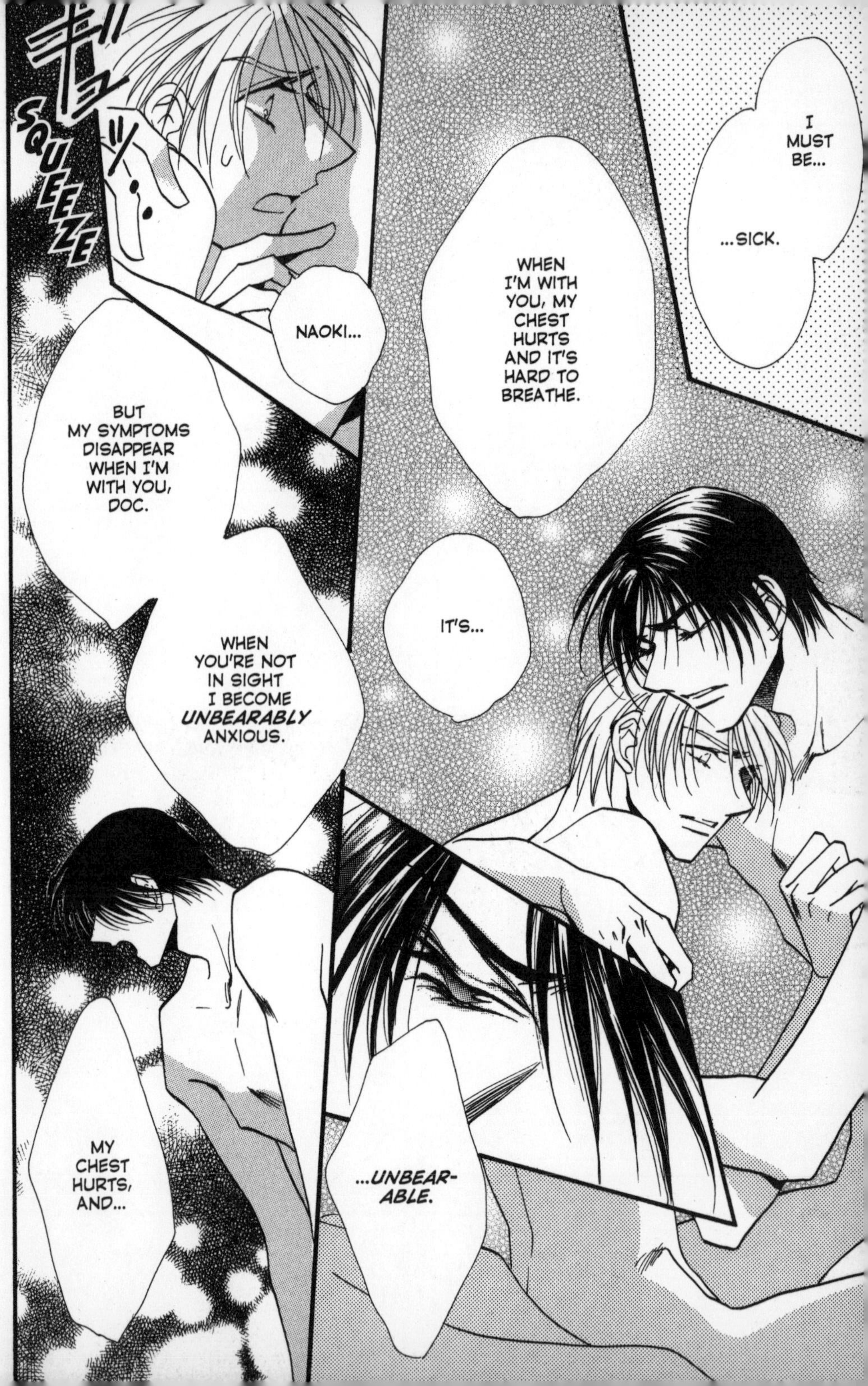
I MUST BE...
...SICK.
WHEN I'M WITH YOU, MY CHEST HURTS AND IT'S HARD TO BREATHE.
IT'S...
...*UNBEAR-ABLE.*
SQUEEZE
NAOKI...
BUT MY SYMPTOMS DISAPPEAR WHEN I'M WITH YOU, DOC.
WHEN YOU'RE NOT IN SIGHT I BECOME *UNBEARABLY* ANXIOUS.
MY CHEST HURTS, AND...

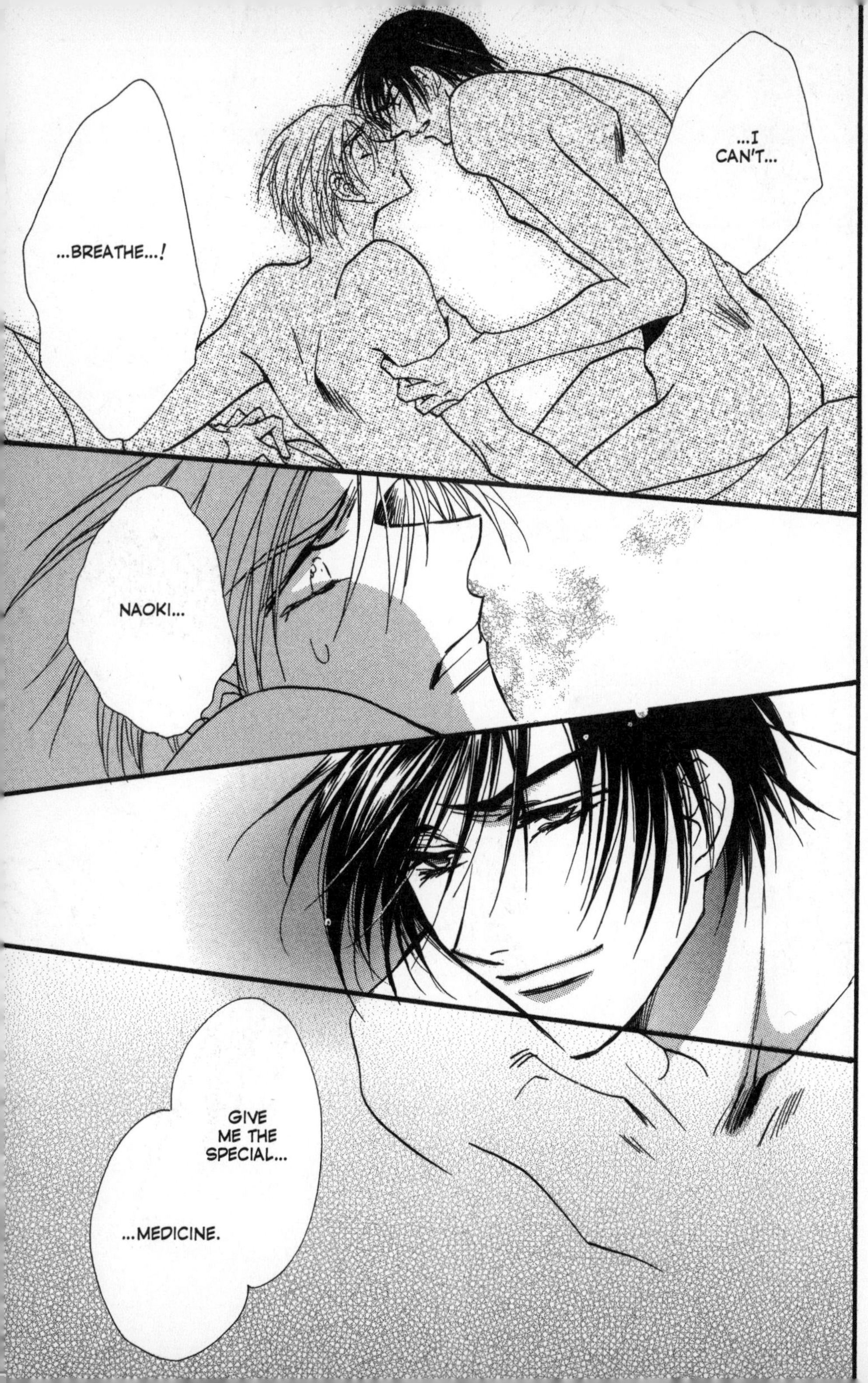
...I CAN'T...
...BREATHE...!
NAOKI...
GIVE ME THE SPECIAL...
...MEDICINE.

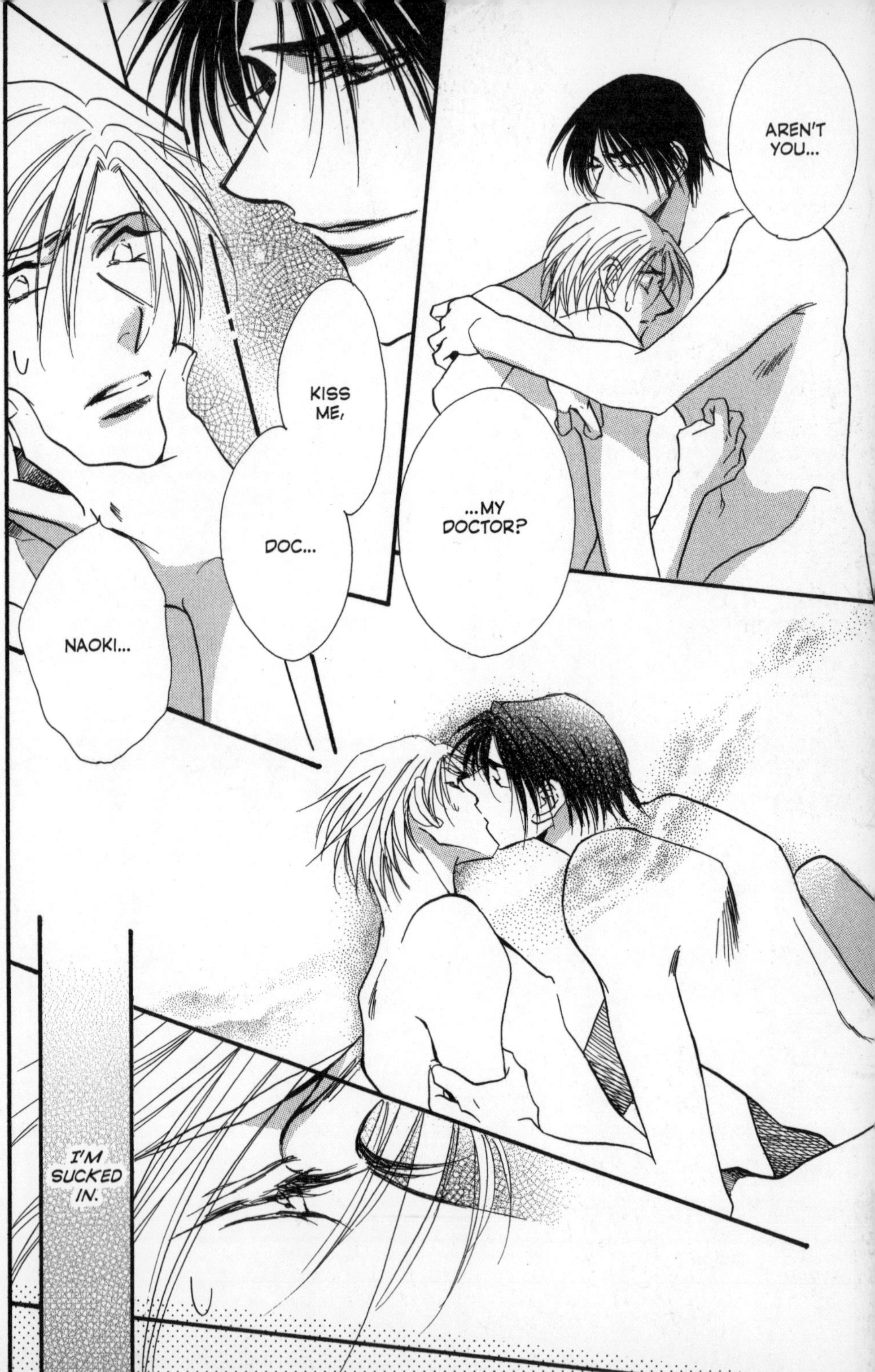
AREN'T YOU...
...MY DOCTOR?
KISS ME,
DOC...
NAOKI...
I'M SUCKED IN.

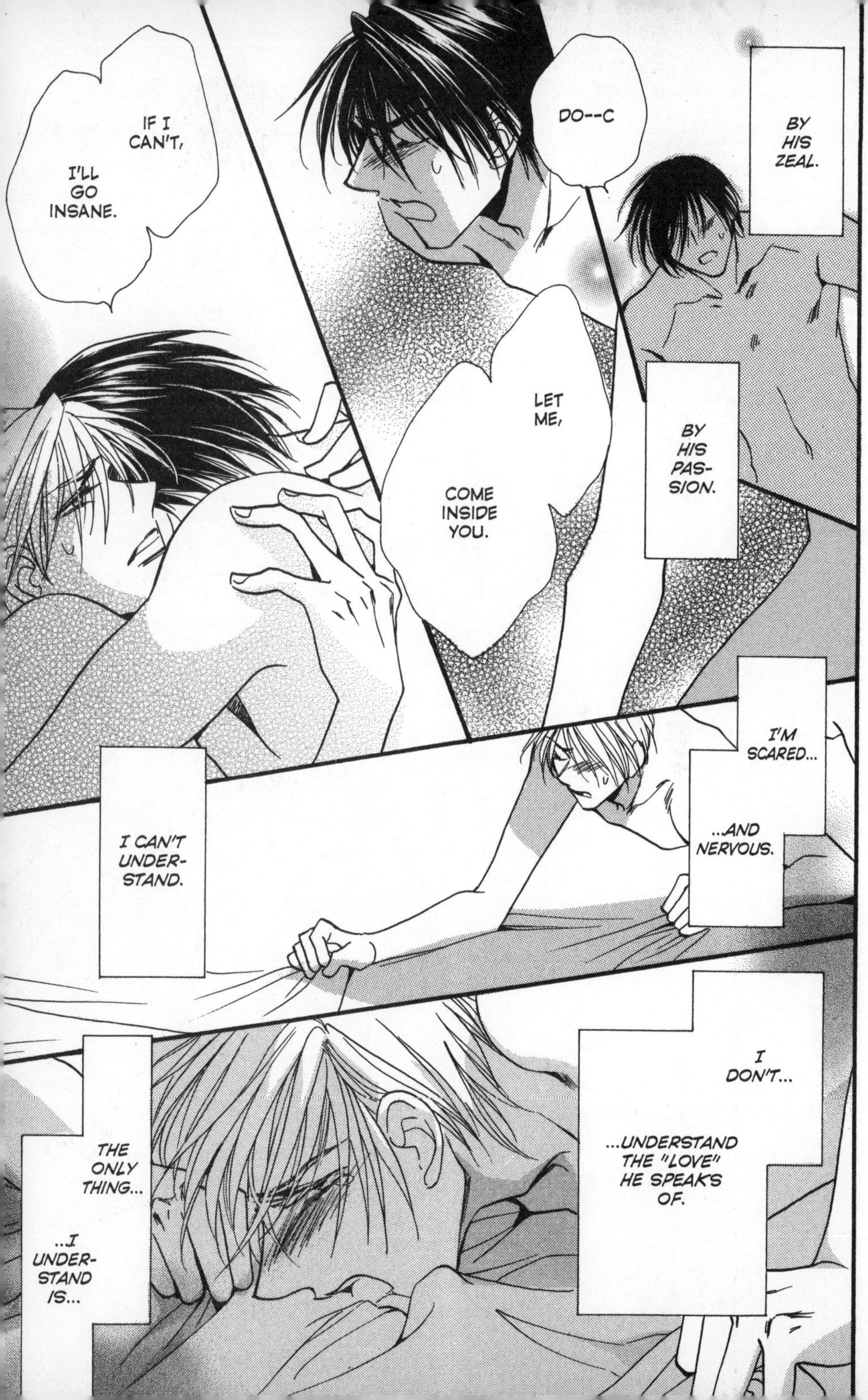
BY HIS ZEAL.
BY HIS PASSION.
DO--C
LET ME,
COME INSIDE YOU.
IF I CAN'T,
I'LL GO INSANE.
I'M SCARED...
...AND NERVOUS.
I CAN'T UNDERSTAND.
I DON'T...
...UNDERSTAND THE "LOVE" HE SPEAKS OF.
THE ONLY THING...
...I UNDERSTAND IS...

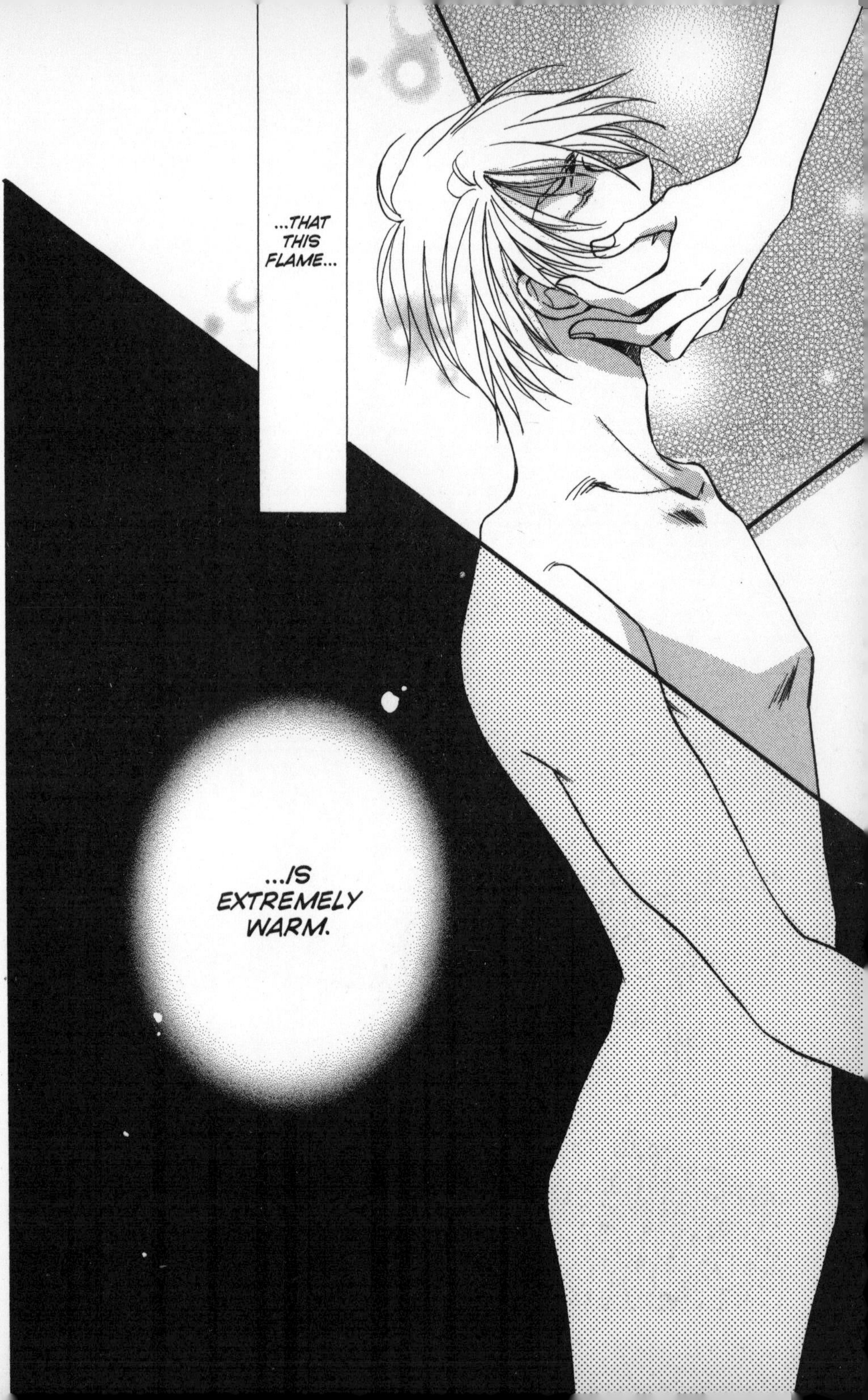
...THAT THIS FLAME...
...IS EXTREMELY WARM.

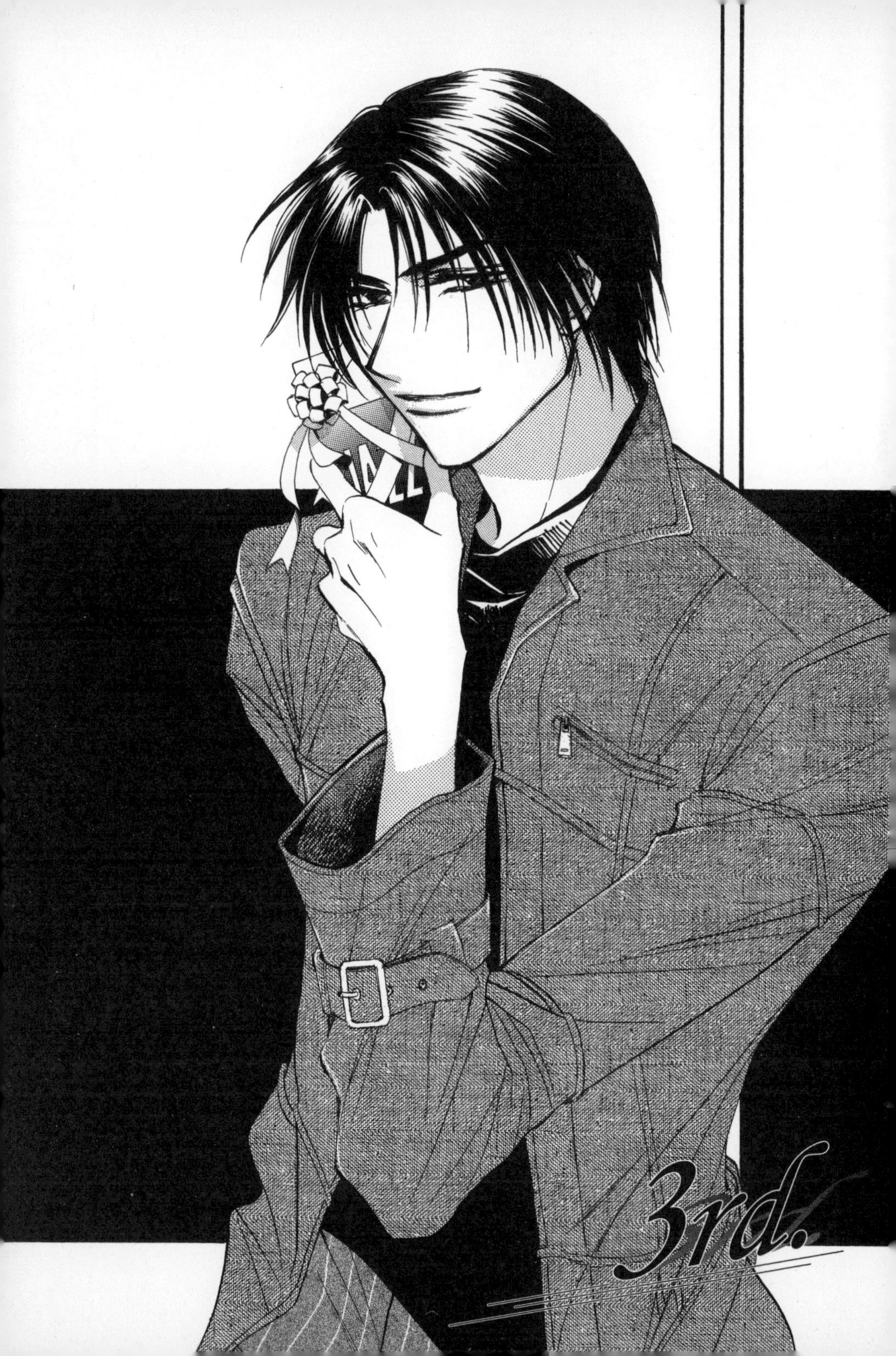
3rd.

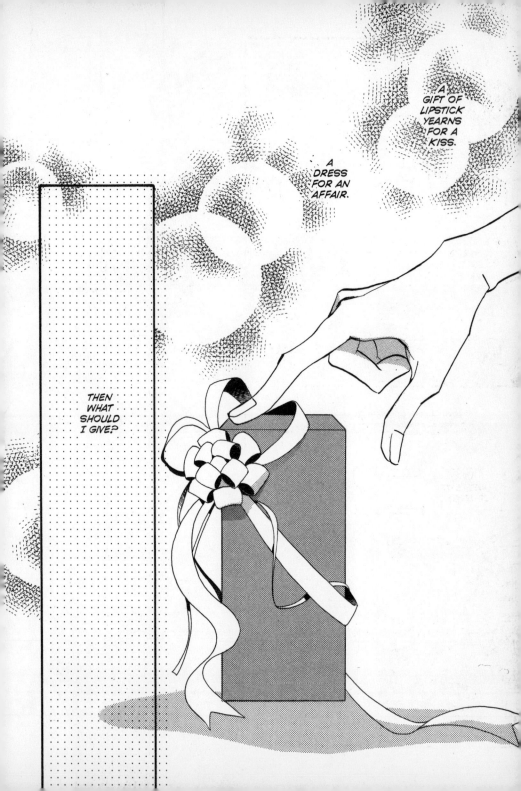

A GIFT OF LIPSTICK YEARNS FOR A KISS.

A DRESS FOR AN AFFAIR.

THEN WHAT SHOULD I GIVE?

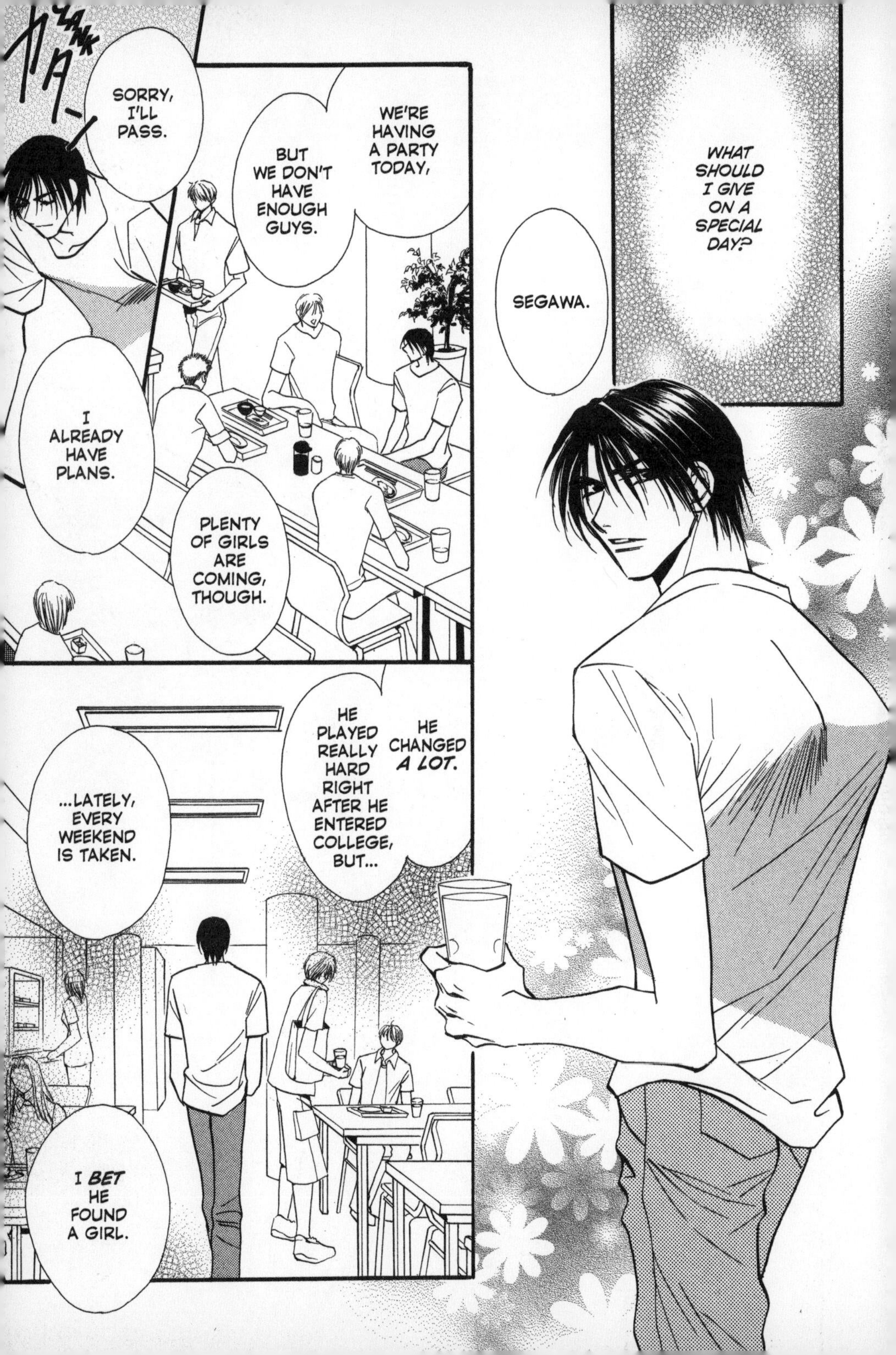

WHAT SHOULD I GIVE ON A SPECIAL DAY?
SEGAWA.
WE'RE HAVING A PARTY TODAY,
BUT WE DON'T HAVE ENOUGH GUYS.
カタ
CLANK
SORRY, I'LL PASS.
I ALREADY HAVE PLANS.
PLENTY OF GIRLS ARE COMING, THOUGH.
HE CHANGED *A LOT*.
HE PLAYED REALLY HARD RIGHT AFTER HE ENTERED COLLEGE, BUT...
...LATELY, EVERY WEEKEND IS TAKEN.
I *BET* HE FOUND A GIRL.

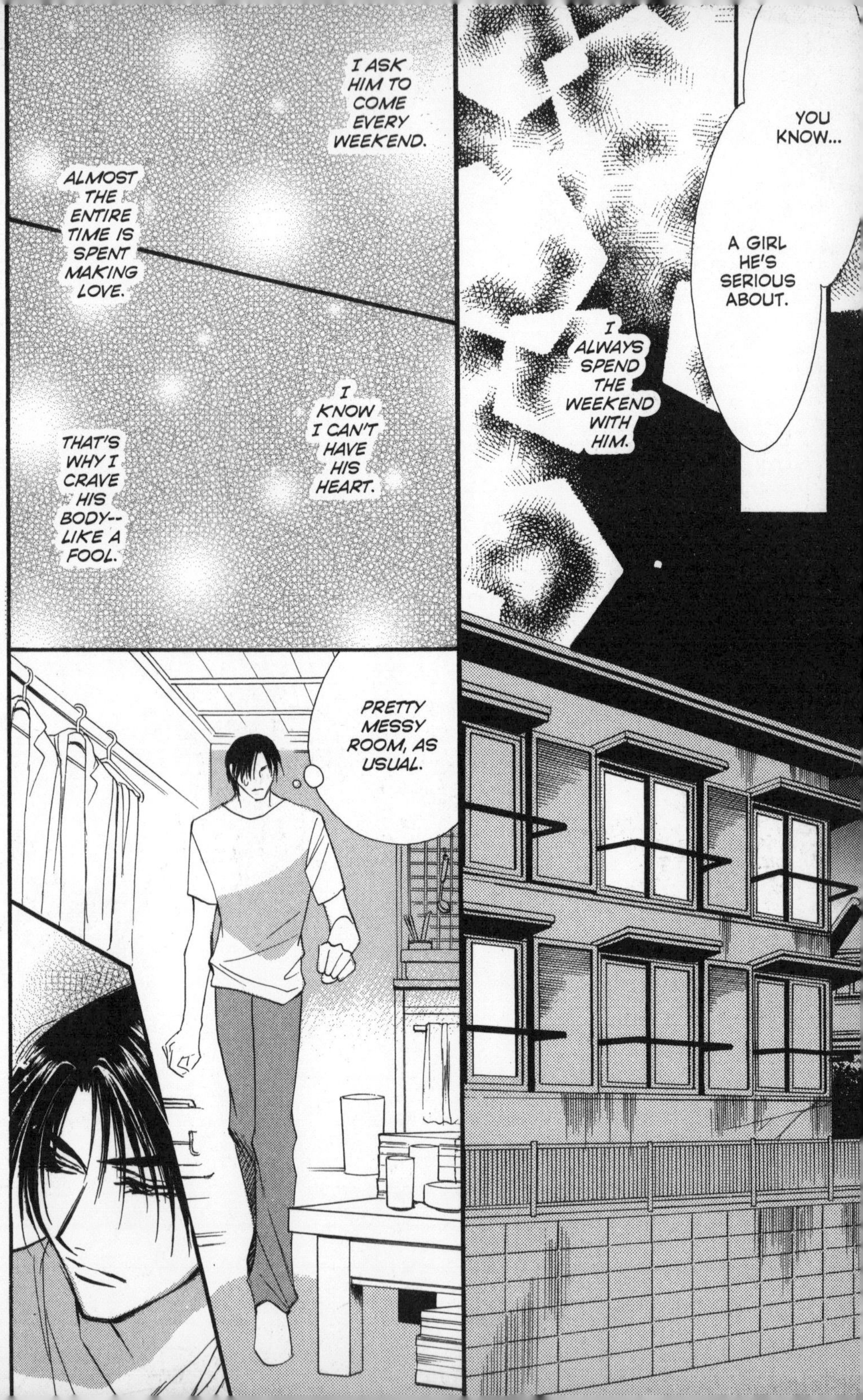
YOU KNOW...
A GIRL HE'S SERIOUS ABOUT.
I ALWAYS SPEND THE WEEKEND WITH HIM.
I ASK HIM TO COME EVERY WEEKEND.
ALMOST THE ENTIRE TIME IS SPENT MAKING LOVE.
I KNOW I CAN'T HAVE HIS HEART.
THAT'S WHY I CRAVE HIS BODY-- LIKE A FOOL.
PRETTY MESSY ROOM, AS USUAL.

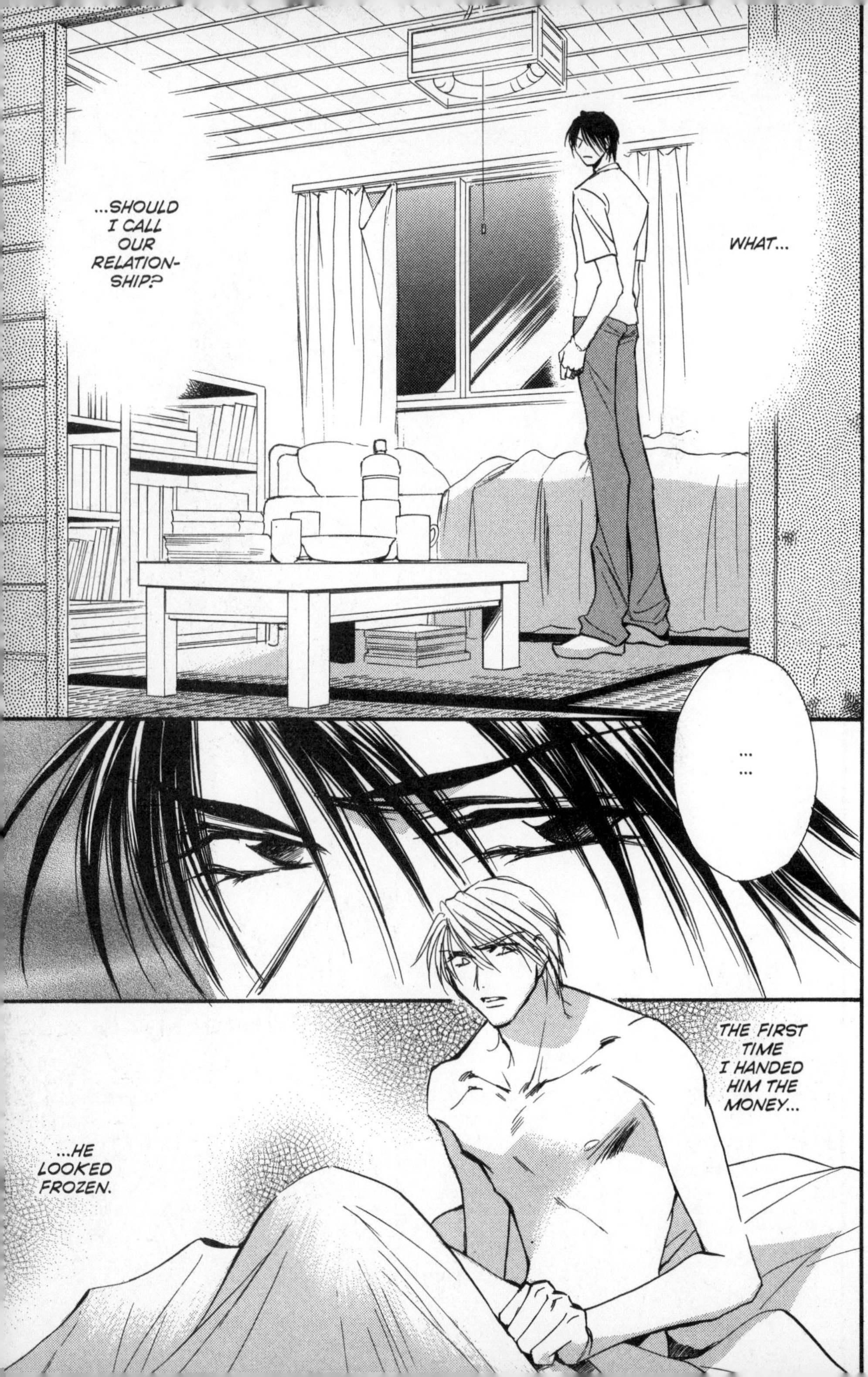
WHAT...
...SHOULD I CALL OUR RELATION-SHIP?
... ...
THE FIRST TIME I HANDED HIM THE MONEY...
...HE LOOKED FROZEN.

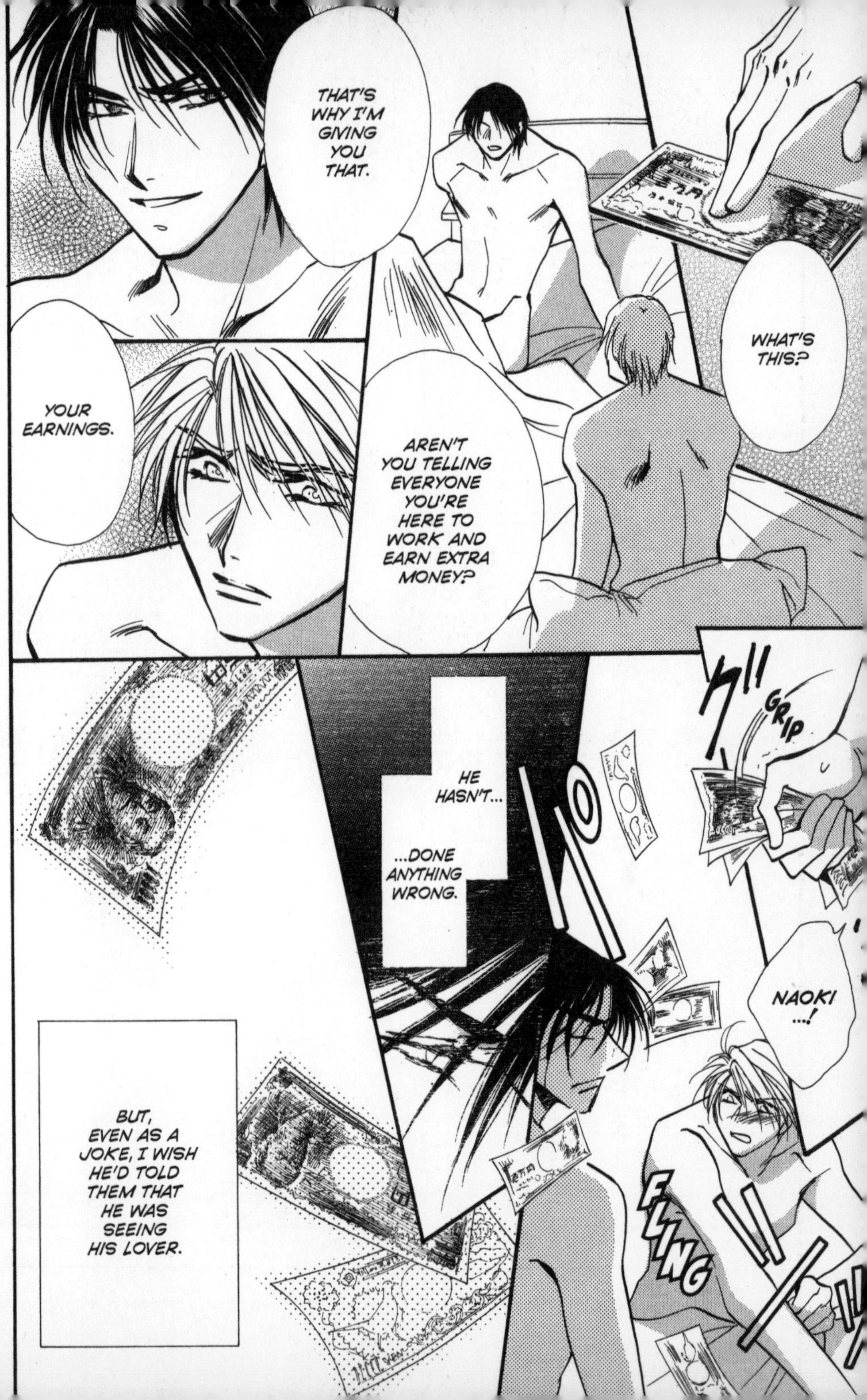
WHAT'S THIS?
YOUR EARNINGS.
AREN'T YOU TELLING EVERYONE YOU'RE HERE TO WORK AND EARN EXTRA MONEY?
THAT'S WHY I'M GIVING YOU THAT.
GRIP
NAOKI ...!
FLING
HE HASN'T...
...DONE ANYTHING WRONG.
BUT, EVEN AS A JOKE, I WISH HE'D TOLD THEM THAT HE WAS SEEING HIS LOVER.

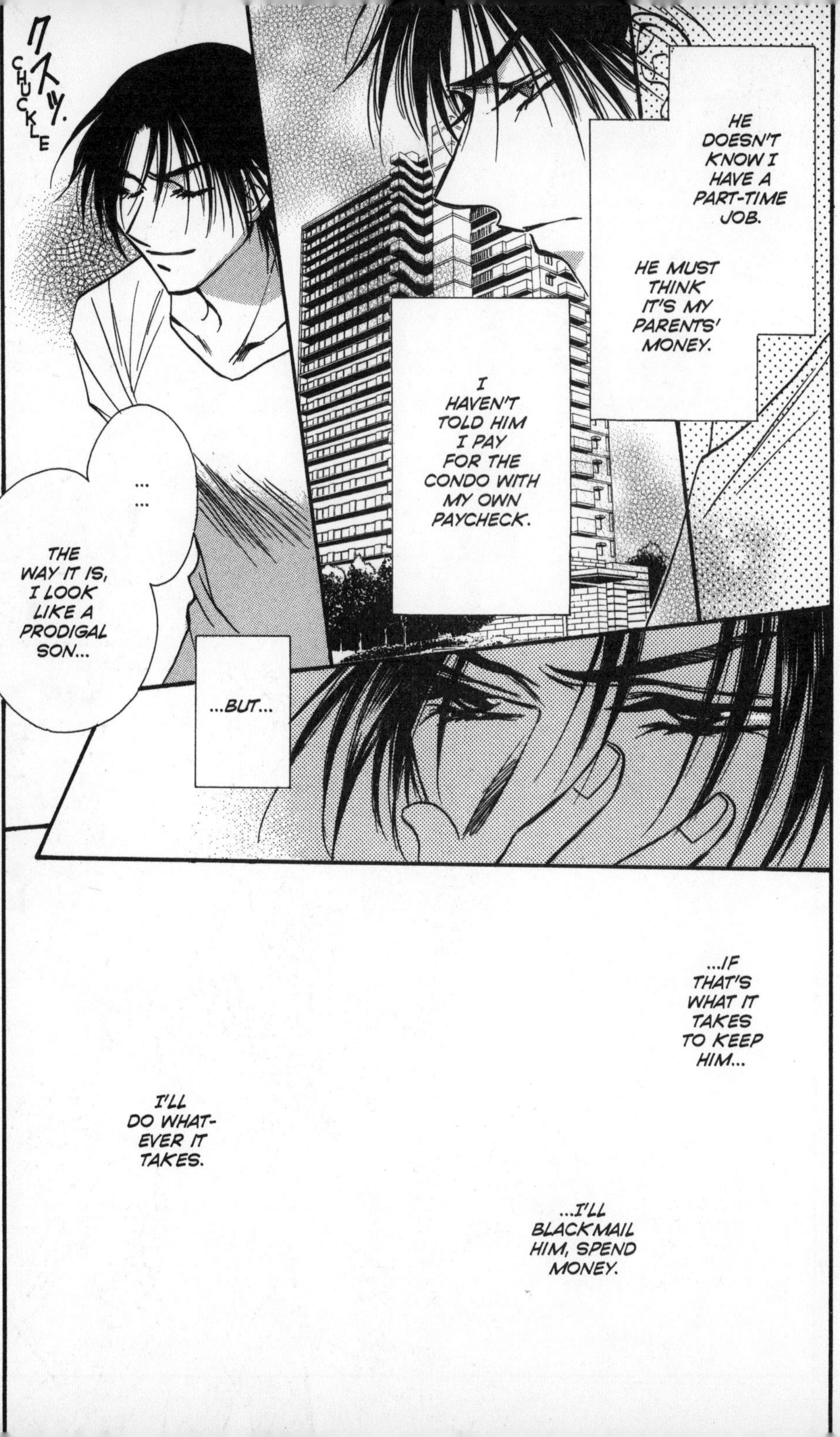
HE DOESN'T KNOW I HAVE A PART-TIME JOB.
HE MUST THINK IT'S MY PARENTS' MONEY.
I HAVEN'T TOLD HIM I PAY FOR THE CONDO WITH MY OWN PAYCHECK.
クスッ. CHUCKLE
...... THE WAY IT IS, I LOOK LIKE A PRODIGAL SON...
...BUT...
...IF THAT'S WHAT IT TAKES TO KEEP HIM...
...I'LL BLACKMAIL HIM, SPEND MONEY.
I'LL DO WHAT-EVER IT TAKES.

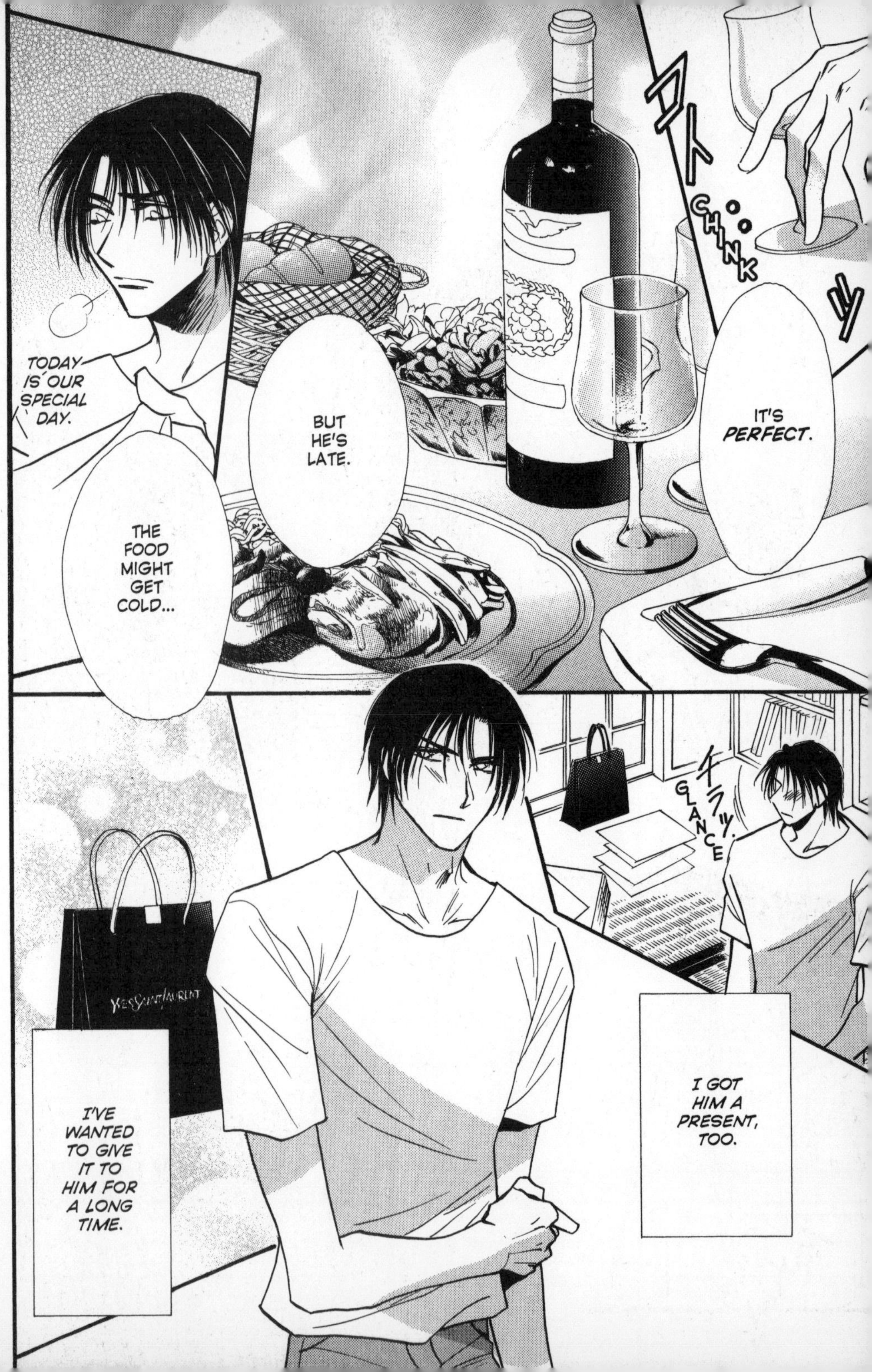
CHINK
IT'S PERFECT.
BUT HE'S LATE.
TODAY IS OUR SPECIAL DAY.
THE FOOD MIGHT GET COLD...
GLANCE
I GOT HIM A PRESENT, TOO.
YVES SAINT LAURENT
I'VE WANTED TO GIVE IT TO HIM FOR A LONG TIME.

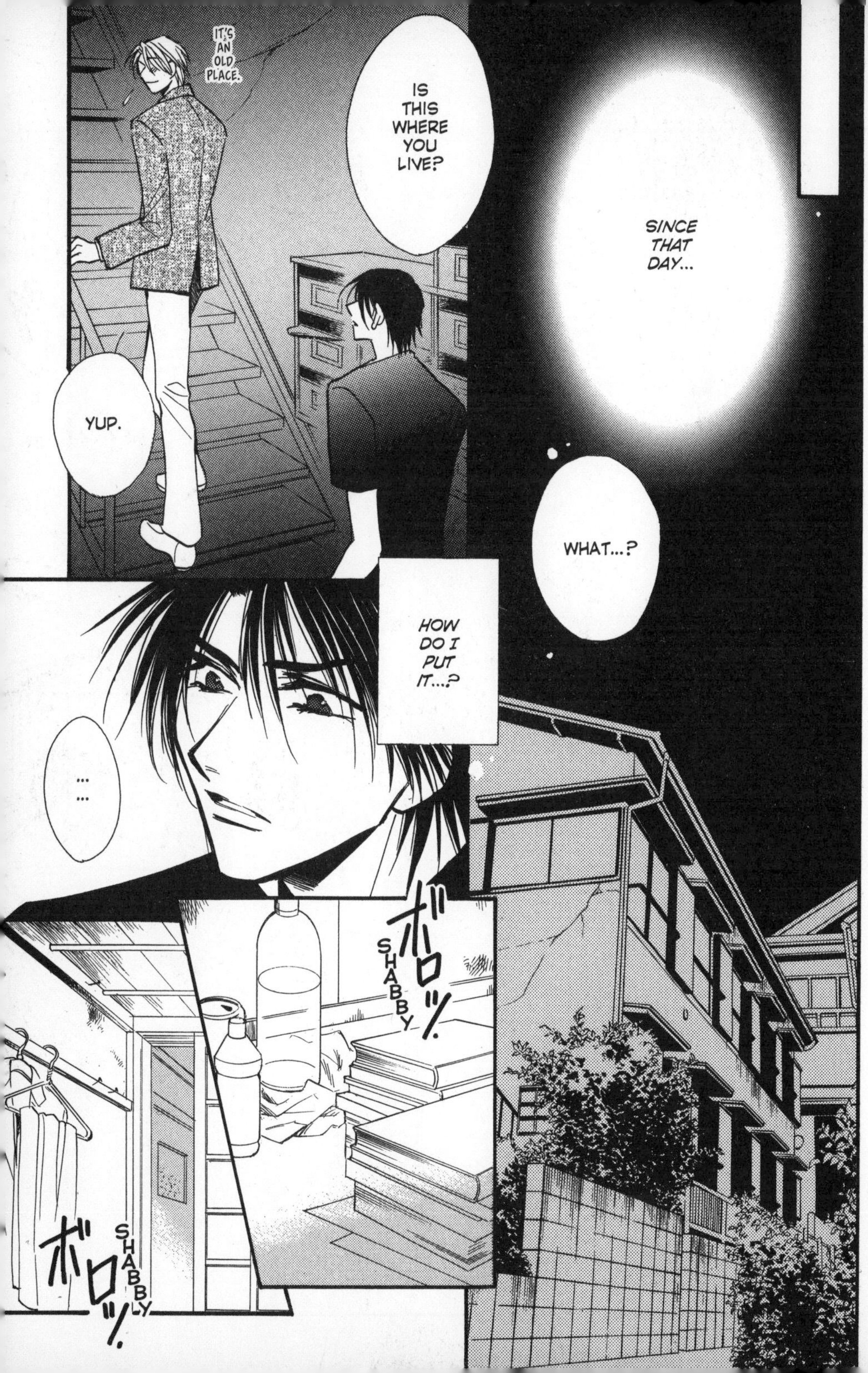
SINCE THAT DAY...
WHAT...?
IS THIS WHERE YOU LIVE?
IT'S AN OLD PLACE.
YUP.
HOW DO I PUT IT...?
......
SHABBY
SHABBY

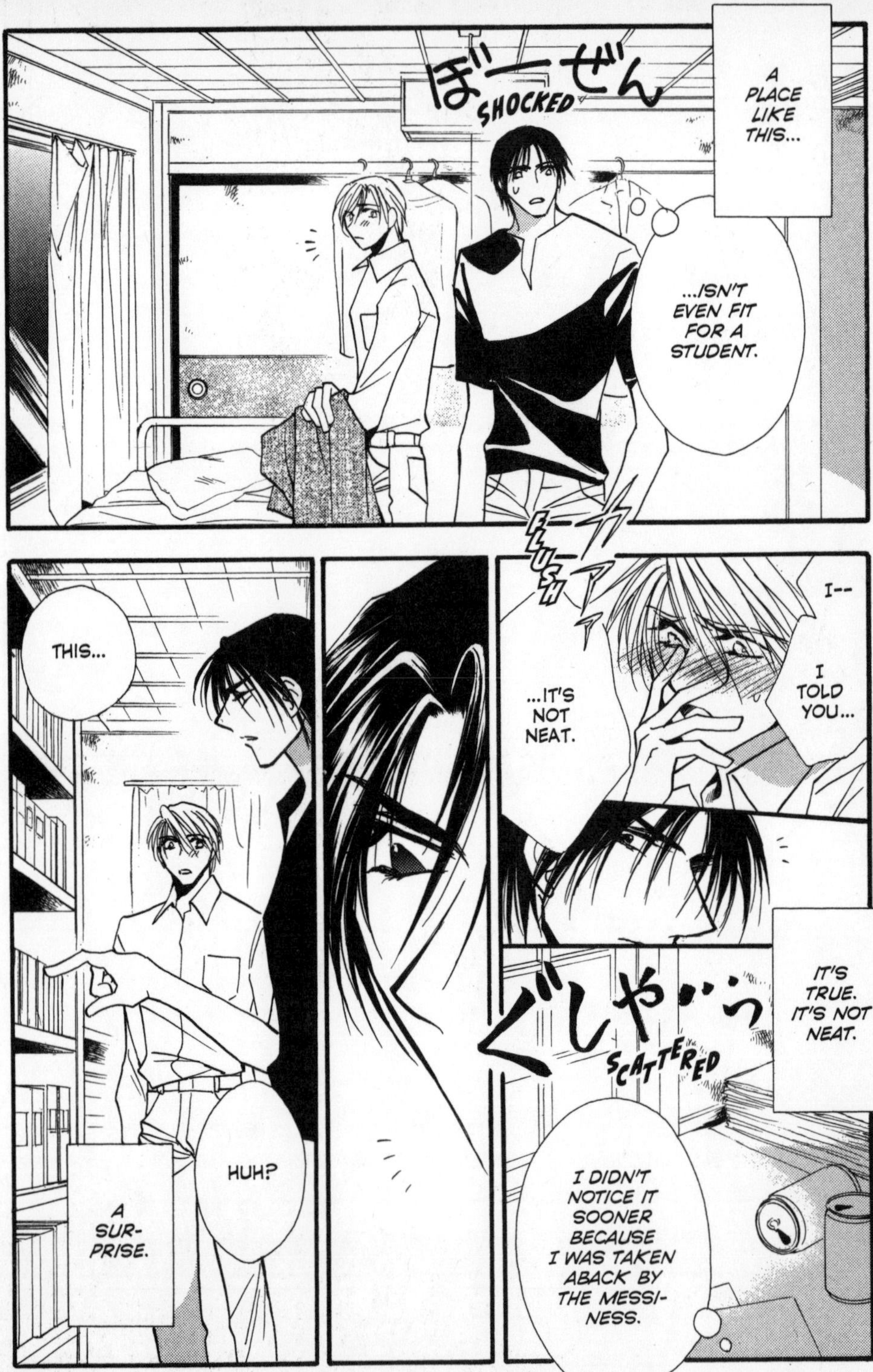
A PLACE LIKE THIS...
ぼーぜん SHOCKED
...ISN'T EVEN FIT FOR A STUDENT.
カアァァ FLUSH
I--
I TOLD YOU...
...IT'S NOT NEAT.
IT'S TRUE. IT'S NOT NEAT.
ぐしゃっ SCATTERED
I DIDN'T NOTICE IT SOONER BECAUSE I WAS TAKEN ABACK BY THE MESSINESS.
THIS...
HUH?
A SURPRISE.

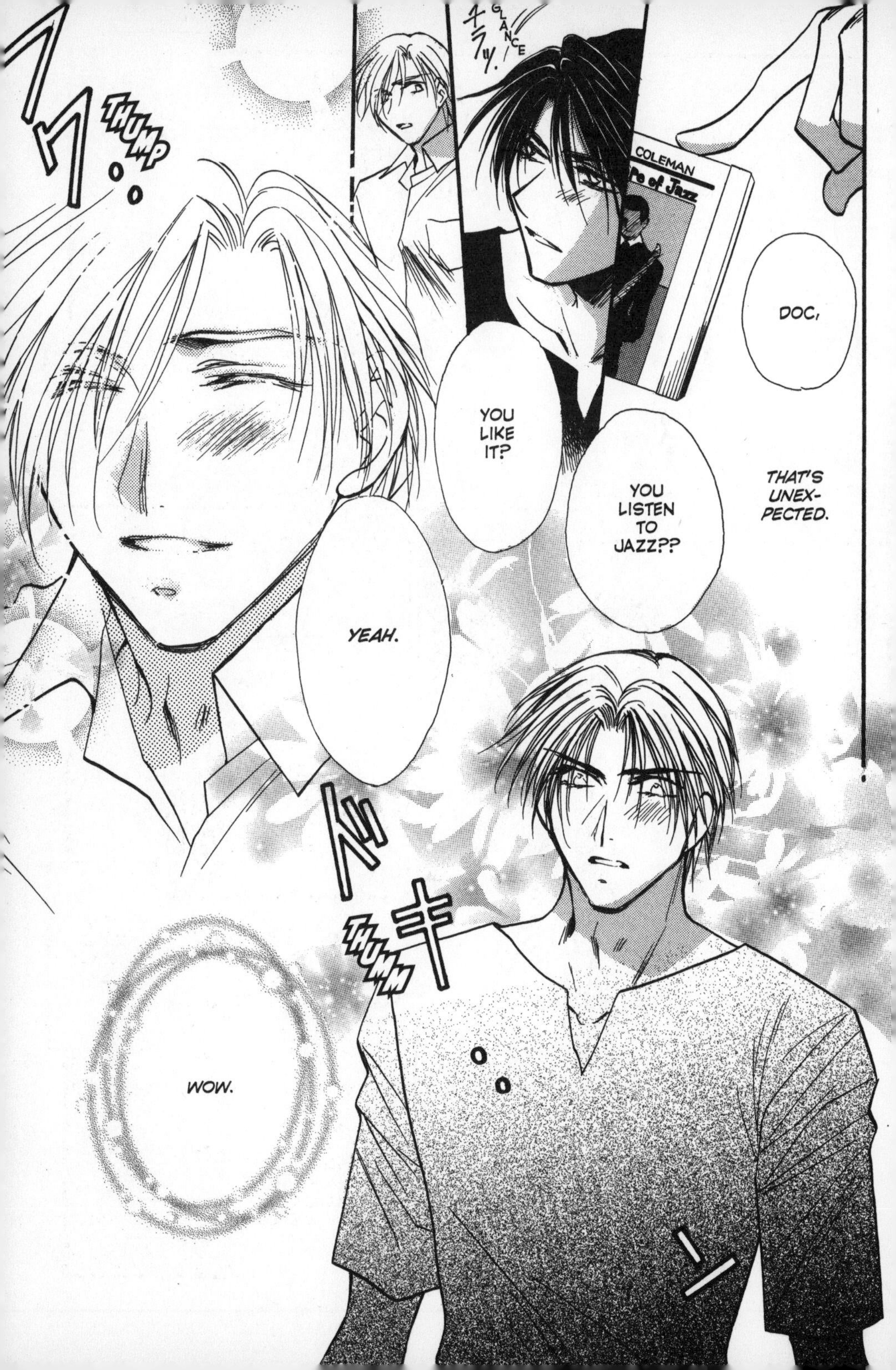
DOC,
THAT'S UNEXPECTED.
チラッ
GLANCE
COLEMAN
YOU LISTEN TO JAZZ??
YOU LIKE IT?
YEAH.
THUMP
ドキ
THUMM
WOW.

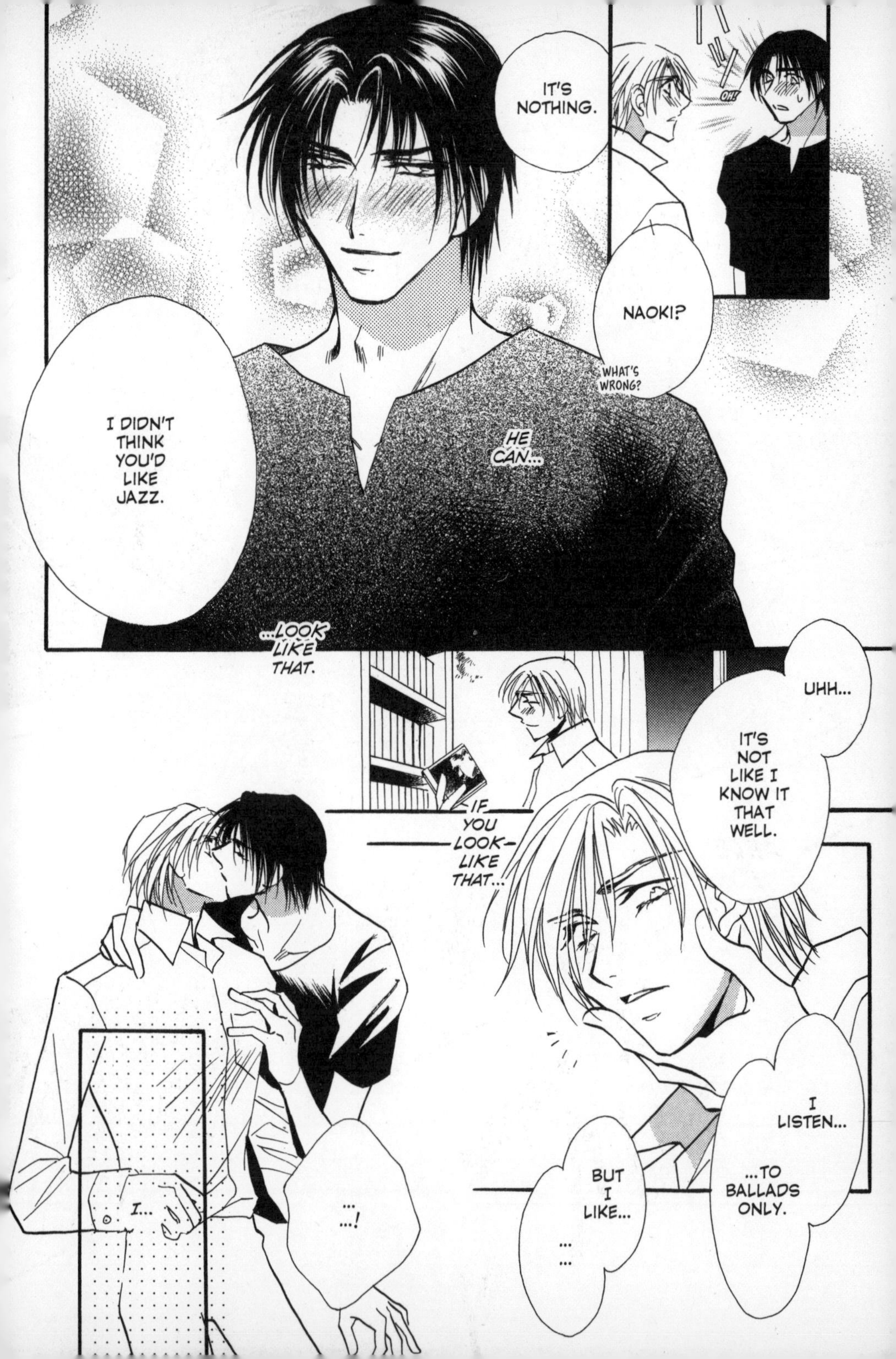
OH!
NAOKI?
WHAT'S WRONG?
IT'S NOTHING.
I DIDN'T THINK YOU'D LIKE JAZZ.
HE CAN...
...LOOK LIKE THAT.
UHH...
IT'S NOT LIKE I KNOW IT THAT WELL.
I LISTEN...
...TO BALLADS ONLY.
BUT I LIKE...
...
...
IF YOU LOOK LIKE THAT...
...
...!
I...

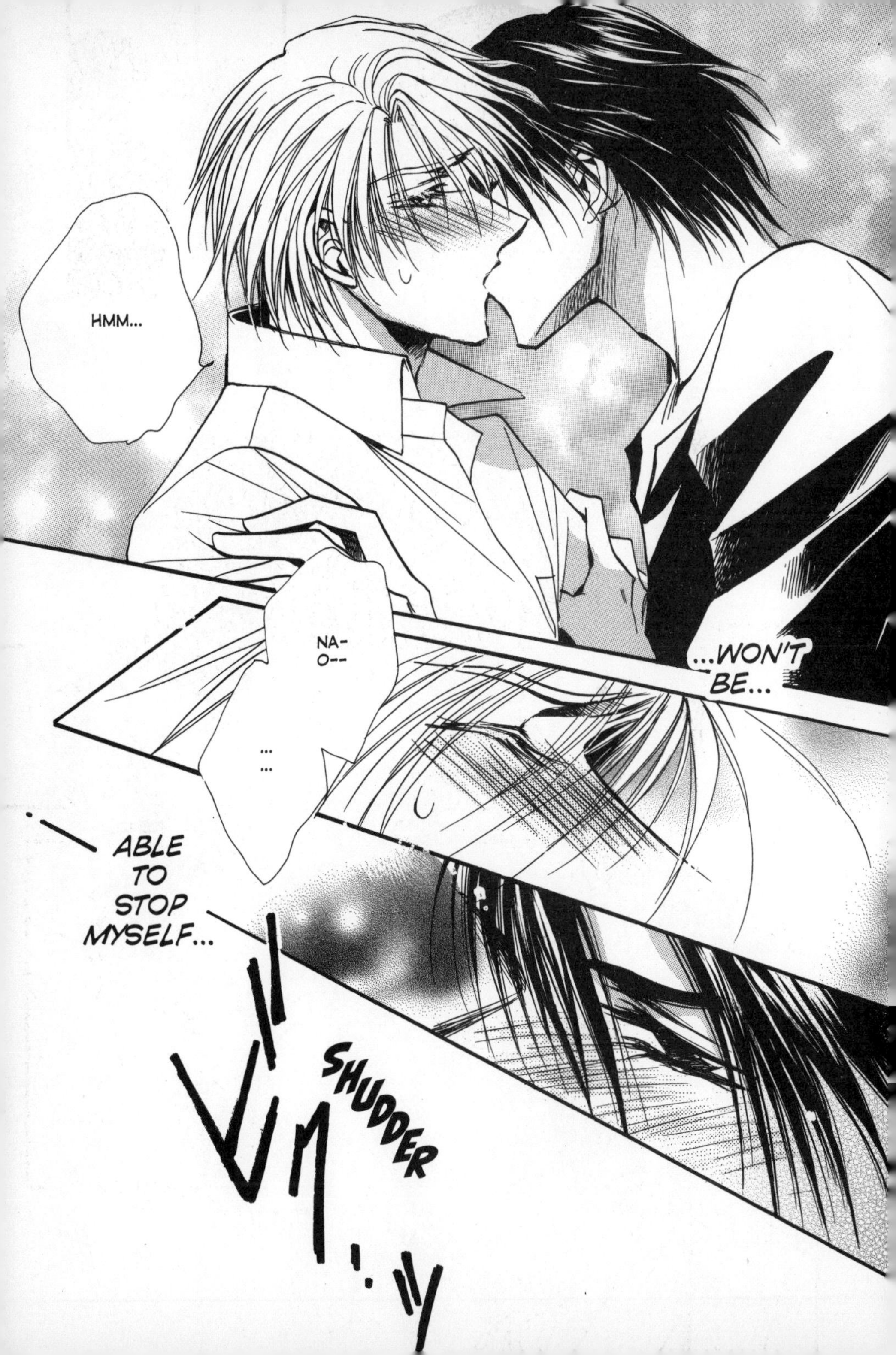
HMM...
...WON'T BE...
NA- O--
... ...
ABLE TO STOP MYSELF...
SHUDDER

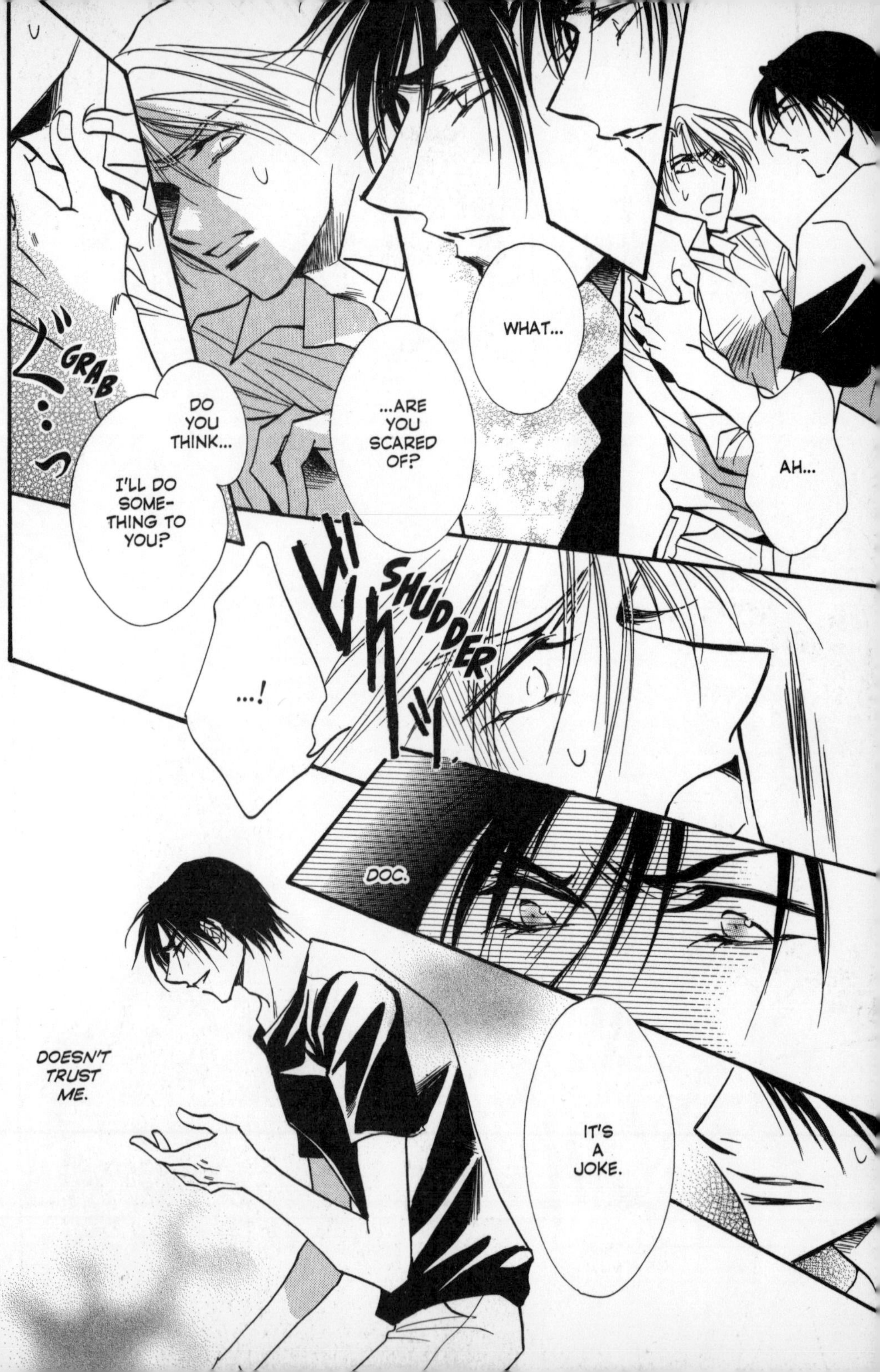
AH...
WHAT...
...ARE YOU SCARED OF?
GRAB
DO YOU THINK...
I'LL DO SOMETHING TO YOU?
SHUDDER
...!
DOC.
IT'S A JOKE.
DOESN'T TRUST ME.

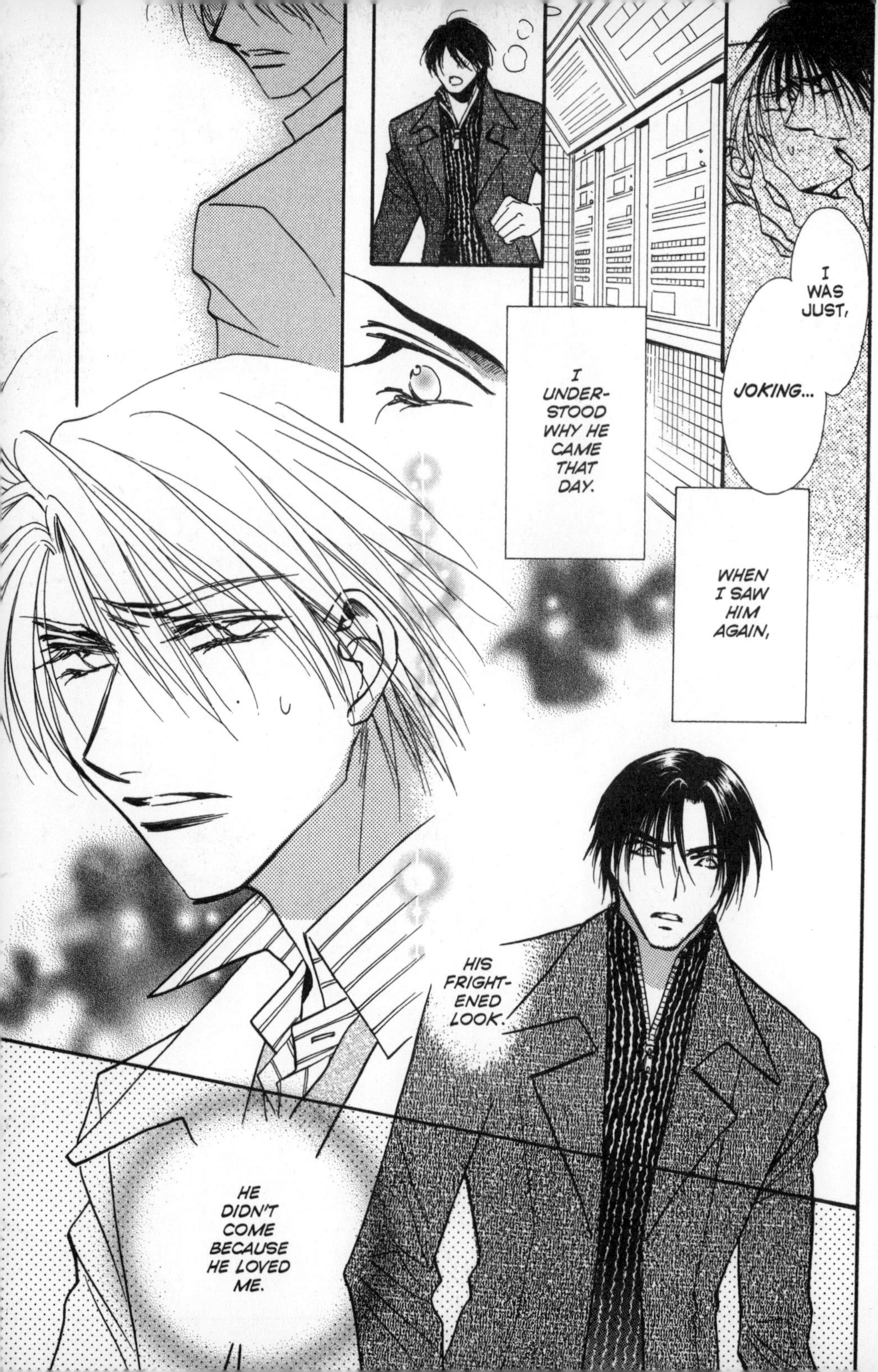
I WAS JUST, JOKING...
I UNDER-STOOD WHY HE CAME THAT DAY.
WHEN I SAW HIM AGAIN,
HIS FRIGHT-ENED LOOK.
HE DIDN'T COME BECAUSE HE LOVED ME.

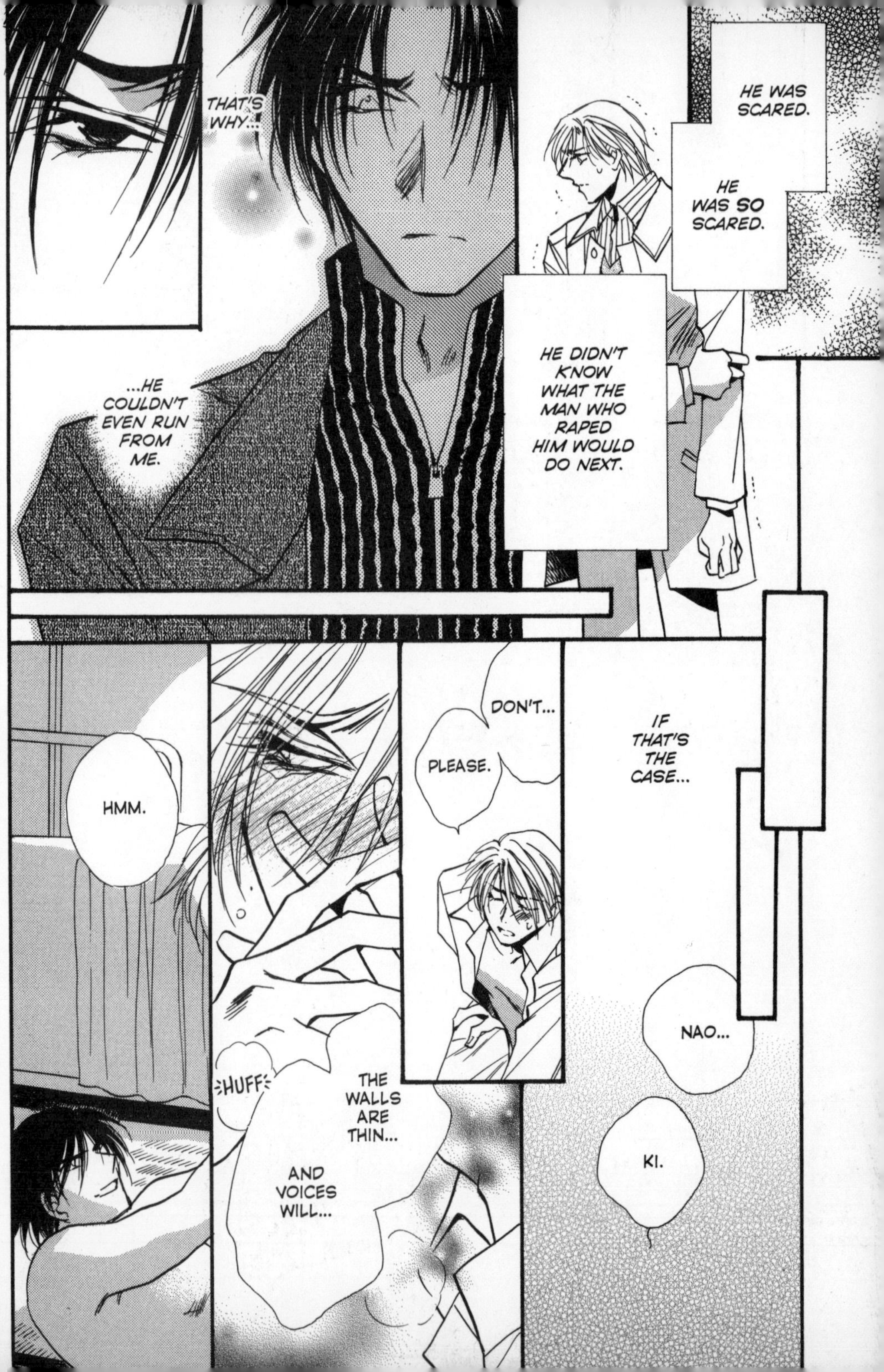
HE WAS SCARED.
HE WAS SO SCARED.
HE DIDN'T KNOW WHAT THE MAN WHO RAPED HIM WOULD DO NEXT.
THAT'S WHY...
...HE COULDN'T EVEN RUN FROM ME.
IF THAT'S THE CASE...
NAO...
KI.
DON'T...
PLEASE.
HUFF
THE WALLS ARE THIN...
AND VOICES WILL...
HMM.

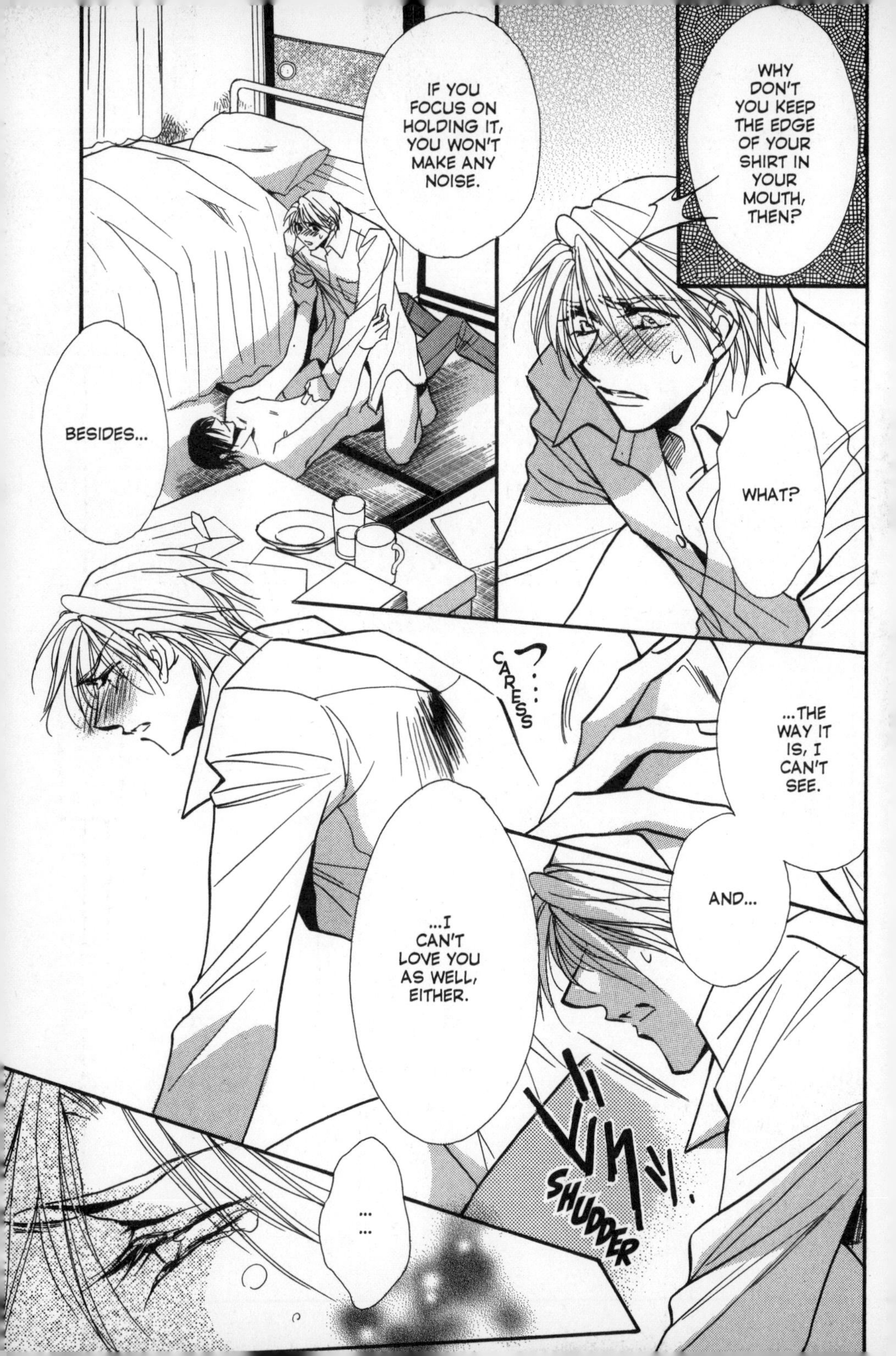

WHY DON'T YOU KEEP THE EDGE OF YOUR SHIRT IN YOUR MOUTH, THEN?
WHAT?
IF YOU FOCUS ON HOLDING IT, YOU WON'T MAKE ANY NOISE.
BESIDES...
CARESS
...THE WAY IT IS, I CAN'T SEE.
AND...
...I CAN'T LOVE YOU AS WELL, EITHER.
SHUDDER
...
...

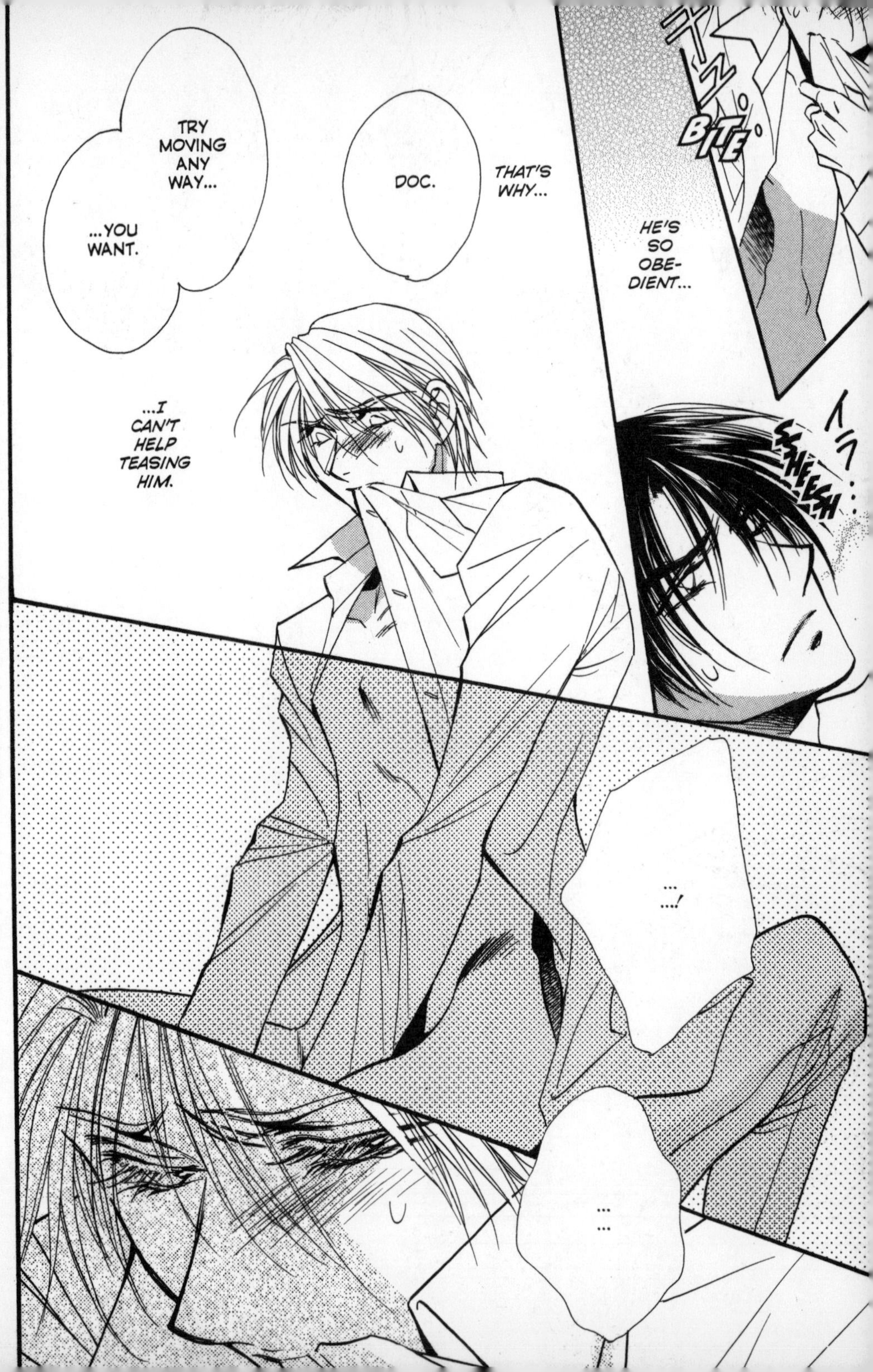
BITE
HE'S SO OBEDIENT...
SHEESH
THAT'S WHY...
DOC.
TRY MOVING ANY WAY...
...YOU WANT.
...I CAN'T HELP TEASING HIM.
... ...!
... ...

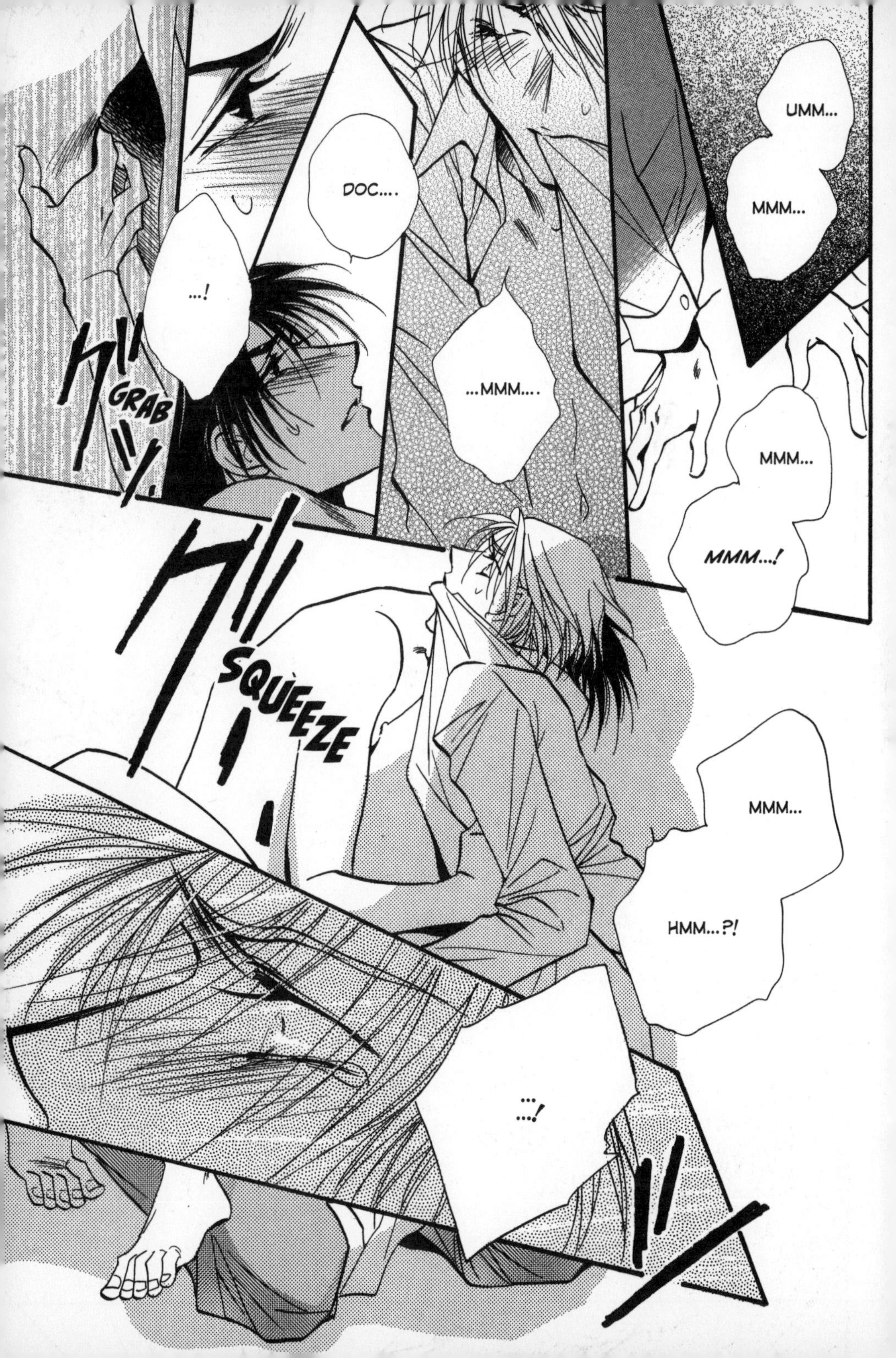
UMM...
MMM...
MMM...
MMM...!
DOC....
...MMM....
...!
GRAB
MMM...
HMM...?!
SQUEEZE
...!

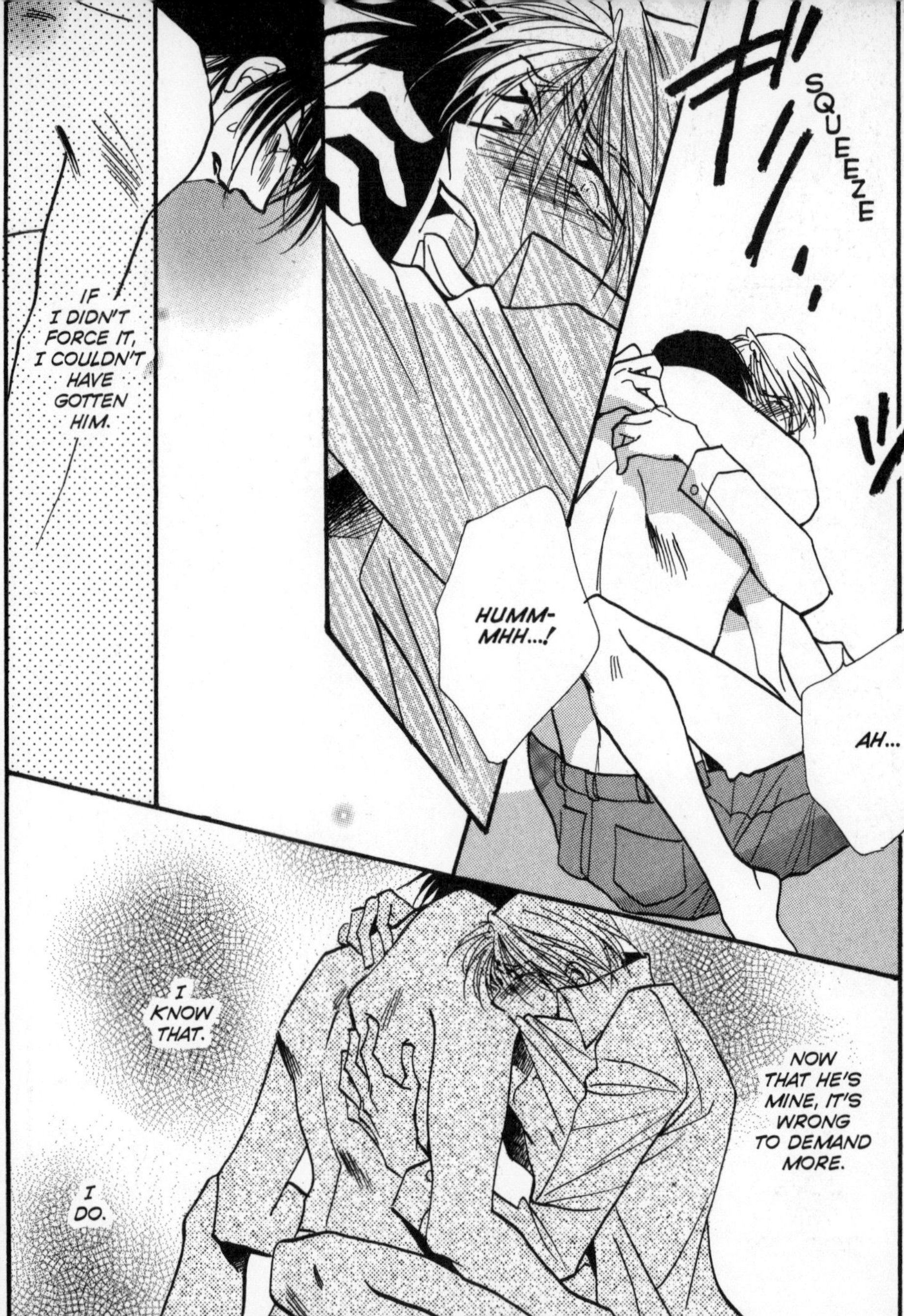
SQUEEZE
HUMM-MHH...!
AH...
IF I DIDN'T FORCE IT, I COULDN'T HAVE GOTTEN HIM.
NOW THAT HE'S MINE, IT'S WRONG TO DEMAND MORE.
I KNOW THAT.
I DO.

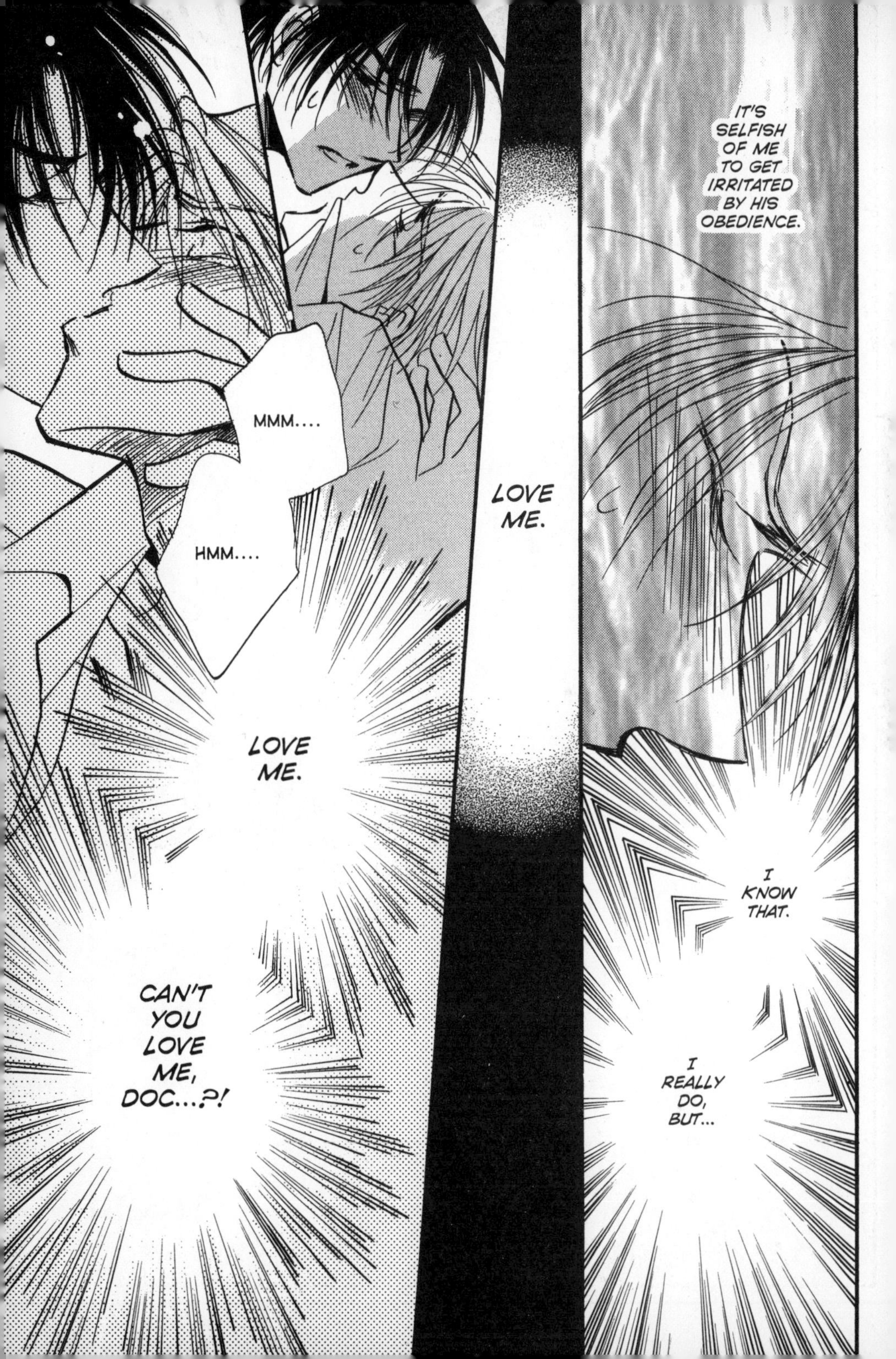
IT'S SELFISH OF ME TO GET IRRITATED BY HIS OBEDIENCE.
I KNOW THAT.
I REALLY DO, BUT...
LOVE ME.
MMM....
HMM....
LOVE ME.
CAN'T YOU LOVE ME, DOC...?!

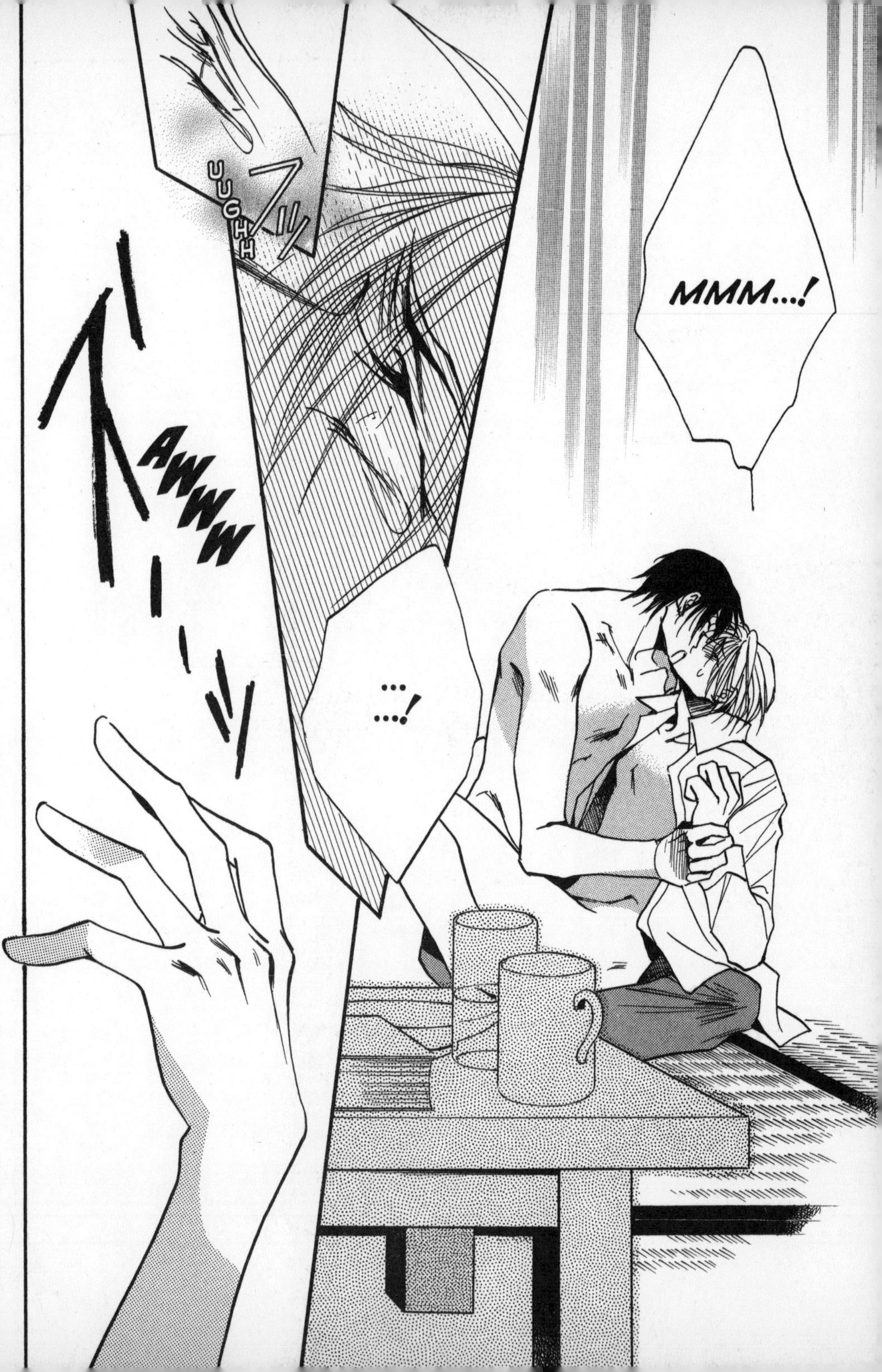
MMM...!
UUGH
... ...!
AWWW

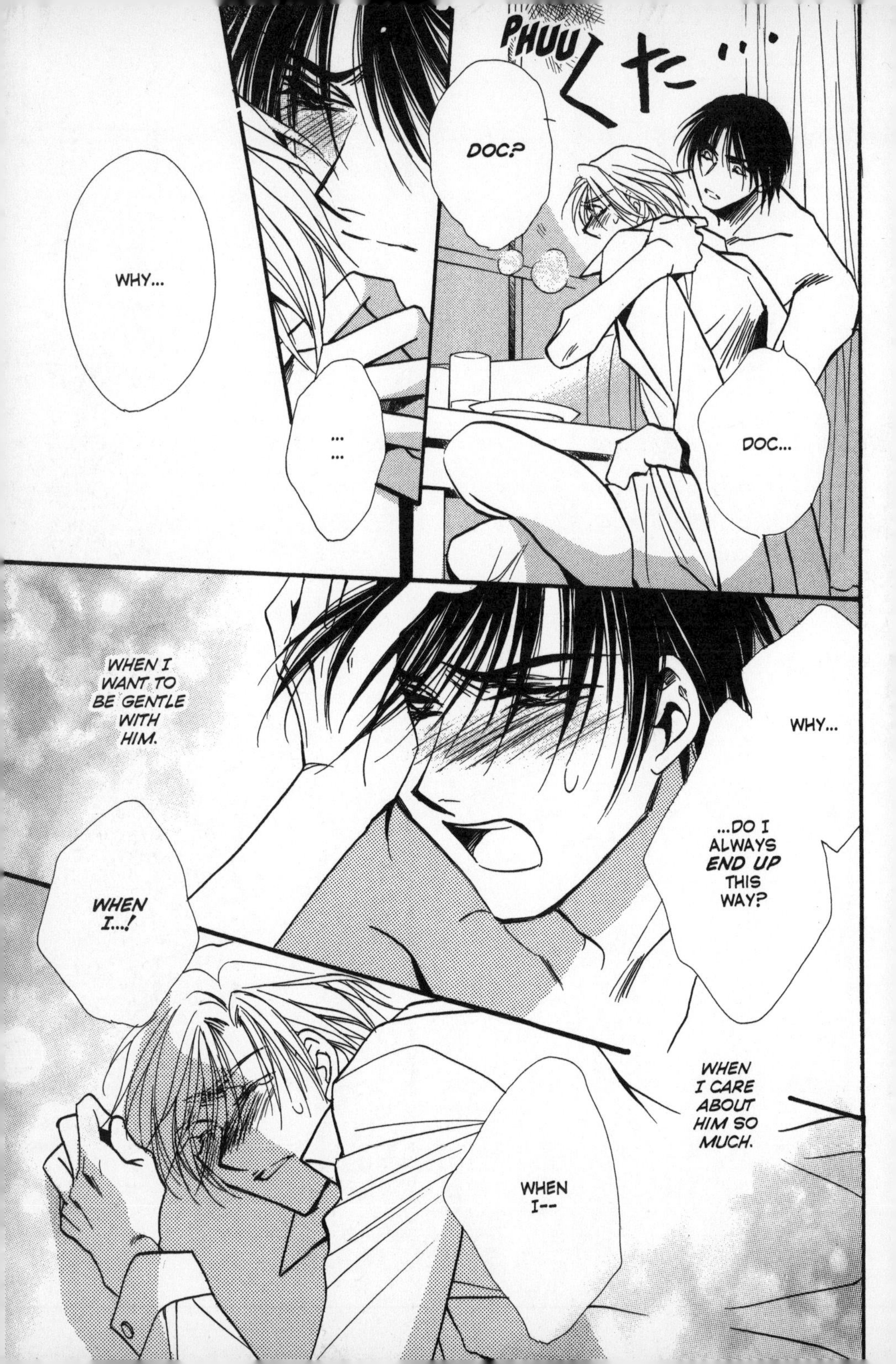
PHUU くたッ
DOC?
DOC...
...
...
WHY...
WHY...
...DO I ALWAYS END UP THIS WAY?
WHEN I WANT TO BE GENTLE WITH HIM.
WHEN I...!
WHEN I CARE ABOUT HIM SO MUCH.
WHEN I--

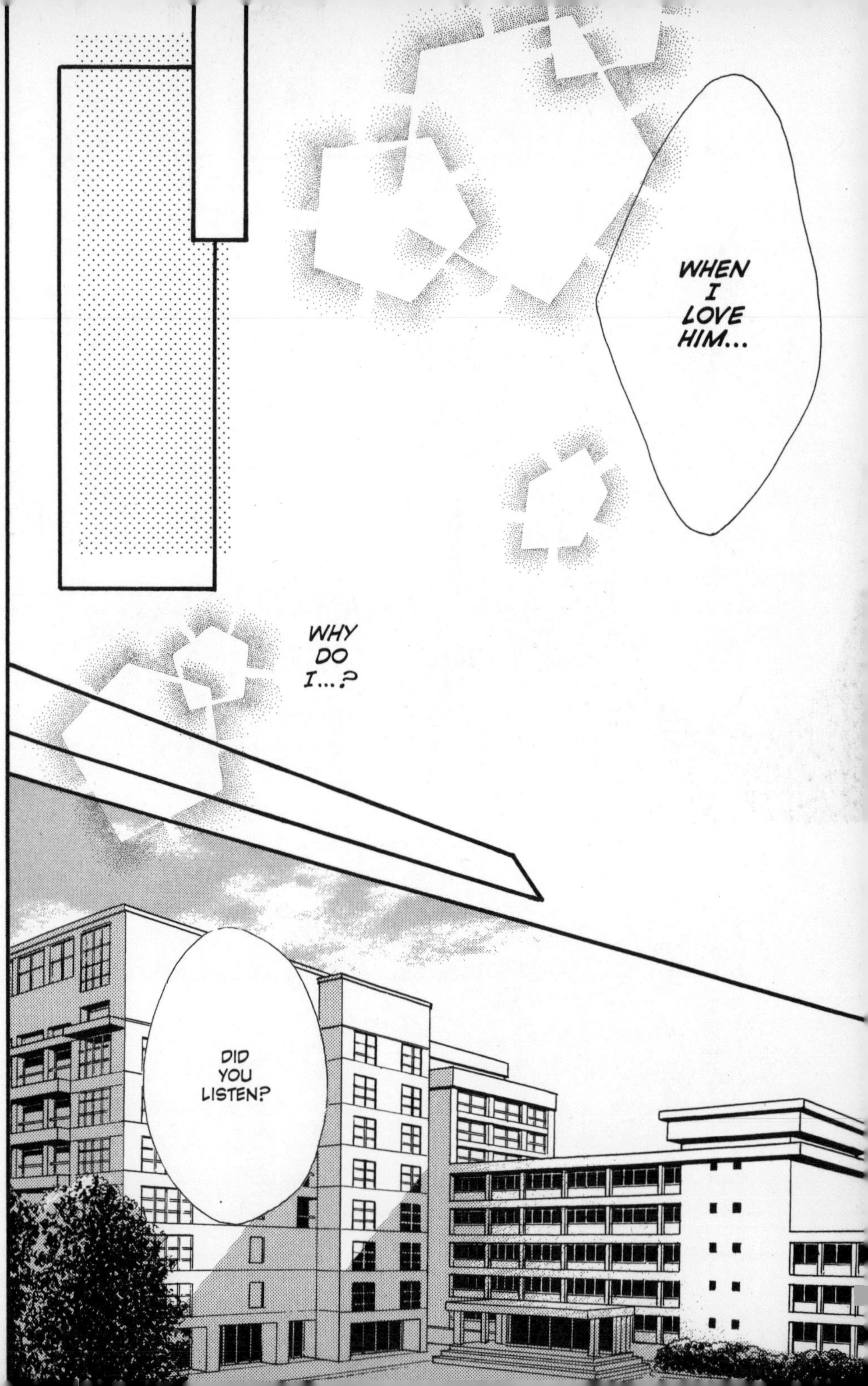
WHEN I LOVE HIM...
WHY DO I...?
DID YOU LISTEN?

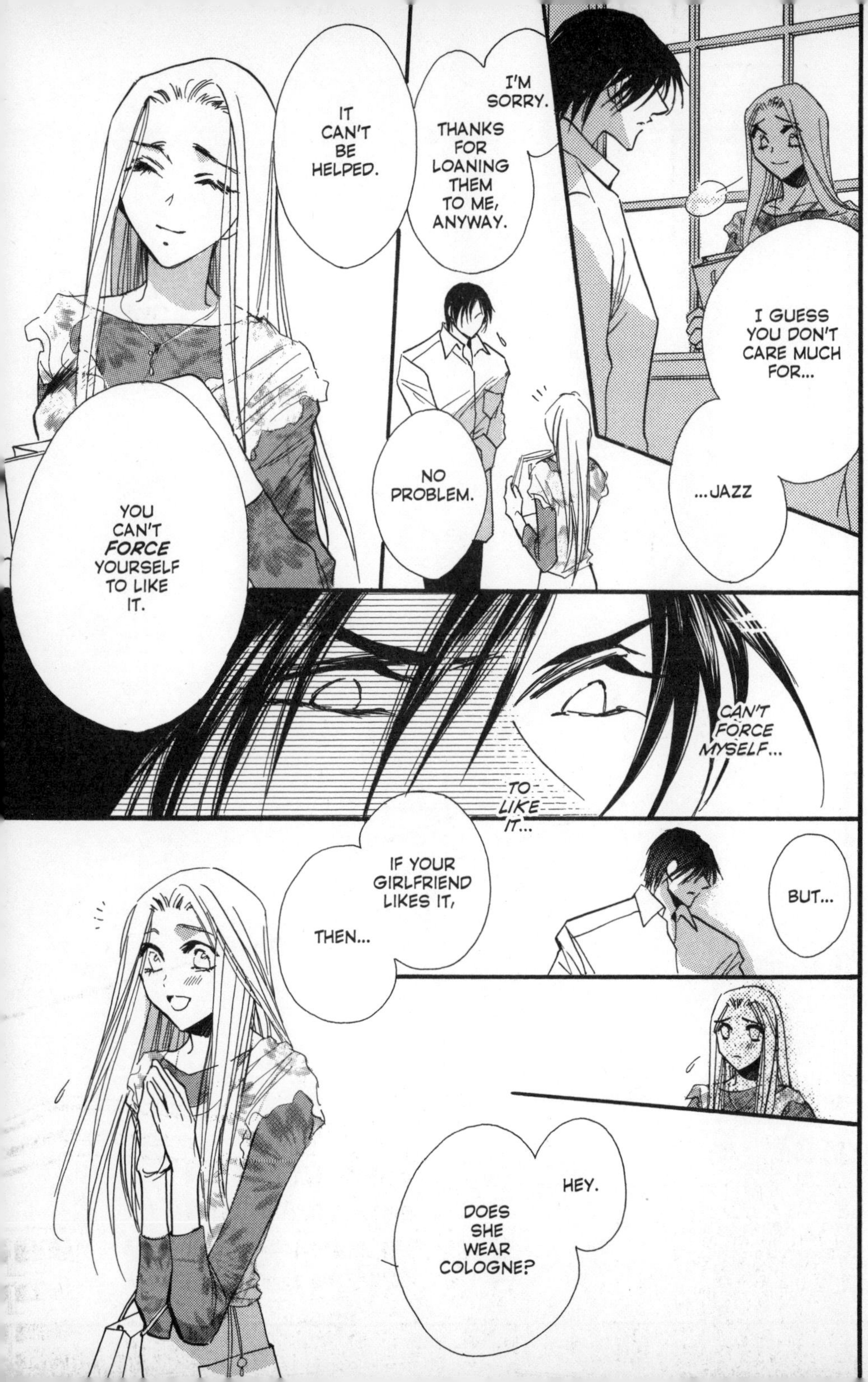
I GUESS YOU DON'T CARE MUCH FOR...
...JAZZ
I'M SORRY.
THANKS FOR LOANING THEM TO ME, ANYWAY.
NO PROBLEM.
IT CAN'T BE HELPED.
YOU CAN'T *FORCE* YOURSELF TO LIKE IT.
CAN'T FORCE MYSELF...
TO LIKE IT...
BUT...
IF YOUR GIRLFRIEND LIKES IT,
THEN...
HEY.
DOES SHE WEAR COLOGNE?

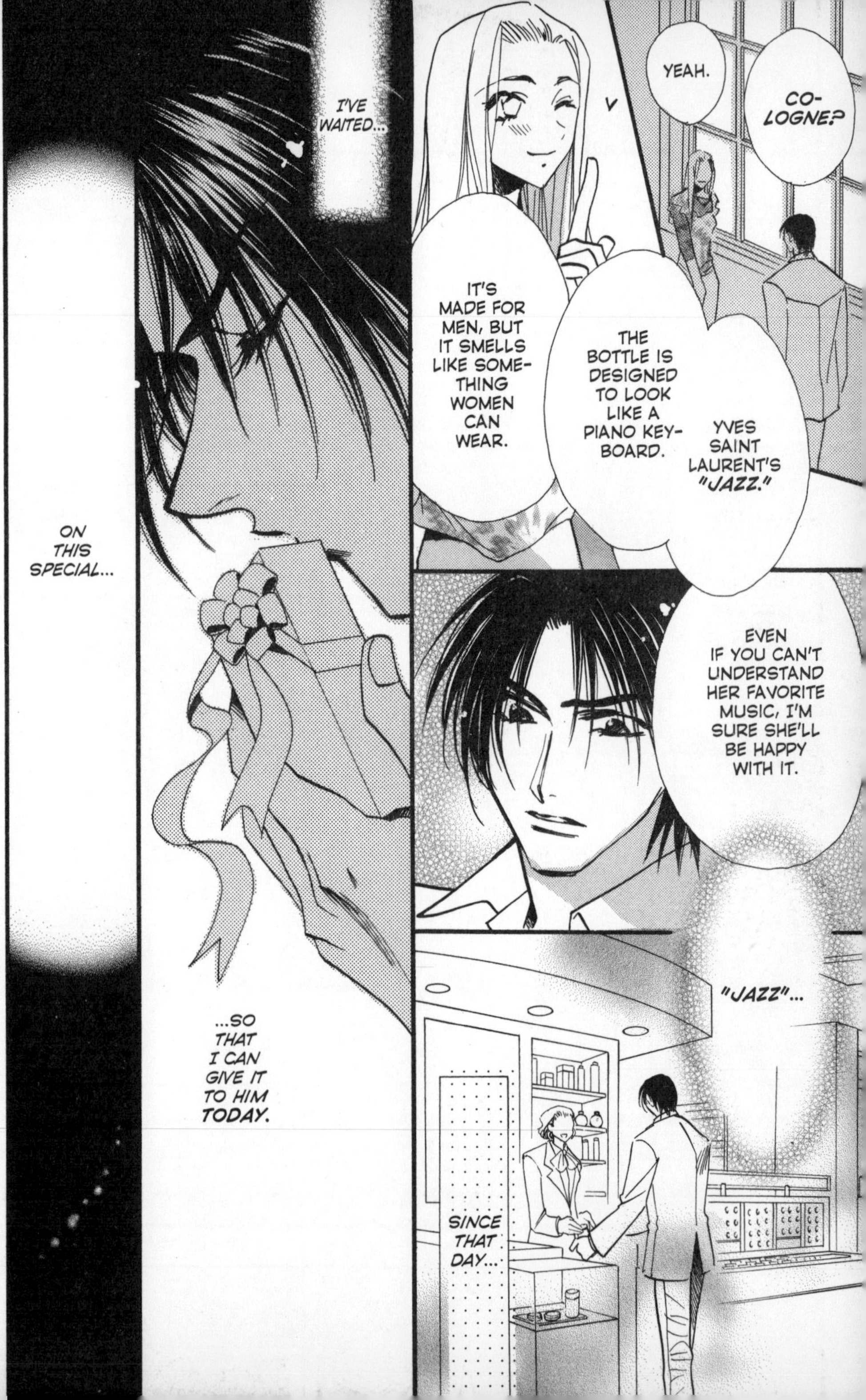
CO-LOGNE?
YEAH.
YVES SAINT LAURENT'S "JAZZ."
THE BOTTLE IS DESIGNED TO LOOK LIKE A PIANO KEY-BOARD.
IT'S MADE FOR MEN, BUT IT SMELLS LIKE SOME-THING WOMEN CAN WEAR.
EVEN IF YOU CAN'T UNDERSTAND HER FAVORITE MUSIC, I'M SURE SHE'LL BE HAPPY WITH IT.
"JAZZ"...
SINCE THAT DAY...
I'VE WAITED...
ON THIS SPECIAL...
...SO THAT I CAN GIVE IT TO HIM TODAY.

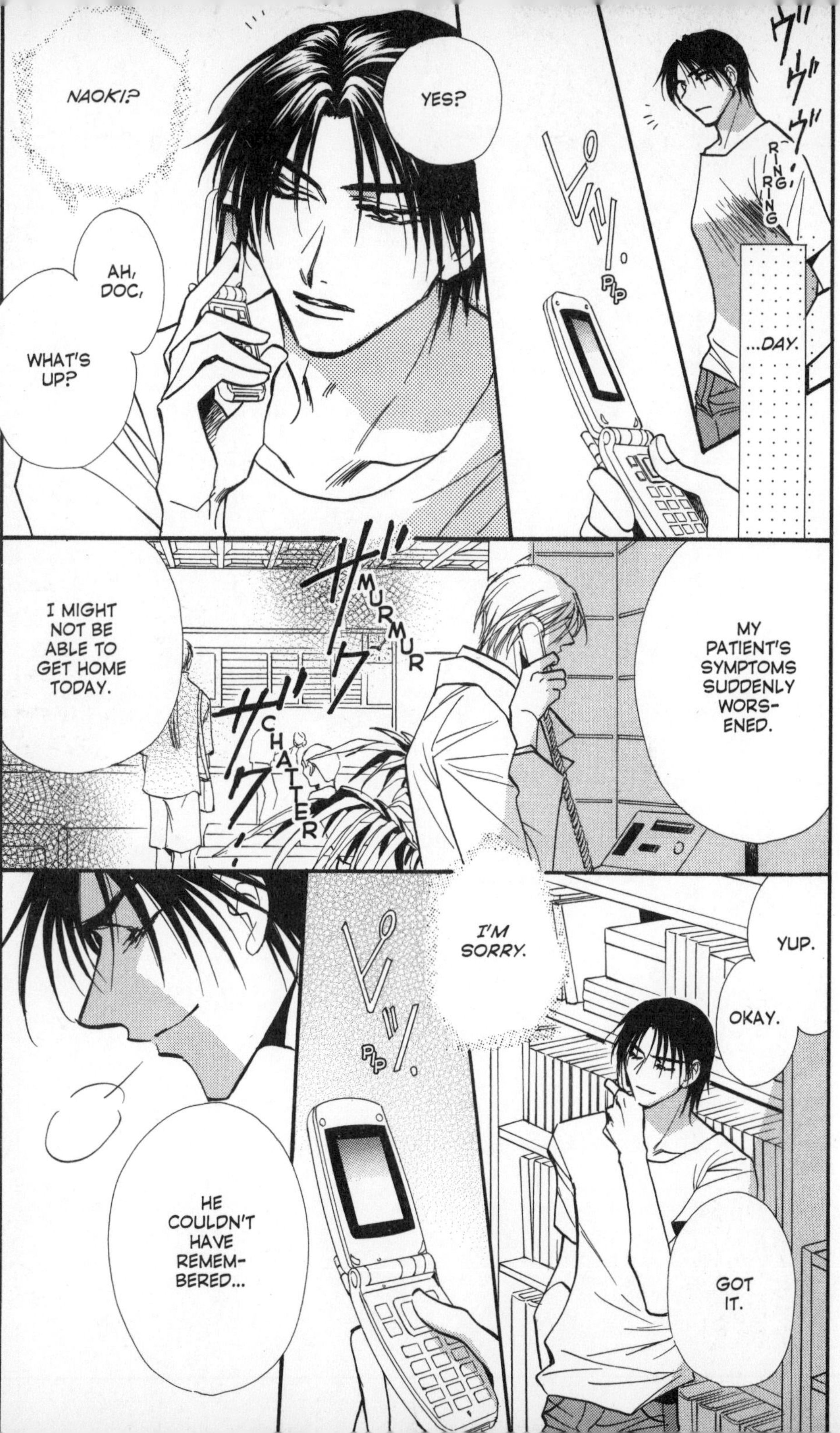
RING RING
...DAY.
PIP
YES?
NAOKI!?
AH, DOC, WHAT'S UP?
MY PATIENT'S SYMPTOMS SUDDENLY WORSENED.
MURMUR
CHATTER
I MIGHT NOT BE ABLE TO GET HOME TODAY.
YUP.
OKAY.
I'M SORRY.
GOT IT.
PIP
HE COULDN'T HAVE REMEMBERED...

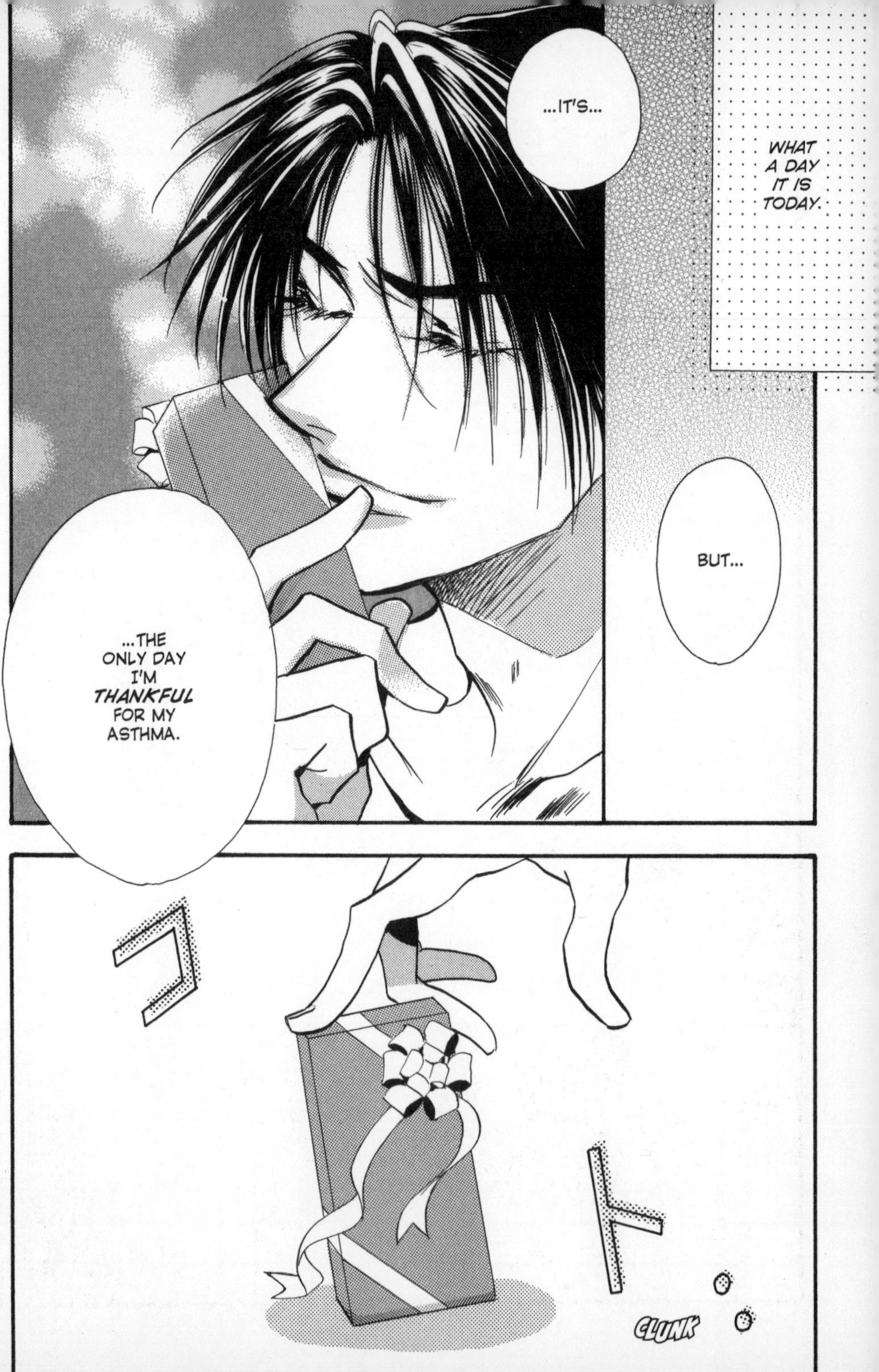
WHAT A DAY IT IS TODAY.
BUT...
...IT'S...
...THE ONLY DAY I'M *THANKFUL* FOR MY ASTHMA.
CLUNK

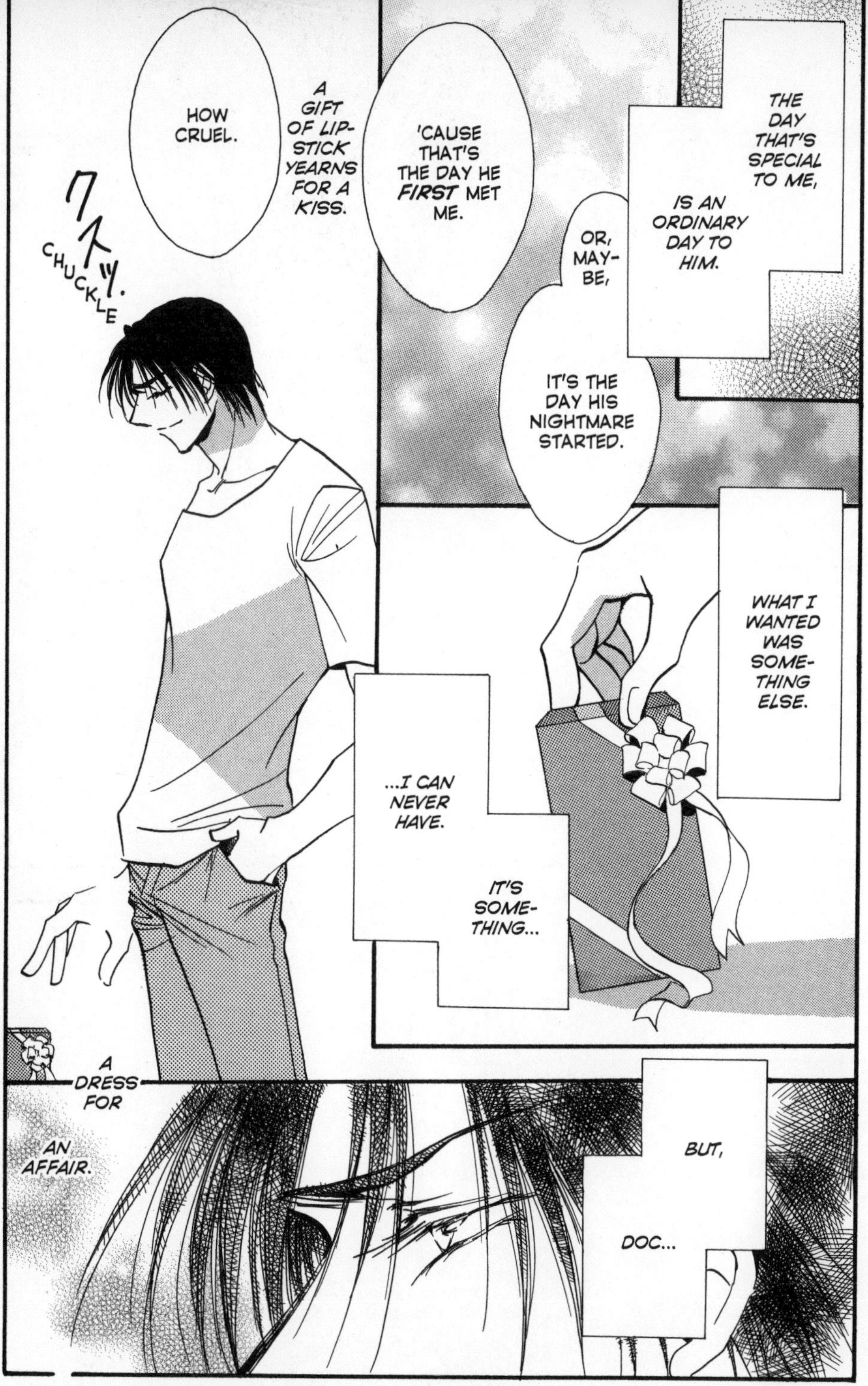

THE DAY THAT'S SPECIAL TO ME,
IS AN ORDINARY DAY TO HIM.
OR, MAYBE,
IT'S THE DAY HIS NIGHTMARE STARTED.
'CAUSE THAT'S THE DAY HE *FIRST* MET ME.
WHAT I WANTED WAS SOMETHING ELSE.
IT'S SOMETHING...
...I CAN NEVER HAVE.
A GIFT OF LIPSTICK YEARNS FOR A KISS.
HOW CRUEL.
クスッ.
CHUCKLE
BUT, DOC...
A DRESS FOR AN AFFAIR.

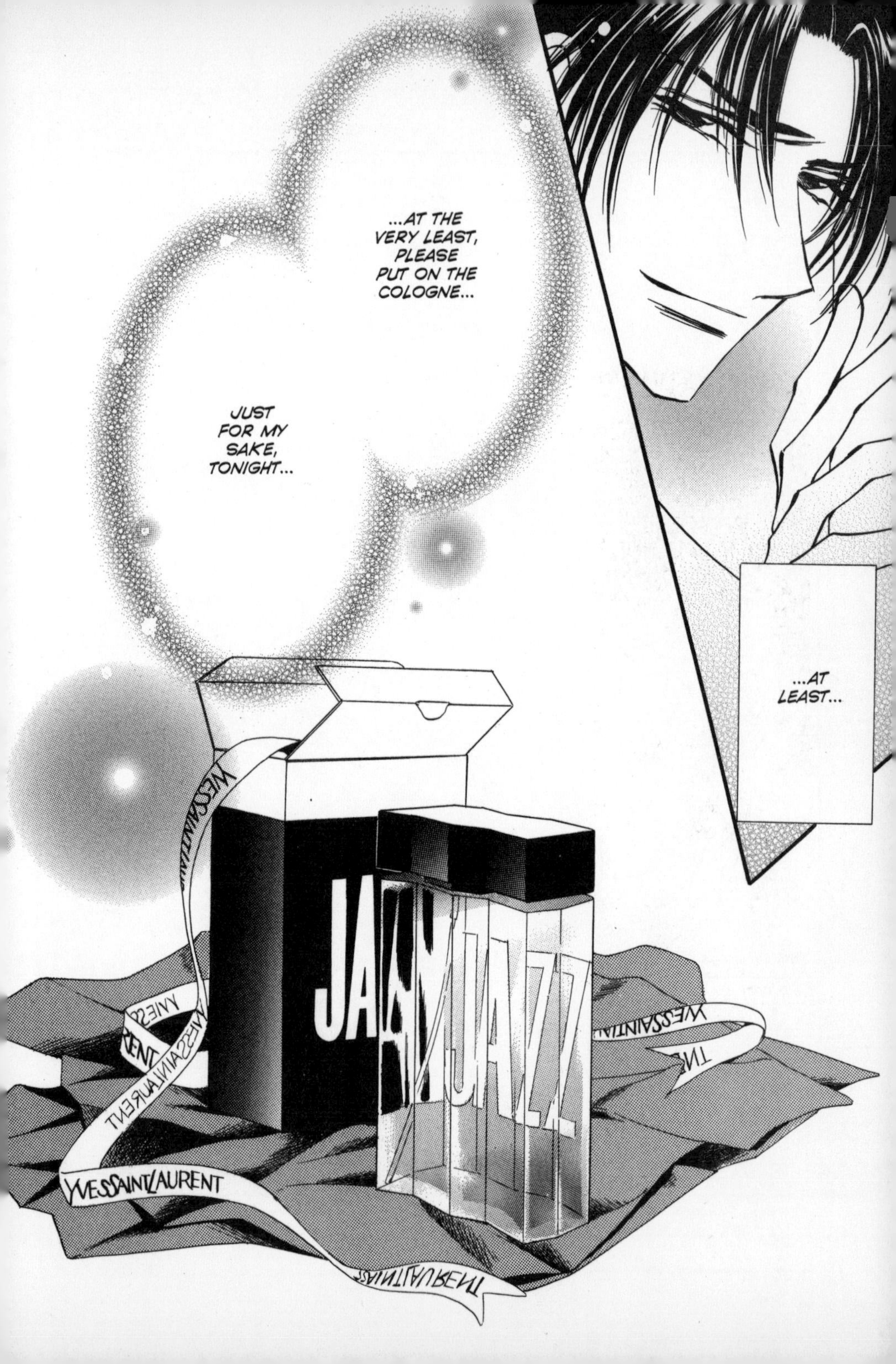
...AT LEAST...
...AT THE VERY LEAST, PLEASE PUT ON THE COLOGNE...
JUST FOR MY SAKE, TONIGHT...
JAZZ
YVESSAINTLAURENT

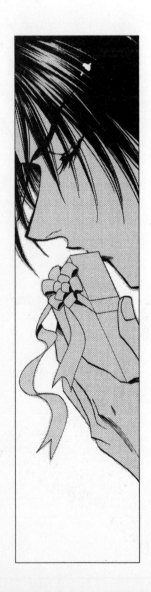

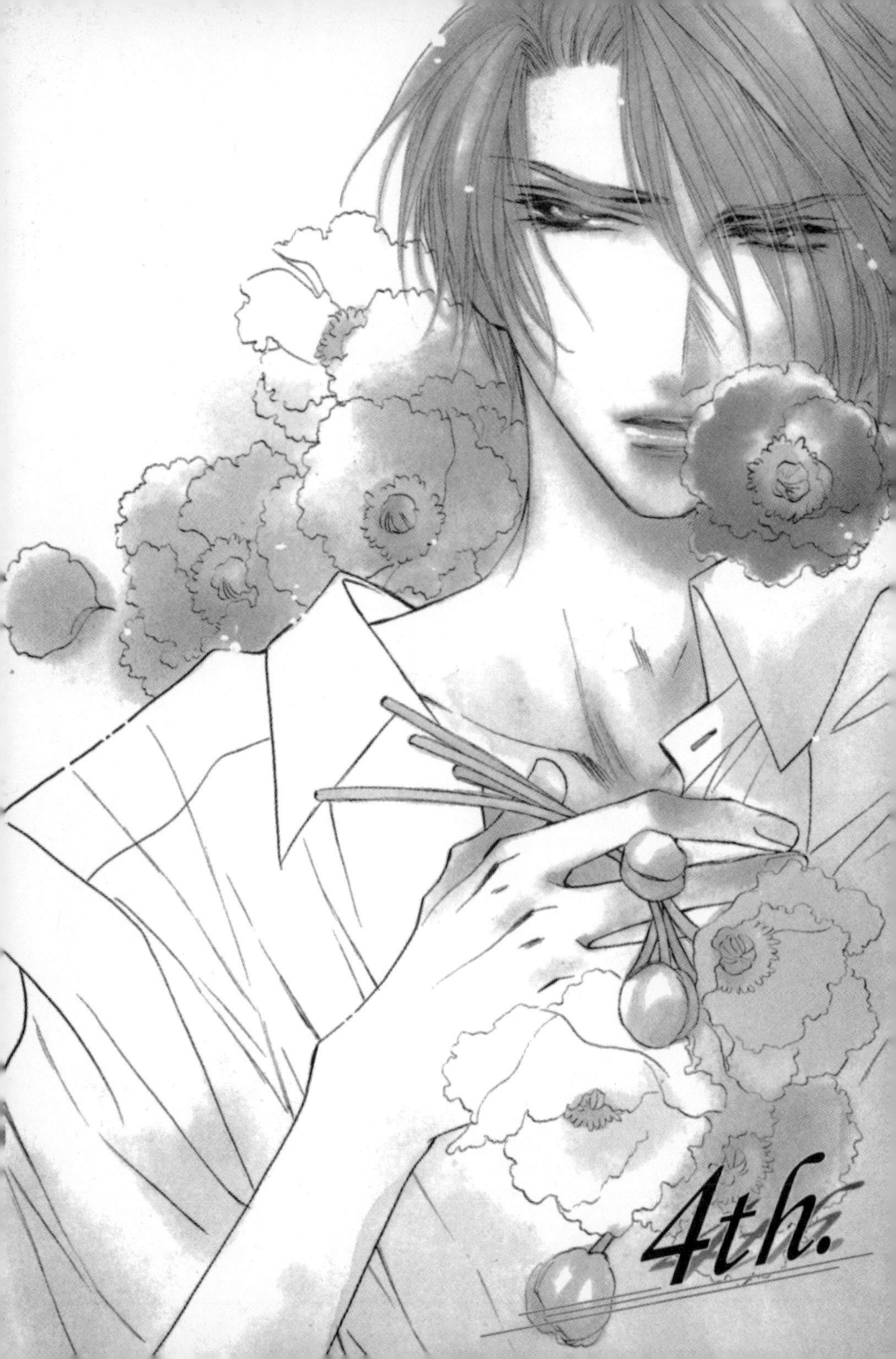
4th.

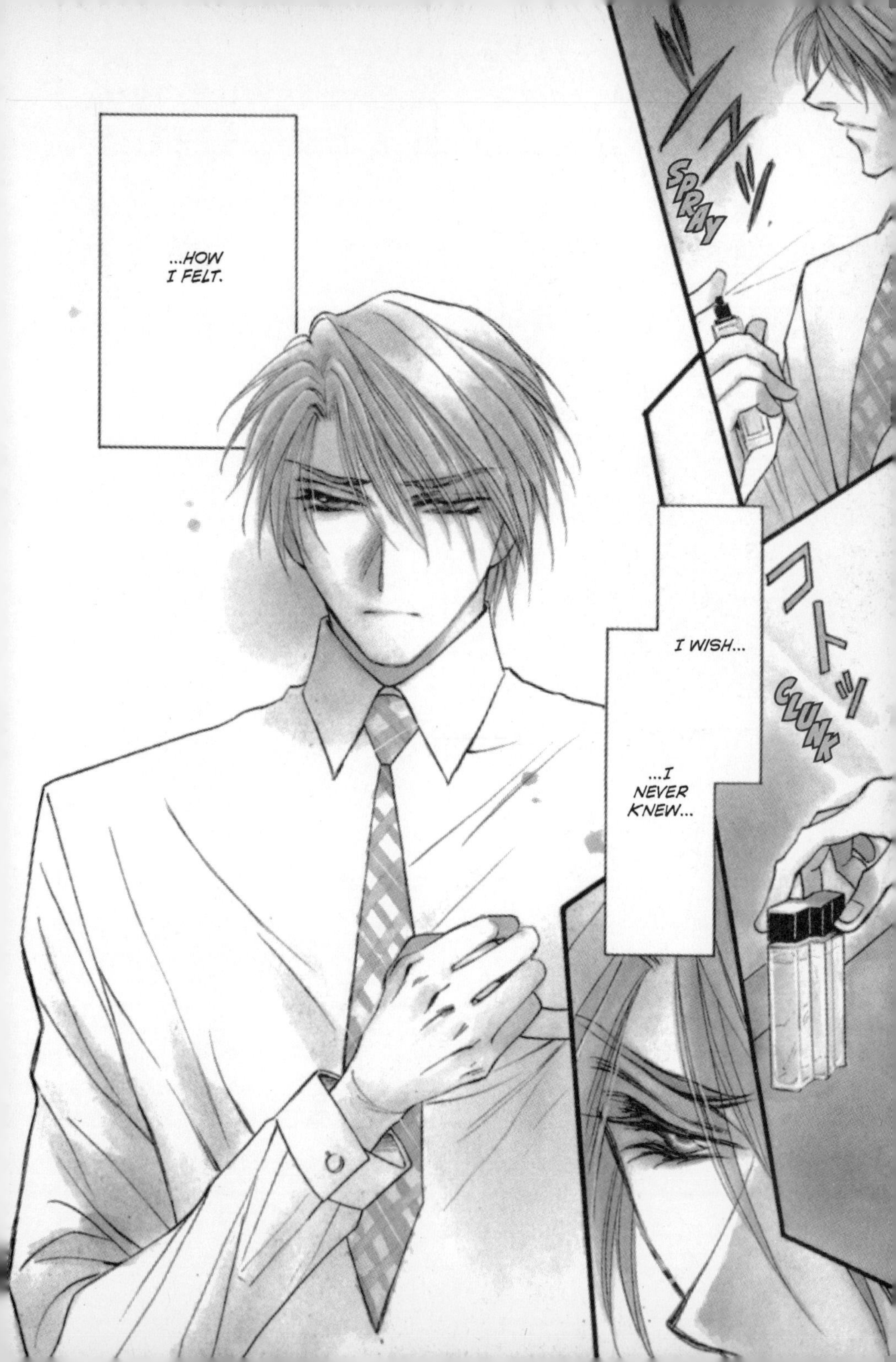
SPRAY
I WISH...
...I NEVER KNEW...
CLUNK
...HOW I FELT.

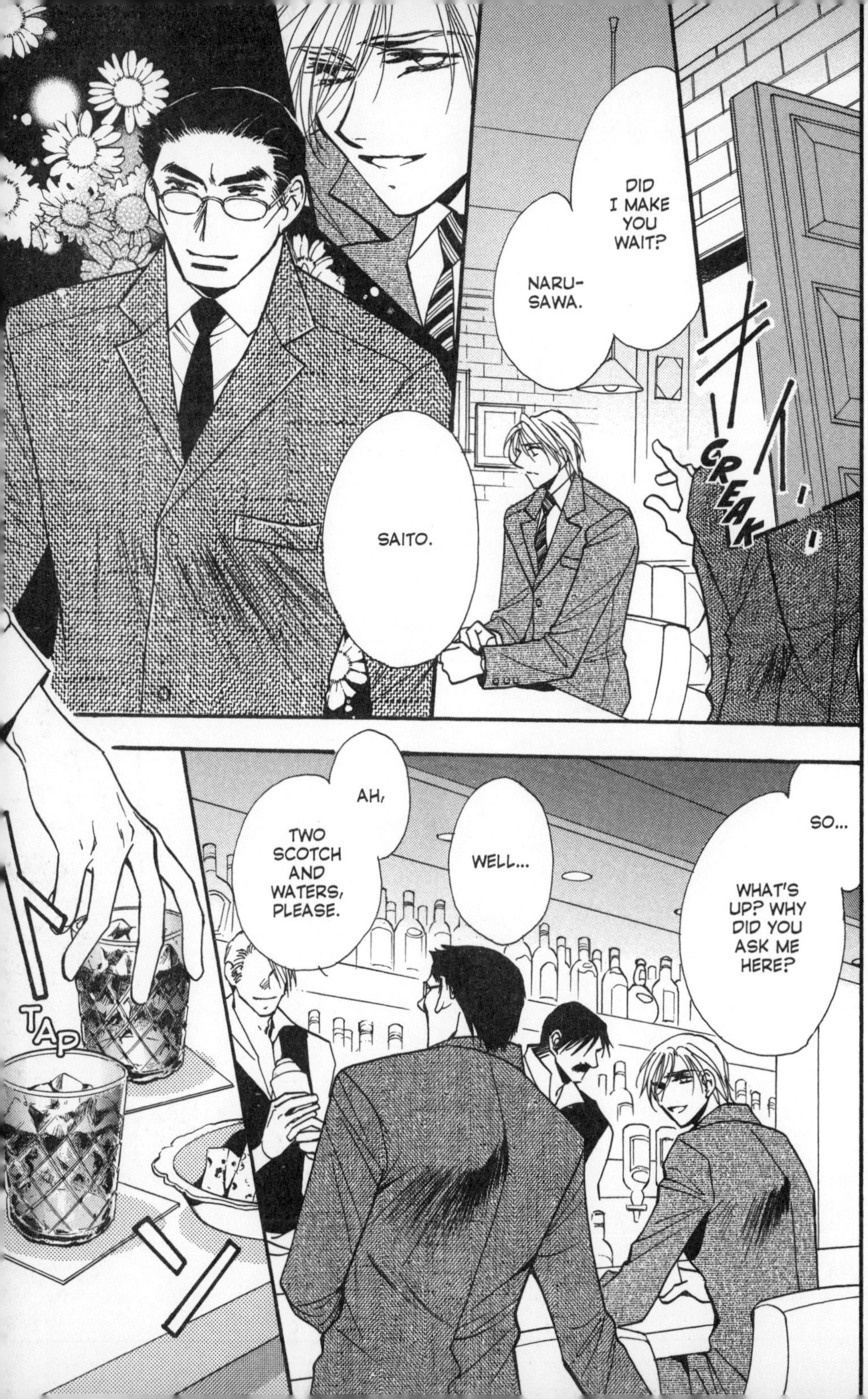
CREAK
DID I MAKE YOU WAIT?
NARU-SAWA.
SAITO.
SO...
WHAT'S UP? WHY DID YOU ASK ME HERE?
WELL...
AH,
TWO SCOTCH AND WATERS, PLEASE.
TAP

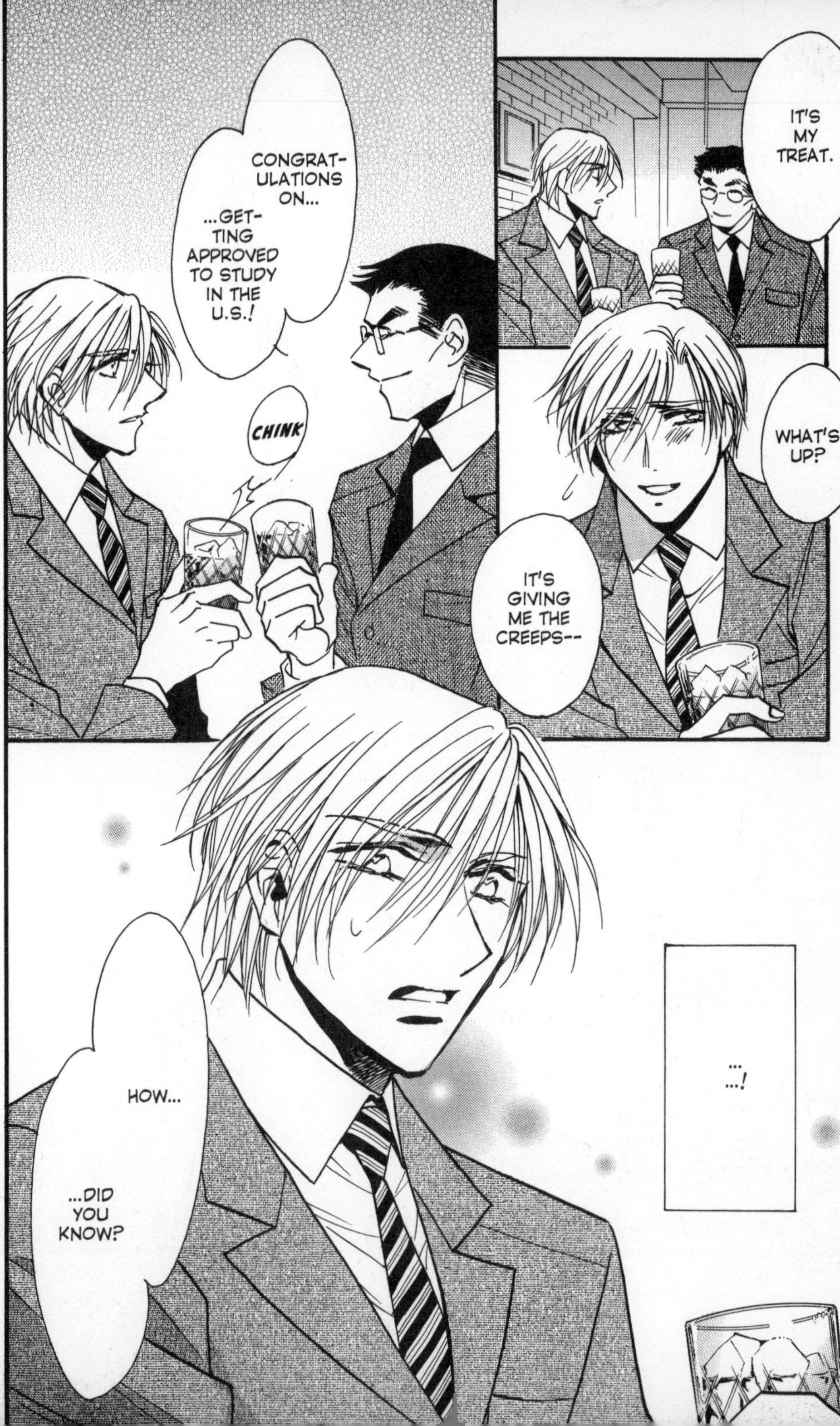
IT'S MY TREAT.
WHAT'S UP?
IT'S GIVING ME THE CREEPS--
CONGRAT-ULATIONS ON...
...GET-TING APPROVED TO STUDY IN THE U.S.!
CHINK
...
...!
HOW...
...DID YOU KNOW?

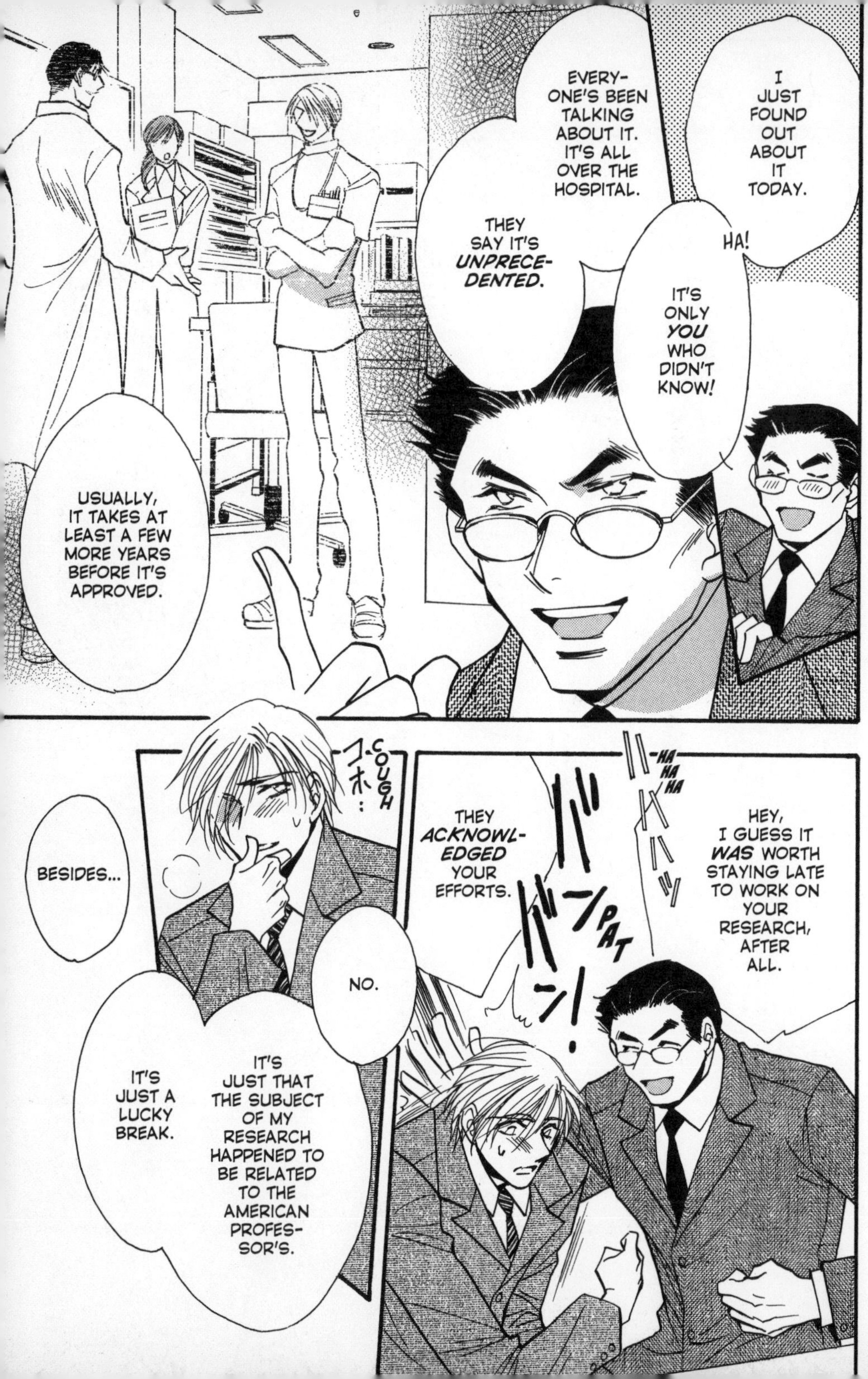
I JUST FOUND OUT ABOUT IT TODAY.
EVERY-ONE'S BEEN TALKING ABOUT IT. IT'S ALL OVER THE HOSPITAL.
THEY SAY IT'S *UNPRECE-DENTED*.
HA!
IT'S ONLY *YOU* WHO DIDN'T KNOW!
USUALLY, IT TAKES AT LEAST A FEW MORE YEARS BEFORE IT'S APPROVED.
HEY, I GUESS IT *WAS* WORTH STAYING LATE TO WORK ON YOUR RESEARCH, AFTER ALL.
HA HA HA
THEY *ACKNOWL-EDGED* YOUR EFFORTS.
PAT
NO.
COUGH
BESIDES...
IT'S JUST THAT THE SUBJECT OF MY RESEARCH HAPPENED TO BE RELATED TO THE AMERICAN PROFES-SOR'S.
IT'S JUST A LUCKY BREAK.

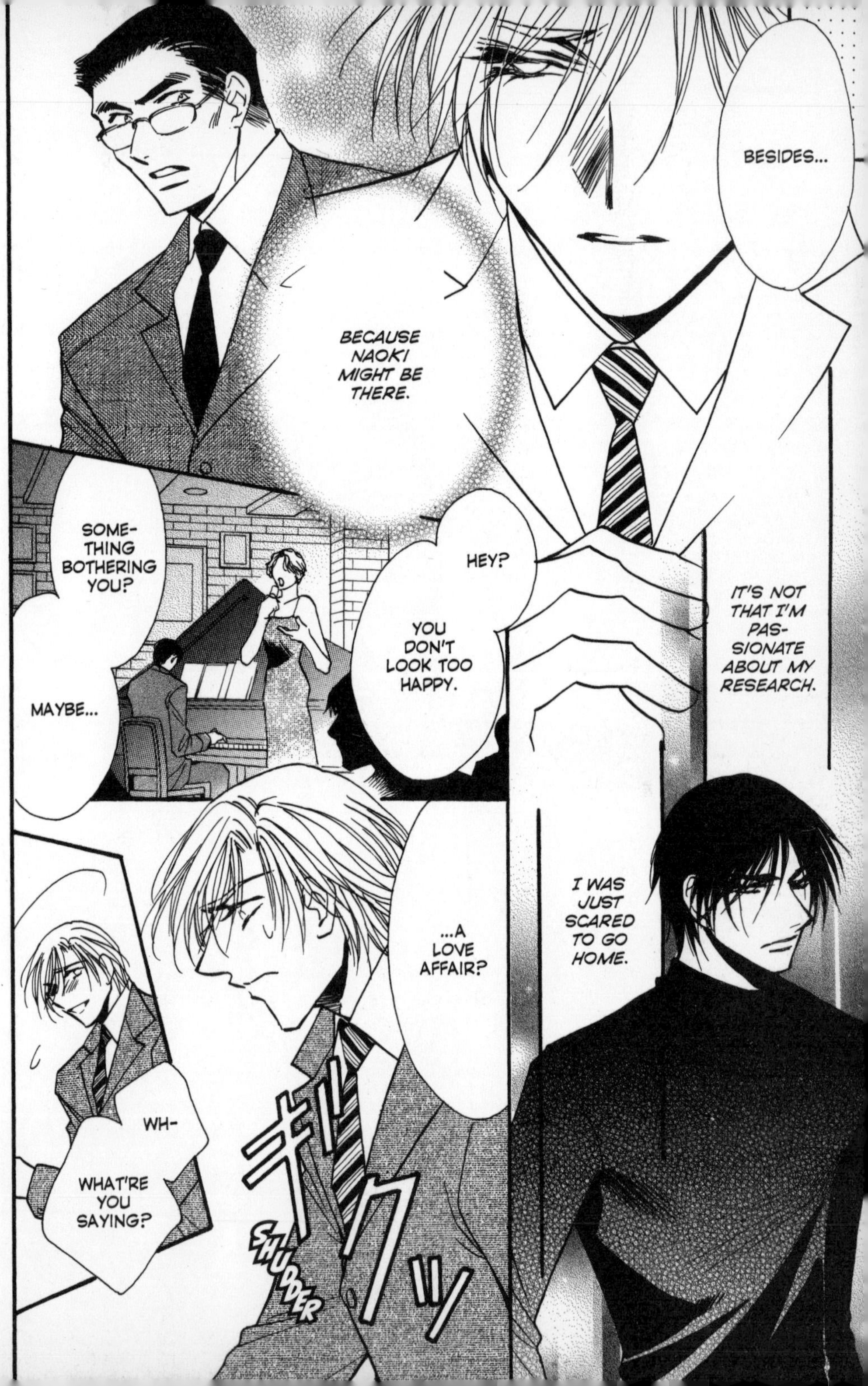
BESIDES...
BECAUSE NAOKI MIGHT BE THERE.
IT'S NOT THAT I'M PAS-SIONATE ABOUT MY RESEARCH.
I WAS JUST SCARED TO GO HOME.
HEY?
YOU DON'T LOOK TOO HAPPY.
SOME-THING BOTHERING YOU?
MAYBE...
...A LOVE AFFAIR?
SHUDDER
WH-
WHAT'RE YOU SAYING?

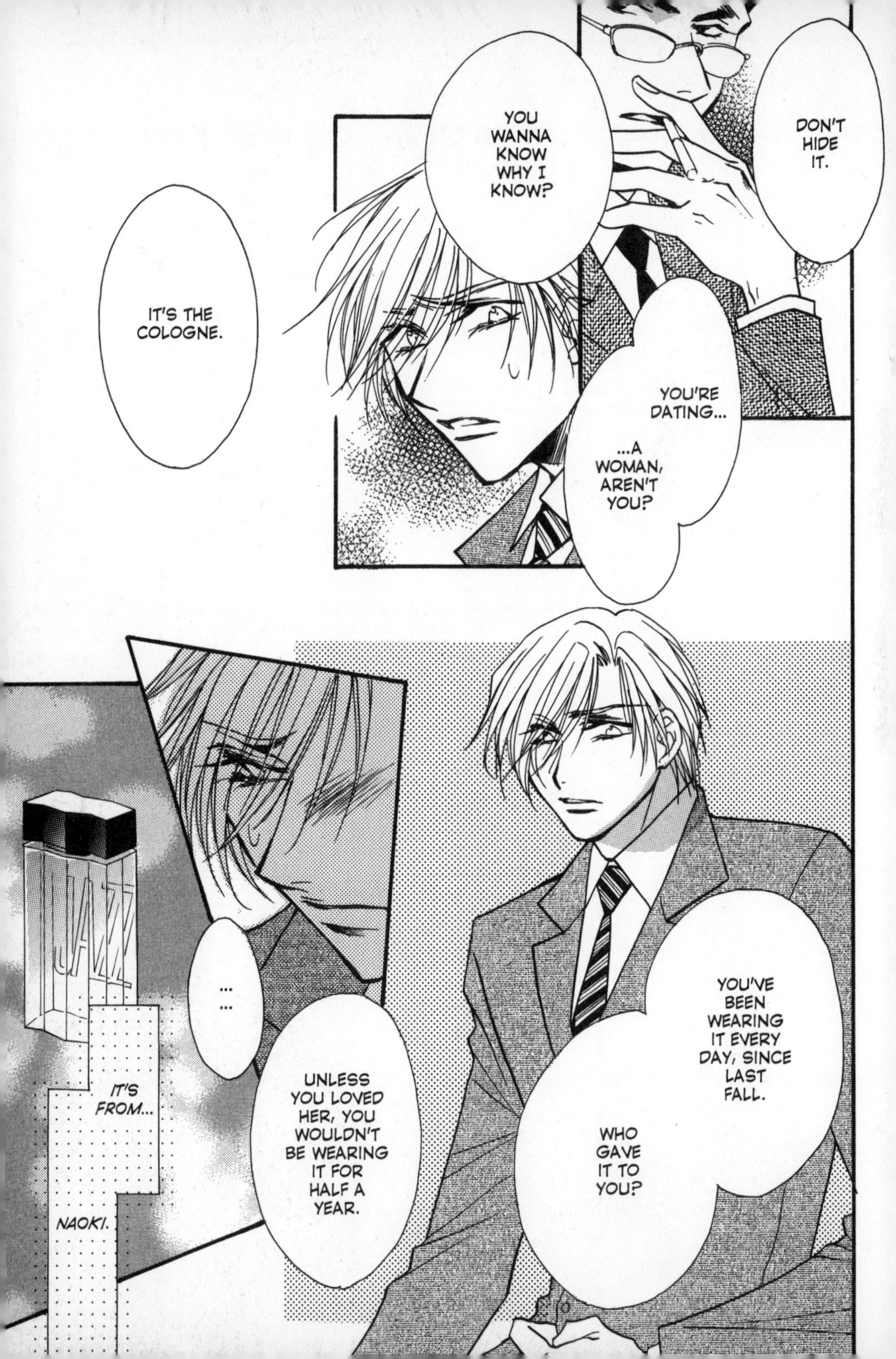
DON'T HIDE IT.
YOU'RE DATING...
...A WOMAN, AREN'T YOU?
YOU WANNA KNOW WHY I KNOW?
IT'S THE COLOGNE.
YOU'VE BEEN WEARING IT EVERY DAY, SINCE LAST FALL.
WHO GAVE IT TO YOU?
UNLESS YOU LOVED HER, YOU WOULDN'T BE WEARING IT FOR HALF A YEAR.
......
JAZZ
IT'S FROM...
NAOKI.

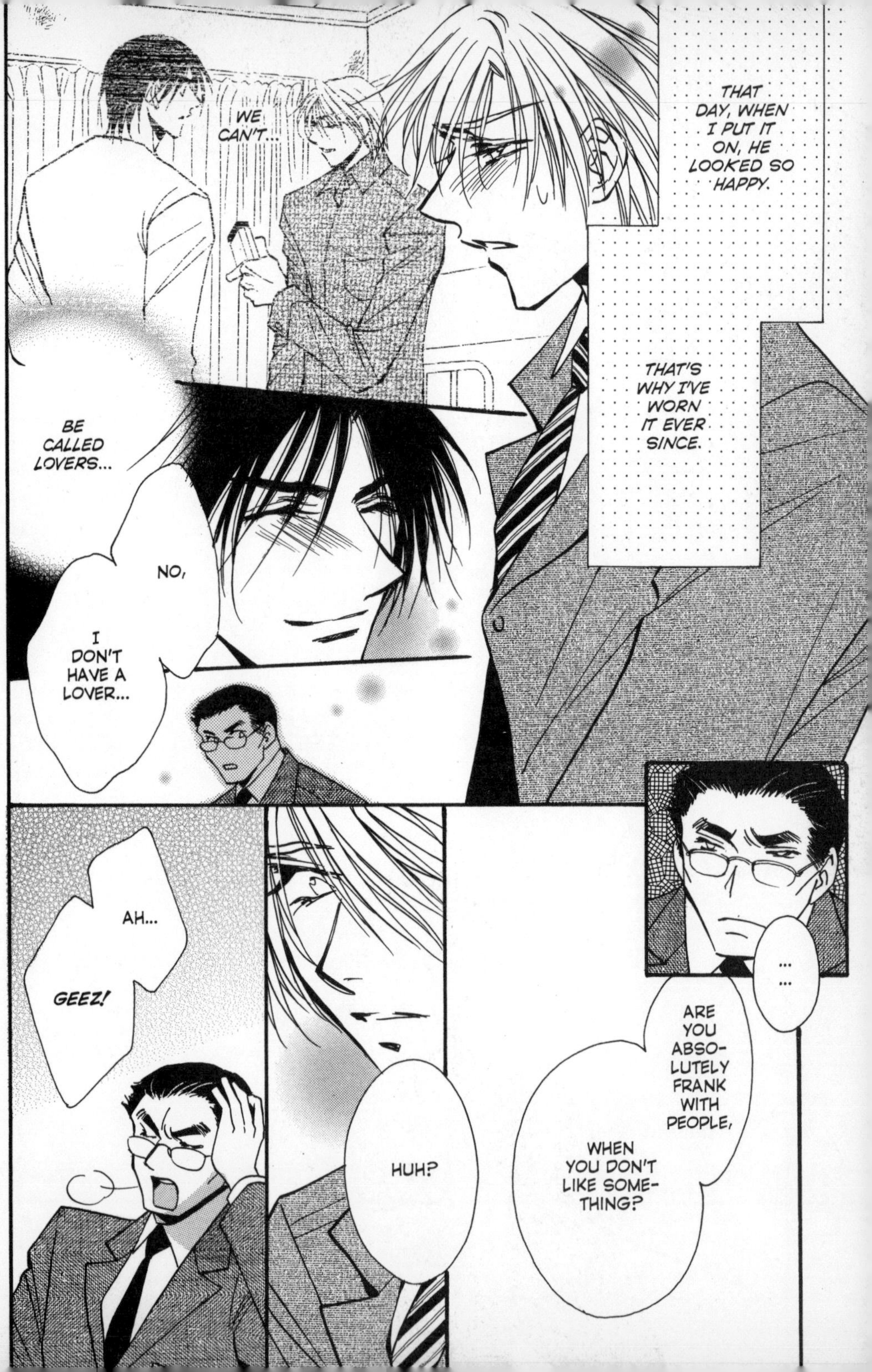
THAT DAY, WHEN I PUT IT ON, HE LOOKED SO HAPPY.
THAT'S WHY I'VE WORN IT EVER SINCE.
WE CAN'T...
BE CALLED LOVERS...
NO,
I DON'T HAVE A LOVER...
......
ARE YOU ABSOLUTELY FRANK WITH PEOPLE,
WHEN YOU DON'T LIKE SOMETHING?
HUH?
AH...
GEEZ!

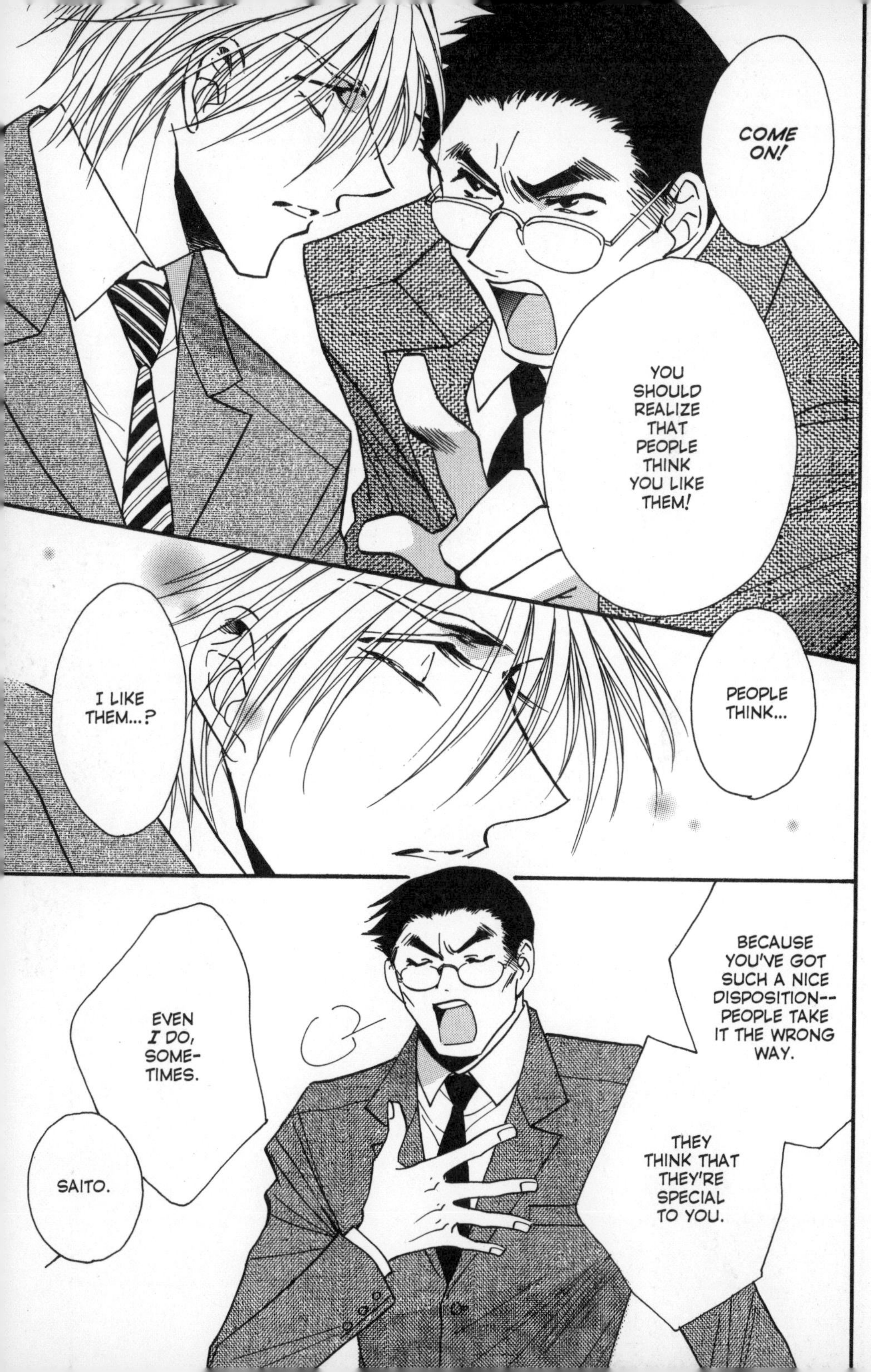
COME ON!
YOU SHOULD REALIZE THAT PEOPLE THINK YOU LIKE THEM!
PEOPLE THINK...
I LIKE THEM...?
BECAUSE YOU'VE GOT SUCH A NICE DISPOSITION-- PEOPLE TAKE IT THE WRONG WAY.
THEY THINK THAT THEY'RE SPECIAL TO YOU.
EVEN *I* DO, SOME-TIMES.
SAITO.

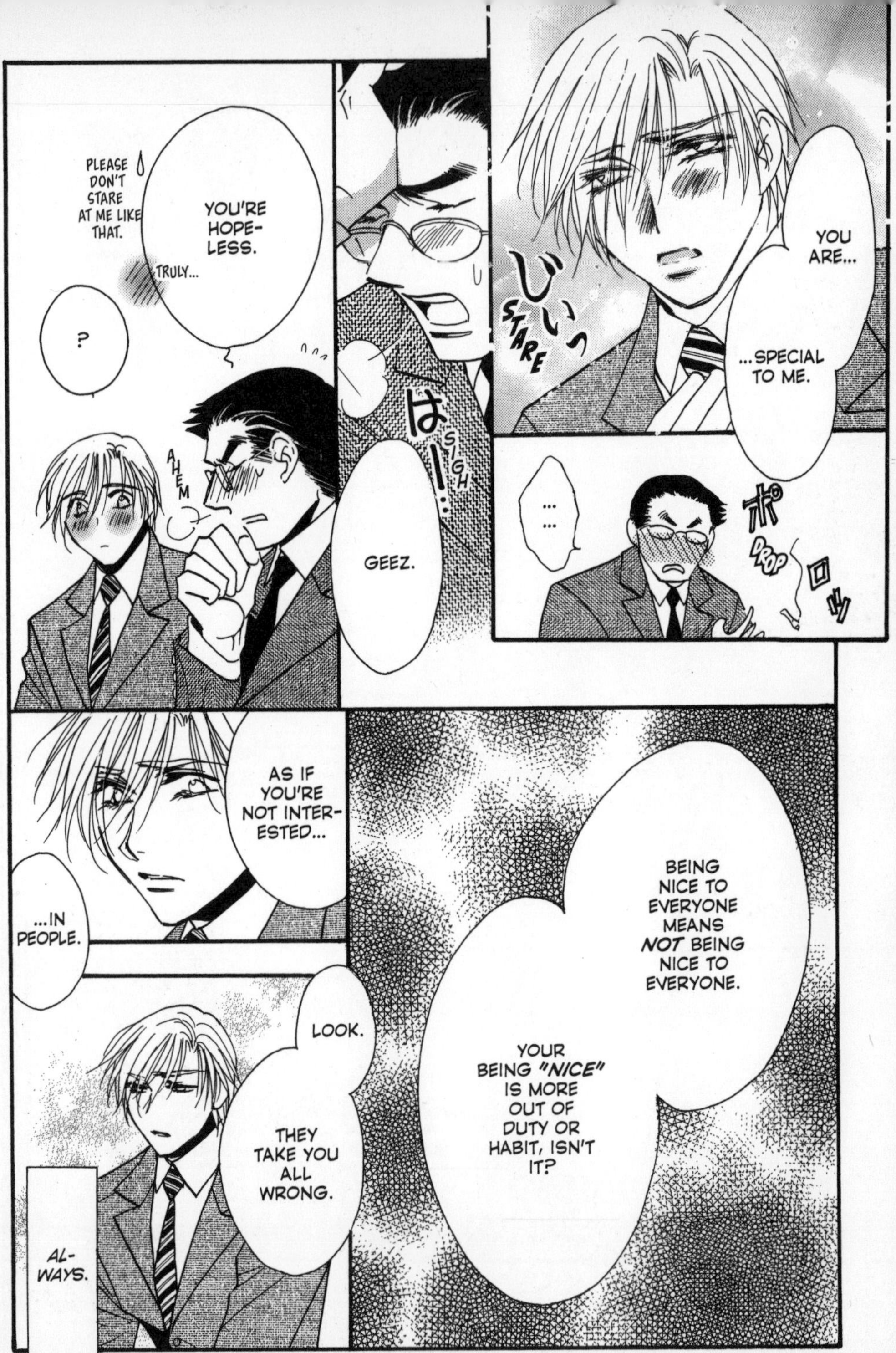
YOU ARE...
...SPECIAL TO ME.
じぃっ
STARE
...
...
ポロッ
DROP
はー!!
SIGH
GEEZ.
YOU'RE HOPELESS.
TRULY...
PLEASE DON'T STARE AT ME LIKE THAT.
?
AHEM
BEING NICE TO EVERYONE MEANS *NOT* BEING NICE TO EVERYONE.
YOUR BEING *"NICE"* IS MORE OUT OF DUTY OR HABIT, ISN'T IT?
AS IF YOU'RE NOT INTERESTED...
...IN PEOPLE.
LOOK.
THEY TAKE YOU ALL WRONG.
AL-WAYS.

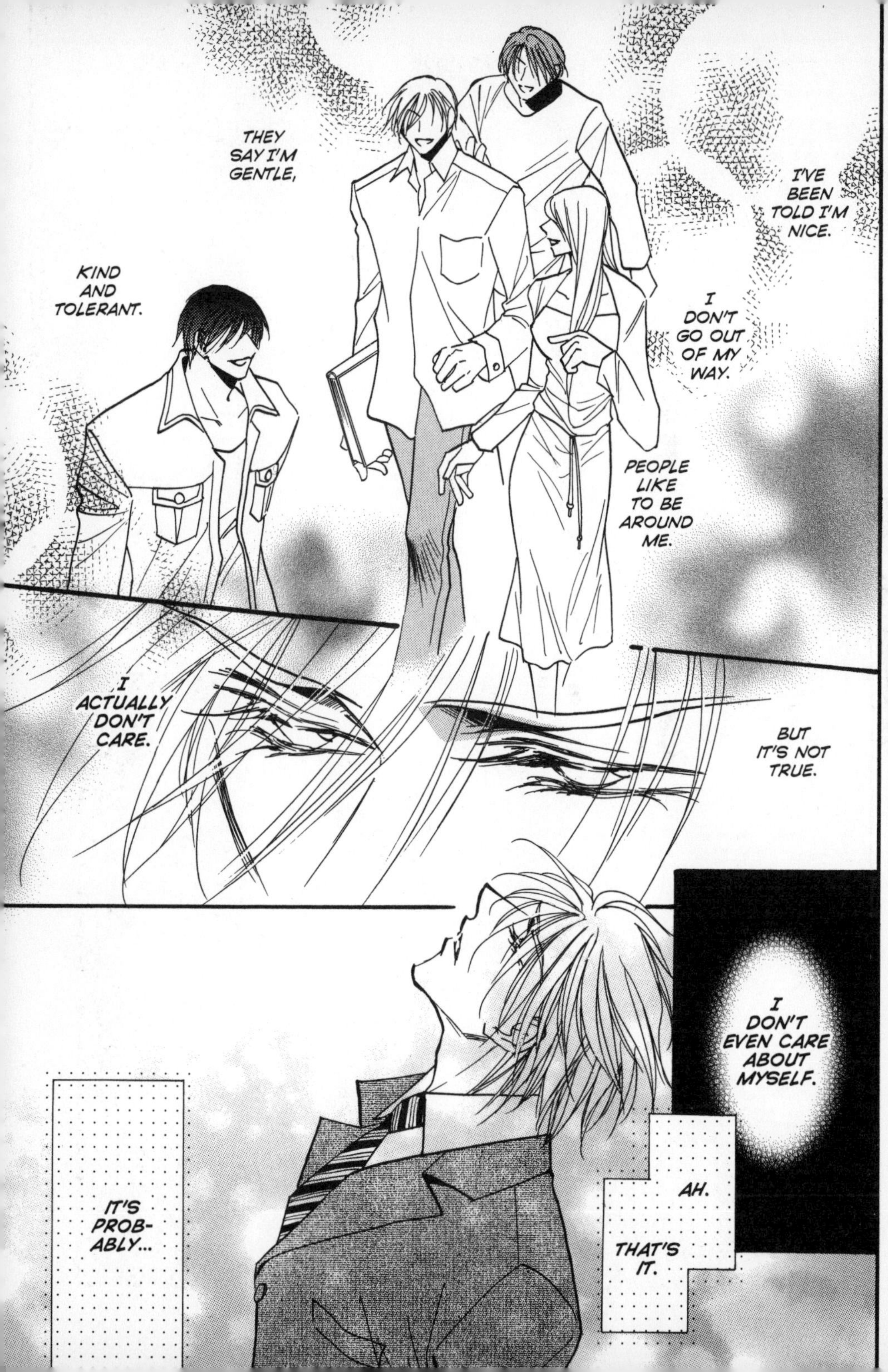
I'VE BEEN TOLD I'M NICE.
THEY SAY I'M GENTLE,
KIND AND TOLERANT.
I DON'T GO OUT OF MY WAY.
PEOPLE LIKE TO BE AROUND ME.
BUT IT'S NOT TRUE.
I ACTUALLY DON'T CARE.
I DON'T EVEN CARE ABOUT MYSELF.
AH.
THAT'S IT.
IT'S PROBABLY...

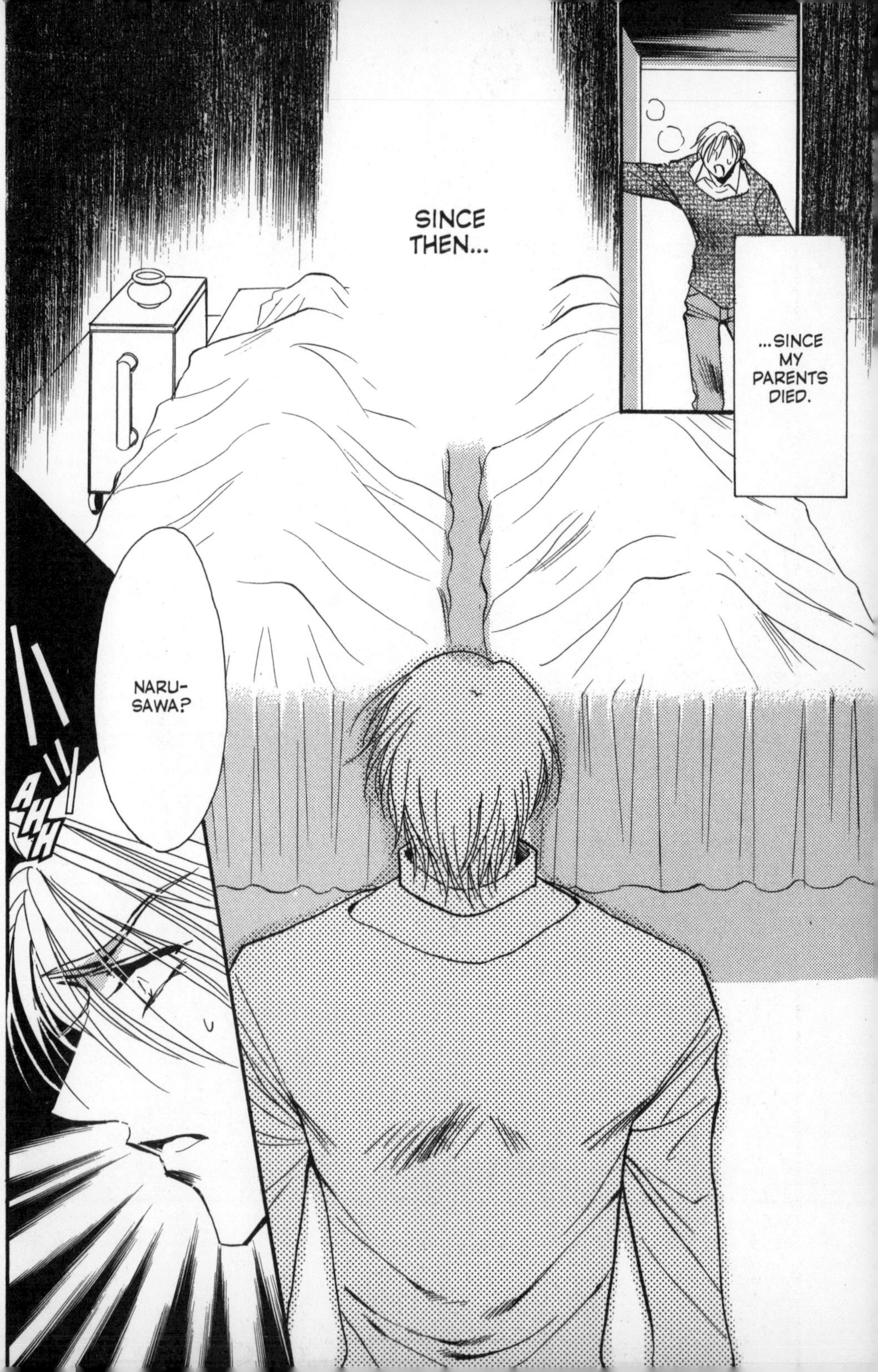
SINCE THEN...
...SINCE MY PARENTS DIED.
NARU-SAWA?
AHH

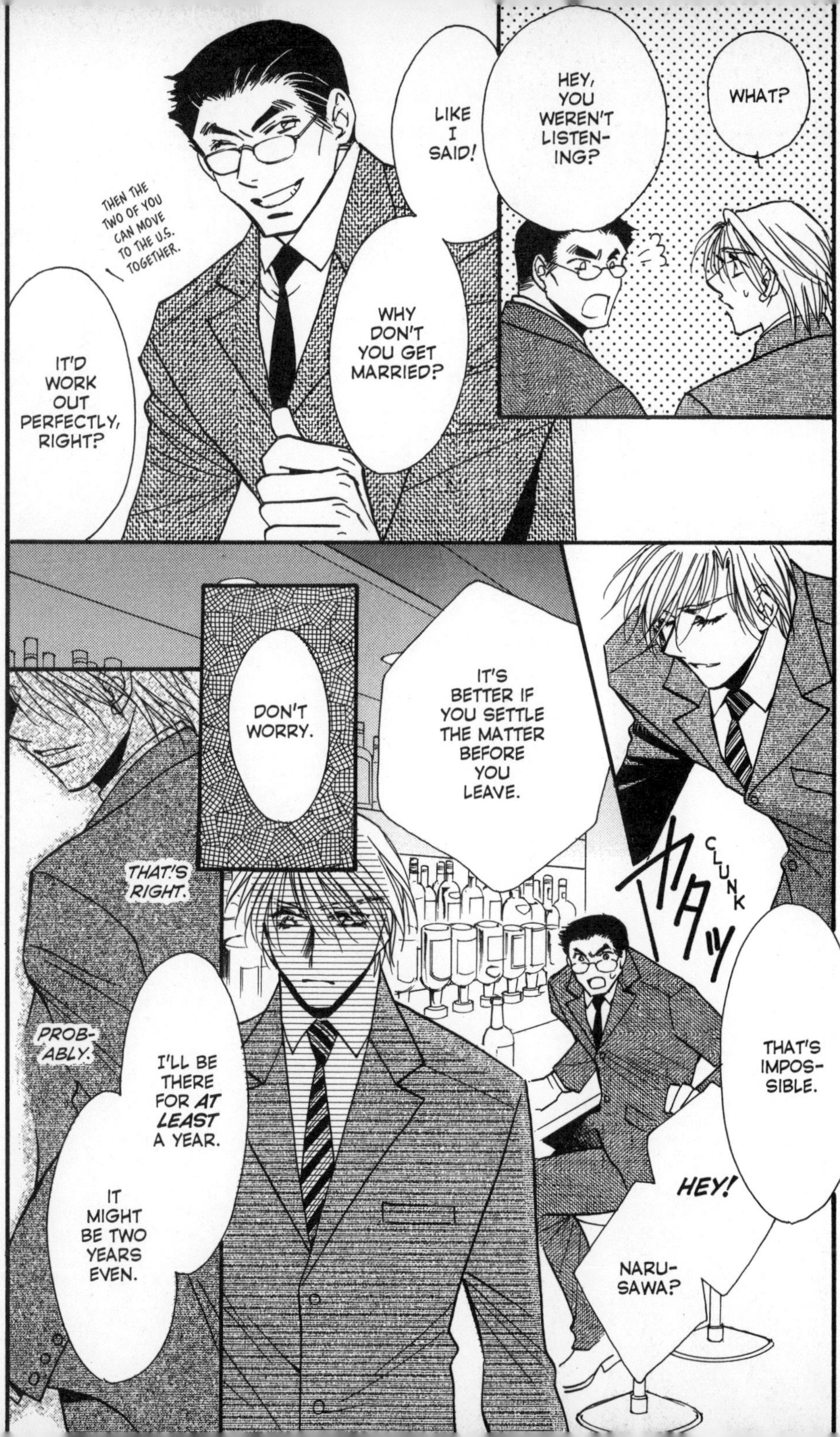
WHAT?
HEY, YOU WEREN'T LISTEN-ING?
LIKE I SAID!
WHY DON'T YOU GET MARRIED?
THEN THE TWO OF YOU CAN MOVE TO THE U.S. TOGETHER.
IT'D WORK OUT PERFECTLY, RIGHT?
IT'S BETTER IF YOU SETTLE THE MATTER BEFORE YOU LEAVE.
DON'T WORRY.
CLUNK
THAT'S IMPOS-SIBLE.
HEY!
NARU-SAWA?
THAT'S RIGHT.
I'LL BE THERE FOR *AT LEAST* A YEAR.
IT MIGHT BE TWO YEARS EVEN.
PROB-ABLY.

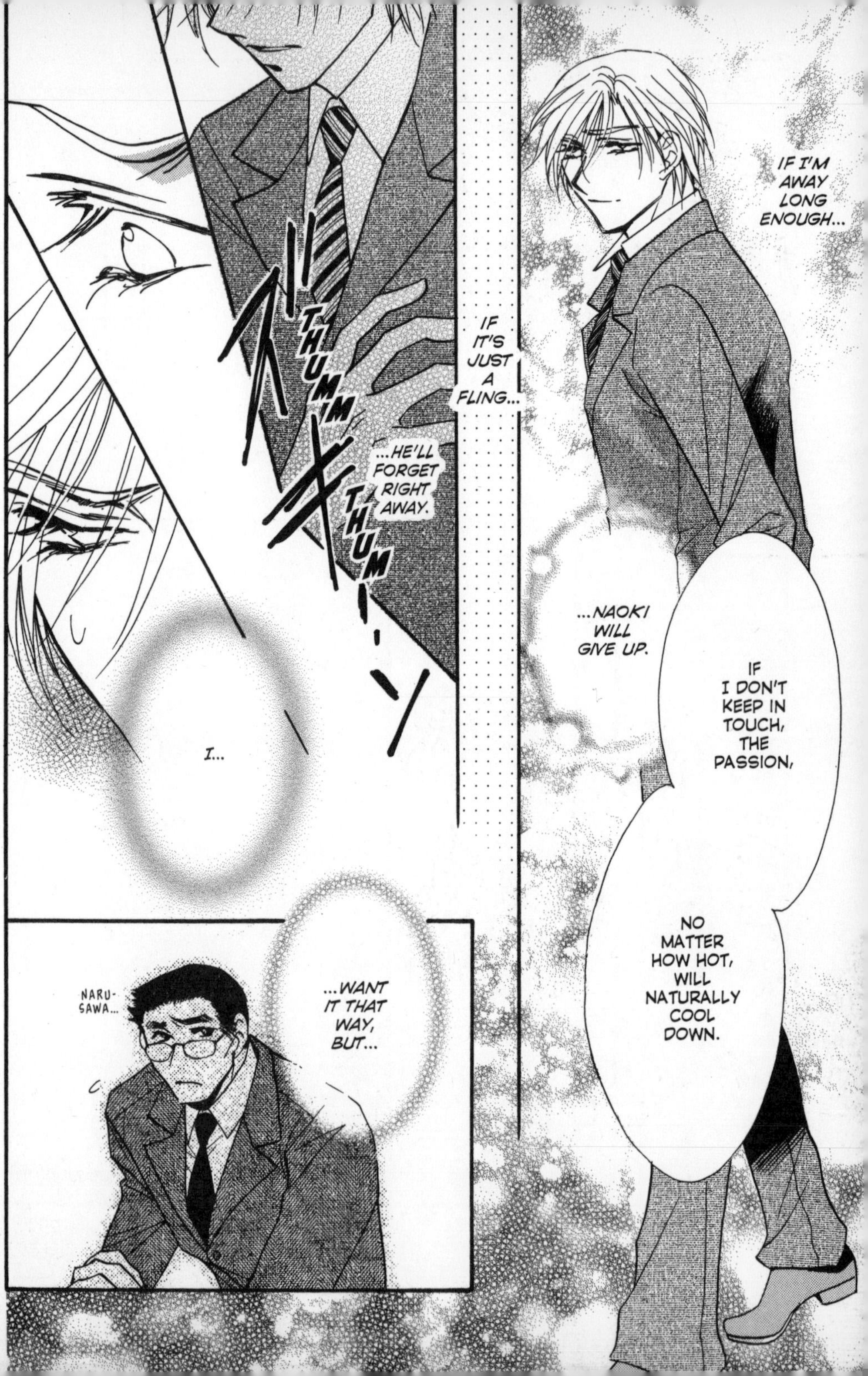
IF I'M AWAY LONG ENOUGH...
...NAOKI WILL GIVE UP.
IF I DON'T KEEP IN TOUCH, THE PASSION,
NO MATTER HOW HOT, WILL NATURALLY COOL DOWN.
IF IT'S JUST A FLING...
...HE'LL FORGET RIGHT AWAY.
THUMM
THUM
I...
...WANT IT THAT WAY, BUT...
NARU-SAWA...

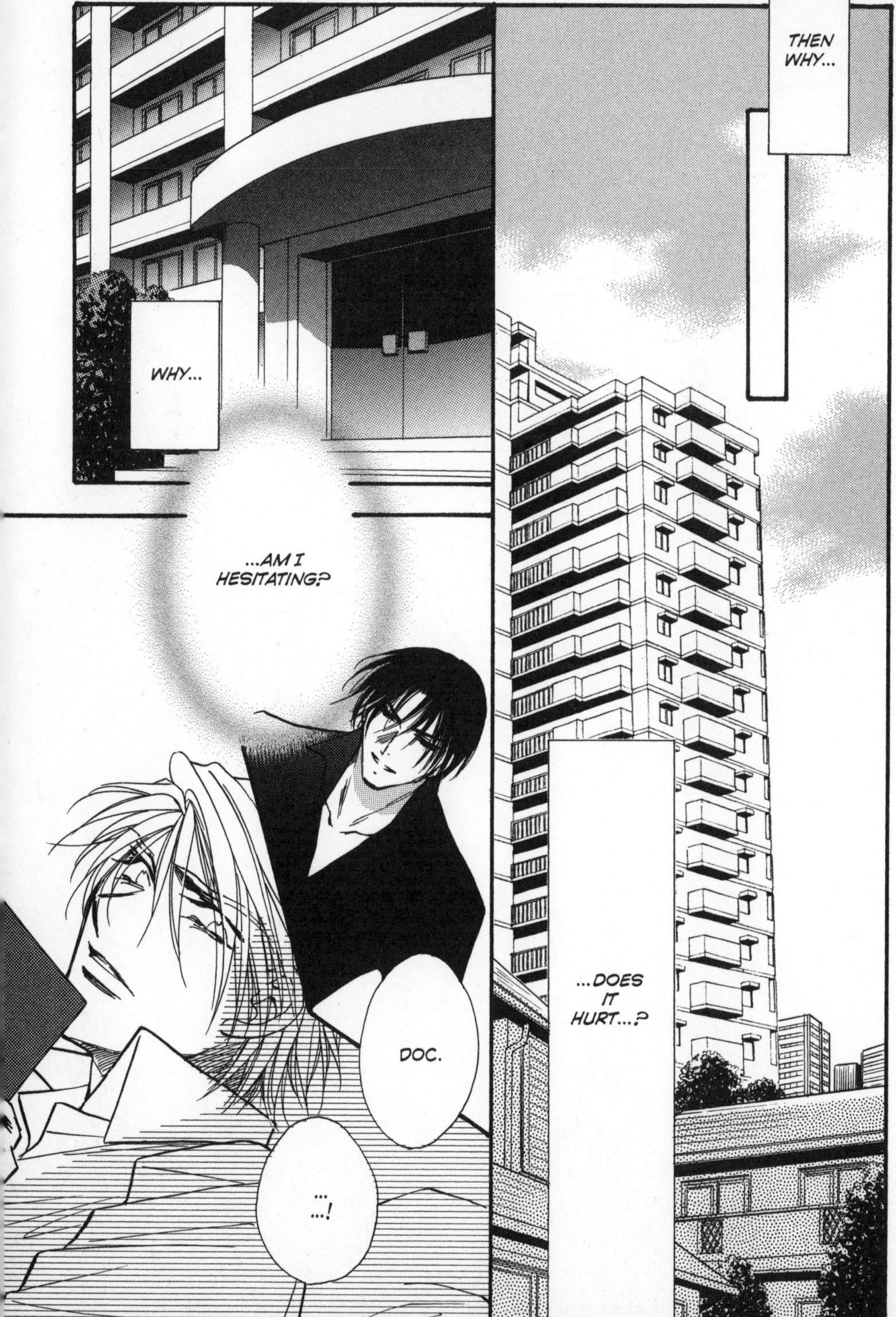
THEN WHY...
...DOES IT HURT...?
WHY...
...AM I HESITATING?
DOC.
... ...!

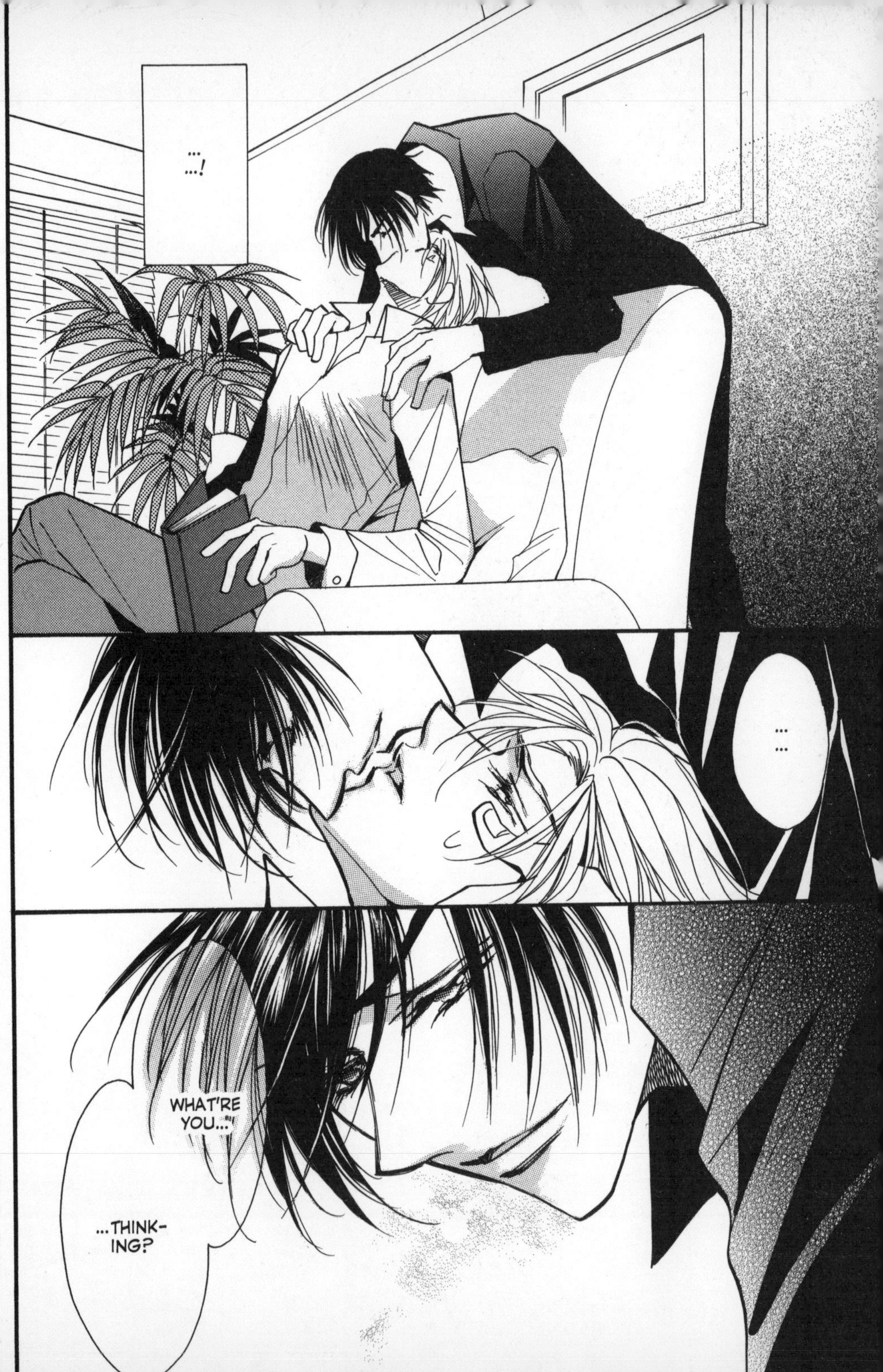
...
...!
...
...
WHAT'RE YOU...
...THINK-ING?

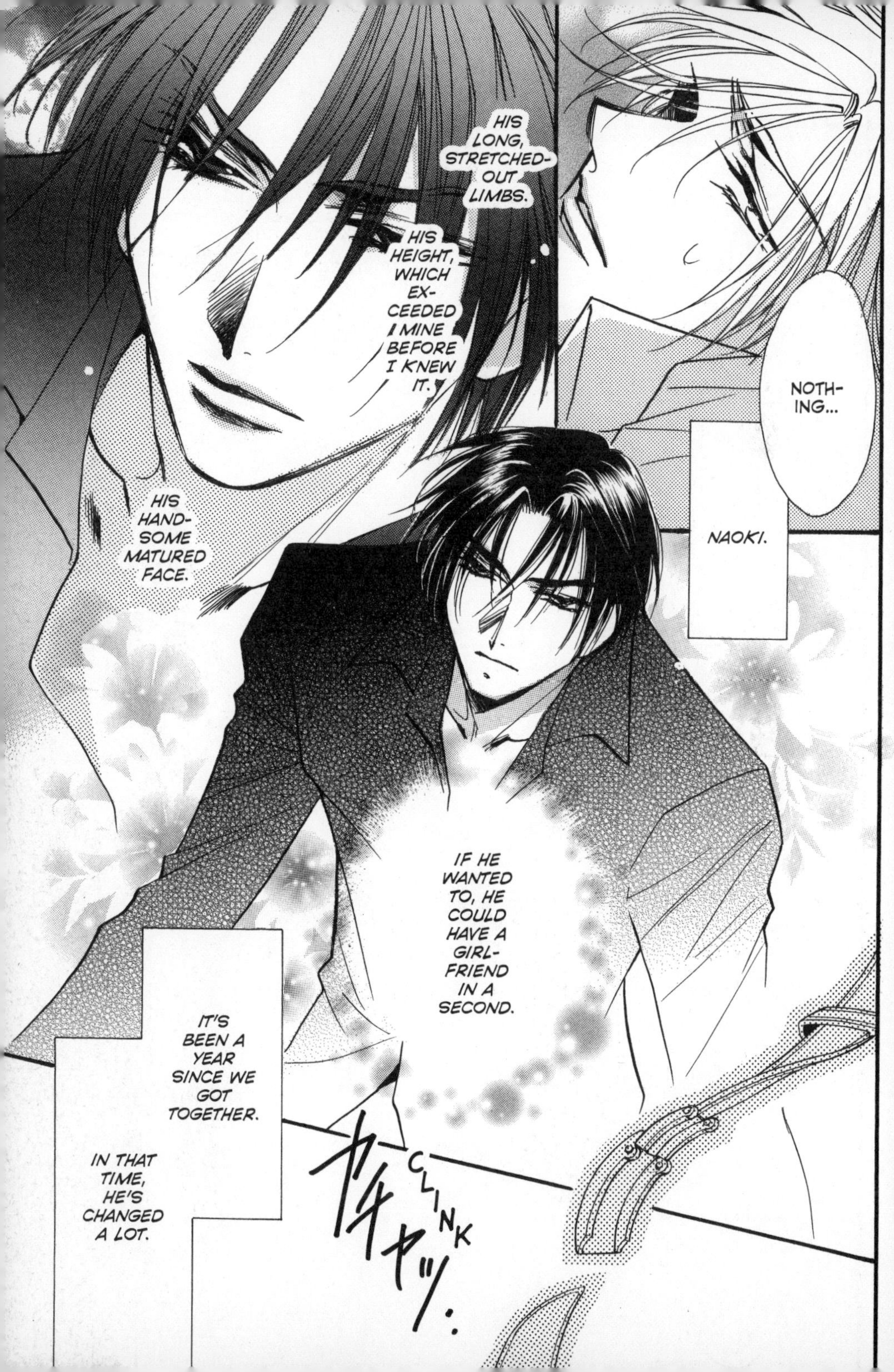
NOTHING...
NAOKI.
HIS LONG, STRETCHED-OUT LIMBS.
HIS HEIGHT, WHICH EXCEEDED MINE BEFORE I KNEW IT.
HIS HANDSOME MATURED FACE.
IF HE WANTED TO, HE COULD HAVE A GIRLFRIEND IN A SECOND.
IT'S BEEN A YEAR SINCE WE GOT TOGETHER.
IN THAT TIME, HE'S CHANGED A LOT.
CLINK
カチャッ

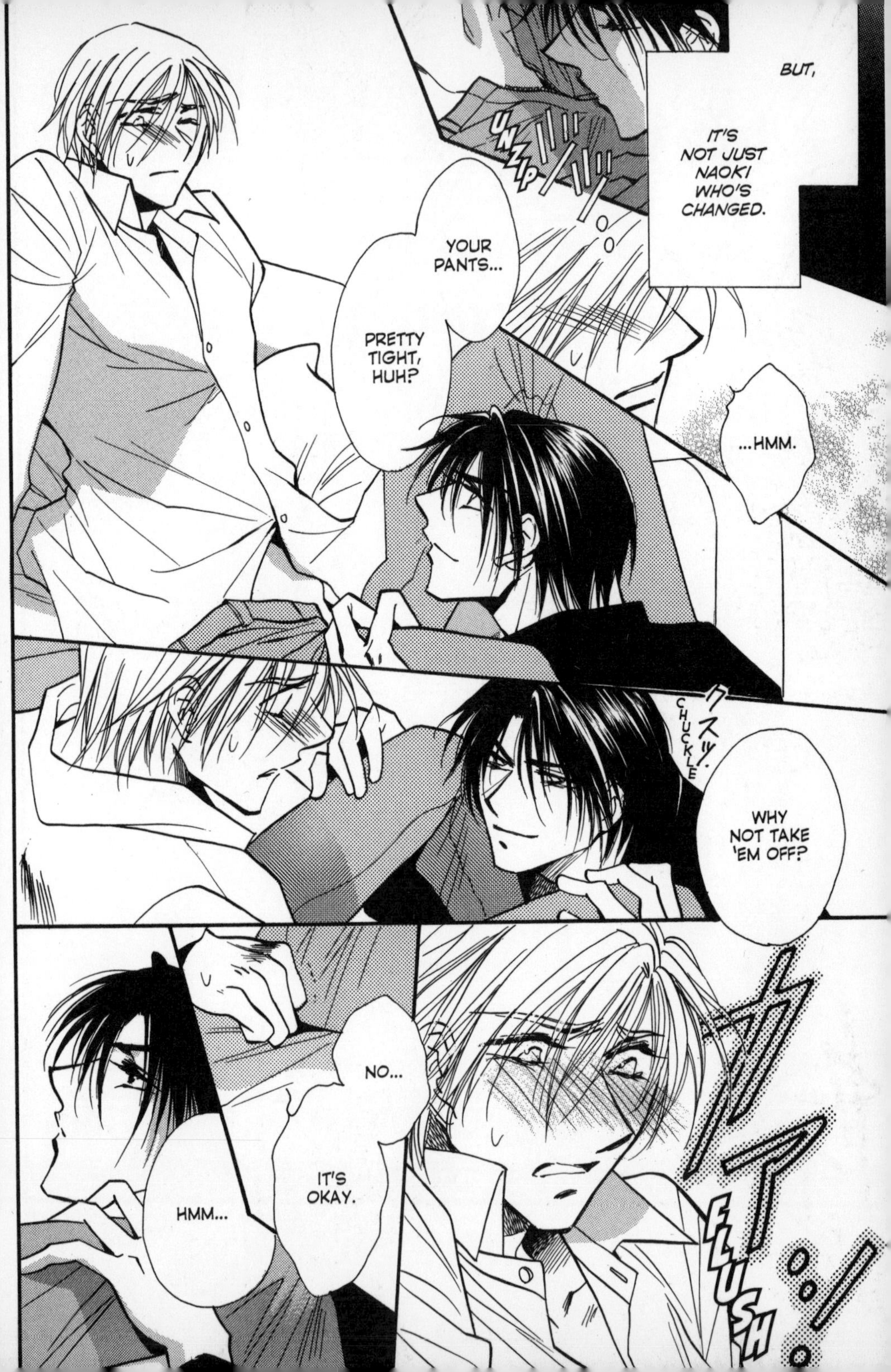
BUT,
IT'S NOT JUST NAOKI WHO'S CHANGED.
UNZIP
YOUR PANTS...
PRETTY TIGHT, HUH?
...HMM.
CHUCKLE
WHY NOT TAKE 'EM OFF?
FLUSH
NO...
IT'S OKAY.
HMM...

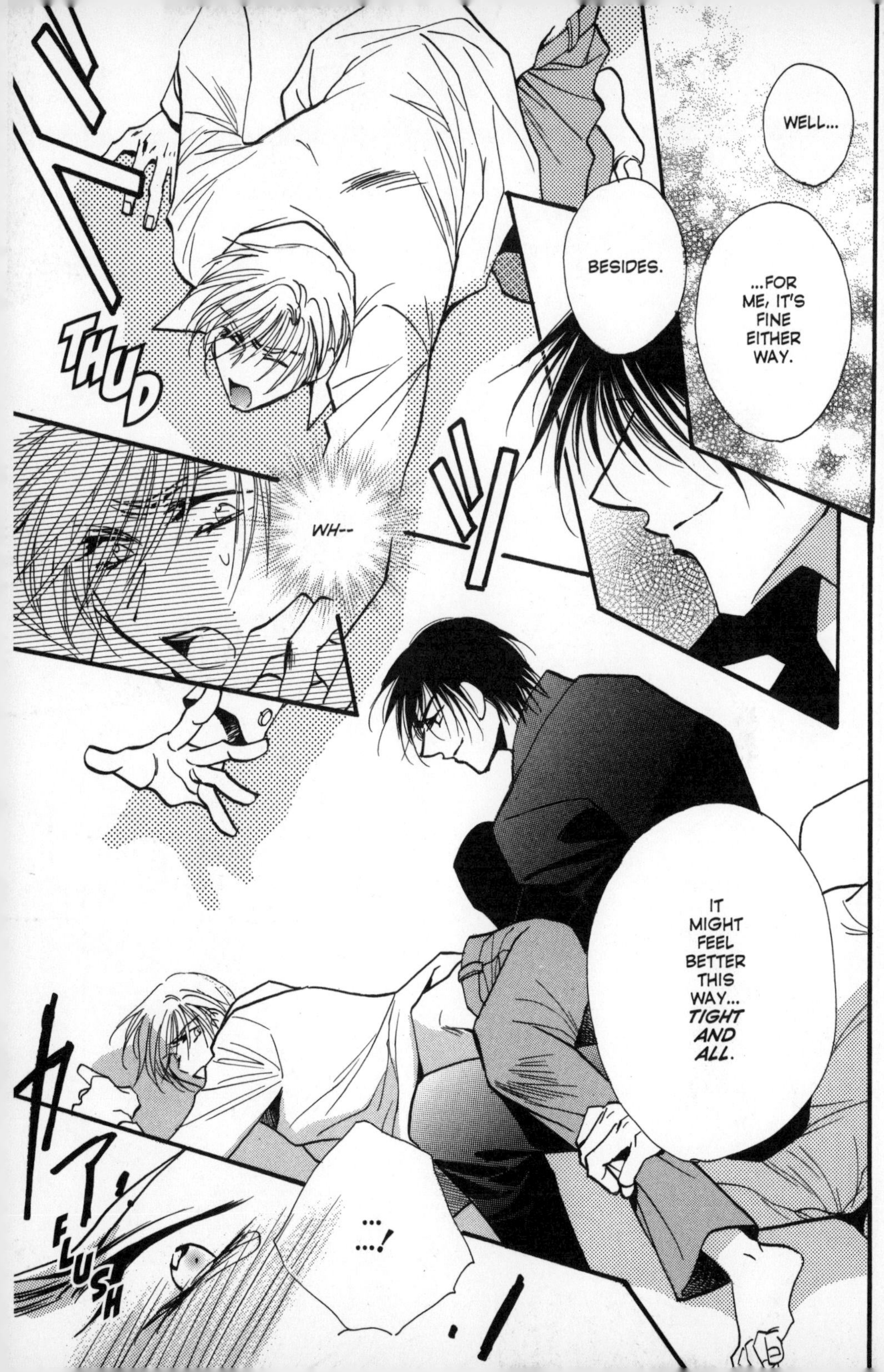

WELL...
...FOR ME, IT'S FINE EITHER WAY.
BESIDES.
THUD
WH--
IT MIGHT FEEL BETTER THIS WAY... *TIGHT AND ALL*.
FLUSH
...
...!

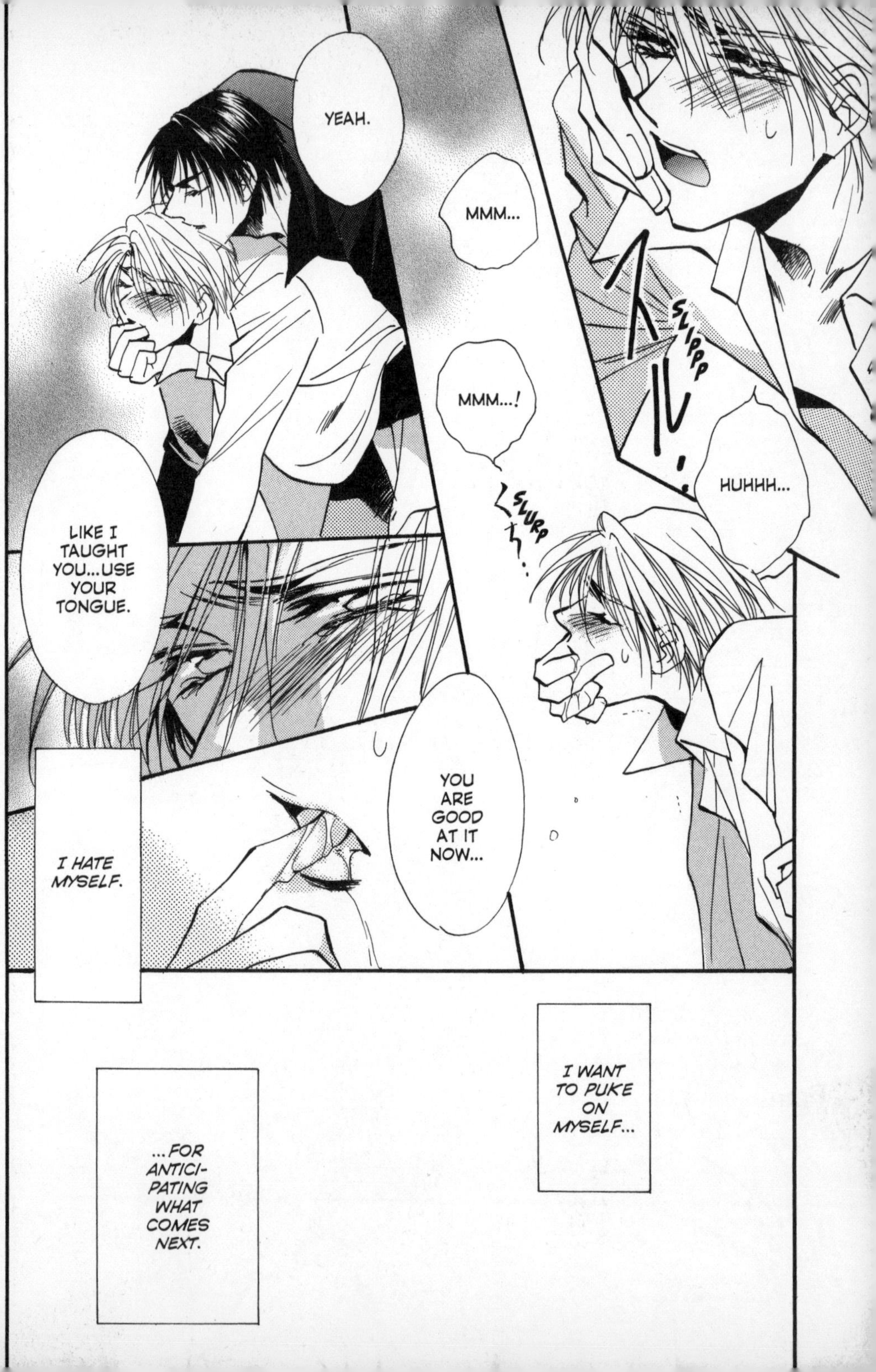
SLIPPP
HUHHH...
MMM...
MMM...!
SLURP
YEAH.
LIKE I TAUGHT YOU...USE YOUR TONGUE.
YOU ARE GOOD AT IT NOW...
I HATE MYSELF.
I WANT TO PUKE ON MYSELF...
...FOR ANTICI-PATING WHAT COMES NEXT.

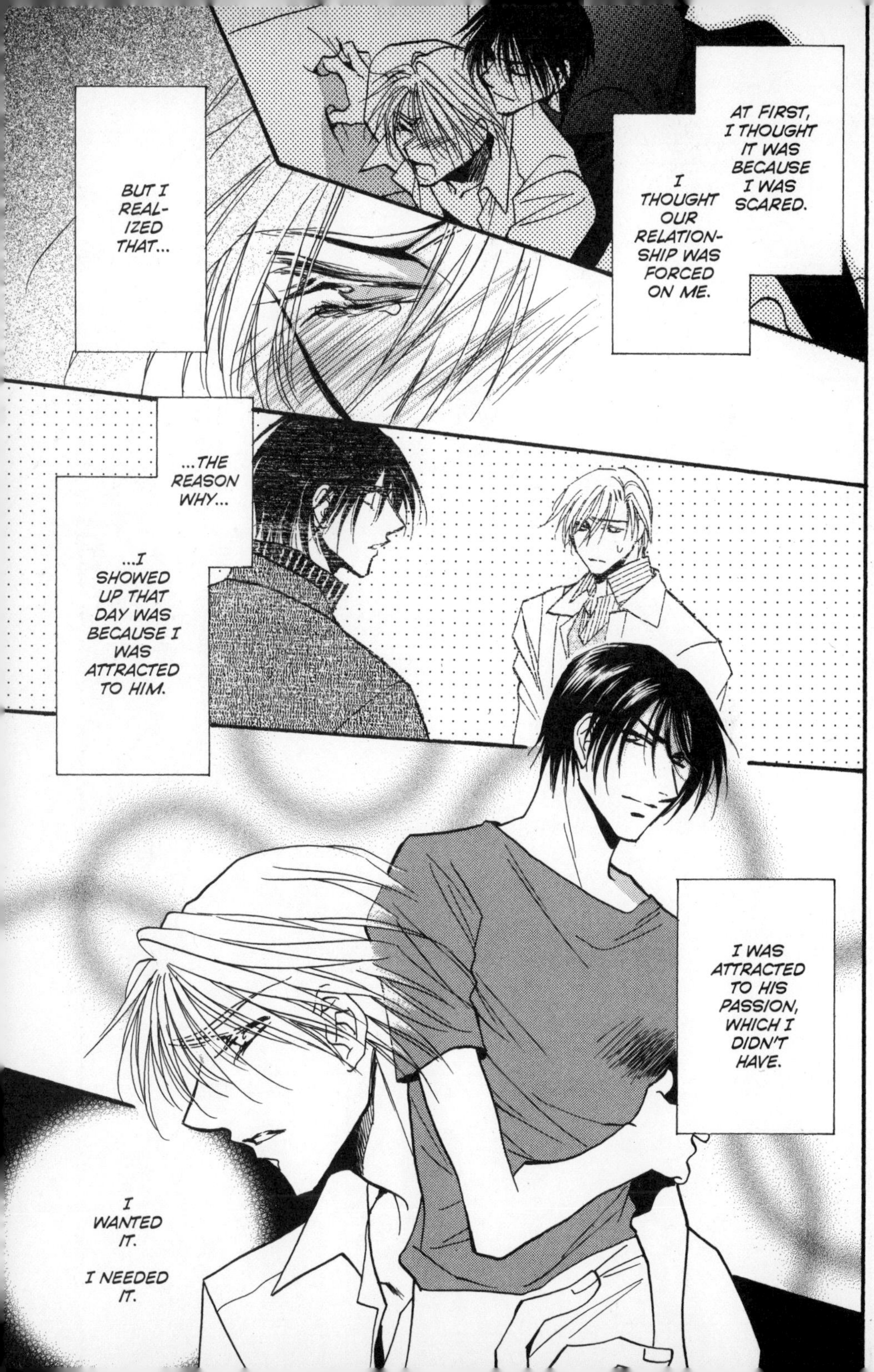
AT FIRST, I THOUGHT IT WAS BECAUSE I WAS SCARED.
I THOUGHT OUR RELATION-SHIP WAS FORCED ON ME.
BUT I REAL-IZED THAT...
...THE REASON WHY...
...I SHOWED UP THAT DAY WAS BECAUSE I WAS ATTRACTED TO HIM.
I WAS ATTRACTED TO HIS PASSION, WHICH I DIDN'T HAVE.
I WANTED IT.
I NEEDED IT.

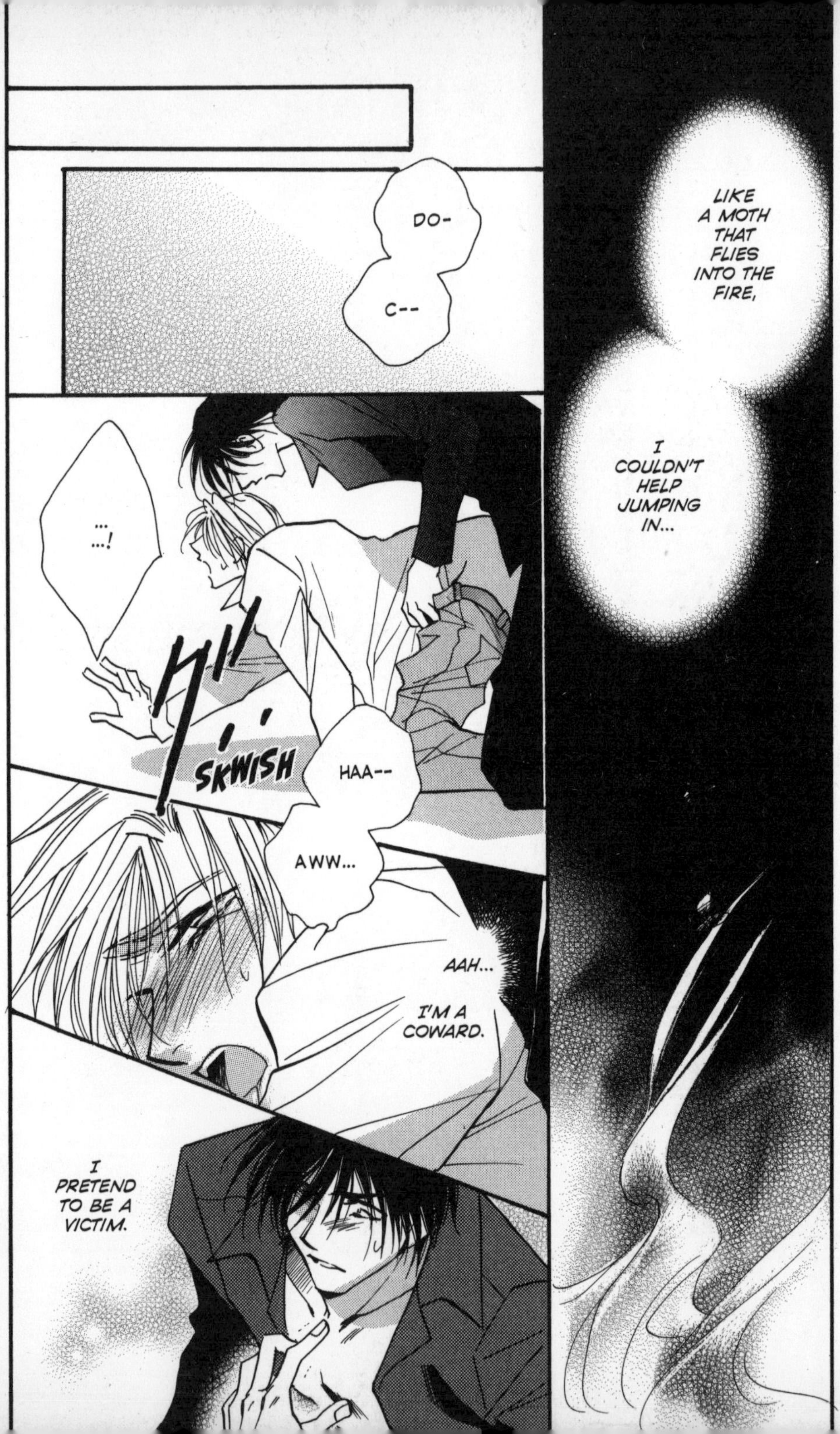
LIKE A MOTH THAT FLIES INTO THE FIRE,
I COULDN'T HELP JUMPING IN...
DO-
C--
... ...!
SKWISH
HAA--
AWW...
AAH...
I'M A COWARD.
I PRETEND TO BE A VICTIM.

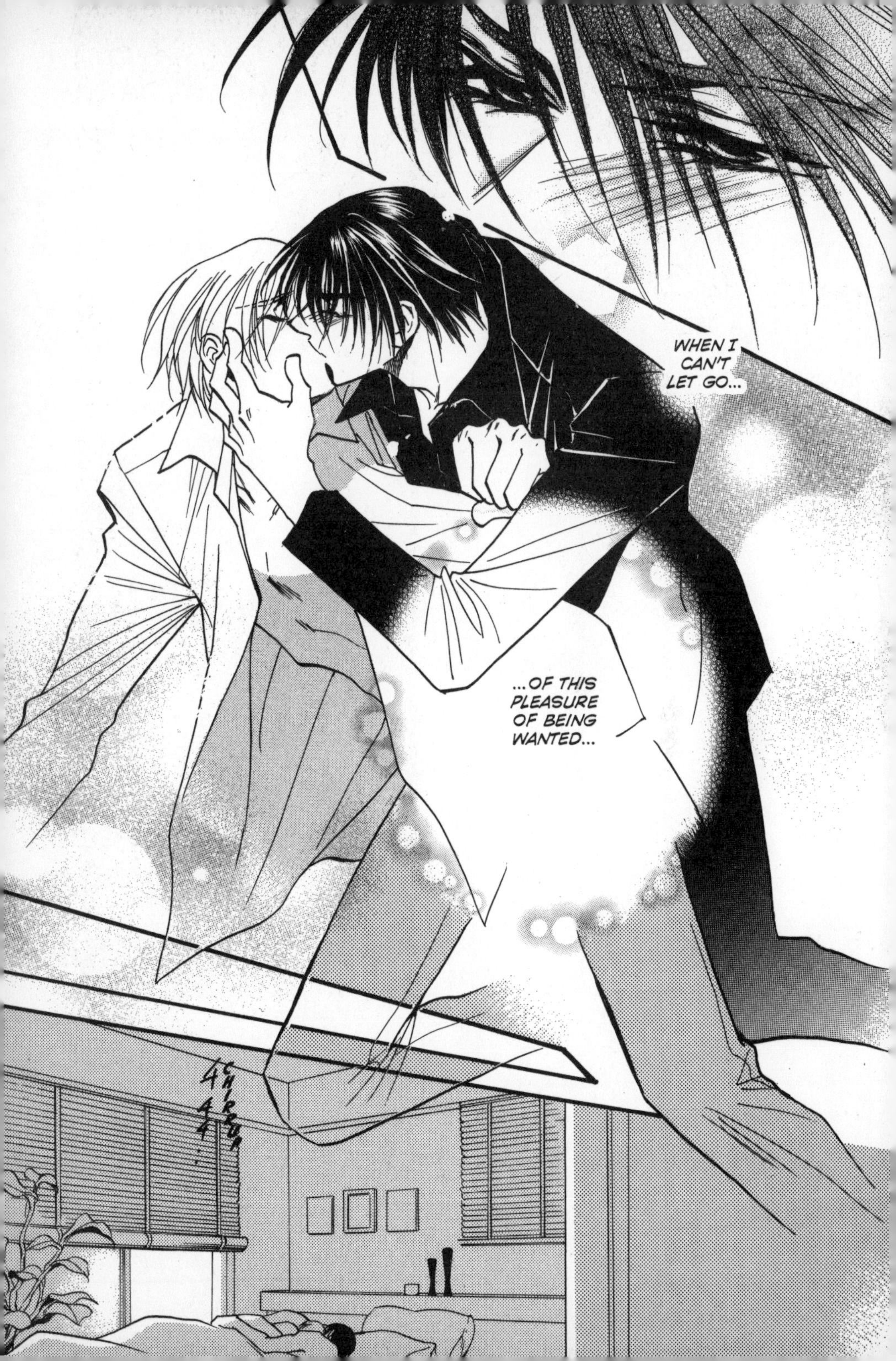
WHEN I CAN'T LET GO...
...OF THIS PLEASURE OF BEING WANTED...
CHIRRUP

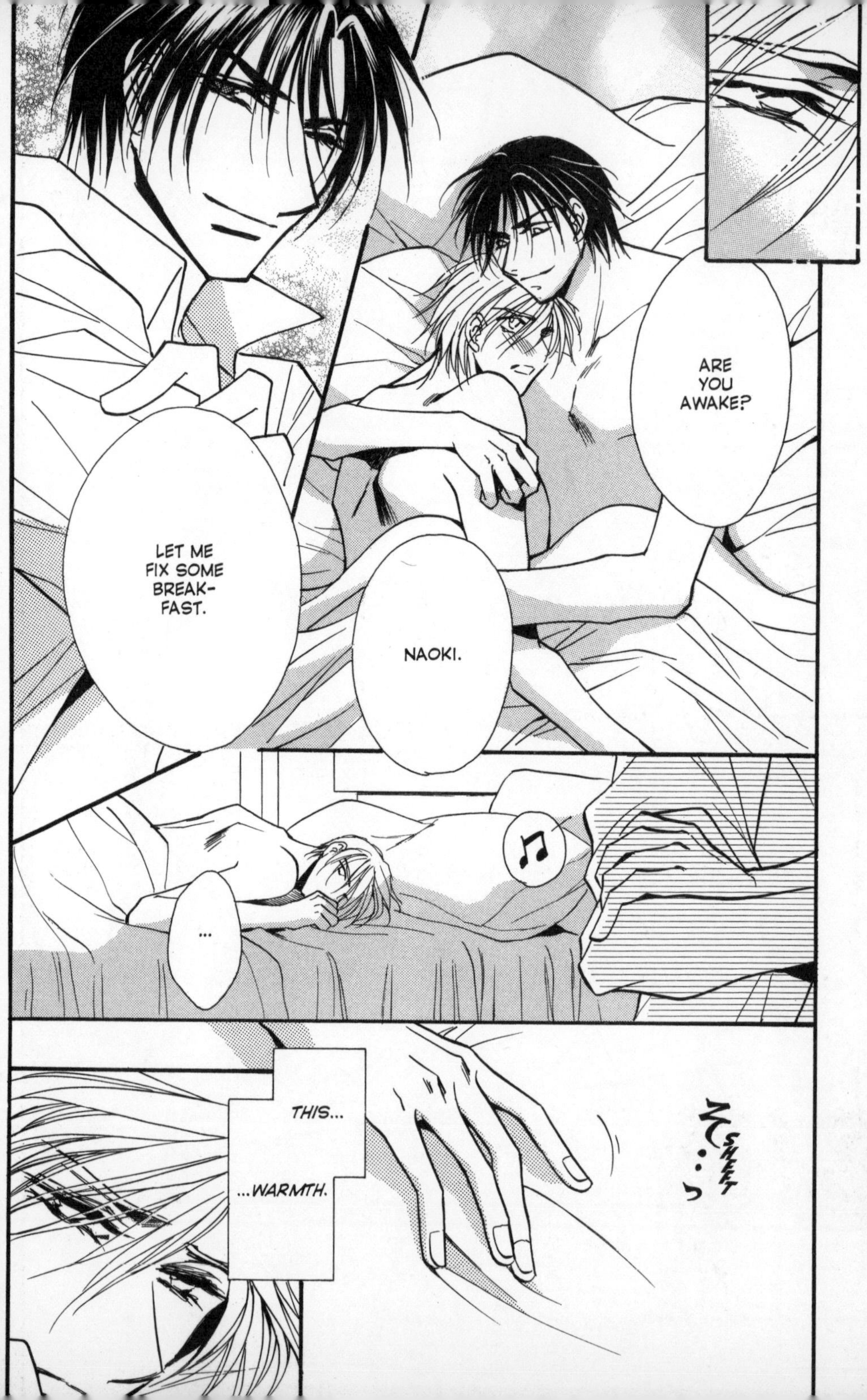
ARE YOU AWAKE?
NAOKI.
LET ME FIX SOME BREAK-FAST.
♫
...
SHEET
THIS...
...WARMTH.

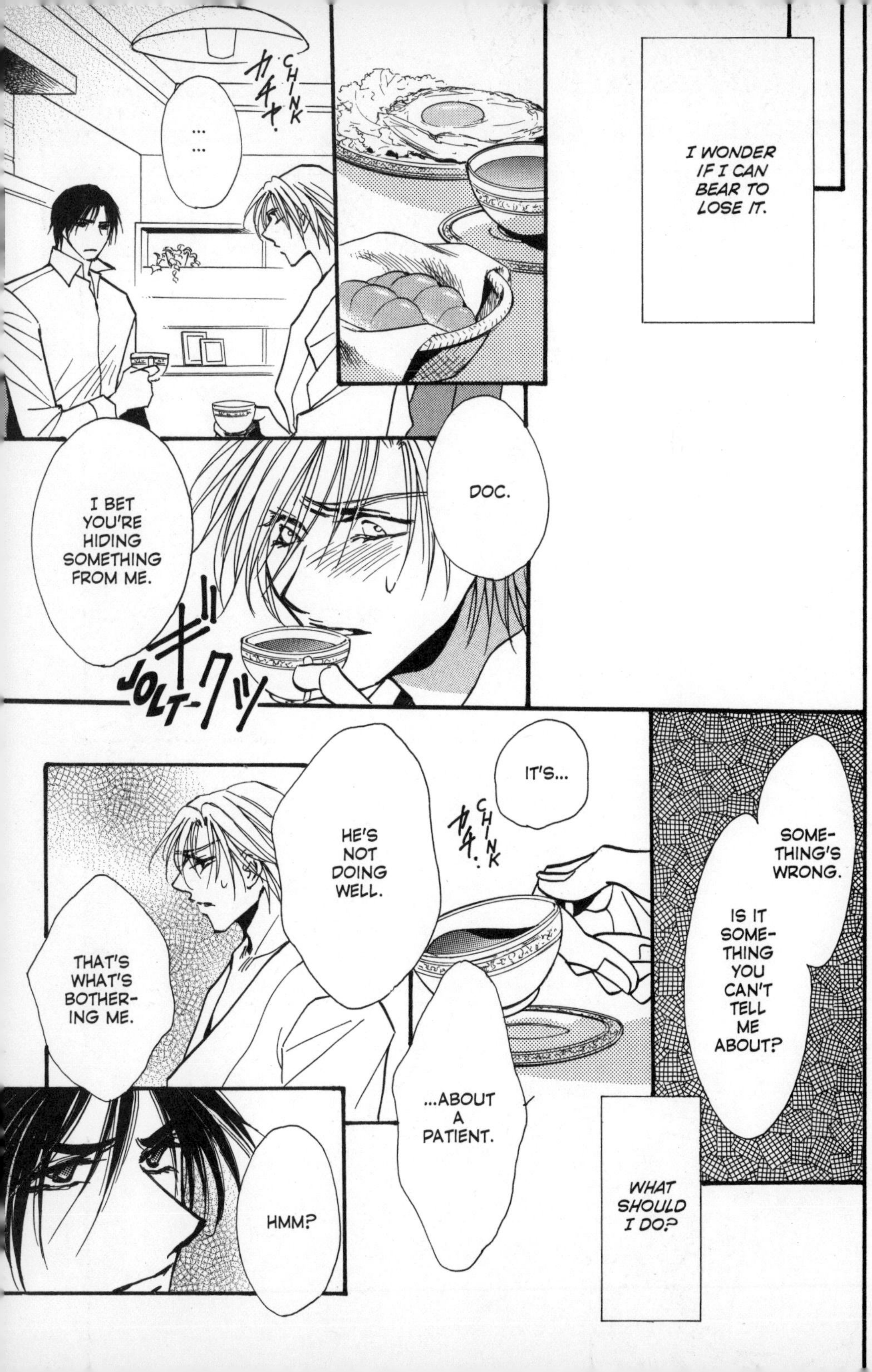

I WONDER IF I CAN BEAR TO LOSE IT.
CHINK
...
...
DOC.
I BET YOU'RE HIDING SOMETHING FROM ME.
JOLT
SOME-THING'S WRONG.
IS IT SOME-THING YOU CAN'T TELL ME ABOUT?
WHAT SHOULD I DO?
IT'S...
CHINK
...ABOUT A PATIENT.
HMM?
HE'S NOT DOING WELL.
THAT'S WHAT'S BOTHERING-ING ME.

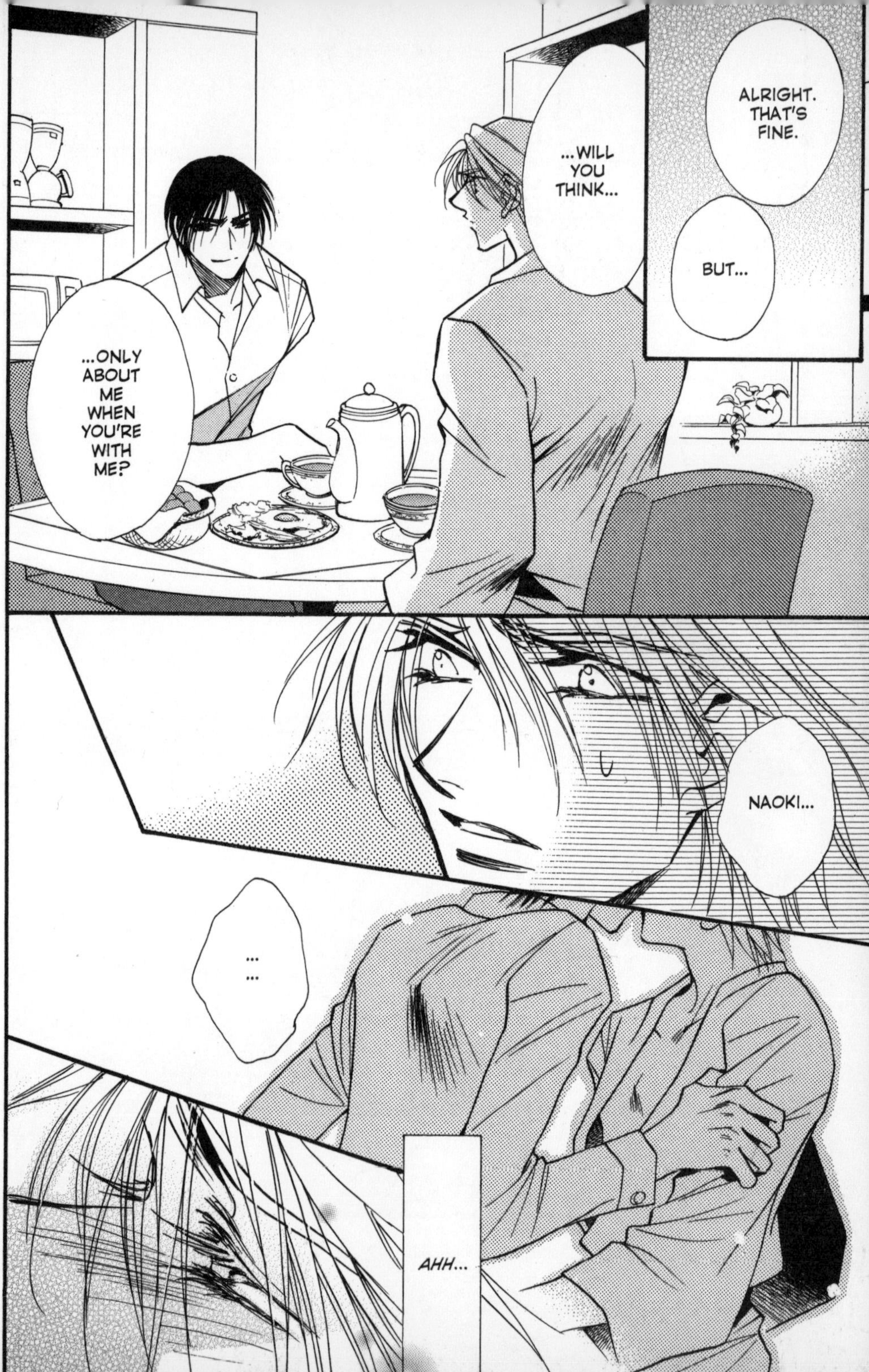
ALRIGHT. THAT'S FINE.
BUT...
...WILL YOU THINK...
...ONLY ABOUT ME WHEN YOU'RE WITH ME?
NAOKI...
... ...
AHH...

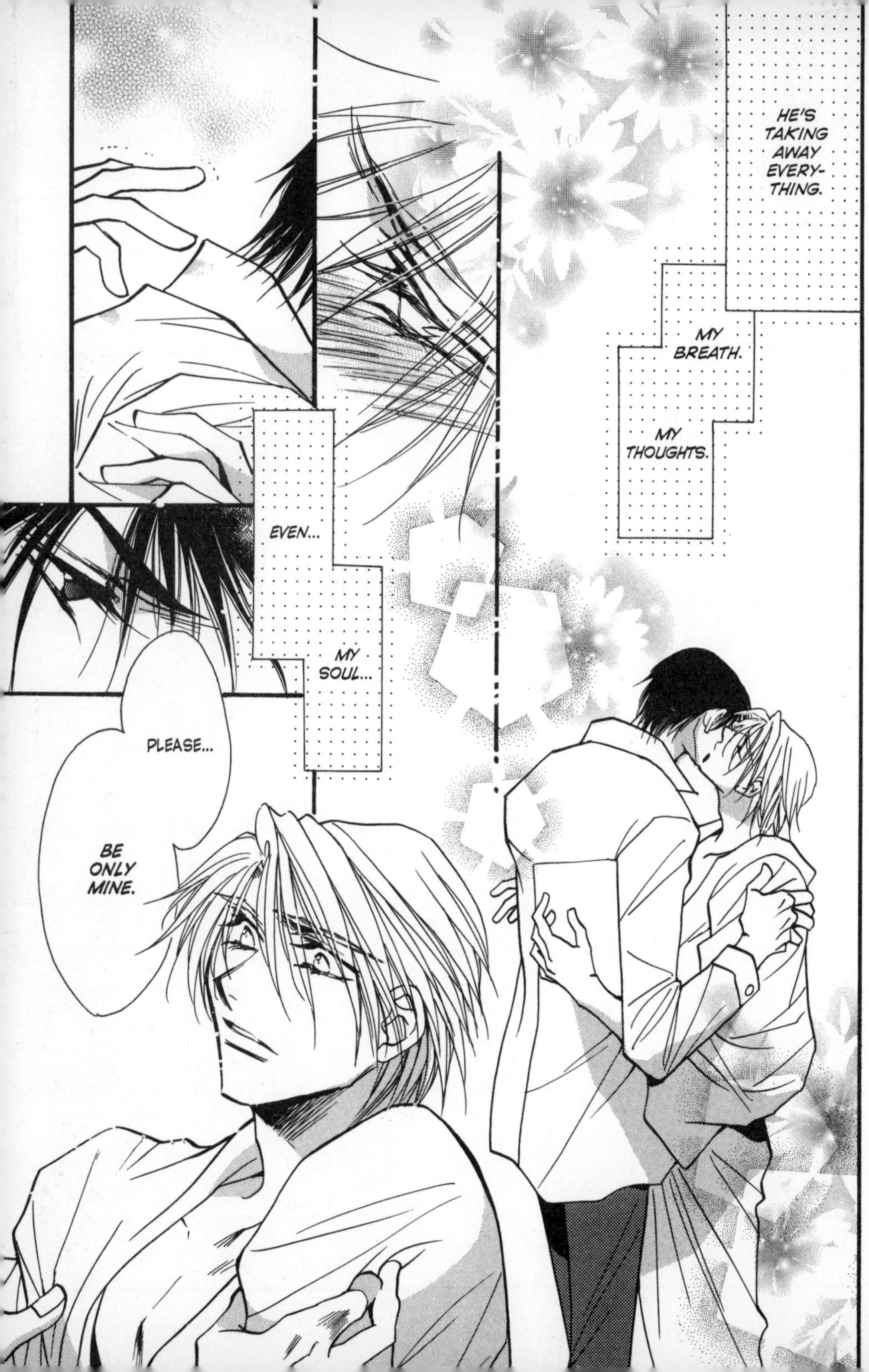
HE'S TAKING AWAY EVERY-THING.
MY BREATH.
MY THOUGHTS.
EVEN...
MY SOUL...
PLEASE...
BE ONLY MINE.

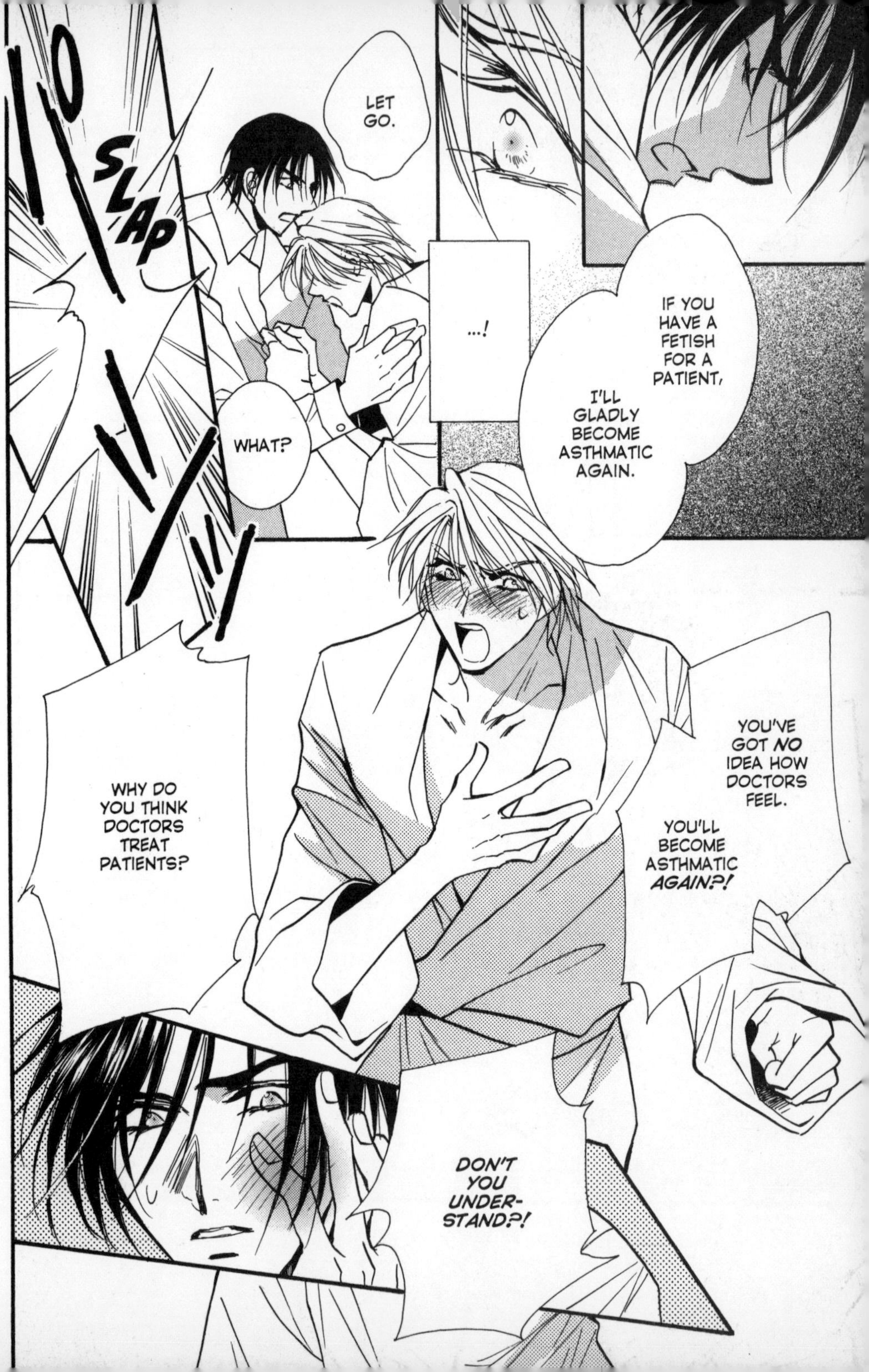
IF YOU HAVE A FETISH FOR A PATIENT,
I'LL GLADLY BECOME ASTHMATIC AGAIN.
...!
LET GO.
WHAT?
SLAP
YOU'VE GOT *NO* IDEA HOW DOCTORS FEEL.
YOU'LL BECOME ASTHMATIC *AGAIN?!*
WHY DO YOU THINK DOCTORS TREAT PATIENTS?
DON'T YOU UNDER-STAND?!

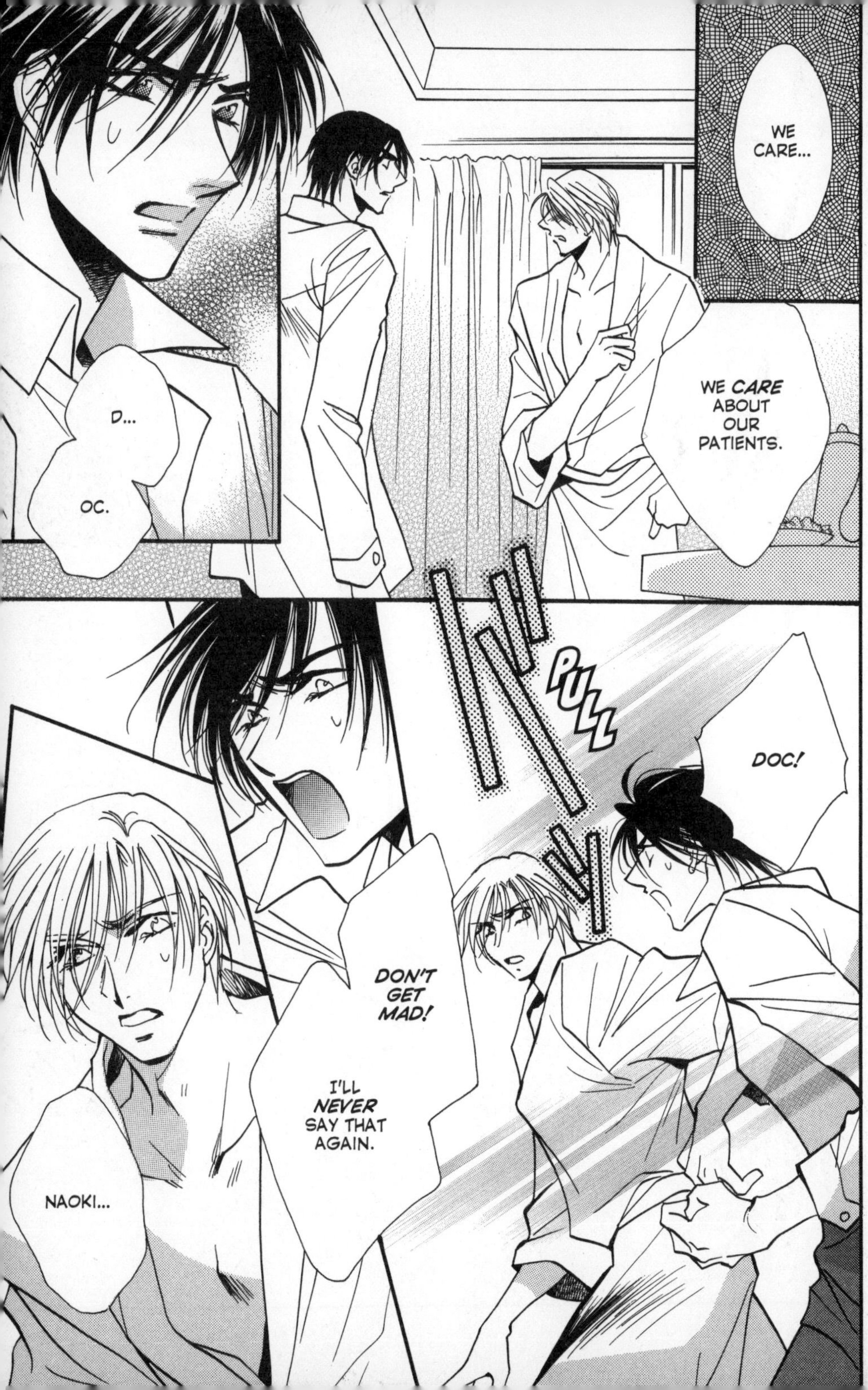
WE CARE...
WE *CARE* ABOUT OUR PATIENTS.
D...
OC.
DOC!
PULL
DON'T GET MAD!
I'LL *NEVER* SAY THAT AGAIN.
NAOKI...

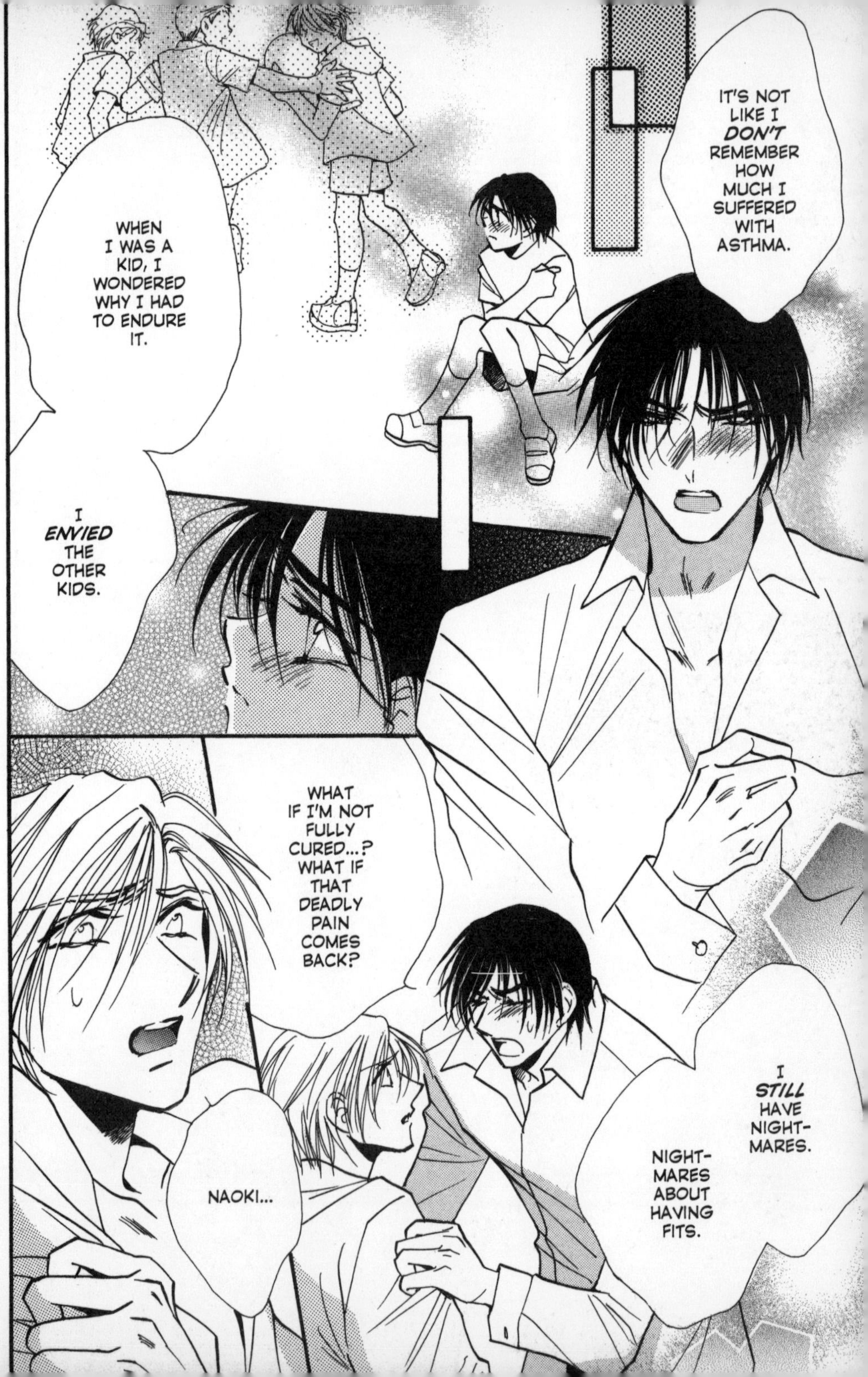
IT'S NOT LIKE I *DON'T* REMEMBER HOW MUCH I SUFFERED WITH ASTHMA.
WHEN I WAS A KID, I WONDERED WHY I HAD TO ENDURE IT.
I *ENVIED* THE OTHER KIDS.
I *STILL* HAVE NIGHT-MARES.
NIGHT-MARES ABOUT HAVING FITS.
WHAT IF I'M NOT FULLY CURED...? WHAT IF THAT DEADLY PAIN COMES BACK?
NAOKI...

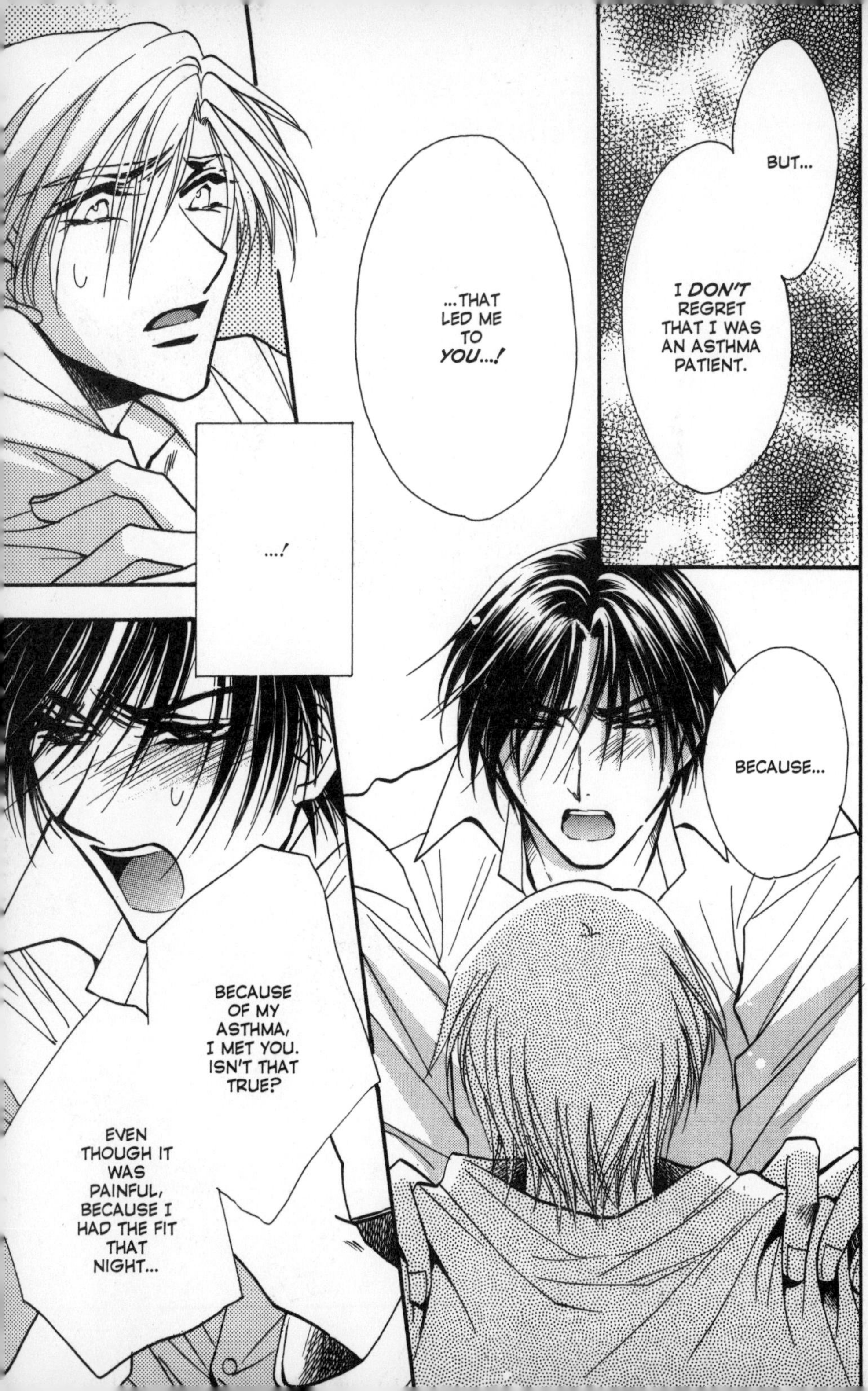
BUT...
I *DON'T* REGRET THAT I WAS AN ASTHMA PATIENT.
...THAT LED ME TO *YOU*...!
...!
BECAUSE...
BECAUSE OF MY ASTHMA, I MET YOU. ISN'T THAT TRUE?
EVEN THOUGH IT WAS PAINFUL, BECAUSE I HAD THE FIT THAT NIGHT...

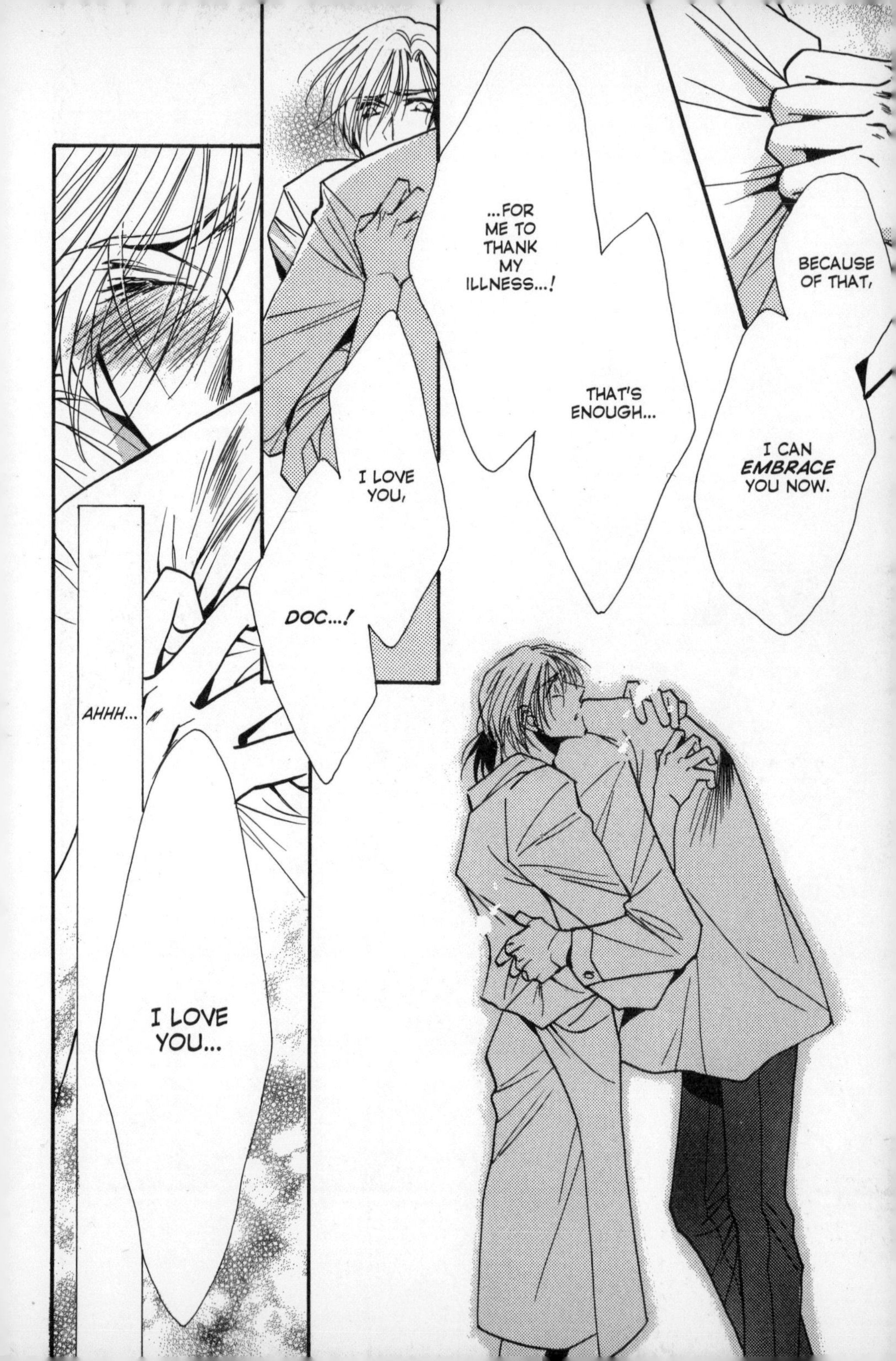

BECAUSE OF THAT,
I CAN *EMBRACE* YOU NOW.
THAT'S ENOUGH...
...FOR ME TO THANK MY ILLNESS...!
I LOVE YOU,
DOC...!
AHHH...
I LOVE YOU...

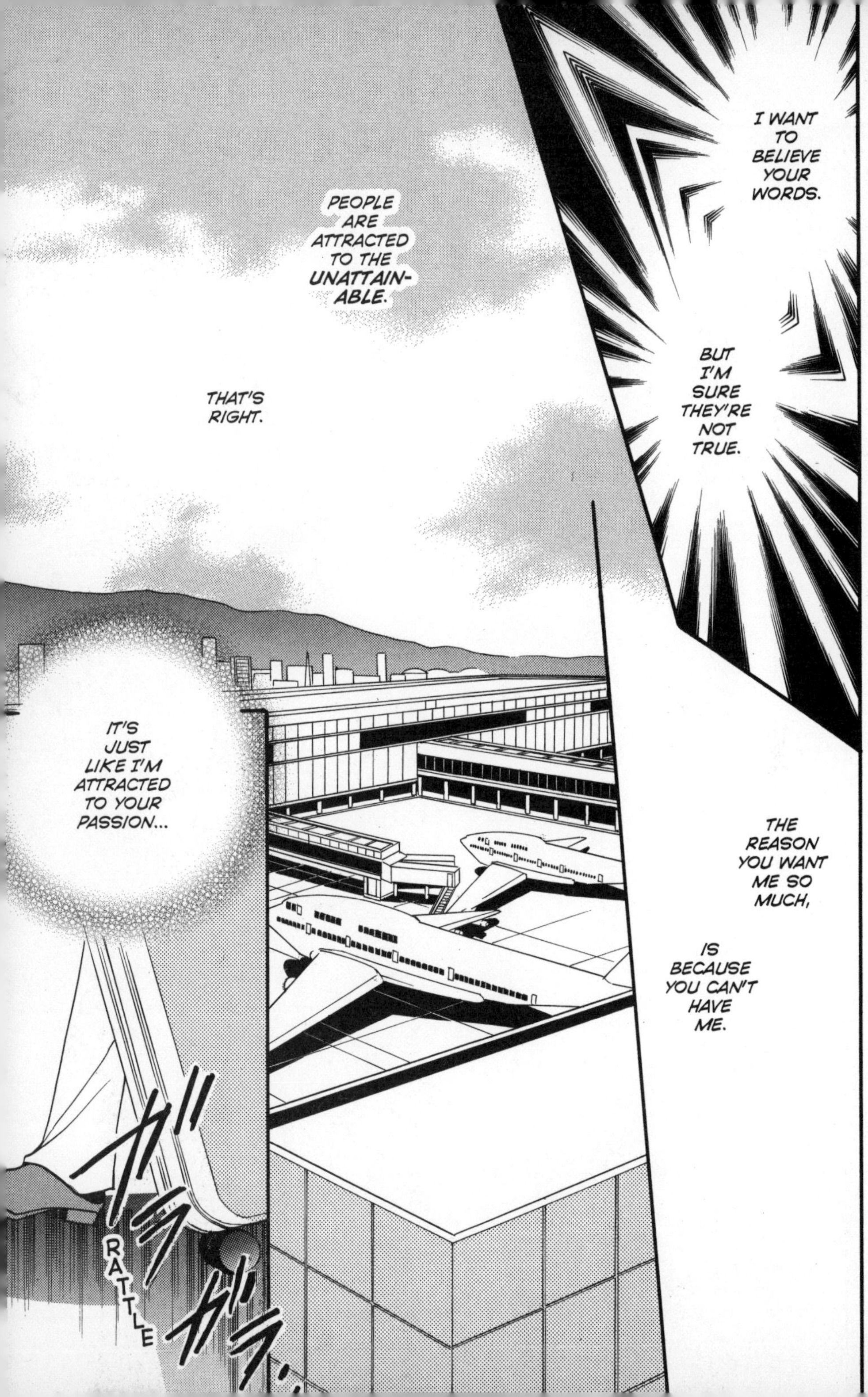
I WANT TO BELIEVE YOUR WORDS.
BUT I'M SURE THEY'RE NOT TRUE.
THE REASON YOU WANT ME SO MUCH,
IS BECAUSE YOU CAN'T HAVE ME.
PEOPLE ARE ATTRACTED TO THE UNATTAIN-ABLE.
THAT'S RIGHT.
IT'S JUST LIKE I'M ATTRACTED TO YOUR PASSION...
RATTLE

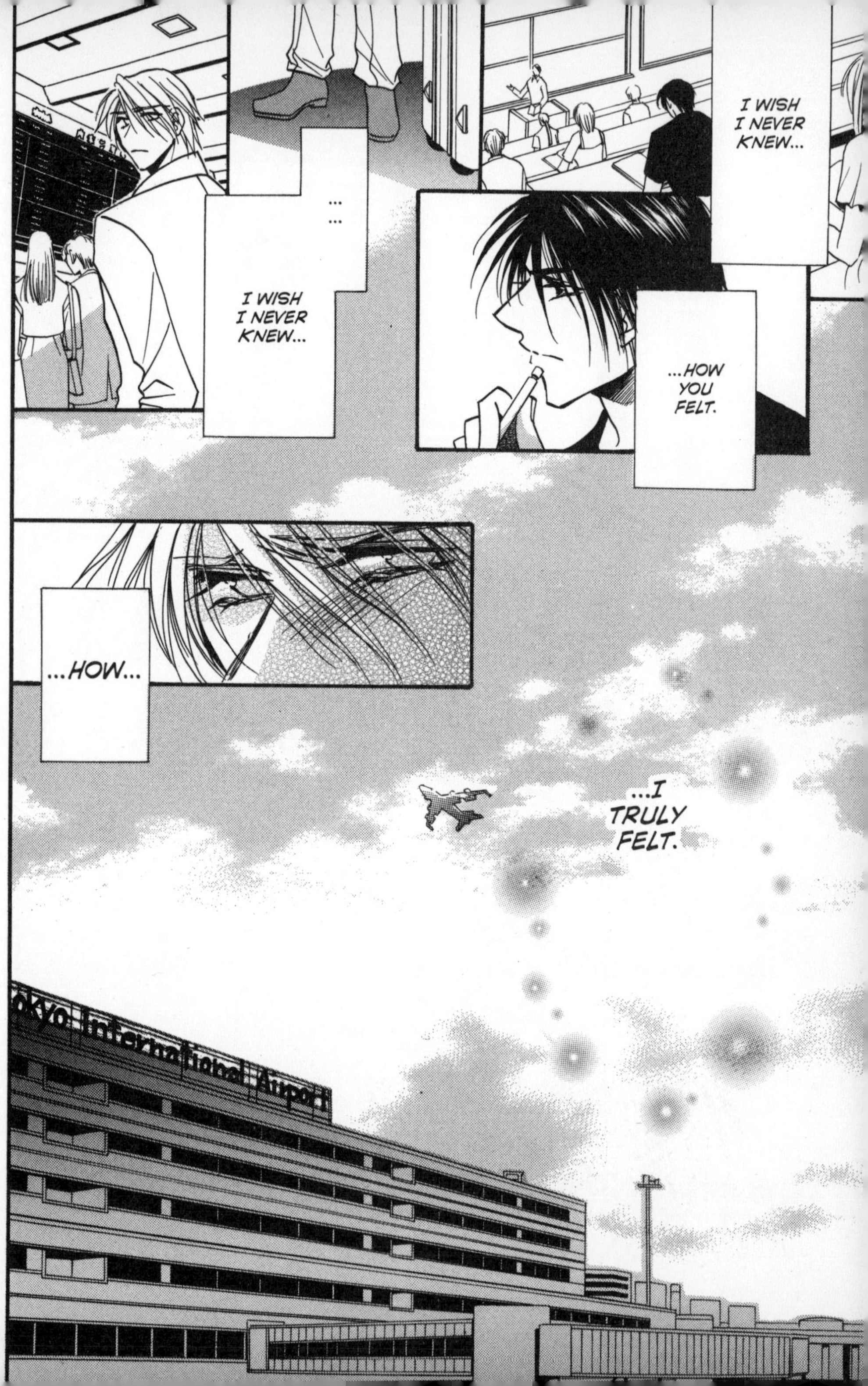
I WISH I NEVER KNEW...
...
...
I WISH I NEVER KNEW...
...HOW YOU FELT.
...HOW...
...I TRULY FELT.
okyo International Airport

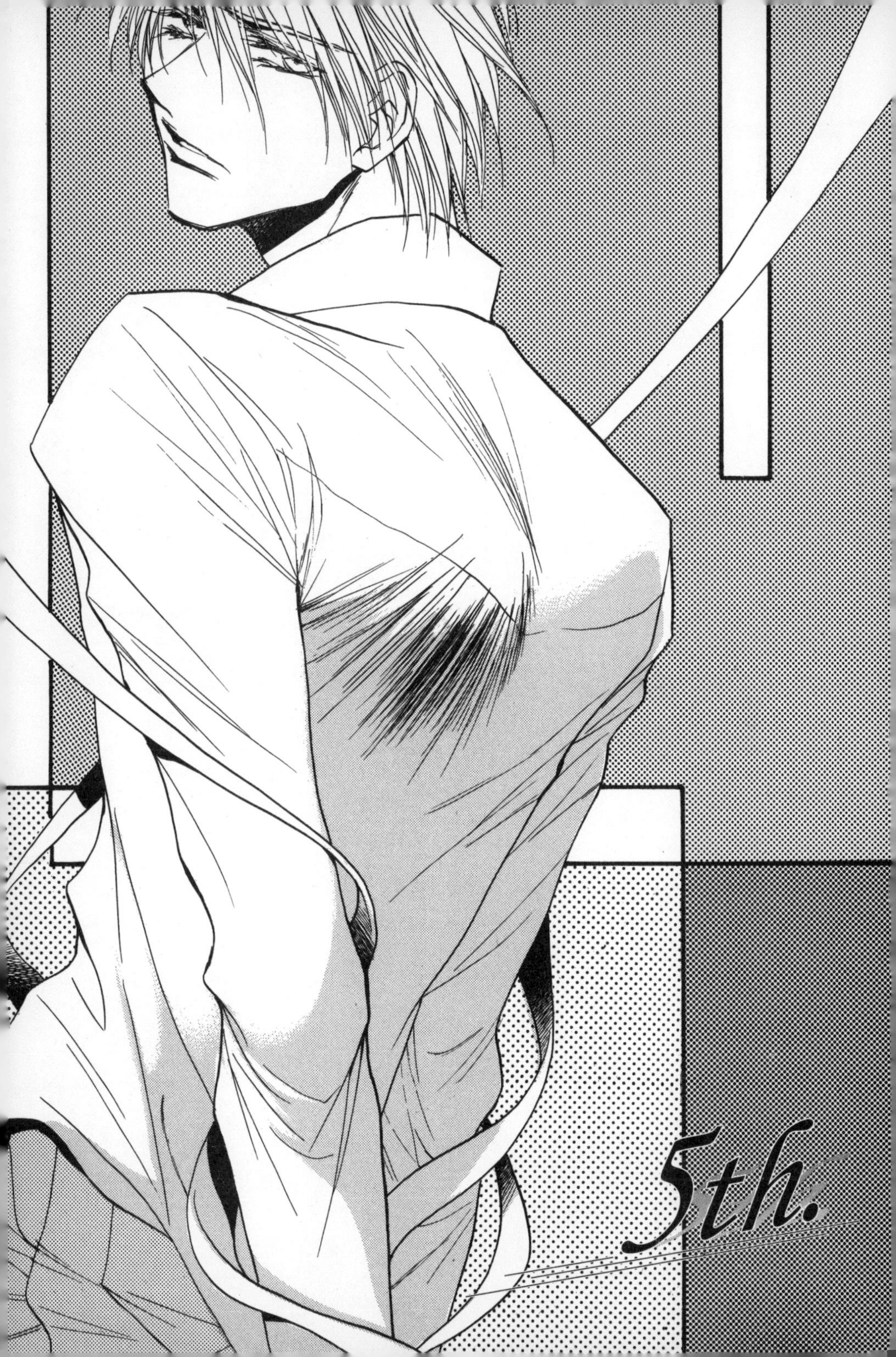
5th.

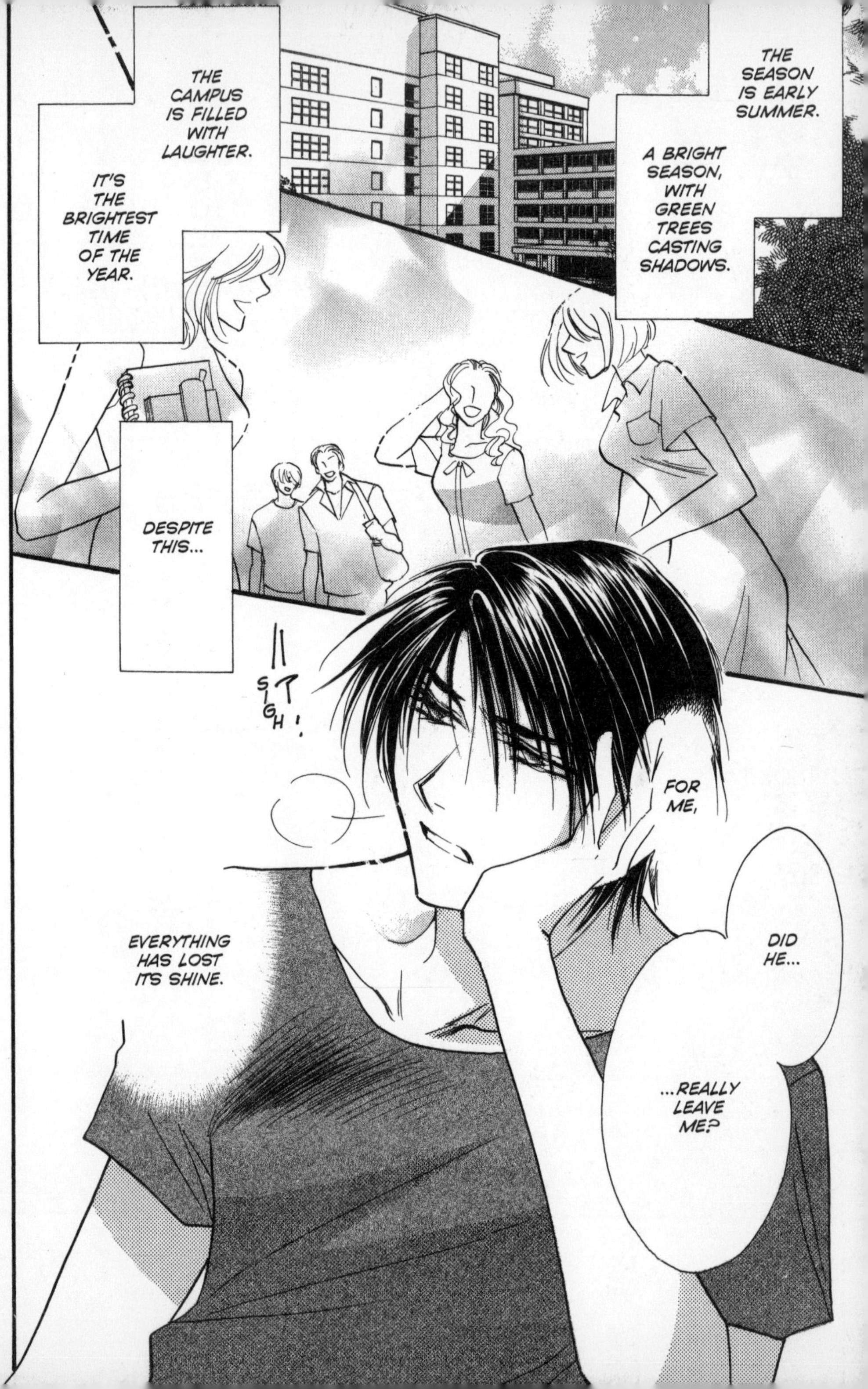
THE SEASON IS EARLY SUMMER.
A BRIGHT SEASON, WITH GREEN TREES CASTING SHADOWS.
THE CAMPUS IS FILLED WITH LAUGHTER.
IT'S THE BRIGHTEST TIME OF THE YEAR.
DESPITE THIS...
SIGH!
FOR ME,
EVERYTHING HAS LOST ITS SHINE.
DID HE...
...REALLY LEAVE ME?

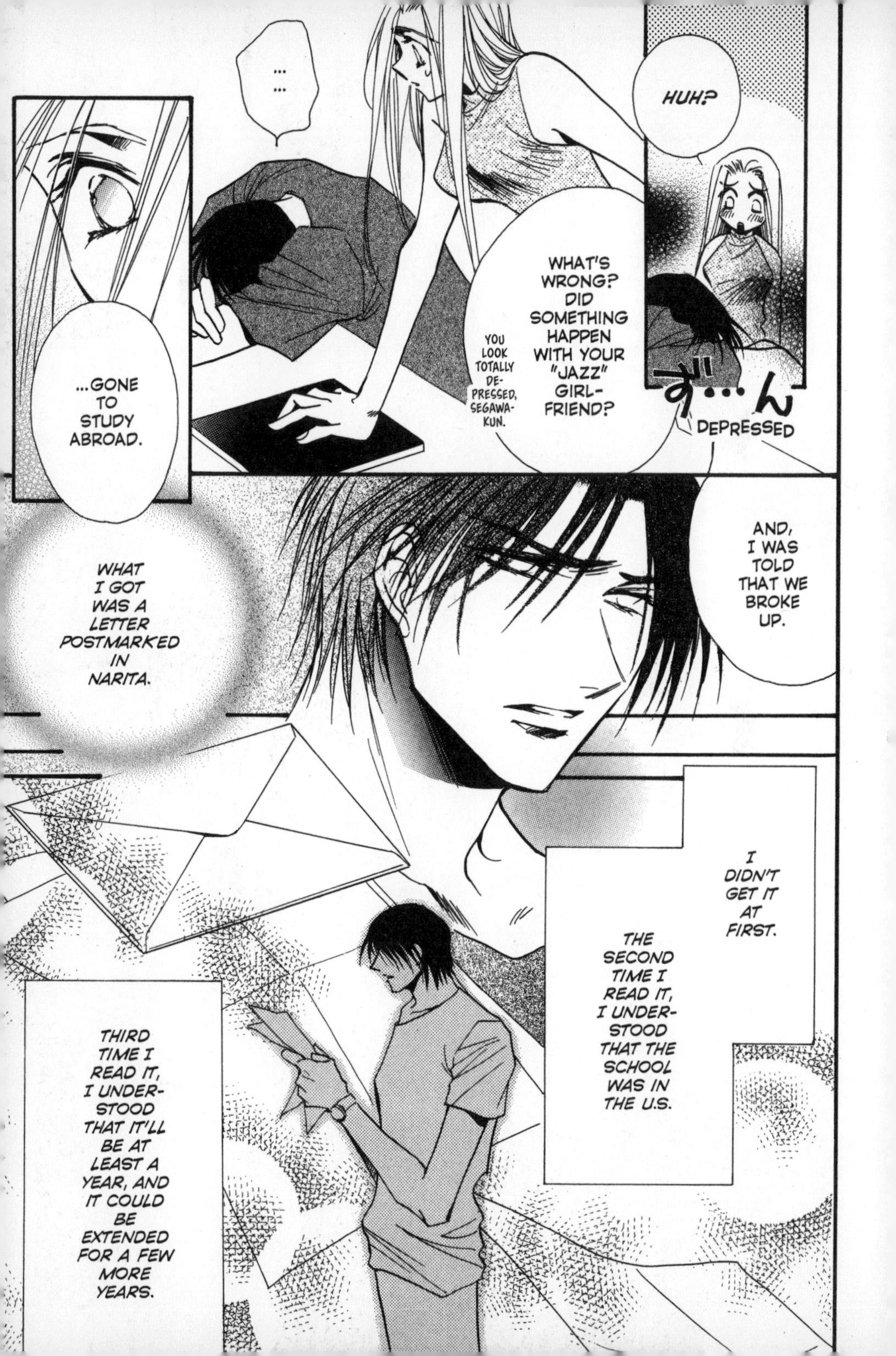
HUH?
ず…ん DEPRESSED
WHAT'S WRONG? DID SOMETHING HAPPEN WITH YOUR "JAZZ" GIRL-FRIEND?
YOU LOOK TOTALLY DE-PRESSED, SEGAWA-KUN.
... ...
...GONE TO STUDY ABROAD.
AND, I WAS TOLD THAT WE BROKE UP.
WHAT I GOT WAS A LETTER POSTMARKED IN NARITA.
I DIDN'T GET IT AT FIRST.
THE SECOND TIME I READ IT, I UNDER-STOOD THAT THE SCHOOL WAS IN THE U.S.
THIRD TIME I READ IT, I UNDER-STOOD THAT IT'LL BE AT LEAST A YEAR, AND IT COULD BE EXTENDED FOR A FEW MORE YEARS.

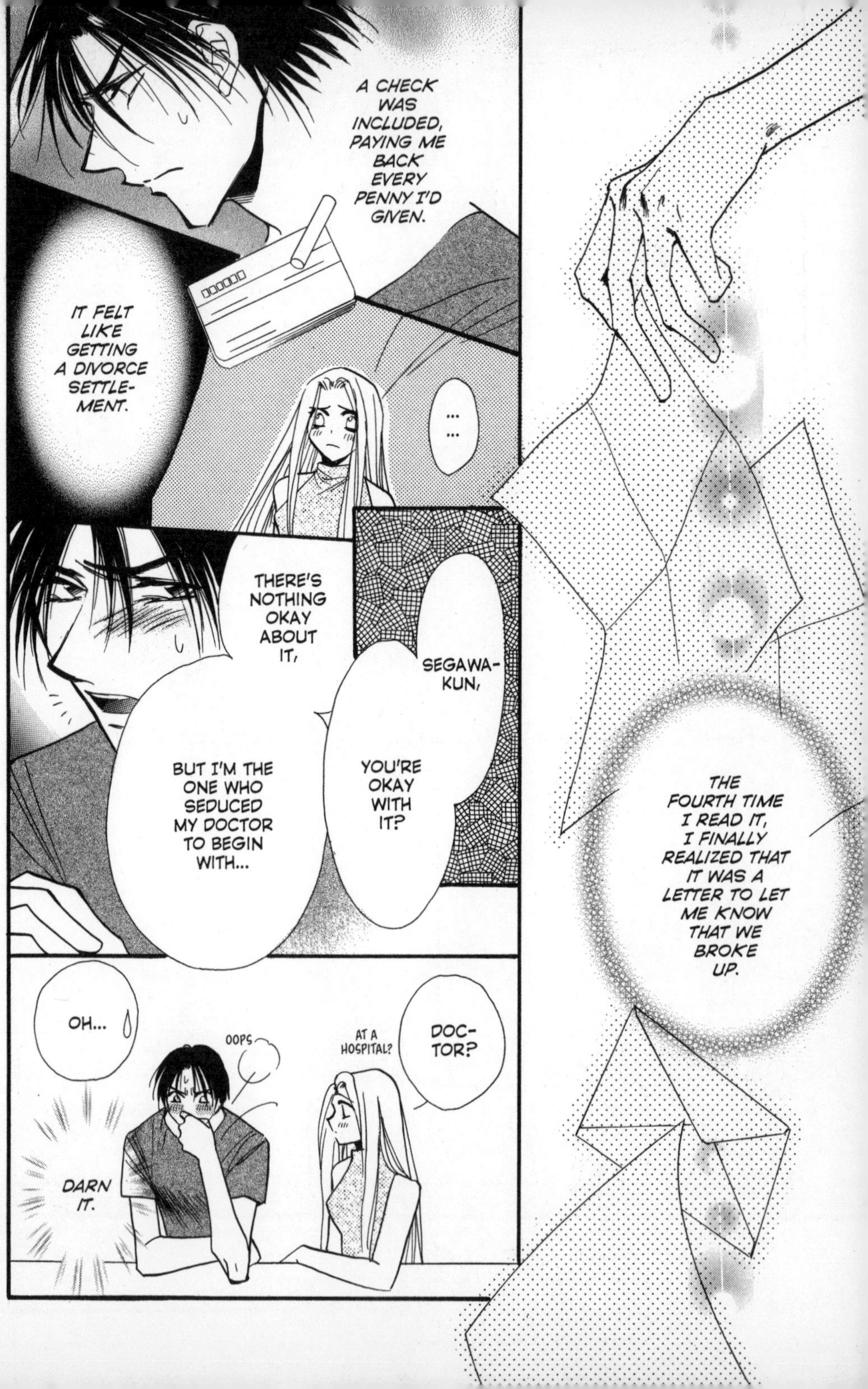
THE FOURTH TIME I READ IT, I FINALLY REALIZED THAT IT WAS A LETTER TO LET ME KNOW THAT WE BROKE UP.
A CHECK WAS INCLUDED, PAYING ME BACK EVERY PENNY I'D GIVEN.
IT FELT LIKE GETTING A DIVORCE SETTLE-MENT.
......
SEGAWA-KUN,
YOU'RE OKAY WITH IT?
THERE'S NOTHING OKAY ABOUT IT,
BUT I'M THE ONE WHO SEDUCED MY DOCTOR TO BEGIN WITH...
DOC-TOR?
AT A HOSPITAL?
OH...
OOPS
DARN IT.

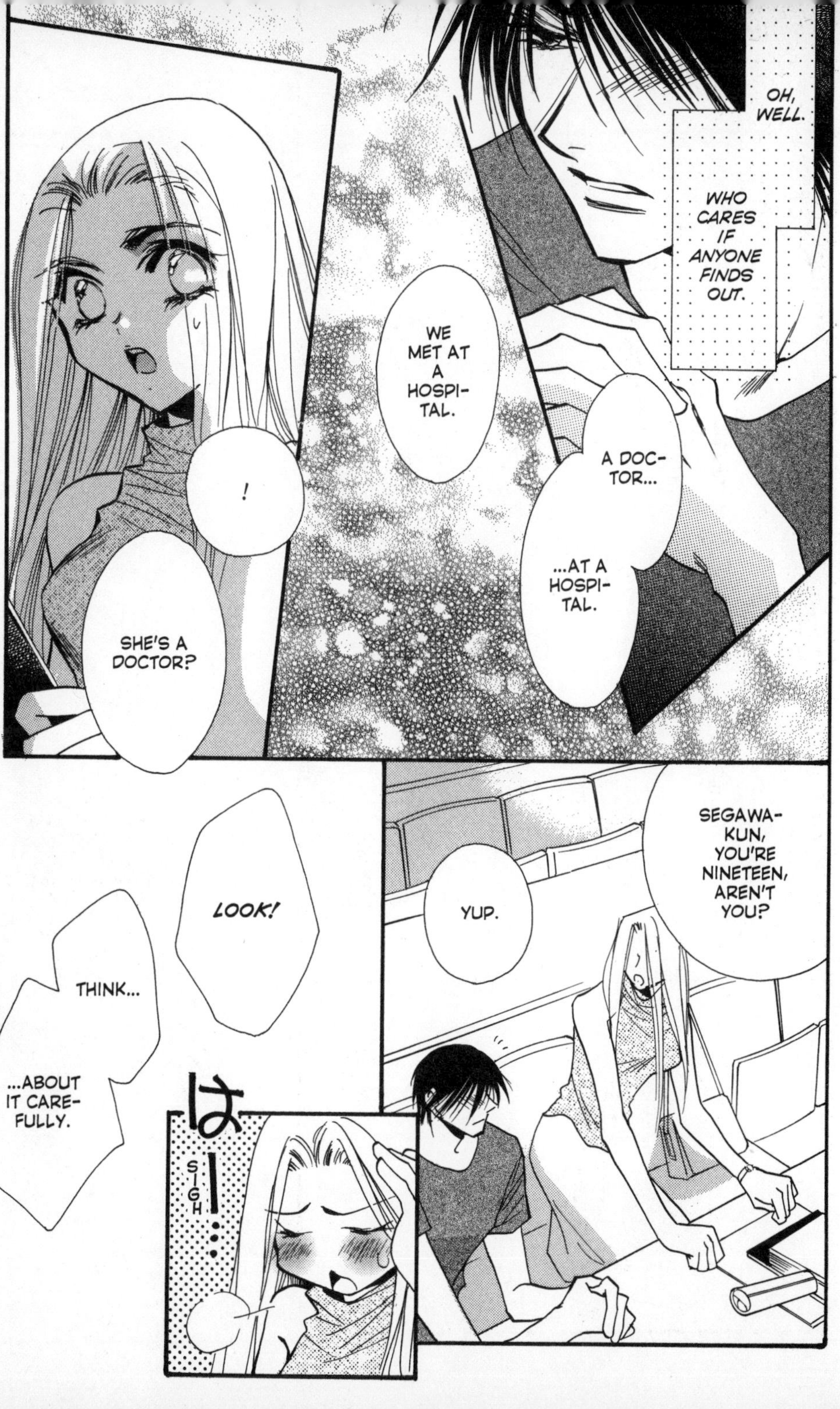
OH, WELL.
WHO CARES IF ANYONE FINDS OUT.
WE MET AT A HOSPITAL.
A DOCTOR...
...AT A HOSPITAL.
!
SHE'S A DOCTOR?
SEGAWA-KUN, YOU'RE NINETEEN, AREN'T YOU?
YUP.
LOOK!
THINK...
...ABOUT IT CAREFULLY.
は一...
SIGH

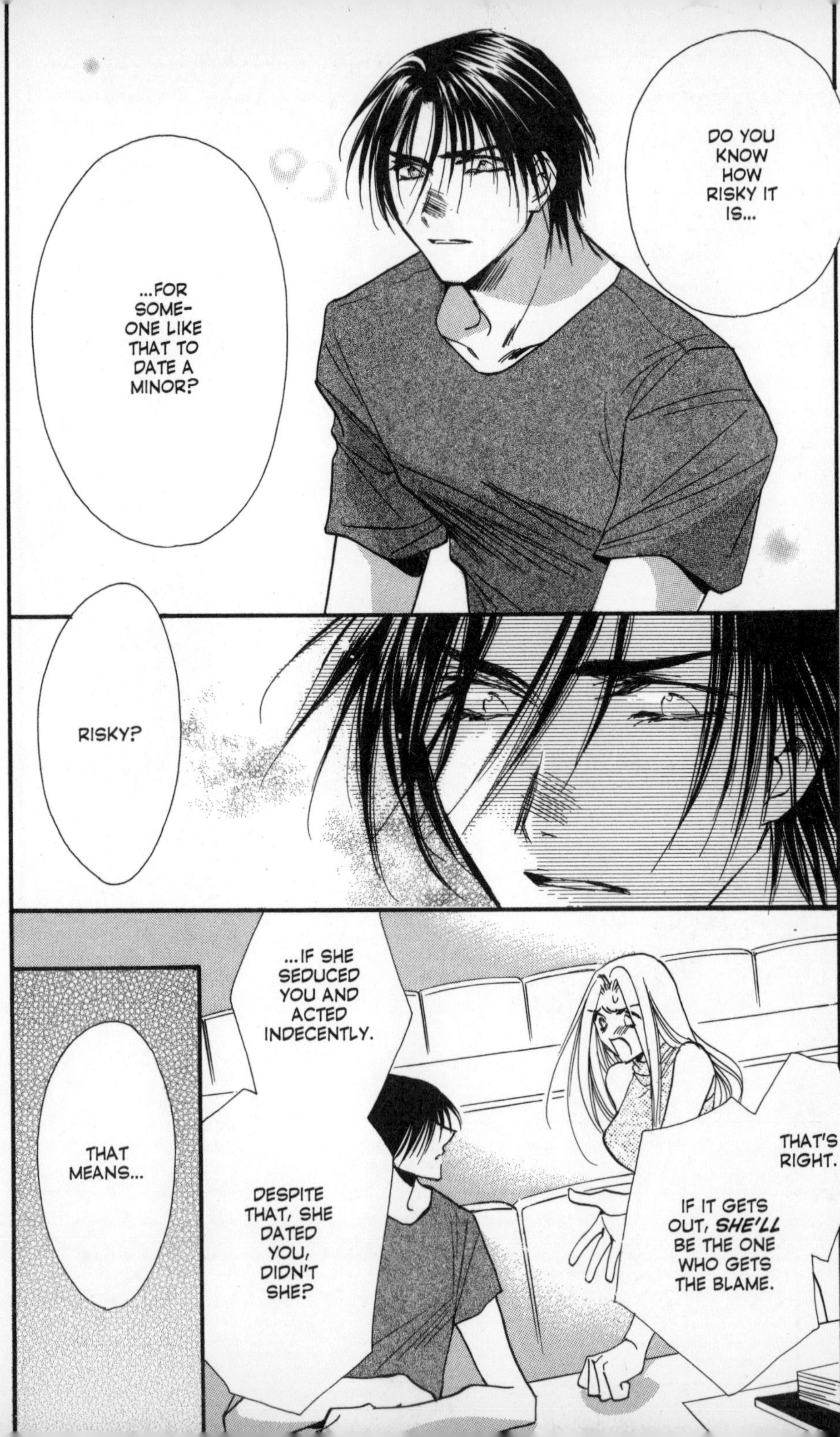
DO YOU KNOW HOW RISKY IT IS...
...FOR SOME-ONE LIKE THAT TO DATE A MINOR?
RISKY?
THAT'S RIGHT.
IF IT GETS OUT, ***SHE'LL*** BE THE ONE WHO GETS THE BLAME.
...IF SHE SEDUCED YOU AND ACTED INDECENTLY.
DESPITE THAT, SHE DATED YOU, DIDN'T SHE?
THAT MEANS...

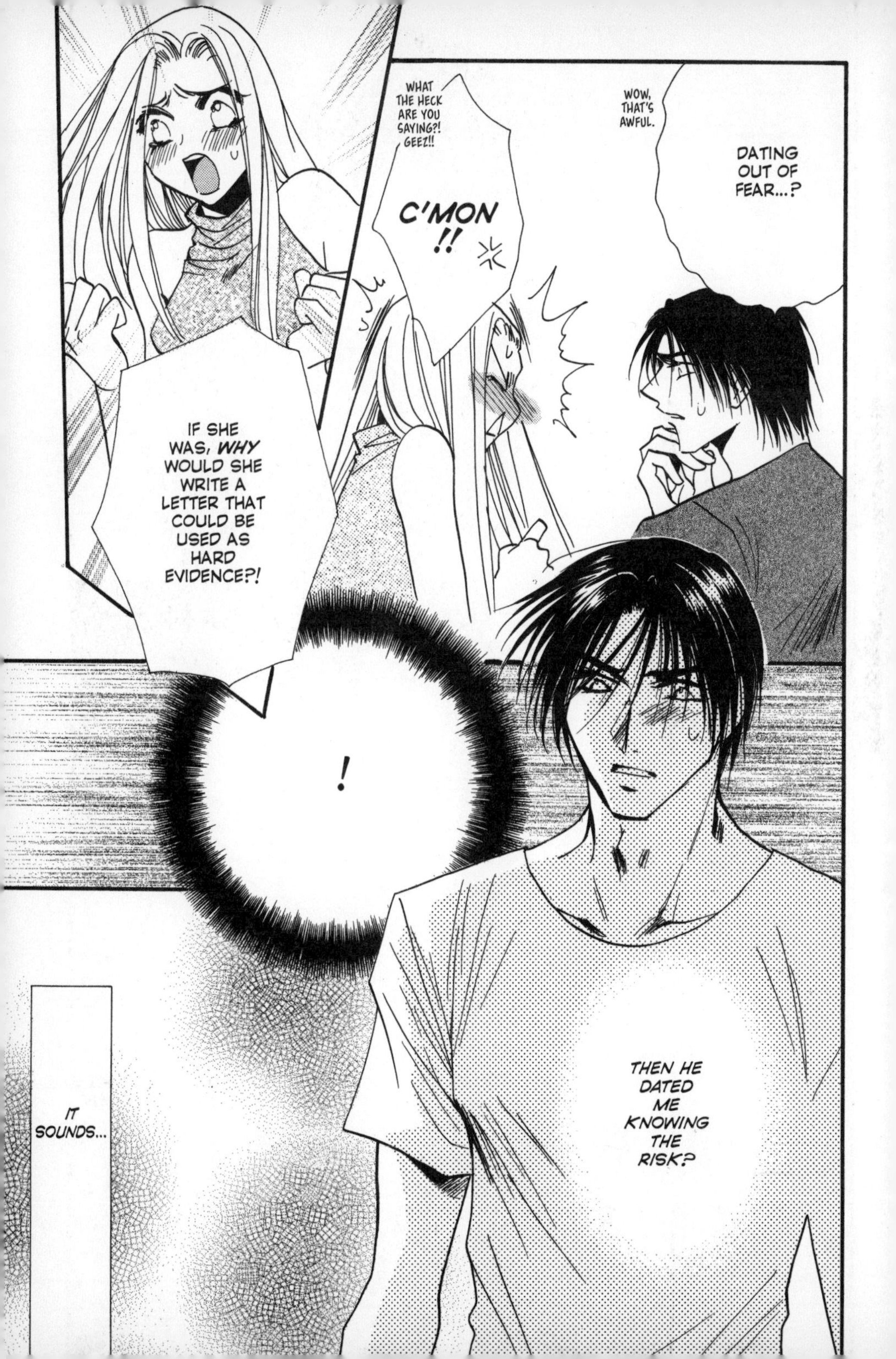

WOW, THAT'S AWFUL.
DATING OUT OF FEAR...?
WHAT THE HECK ARE YOU SAYING?! GEEZ!!
C'MON!!
IF SHE WAS, *WHY* WOULD SHE WRITE A LETTER THAT COULD BE USED AS HARD EVIDENCE?!
!
THEN HE DATED ME KNOWING THE RISK?
IT SOUNDS...

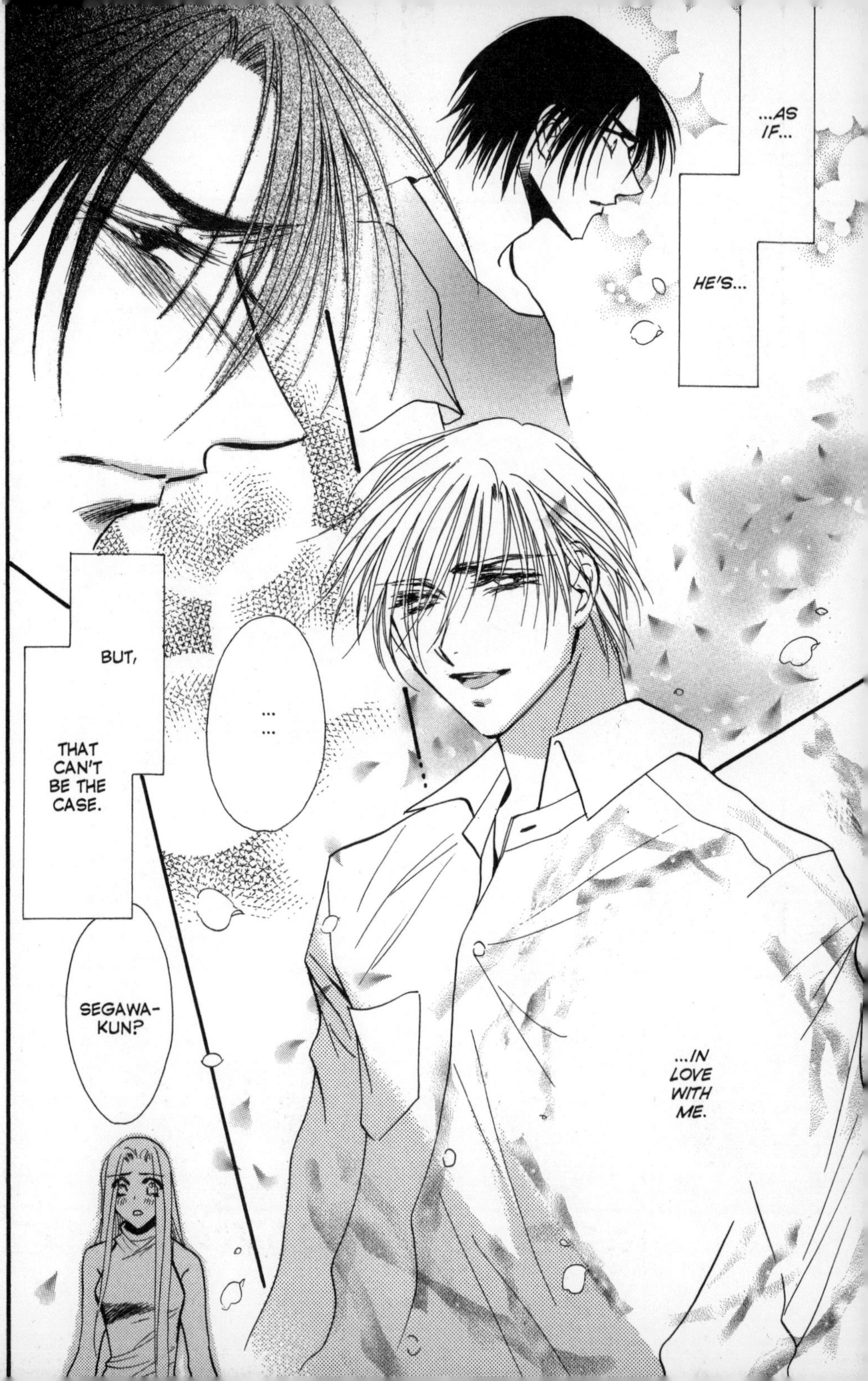
...AS IF...
HE'S...
...IN LOVE WITH ME.
......
BUT,
THAT CAN'T BE THE CASE.
SEGAWA-KUN?

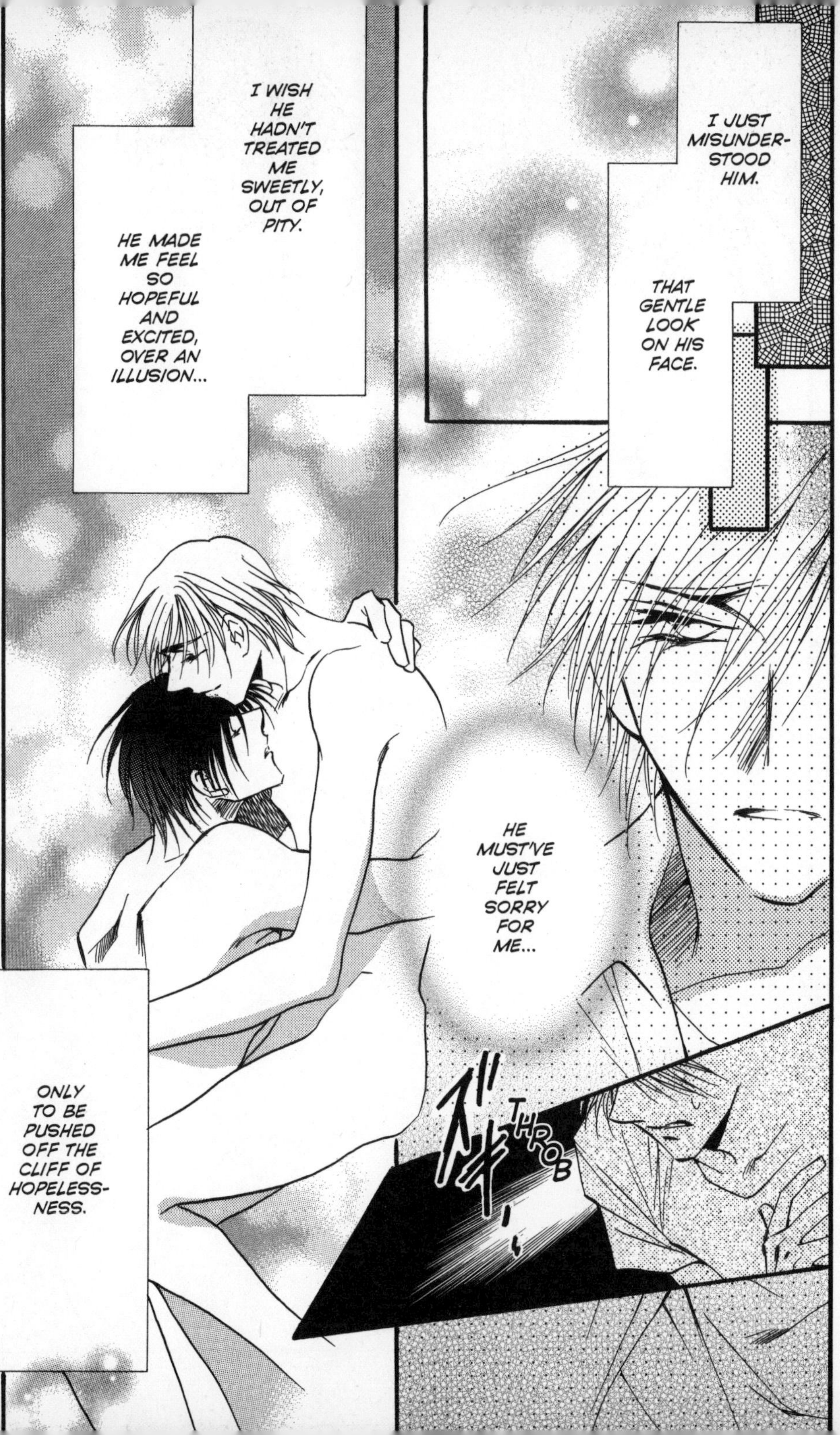
I JUST MISUNDERSTOOD HIM.
THAT GENTLE LOOK ON HIS FACE.
HE MUST'VE JUST FELT SORRY FOR ME...
THROB
I WISH HE HADN'T TREATED ME SWEETLY, OUT OF PITY.
HE MADE ME FEEL SO HOPEFUL AND EXCITED, OVER AN ILLUSION...
ONLY TO BE PUSHED OFF THE CLIFF OF HOPELESSNESS.

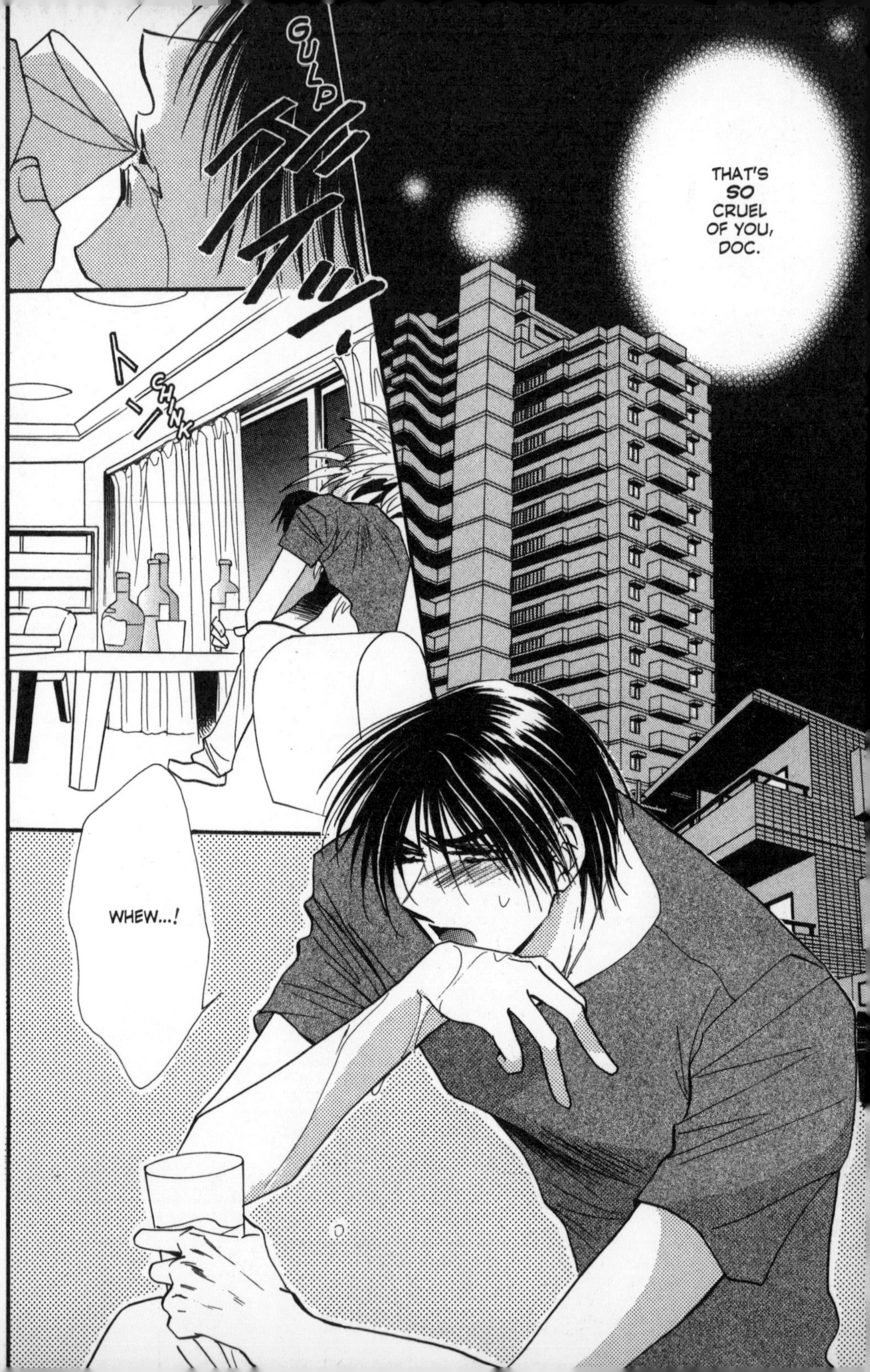
THAT'S SO CRUEL OF YOU, DOC.
GULP
CHINK
WHEW...!

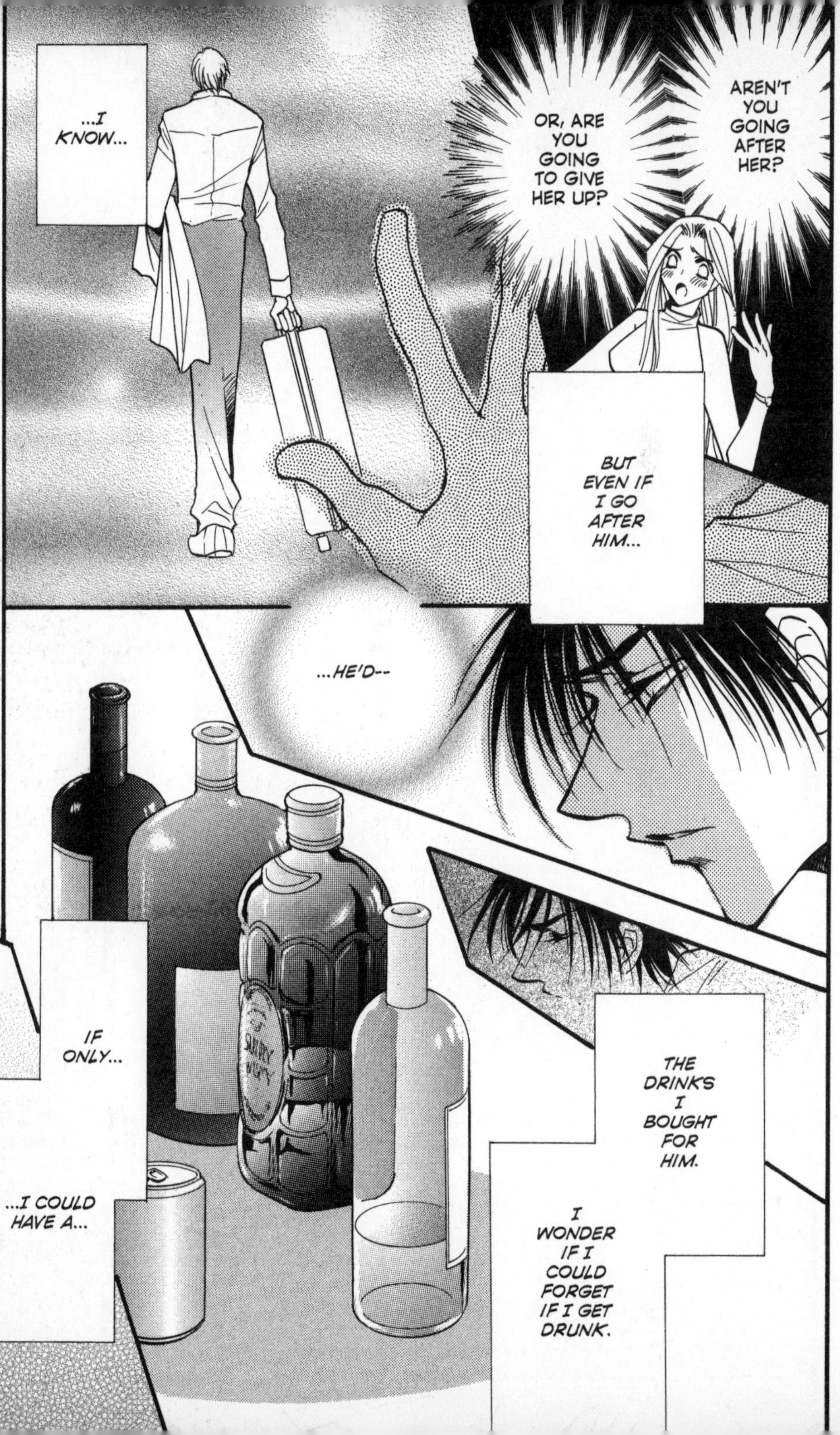
AREN'T YOU GOING AFTER HER?
OR, ARE YOU GOING TO GIVE HER UP?
BUT EVEN IF I GO AFTER HIM...
...I KNOW...
...HE'D--
THE DRINKS I BOUGHT FOR HIM.
I WONDER IF I COULD FORGET IF I GET DRUNK.
IF ONLY...
...I COULD HAVE A...

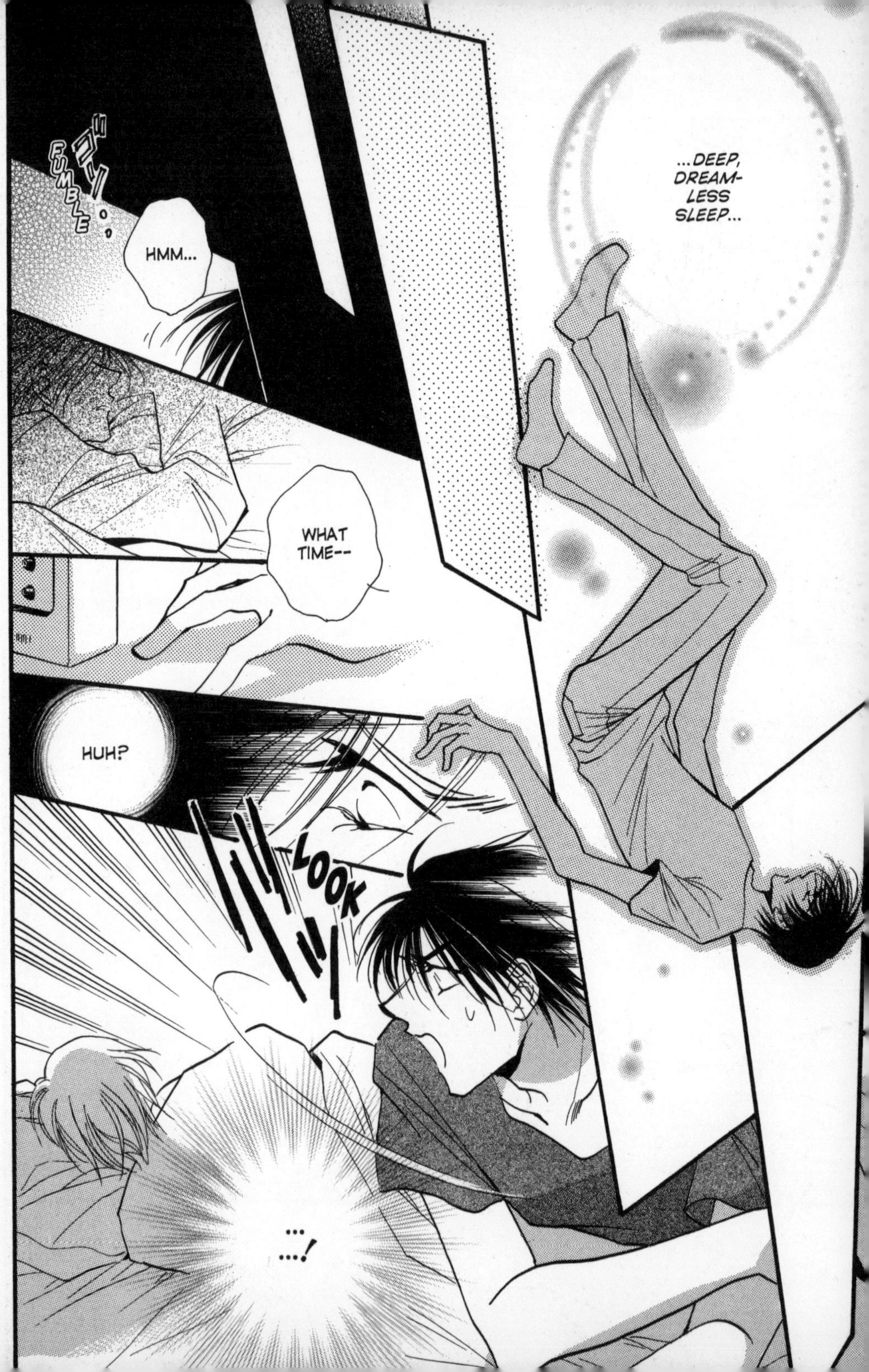
...DEEP, DREAMLESS SLEEP...
FUMBLE
HMM...
WHAT TIME--
HUH?
LOOK
...
...!

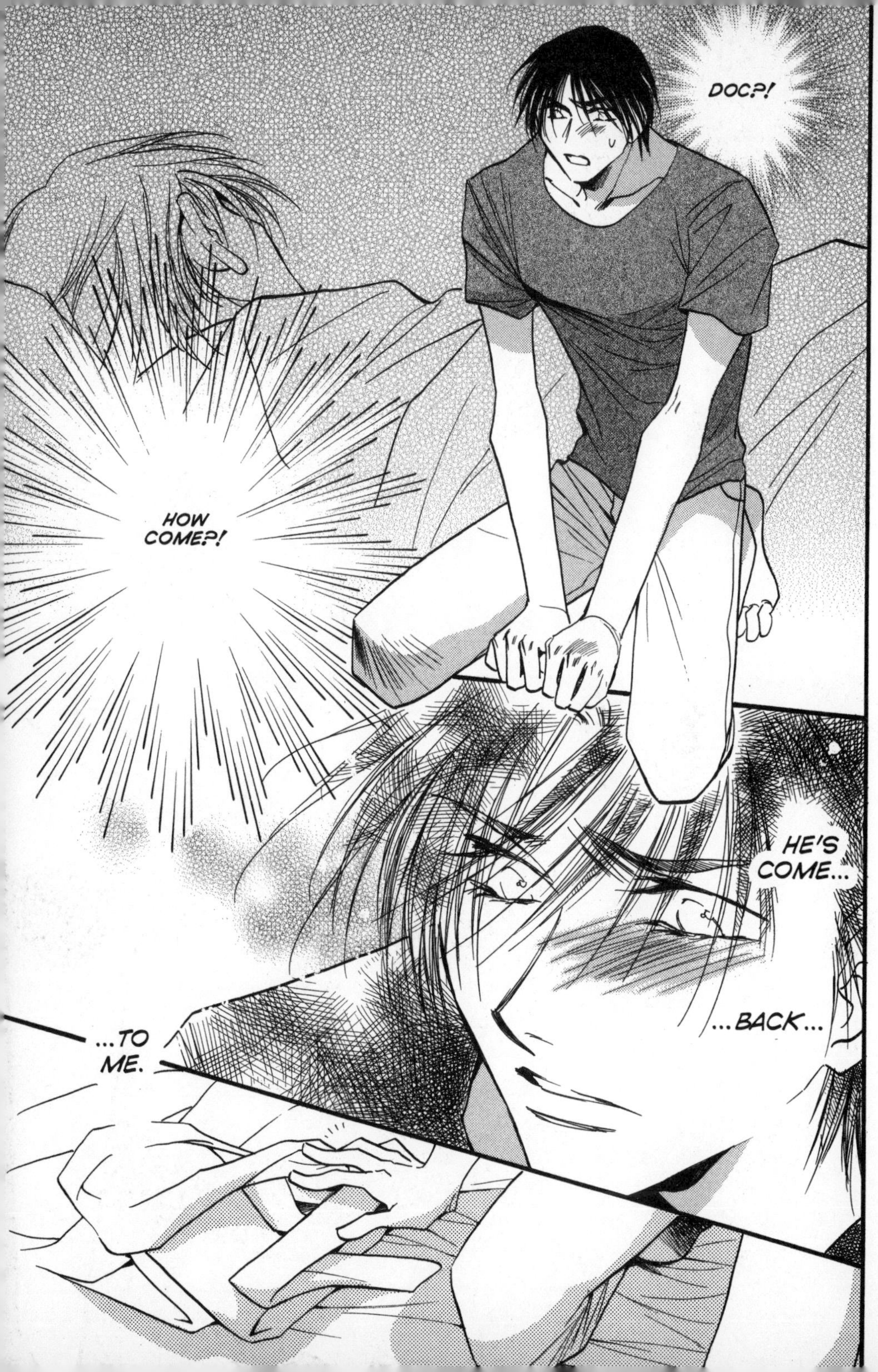
DOC?!
HOW COME?!
HE'S COME...
...BACK...
...TO ME.

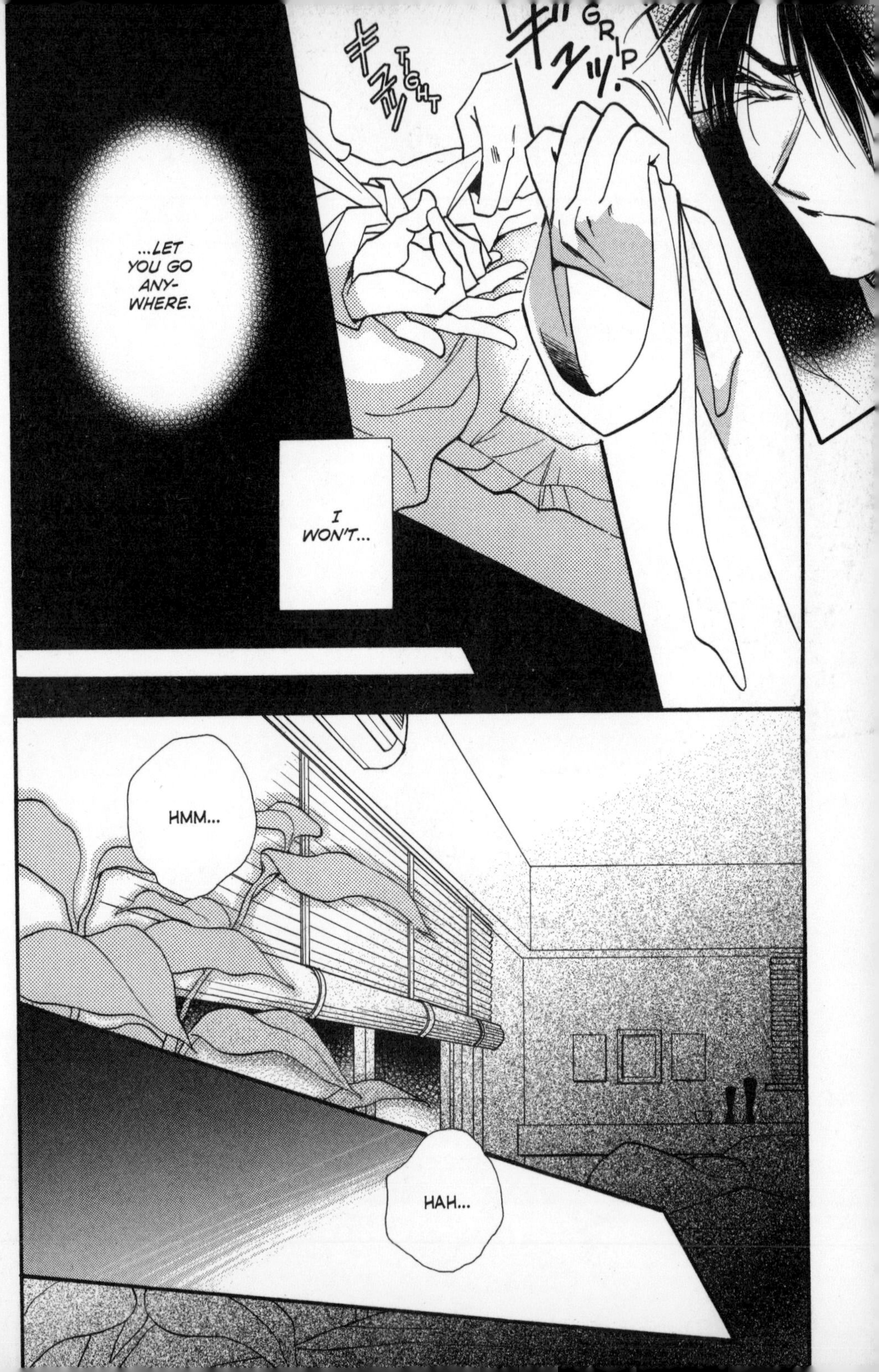
GRIP
TIGHT
I WON'T...
...LET YOU GO ANY-WHERE.
HMM...
HAH...

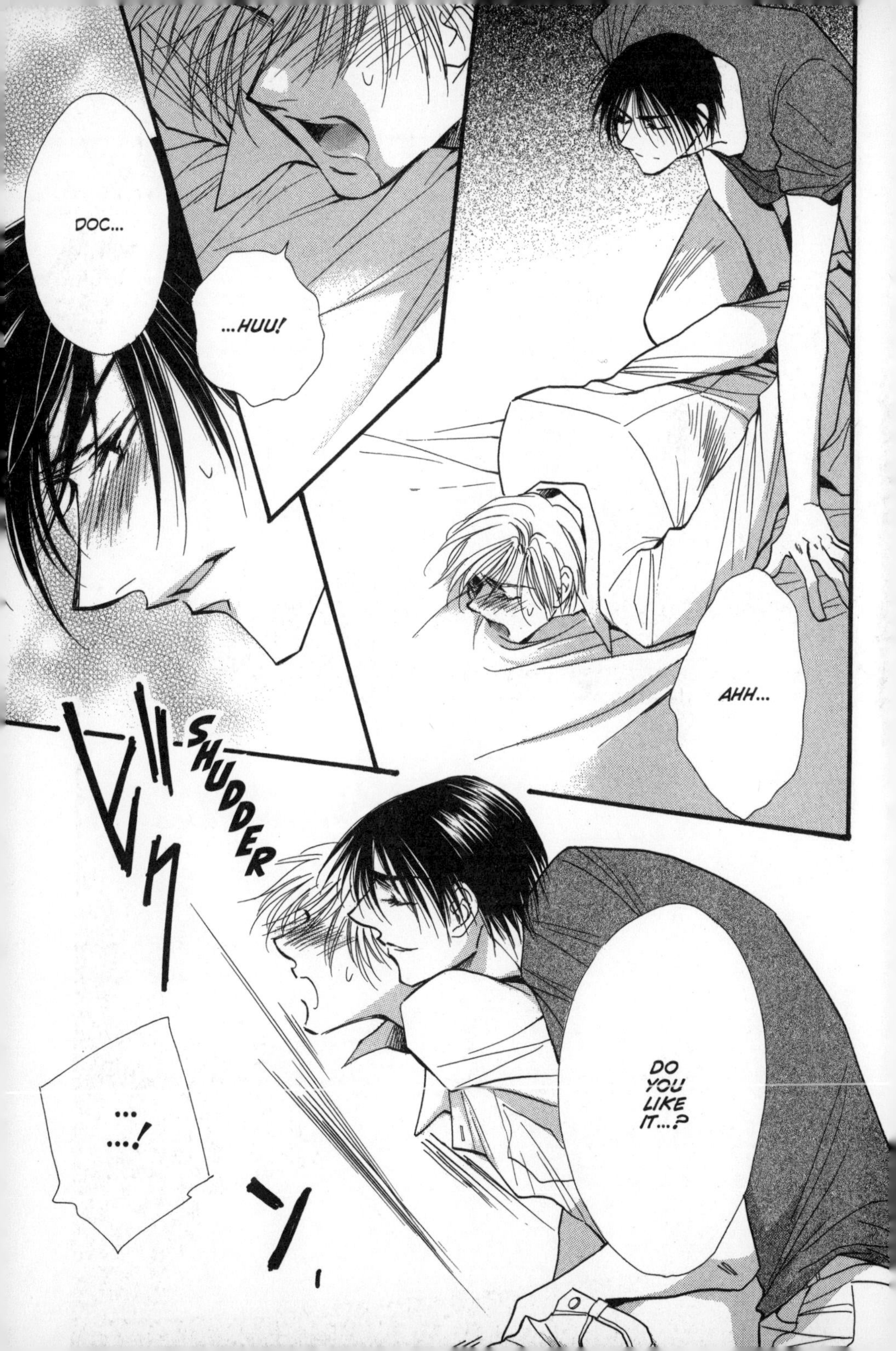
AHH...
DOC...
...HUU!
SHUDDER
DO YOU LIKE IT...?
...
...!

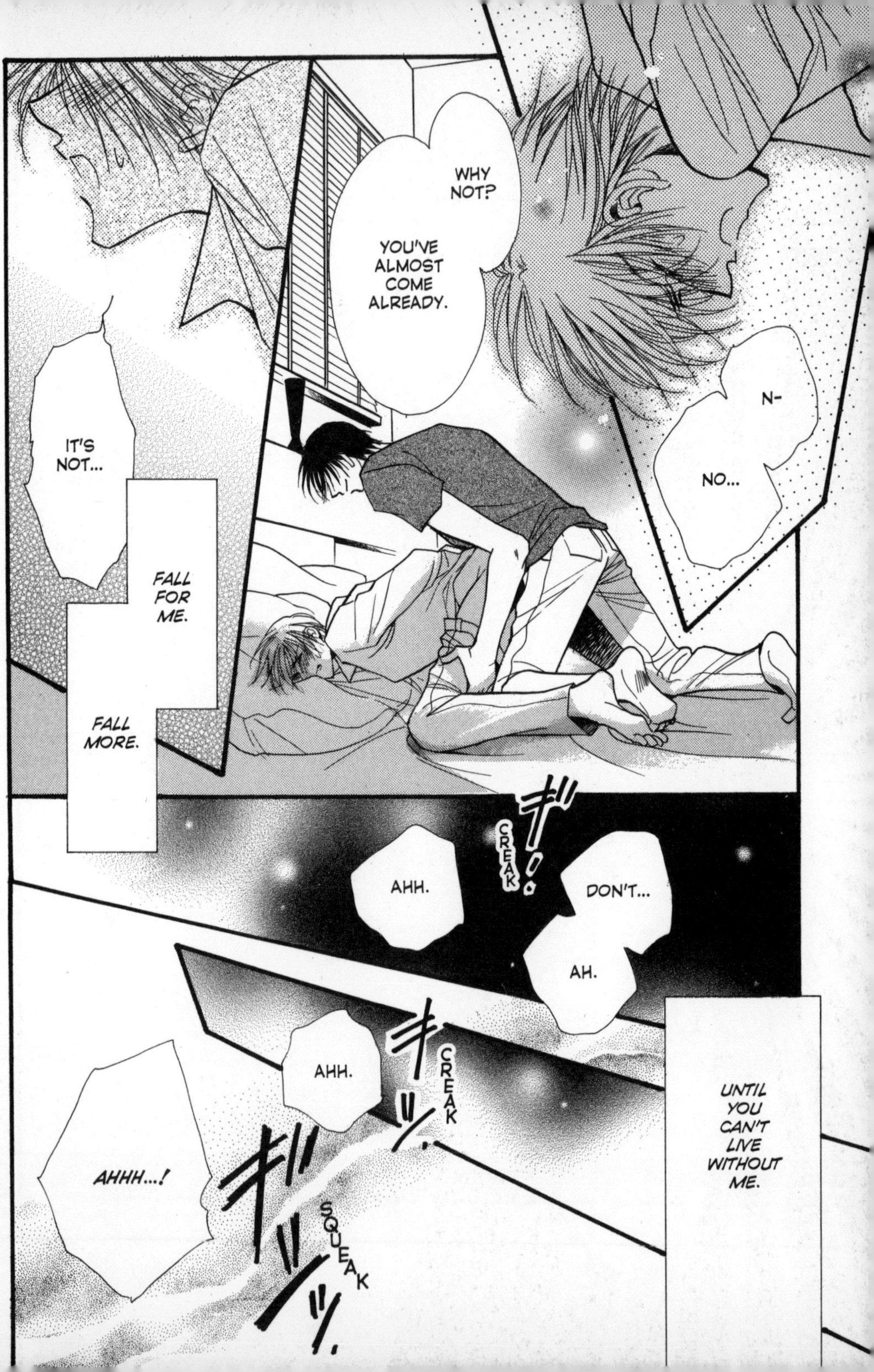
N-
NO...
WHY NOT?
YOU'VE ALMOST COME ALREADY.
IT'S NOT...
FALL FOR ME.
FALL MORE.
UNTIL YOU CAN'T LIVE WITHOUT ME.
DON'T...
AH.
CREAK
AHH.
AHH.
CREAK
AHHH...!
SQUEAK

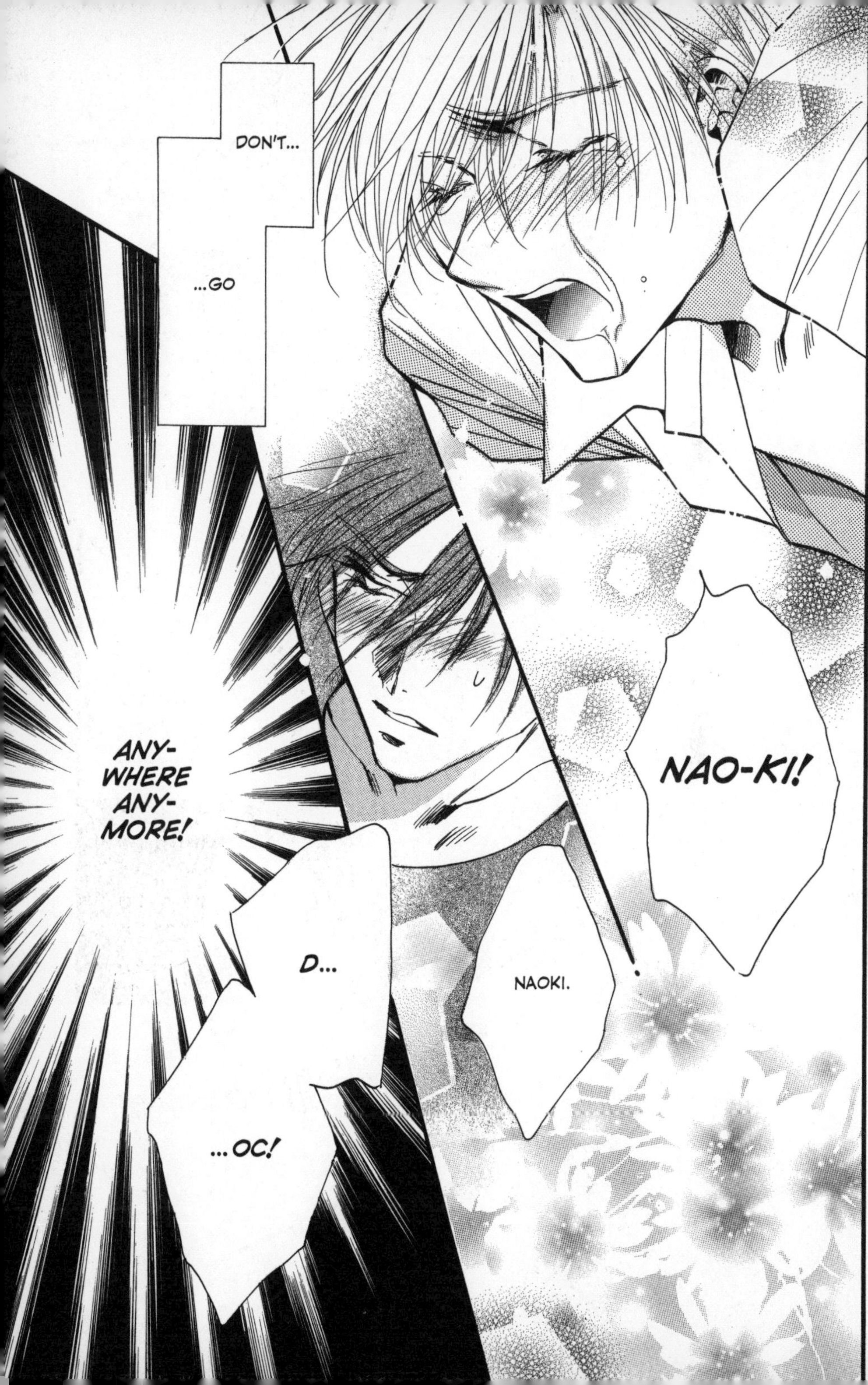
DON'T...
...GO
ANY-WHERE ANY-MORE!
NAO-KI!
NAOKI.
D...
...OC!

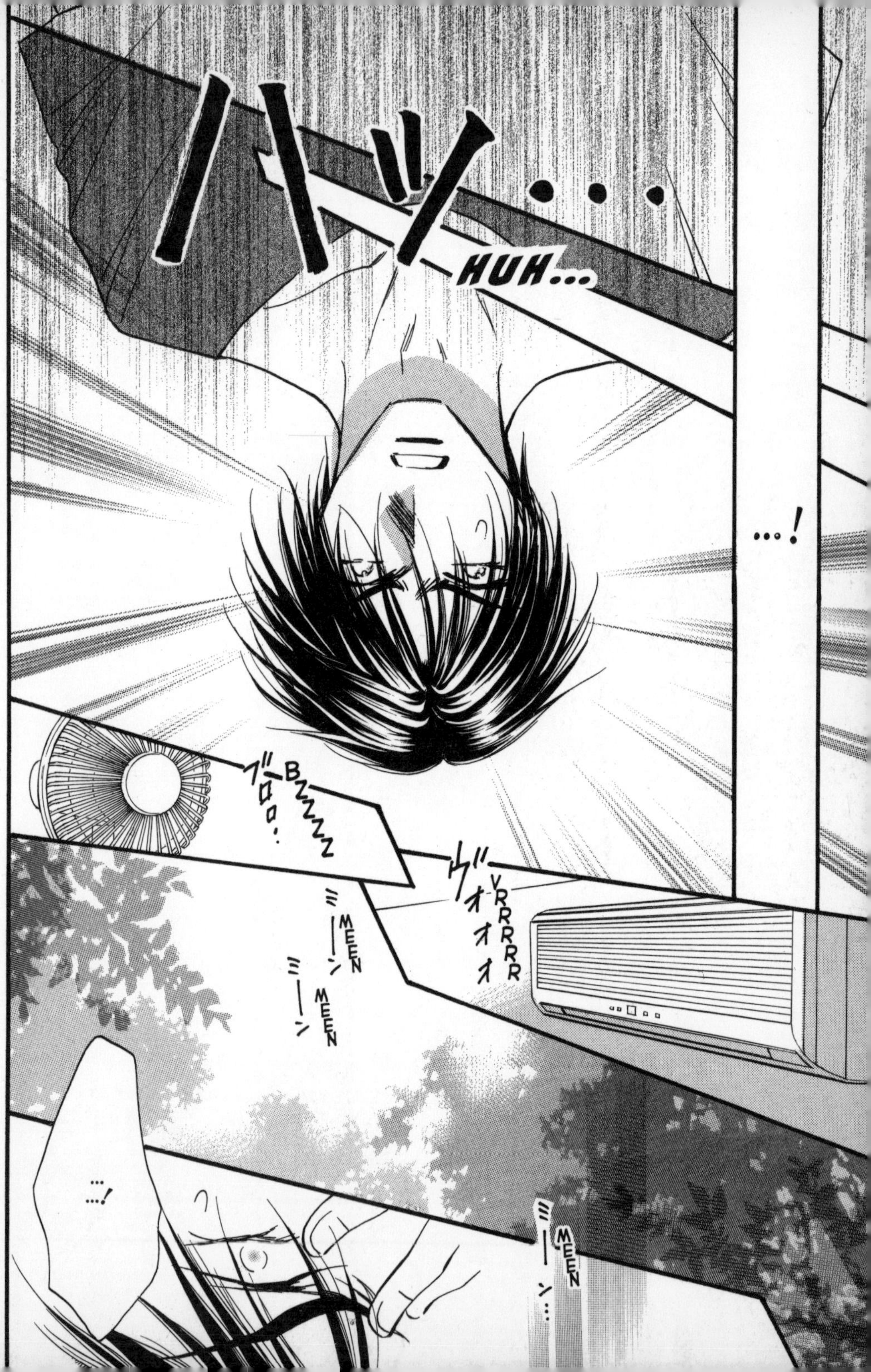

ハッ…
HUH...
...!
ブロロ…
BZZZZZ
ヴォーォォォ
VRRRRR
ミーン
MEEN
ミーン
MEEN
...!
ミーン…
MEEN

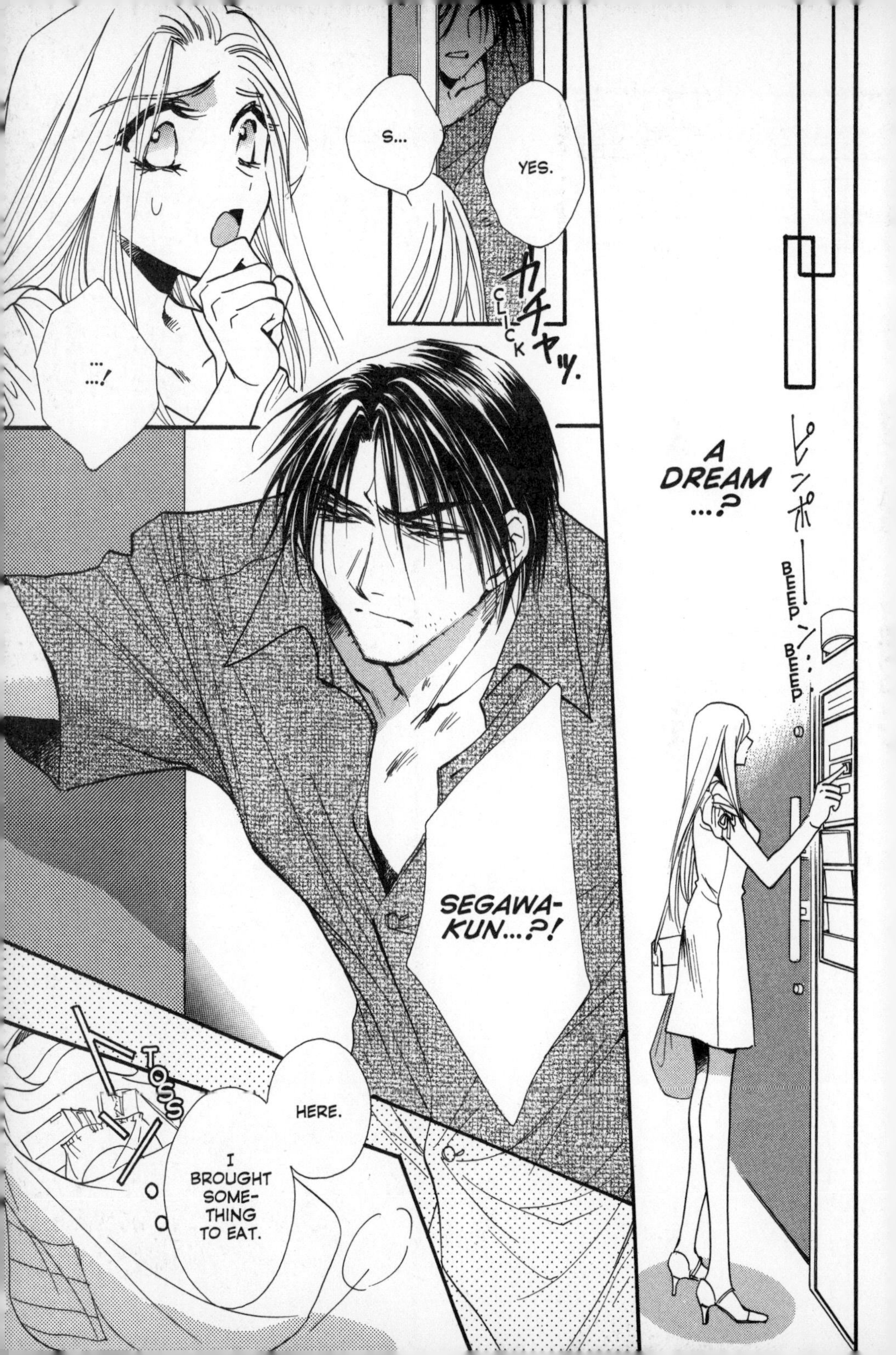

A DREAM ...?
ピンポーン
BEEP BEEP
YES.
S...
カチャッ
CLICK
...!
SEGAWA-KUN...?!
HERE.
I BROUGHT SOMETHING TO EAT.
TOSS

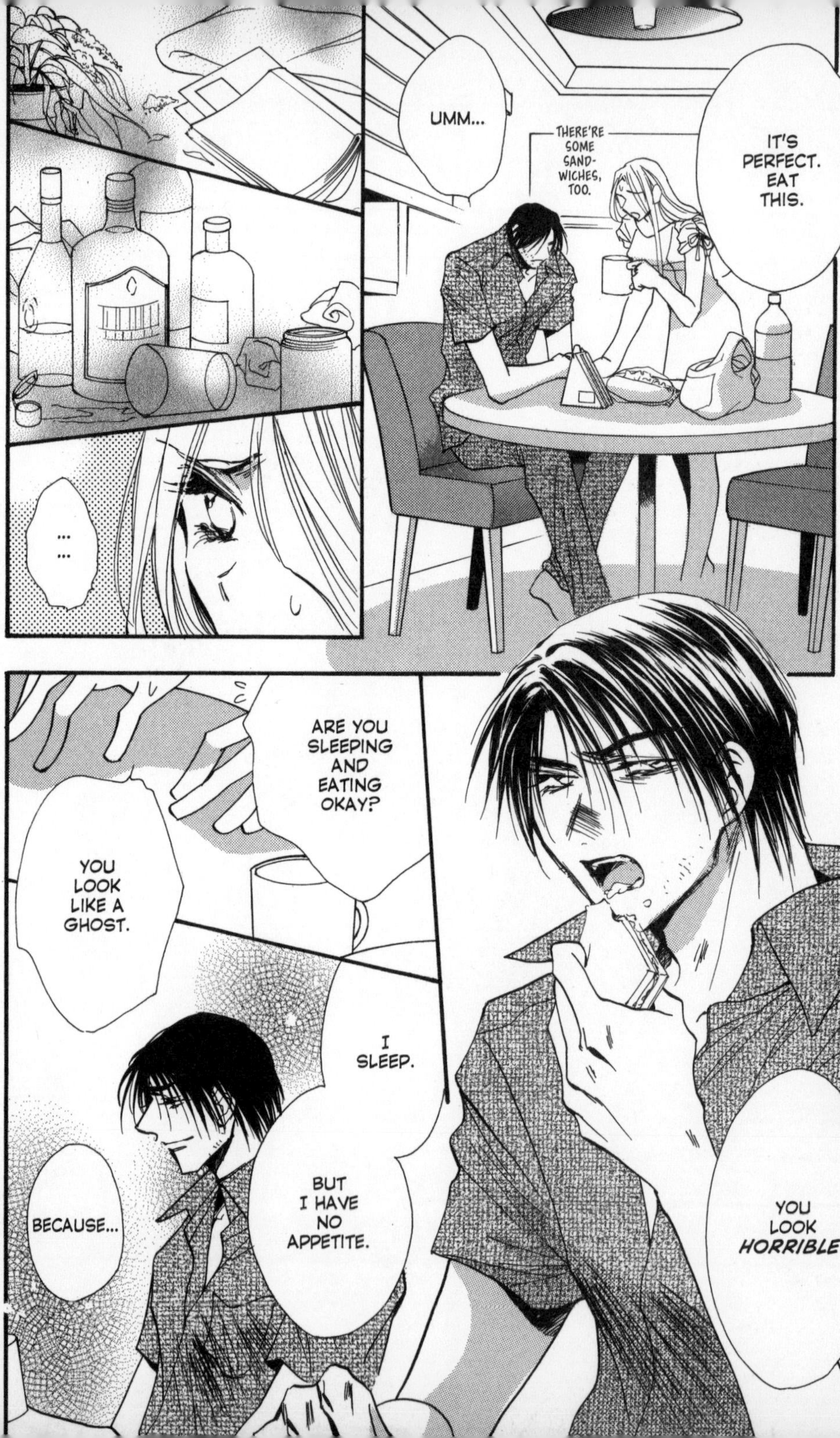
IT'S PERFECT. EAT THIS.
UMM...
THERE'RE SOME SANDWICHES, TOO.
... ...
YOU LOOK *HORRIBLE*.
ARE YOU SLEEPING AND EATING OKAY?
YOU LOOK LIKE A GHOST.
I SLEEP.
BUT I HAVE NO APPETITE.
BECAUSE...

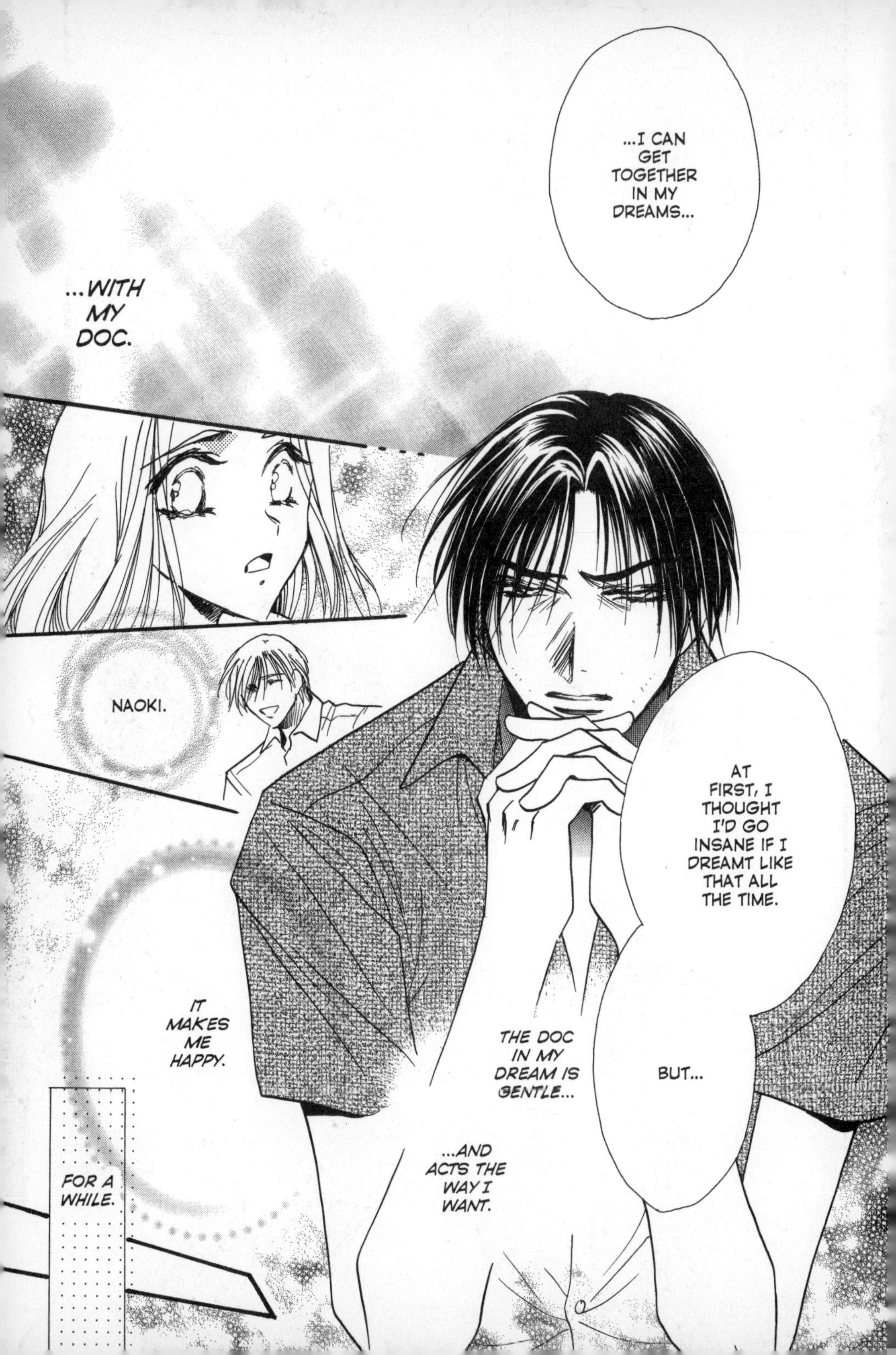
...I CAN GET TOGETHER IN MY DREAMS...
...WITH MY DOC.
AT FIRST, I THOUGHT I'D GO INSANE IF I DREAMT LIKE THAT ALL THE TIME.
BUT...
THE DOC IN MY DREAM IS GENTLE...
...AND ACTS THE WAY I WANT.
NAOKI.
IT MAKES ME HAPPY.
FOR A WHILE.

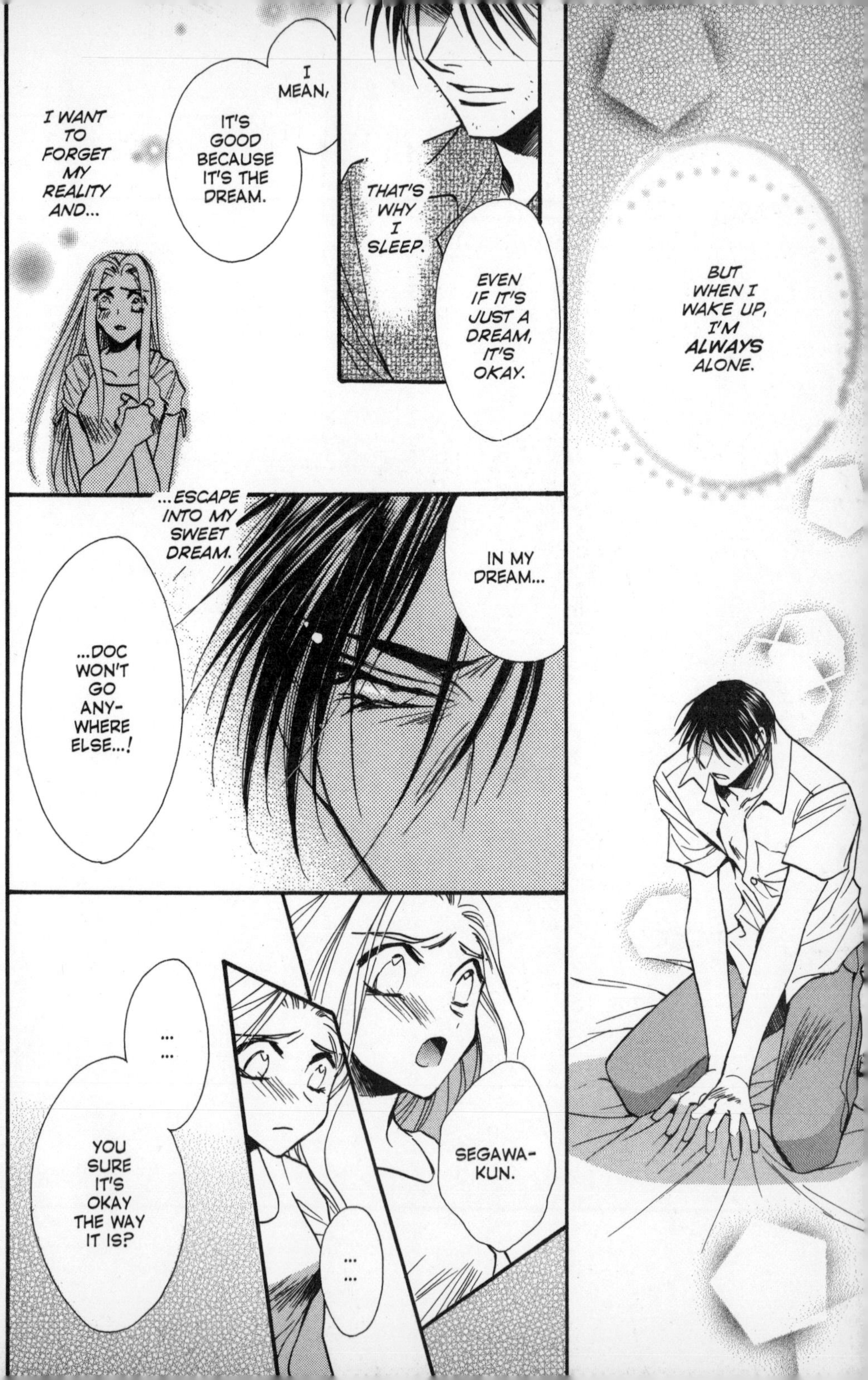
BUT WHEN I WAKE UP, I'M **ALWAYS** ALONE.
I MEAN,
IT'S GOOD BECAUSE IT'S THE DREAM.
THAT'S WHY I SLEEP.
EVEN IF IT'S JUST A DREAM, IT'S OKAY.
I WANT TO FORGET MY REALITY AND...
...ESCAPE INTO MY SWEET DREAM.
IN MY DREAM...
...DOC WON'T GO ANY-WHERE ELSE...!
SEGAWA-KUN.
......
YOU SURE IT'S OKAY THE WAY IT IS?
......

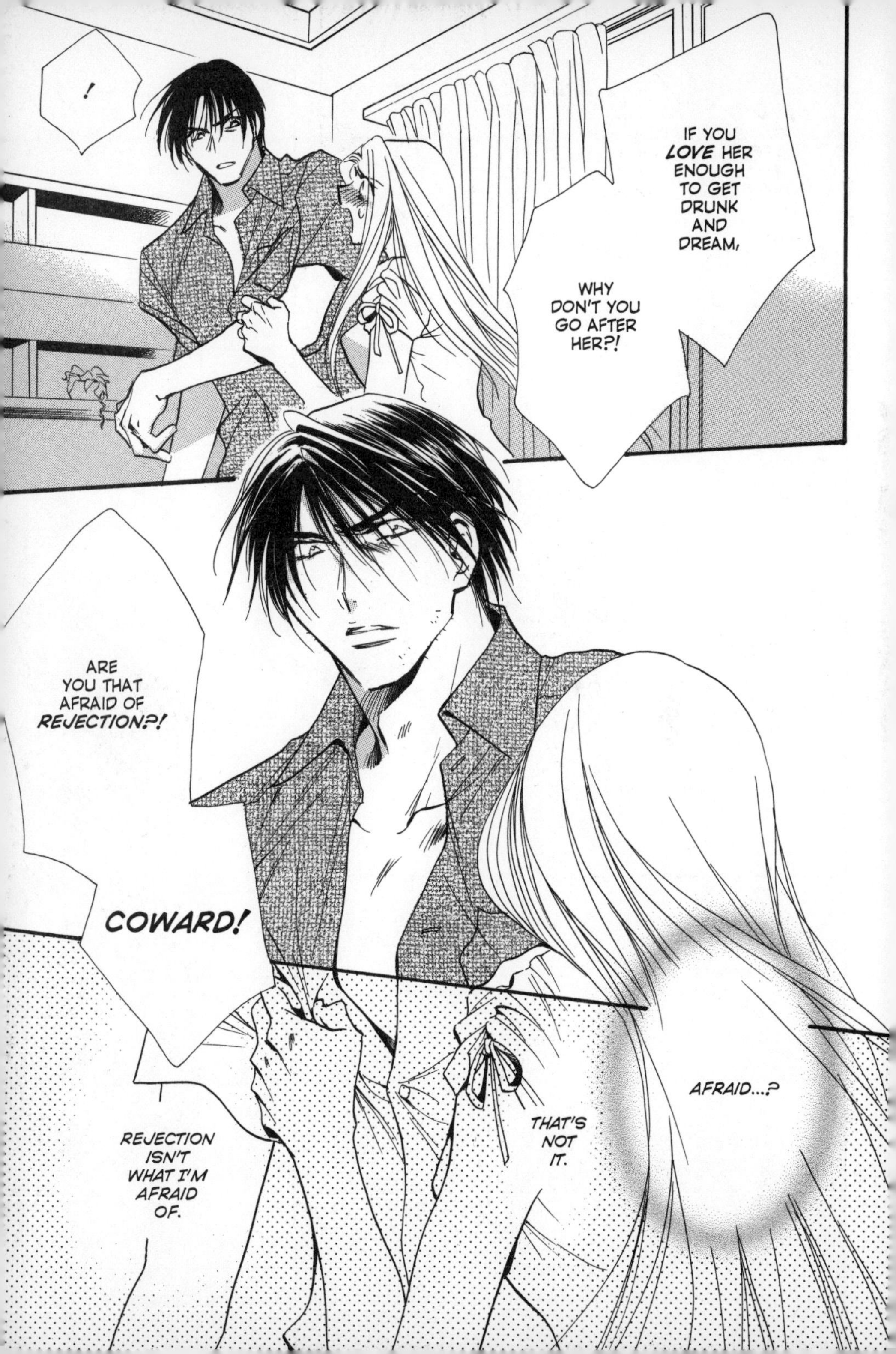
IF YOU LOVE HER ENOUGH TO GET DRUNK AND DREAM,
WHY DON'T YOU GO AFTER HER?!
!
ARE YOU THAT AFRAID OF REJECTION?!
COWARD!
AFRAID...?
THAT'S NOT IT.
REJECTION ISN'T WHAT I'M AFRAID OF.

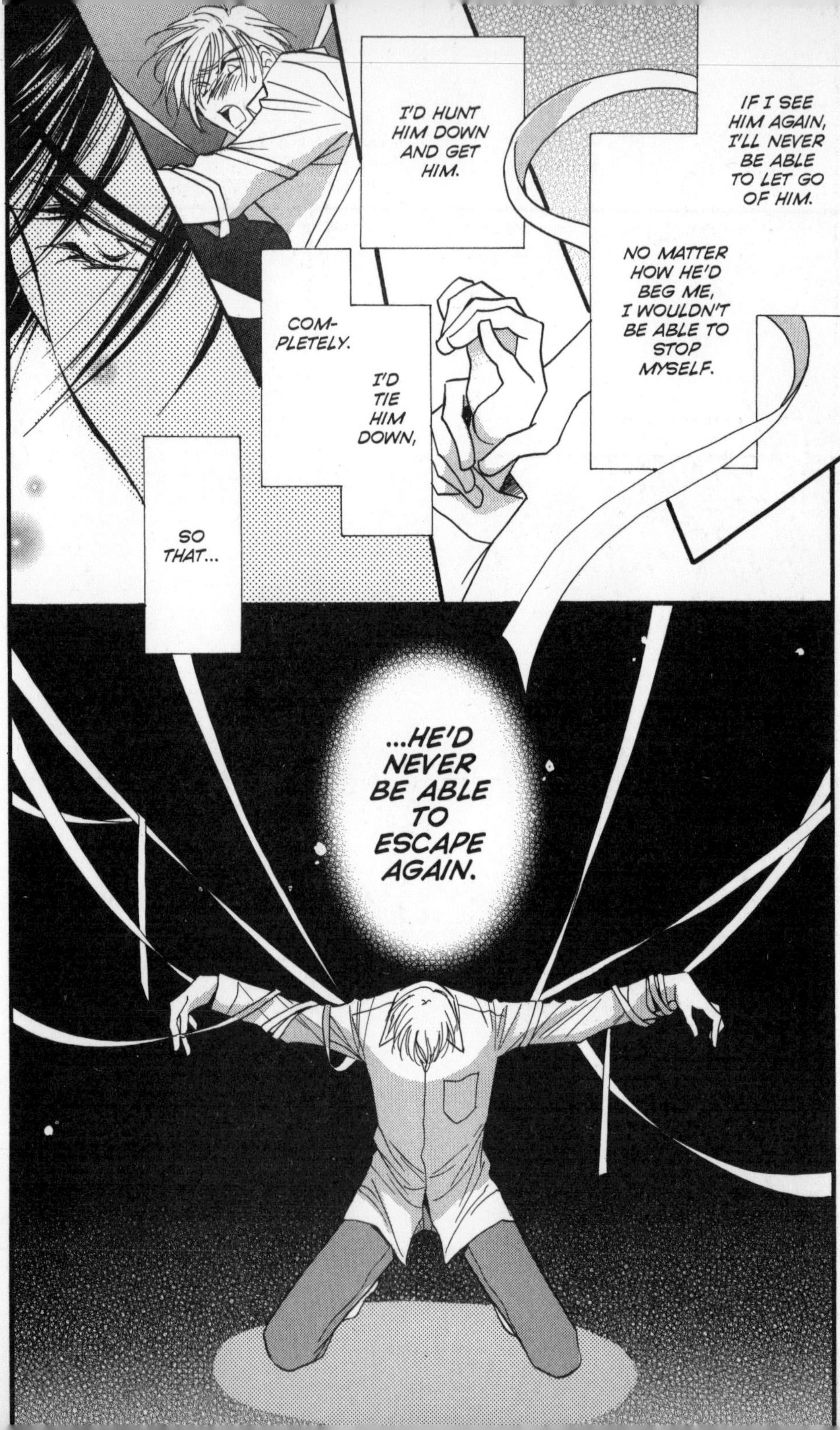

IF I SEE HIM AGAIN, I'LL NEVER BE ABLE TO LET GO OF HIM.
NO MATTER HOW HE'D BEG ME, I WOULDN'T BE ABLE TO STOP MYSELF.
I'D HUNT HIM DOWN AND GET HIM.
COM-PLETELY.
I'D TIE HIM DOWN,
SO THAT...
...HE'D NEVER BE ABLE TO ESCAPE AGAIN.

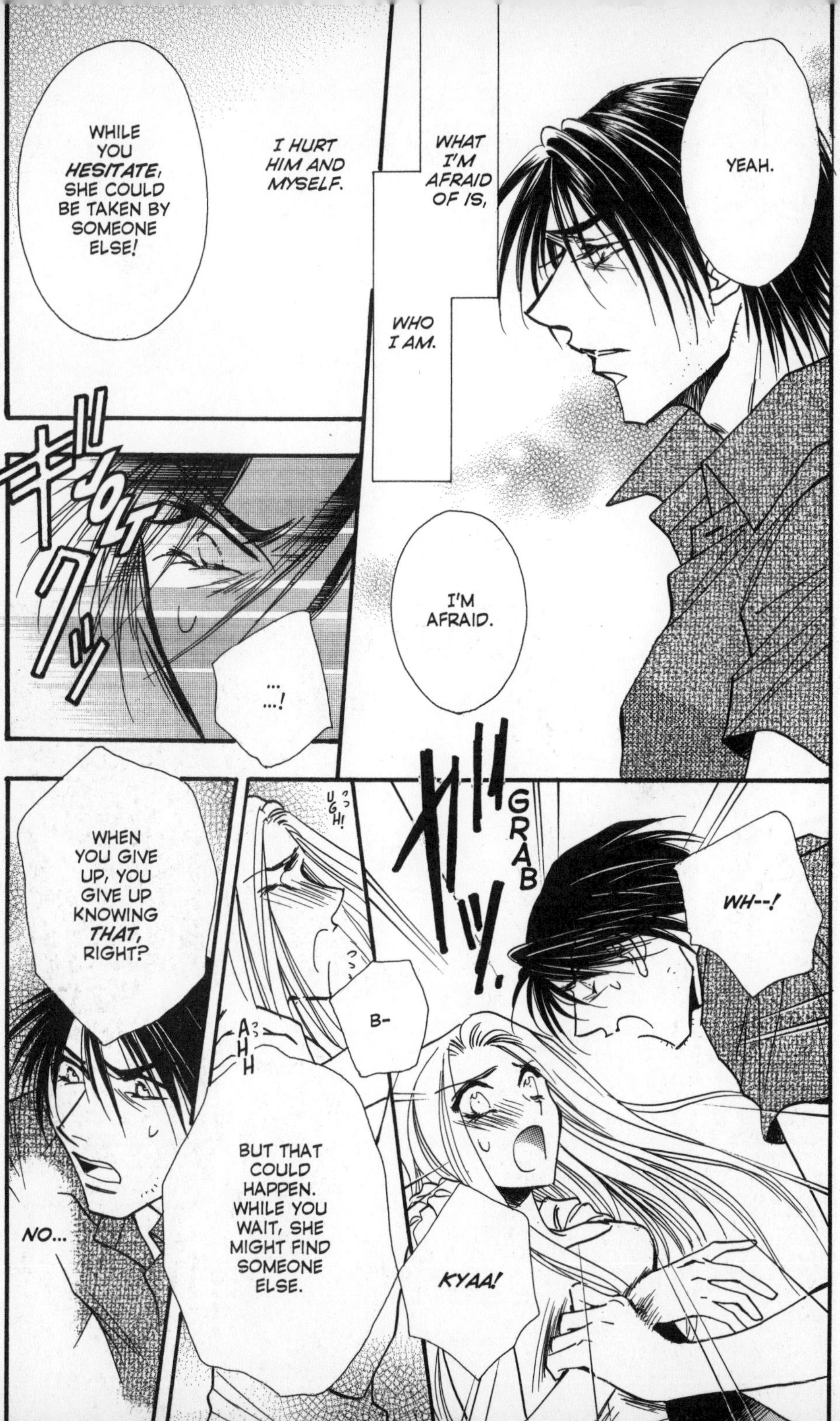

YEAH.
WHAT I'M AFRAID OF IS,
WHO I AM.
I'M AFRAID.
I HURT HIM AND MYSELF.
WHILE YOU HESITATE, SHE COULD BE TAKEN BY SOMEONE ELSE!
JOLT
...
...!
GRAB
WH--!
KYAA!
UGH!
AHH
B-
WHEN YOU GIVE UP, YOU GIVE UP KNOWING THAT, RIGHT?
BUT THAT COULD HAPPEN. WHILE YOU WAIT, SHE MIGHT FIND SOMEONE ELSE.
NO...

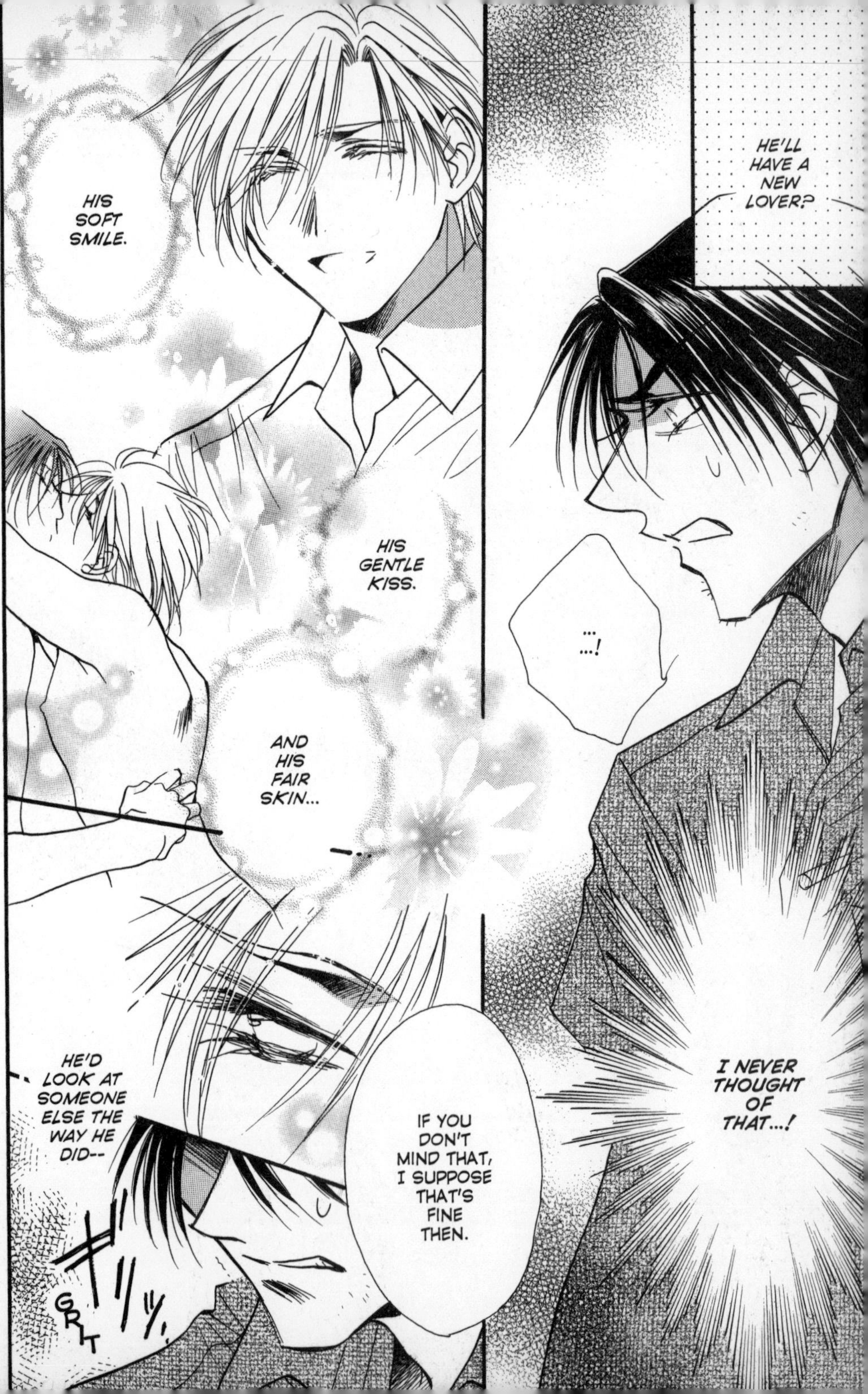
HE'LL HAVE A NEW LOVER?
...!
I NEVER THOUGHT OF THAT...!
HIS SOFT SMILE.
HIS GENTLE KISS.
AND HIS FAIR SKIN...
IF YOU DON'T MIND THAT, I SUPPOSE THAT'S FINE THEN.
HE'D LOOK AT SOMEONE ELSE THE WAY HE DID--
GRIT

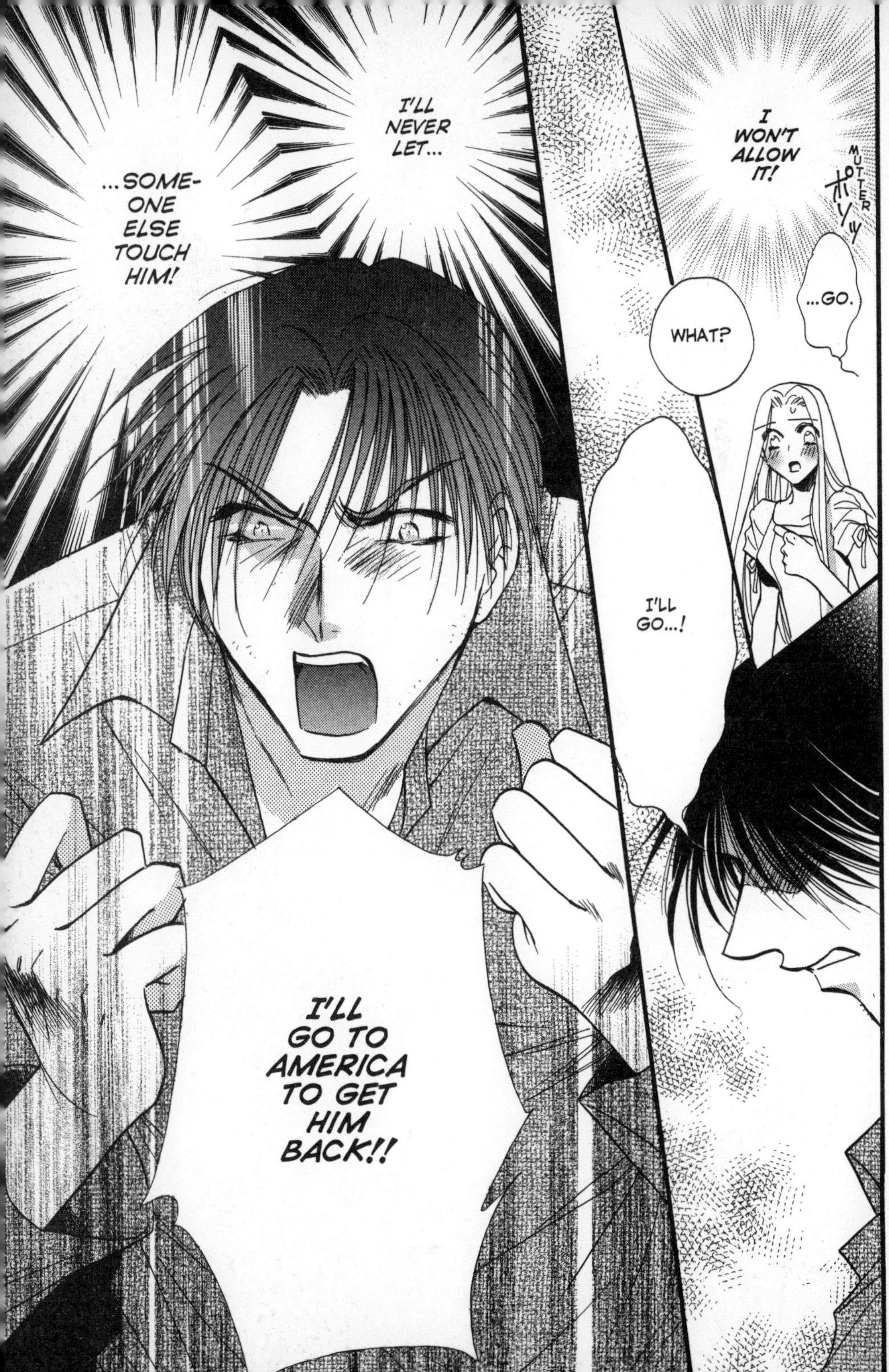
I WON'T ALLOW IT!
MUTTER
...GO.
WHAT?
I'LL GO...!
I'LL NEVER LET...
...SOME-ONE ELSE TOUCH HIM!
I'LL GO TO AMERICA TO GET HIM BACK!!

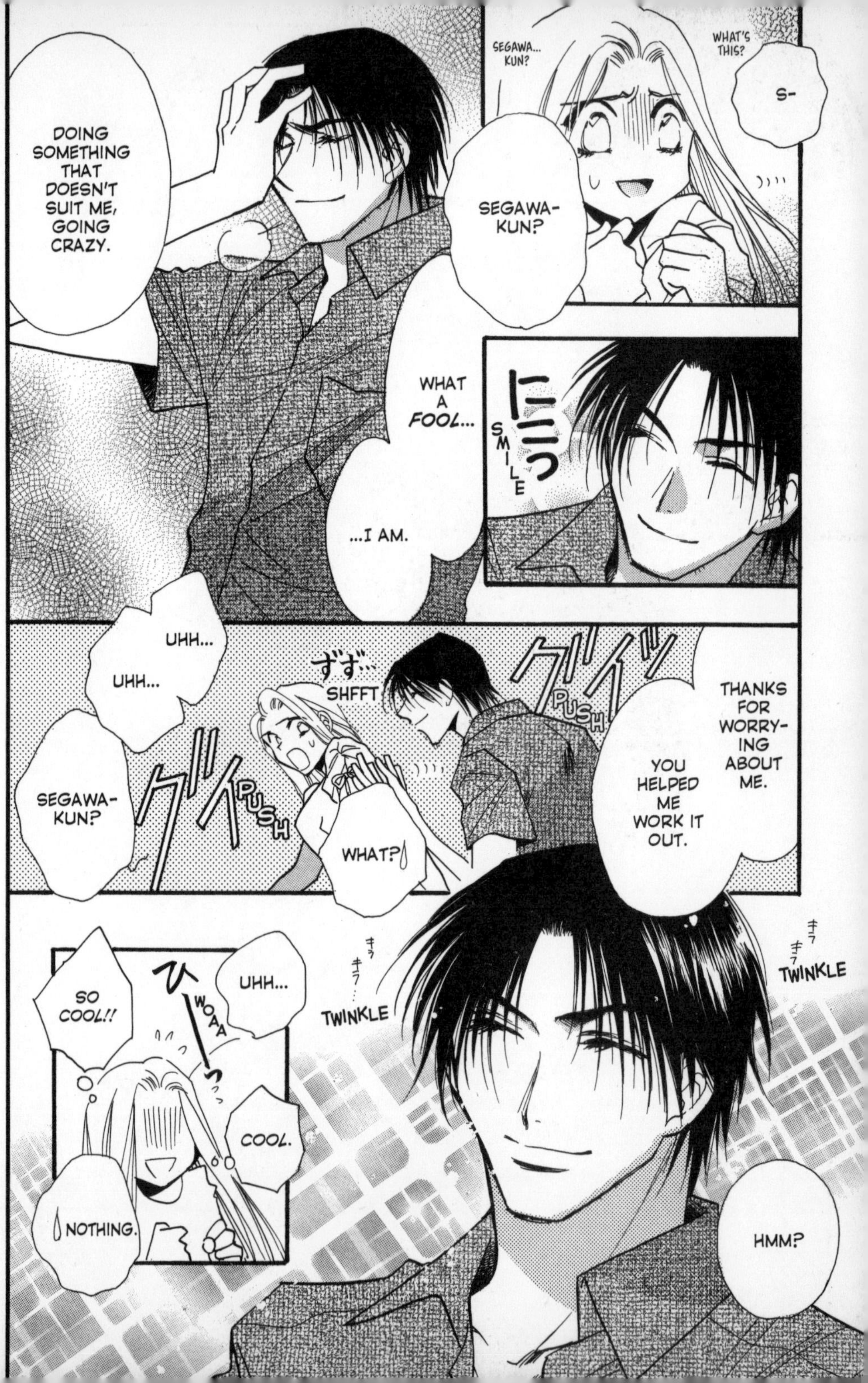
S-
WHAT'S THIS?
SEGAWA... KUN?
SEGAWA-KUN?
WHAT A FOOL...
SMILE
...I AM.
DOING SOMETHING THAT DOESN'T SUIT ME, GOING CRAZY.
THANKS FOR WORRYING ABOUT ME.
YOU HELPED ME WORK IT OUT.
PUSH
SHFFT
UHH...
UHH...
WHAT?
PUSH
SEGAWA-KUN?
TWINKLE
TWINKLE
HMM?
UHH...
SO COOL!!
WOAA
COOL.
NOTHING.

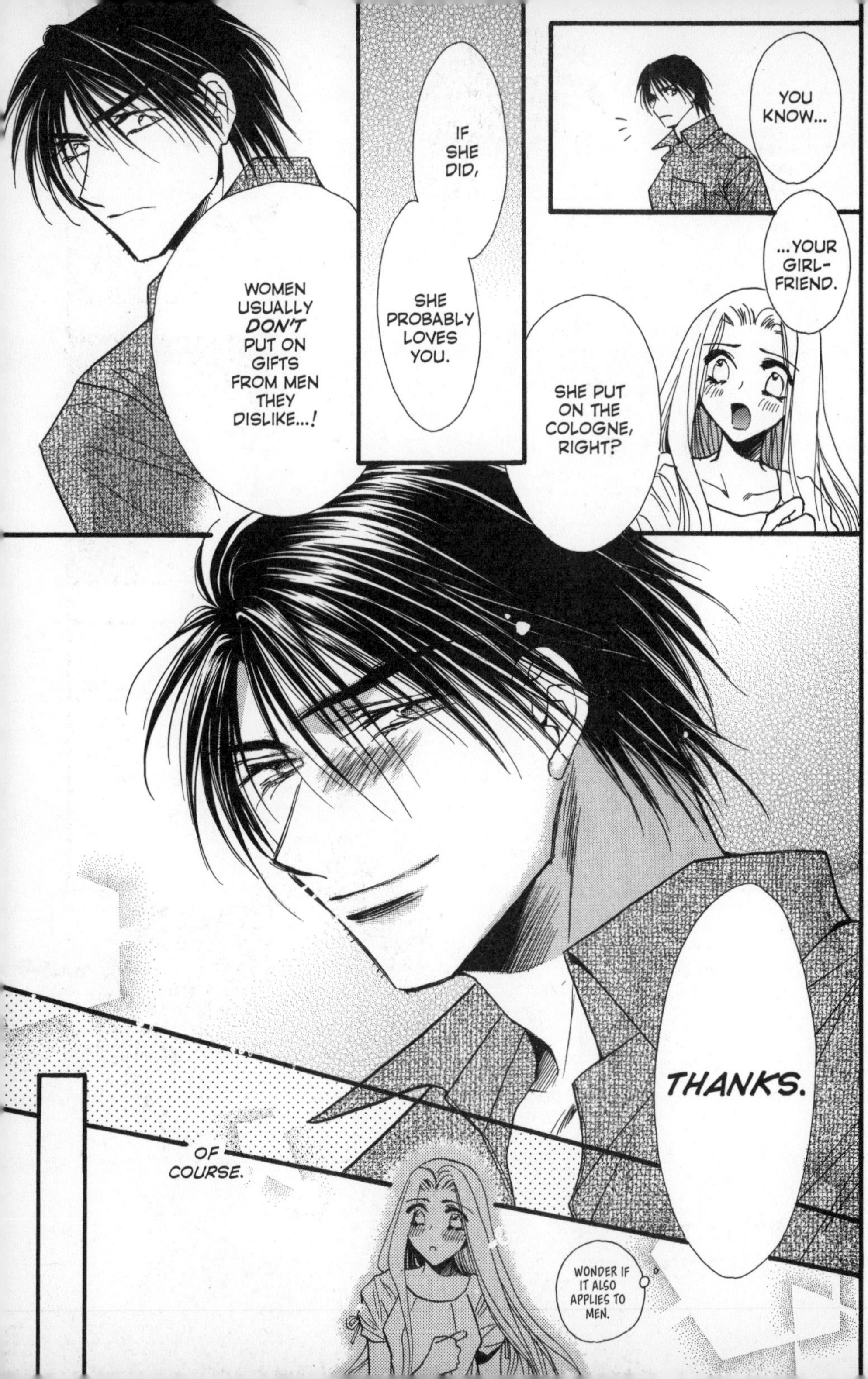
YOU KNOW...
...YOUR GIRL-FRIEND.
SHE PUT ON THE COLOGNE, RIGHT?
IF SHE DID,
SHE PROBABLY LOVES YOU.
WOMEN USUALLY *DON'T* PUT ON GIFTS FROM MEN THEY DISLIKE...!
THANKS.
WONDER IF IT ALSO APPLIES TO MEN.
OF COURSE.

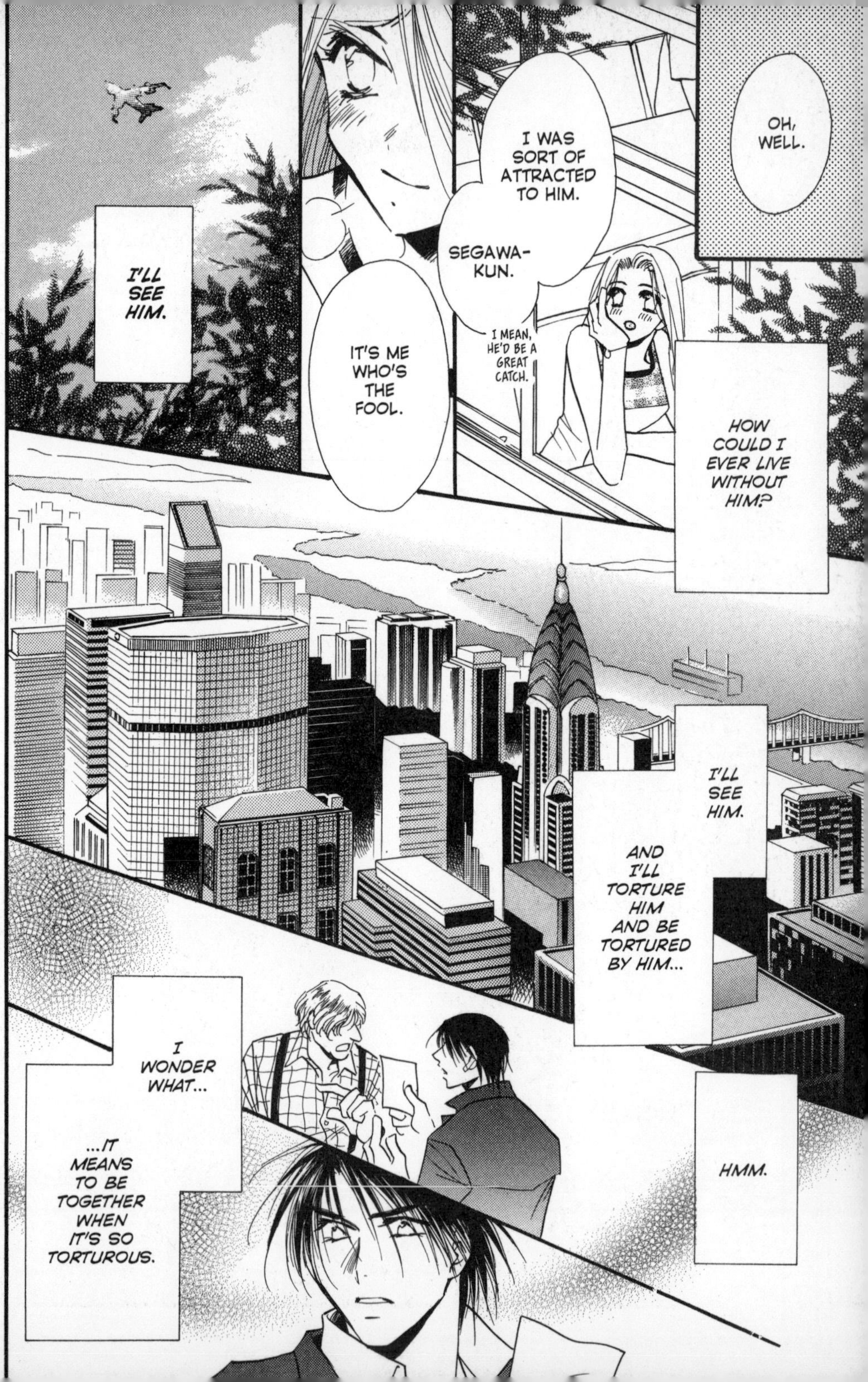
OH, WELL.
I WAS SORT OF ATTRACTED TO HIM.
I MEAN, HE'D BE A GREAT CATCH.
HOW COULD I EVER LIVE WITHOUT HIM?
SEGAWA-KUN.
IT'S ME WHO'S THE FOOL.
I'LL SEE HIM.
I'LL SEE HIM.
AND I'LL TORTURE HIM AND BE TORTURED BY HIM...
HMM.
I WONDER WHAT...
...IT MEANS TO BE TOGETHER WHEN IT'S SO TORTUROUS.

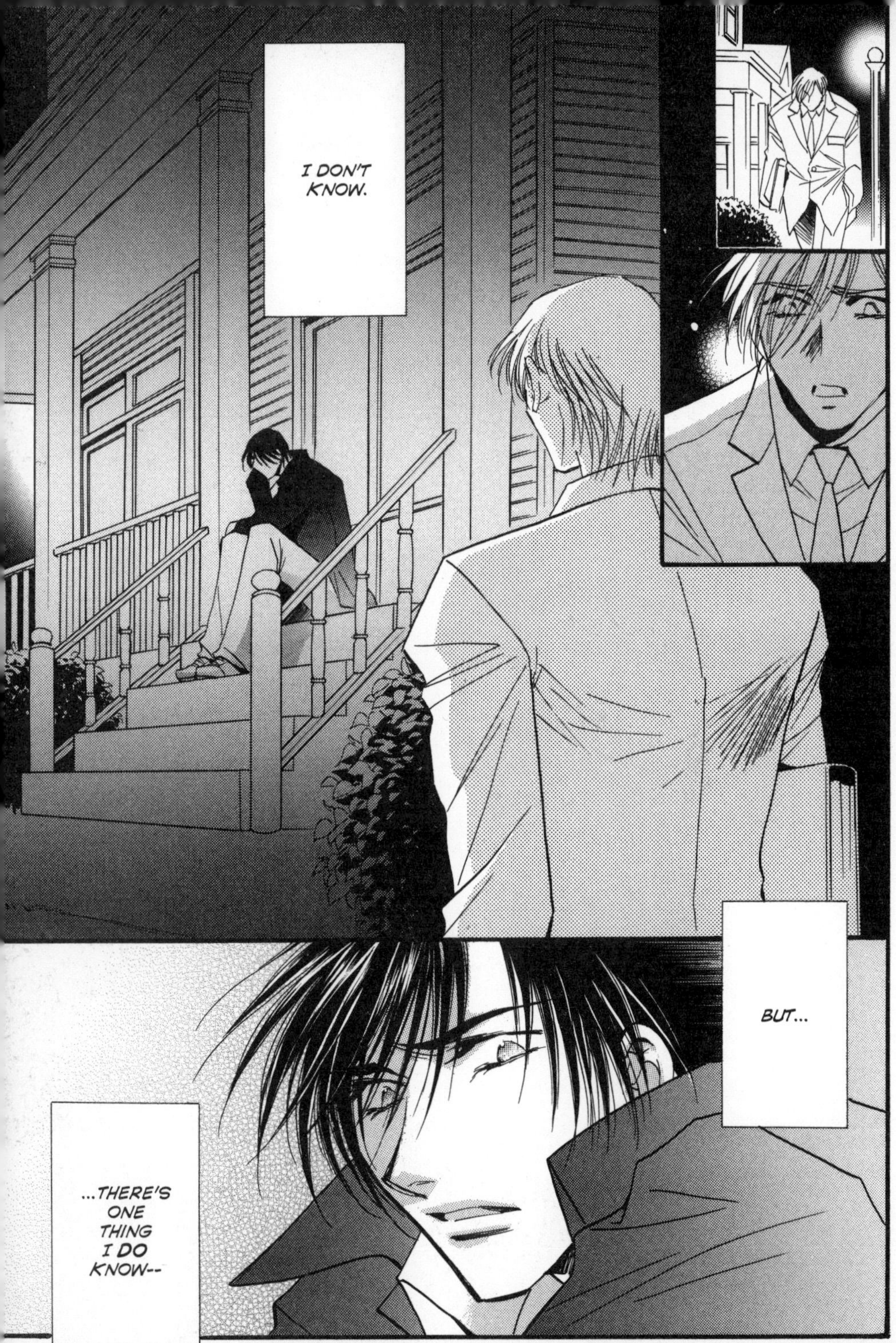
I DON'T KNOW.
BUT...
...THERE'S ONE THING I DO KNOW--

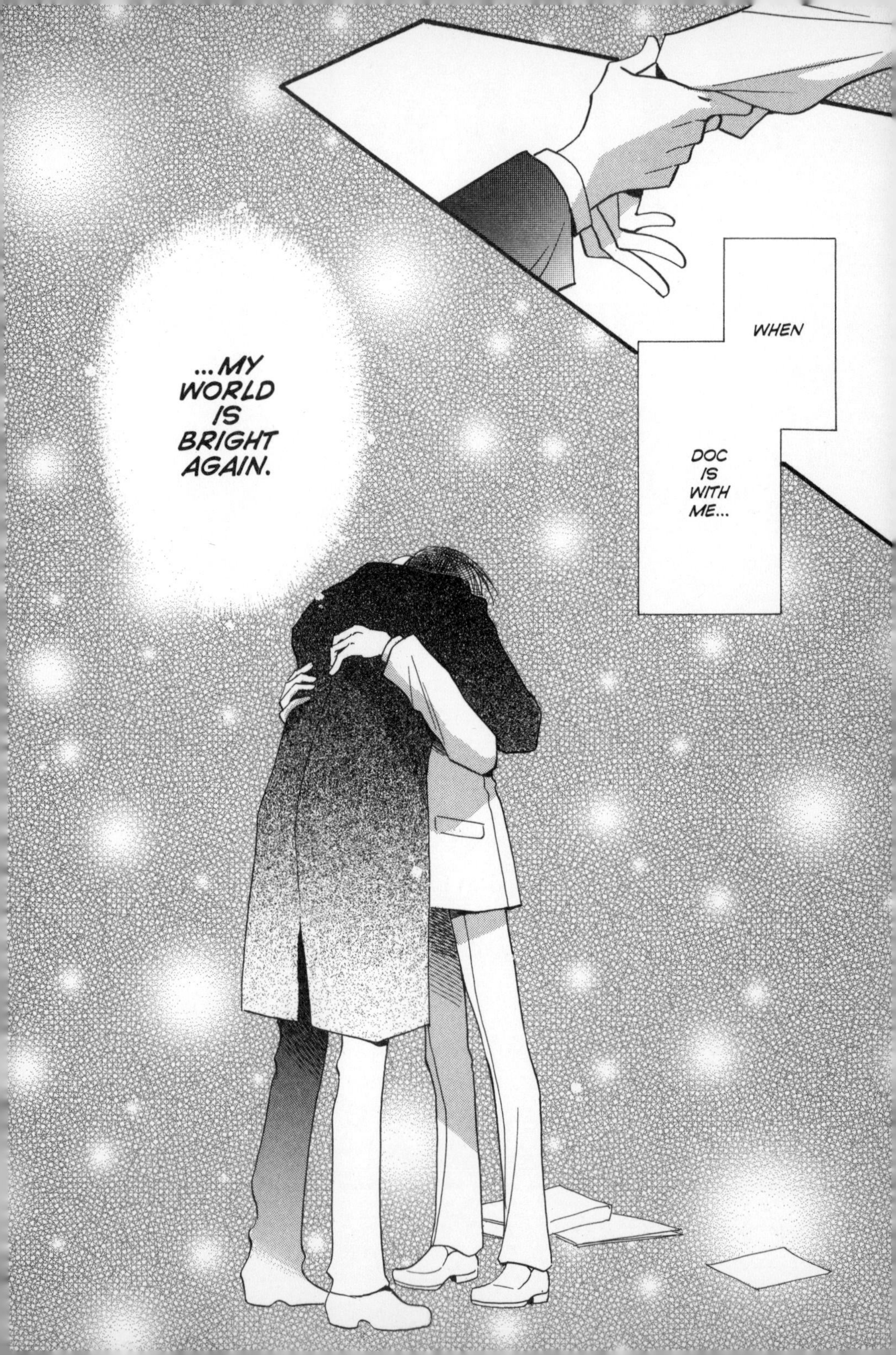
WHEN
DOC IS WITH ME...
...MY WORLD IS BRIGHT AGAIN.

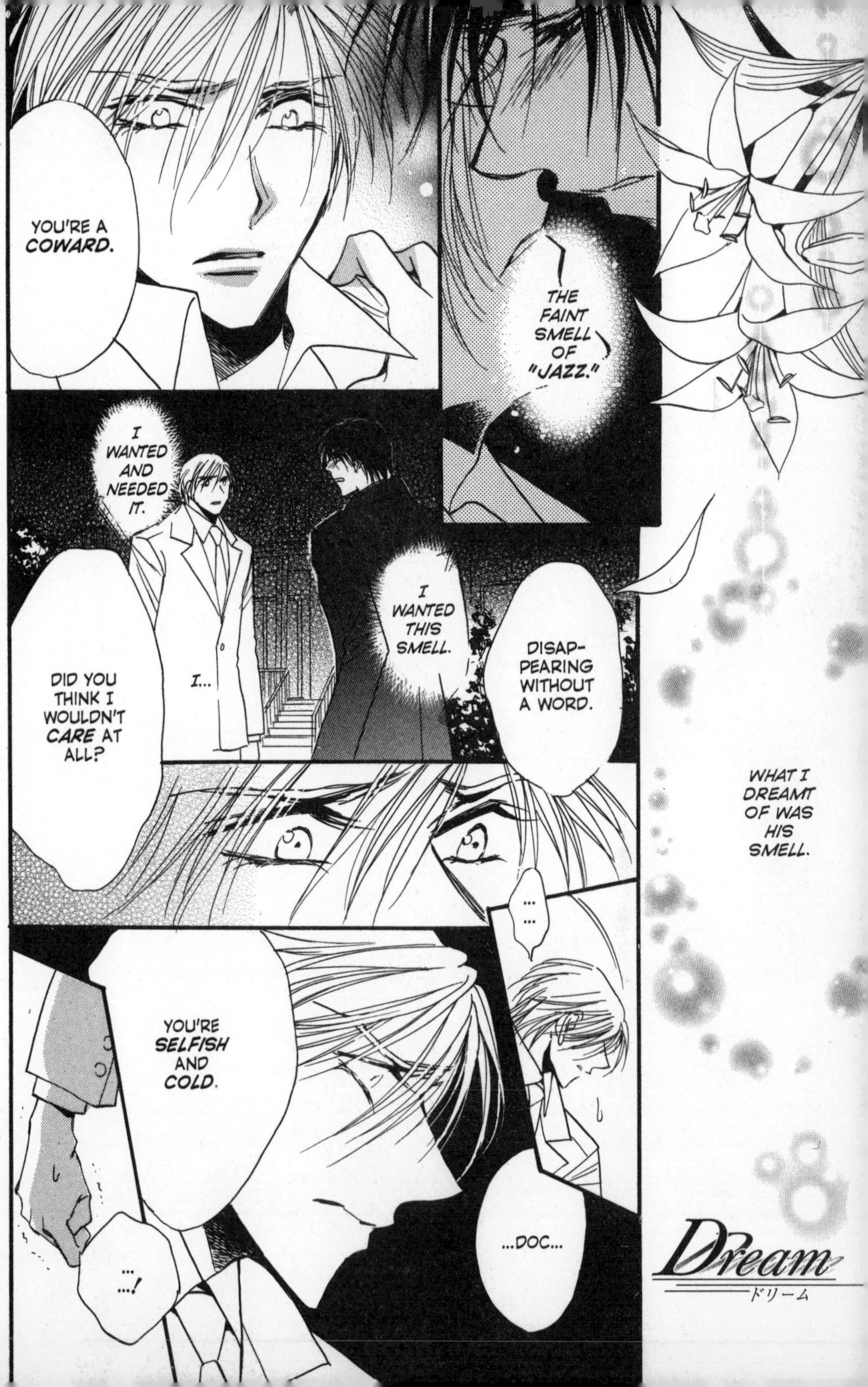
WHAT I DREAMT OF WAS HIS SMELL.
Dream
ドリーム
THE FAINT SMELL OF "JAZZ."
YOU'RE A COWARD.
DISAP-PEARING WITHOUT A WORD.
I WANTED AND NEEDED IT.
I WANTED THIS SMELL.
DID YOU THINK I WOULDN'T CARE AT ALL?
I...
......
YOU'RE SELFISH AND COLD.
...DOC...
...…!

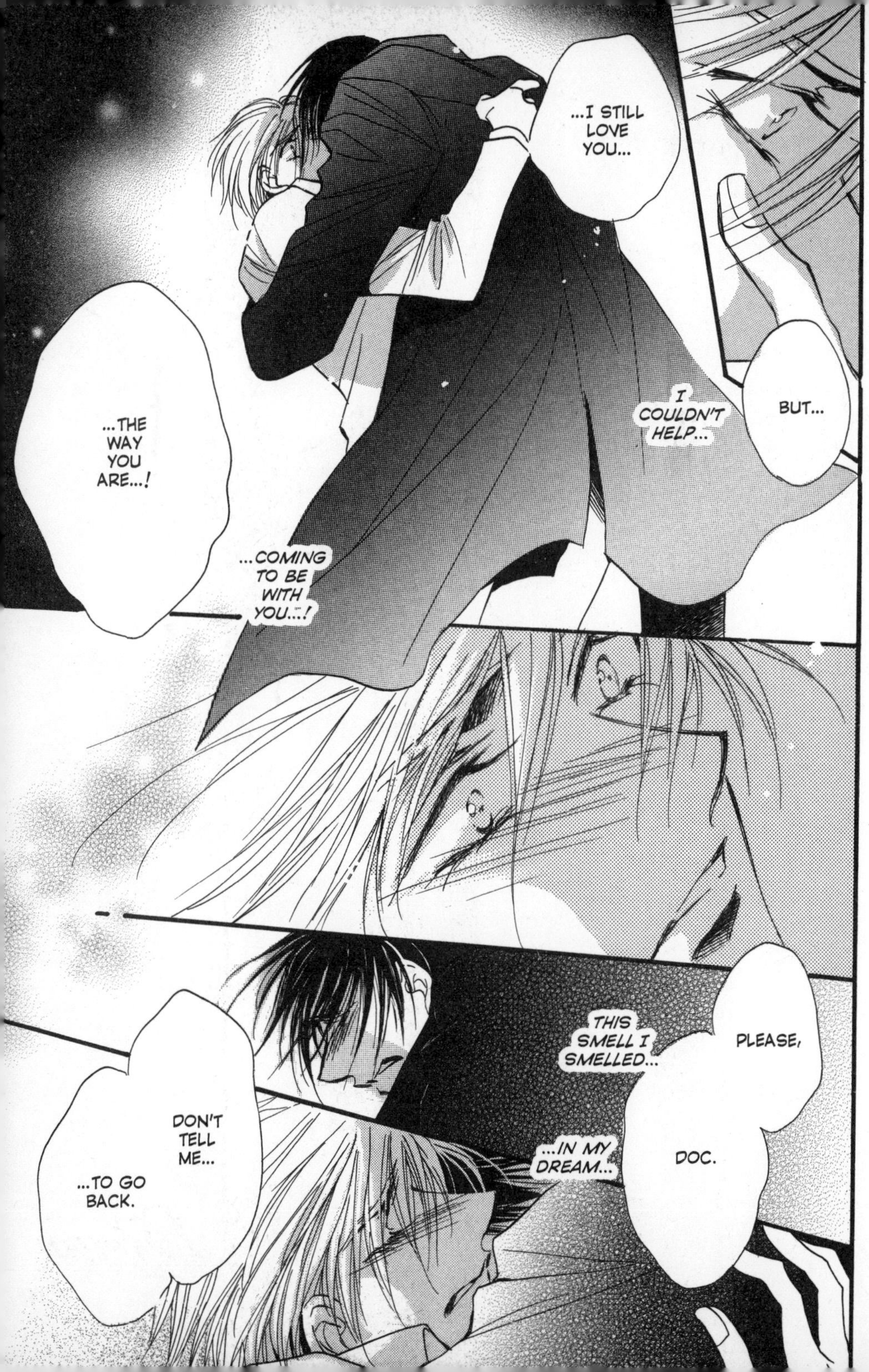
...I STILL LOVE YOU...
BUT...
I COULDN'T HELP...
...COMING TO BE WITH YOU...!
...THE WAY YOU ARE...!
PLEASE,
DOC.
THIS SMELL I SMELLED...
...IN MY DREAM...
DON'T TELL ME...
...TO GO BACK.

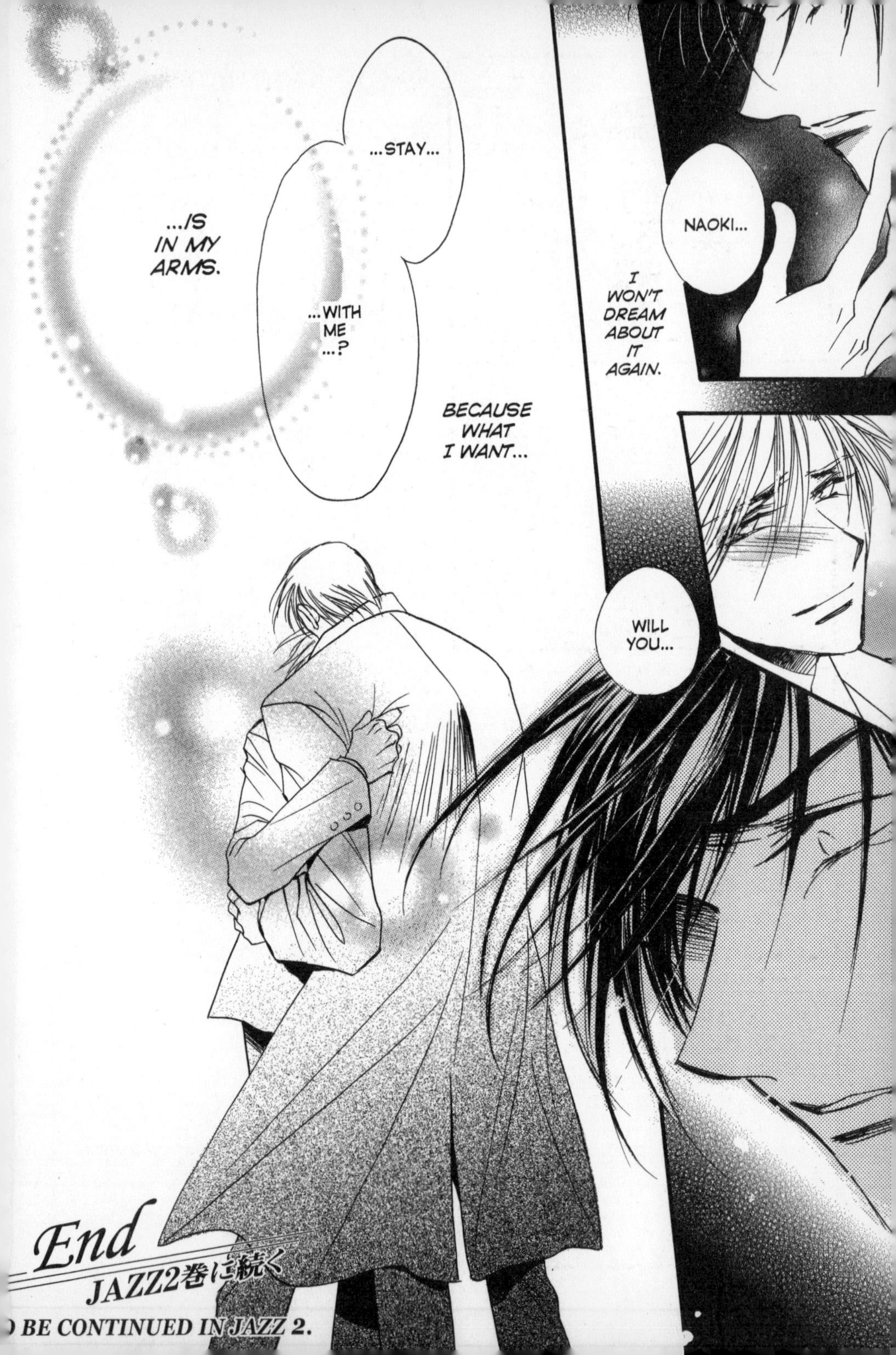
NAOKI...
I WON'T DREAM ABOUT IT AGAIN.
WILL YOU...
BECAUSE WHAT I WANT...
...STAY...
...WITH ME ...?
...IS IN MY ARMS.
End
JAZZ2巻に続く
O BE CONTINUED IN JAZZ 2.

HELLO, THIS IS TAKAMURE.

"JAZZ" STARTED AS A NOVEL WITH ILLUSTRATIONS, WHICH EVENTUALLY DEVELOPED INTO THE MANGA VERSION. IT'S IMPOSSIBLE TO TURN A NOVEL INTO A MANGA WITH EXACTLY THE SAME CONTENT (WITH ISSUES LIKE THE NUMBER OF PAGES TO BE USED AND ALL). SO I REVISED THE CONTENT, AND THE BIGGEST CHANGE WAS MADE WITH DR. NARUSAWA.

THE YOUNGER, ACTIVE PUPS ARE MY FAVORITE TYPE, AND THEREFORE, DR. NARUSAWA, A TOTALLY PASSIVE TYPE, IS A MYSTERY TO ME. I UNDERSTAND WHAT HE THINKS BUT DON'T UNDERSTAND WHY HE ENDS UP THINKING THAT WAY...NO MATTER HOW OFTEN I RE-READ THE ORIGINAL NOVEL, I FEEL SORRY FOR HIS UNFORTUNATE PERSONALITY.

IT'S MY MISSION TO MAKE THIS UNFORTUNATE PERSON HAPPY. I WONDER IF THE STORY WILL HAVE A HAPPY ENDING. (← HOW IRRESPONSIBLE OF ME?)

ANYHOW, I'D BE VERY HAPPY IF YOU COULD STICK WITH "JAZZ" THROUGH THE END.

I'LL SEE YOU AGAIN IN THE NEXT VOLUME.

TAMOTSU TAKAMURE

MAEDA-SAN, EDITOR-IN-CHARGE-SAMA, ASSISTANTS-SAN, THANK YOU FOR LOOKING AFTER ME (← SOME SAY I'M A BURDEN TO THEM). PLEASE CONTINUE TO HELP ME OUT. THANKS AGAIN.

MY NEPHEW IN THE 9TH GRADE.
BASKETBALL PLAYER?
WHEN I SAW HIM AFTER 6 MONTHS, HE GREW LIKE A WEED.
TALL & SKINNY
BABY FACE & SKINNY
WHAT? YOU'VE GOTTEN TALL.
69
BECAUSE MY BROTHER IS A LOT OLDER, HIS KID IS ALREADY THIS BIG.
ANOTHER 6 MONTHS LATER...
BIG MUSCULAR BUILD
HE LOOKED LIKE (NONE OTHER THAN) A COLLEGE STUDENT, SKIPPING THE HIGH SCHOOL PHASE.
A GROWN MAN?!
LAZY
EEK, WHO'S HE?
ONE YEAR LATER...
OVER 180 CM TALL.
TRULY BIG.
HE TURNED HIP HOP...
WHERE'RE YOU GOING NOW?
BIG
RUFF?
THE WORLD OF JAZZ IS REAL!!
BOYS CHANGE A LOT!
PUPS GROW UP IN JUST HALF A YEAR...

JAZZ

ジャズ

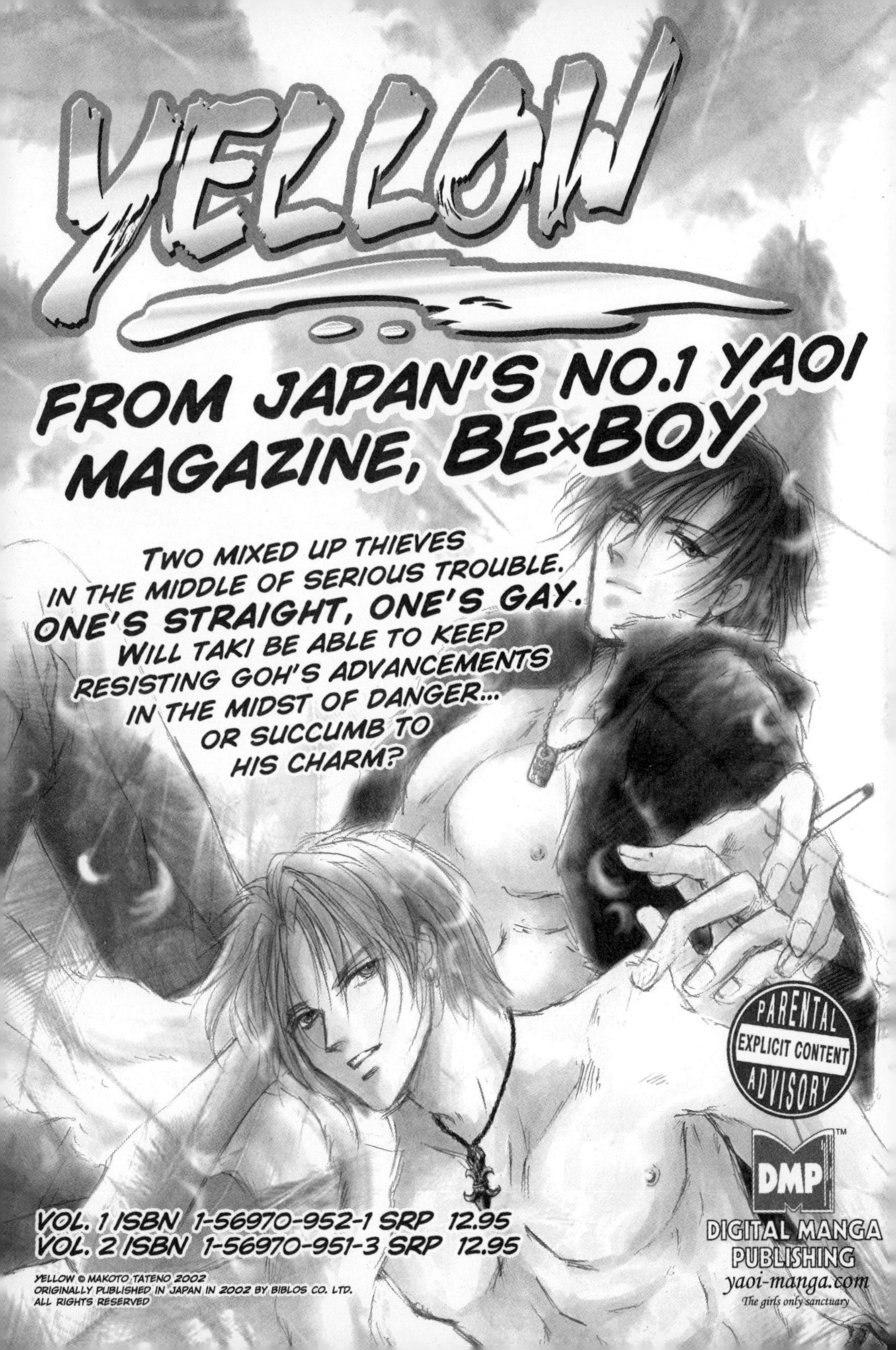
YELLOW
FROM JAPAN'S NO.1 YAOI MAGAZINE, BE×BOY
TWO MIXED UP THIEVES IN THE MIDDLE OF SERIOUS TROUBLE.
ONE'S STRAIGHT, ONE'S GAY.
WILL TAKI BE ABLE TO KEEP RESISTING GOH'S ADVANCEMENTS IN THE MIDST OF DANGER... OR SUCCUMB TO HIS CHARM?
PARENTAL ADVISORY EXPLICIT CONTENT
DMP
VOL. 1 ISBN 1-56970-952-1 SRP 12.95
VOL. 2 ISBN 1-56970-951-3 SRP 12.95
DIGITAL MANGA PUBLISHING
yaoi-manga.com
The girls only sanctuary
YELLOW © MAKOTO TATENO 2002
ORIGINALLY PUBLISHED IN JAPAN IN 2002 BY BIBLOS CO. LTD.
ALL RIGHTS RESERVED

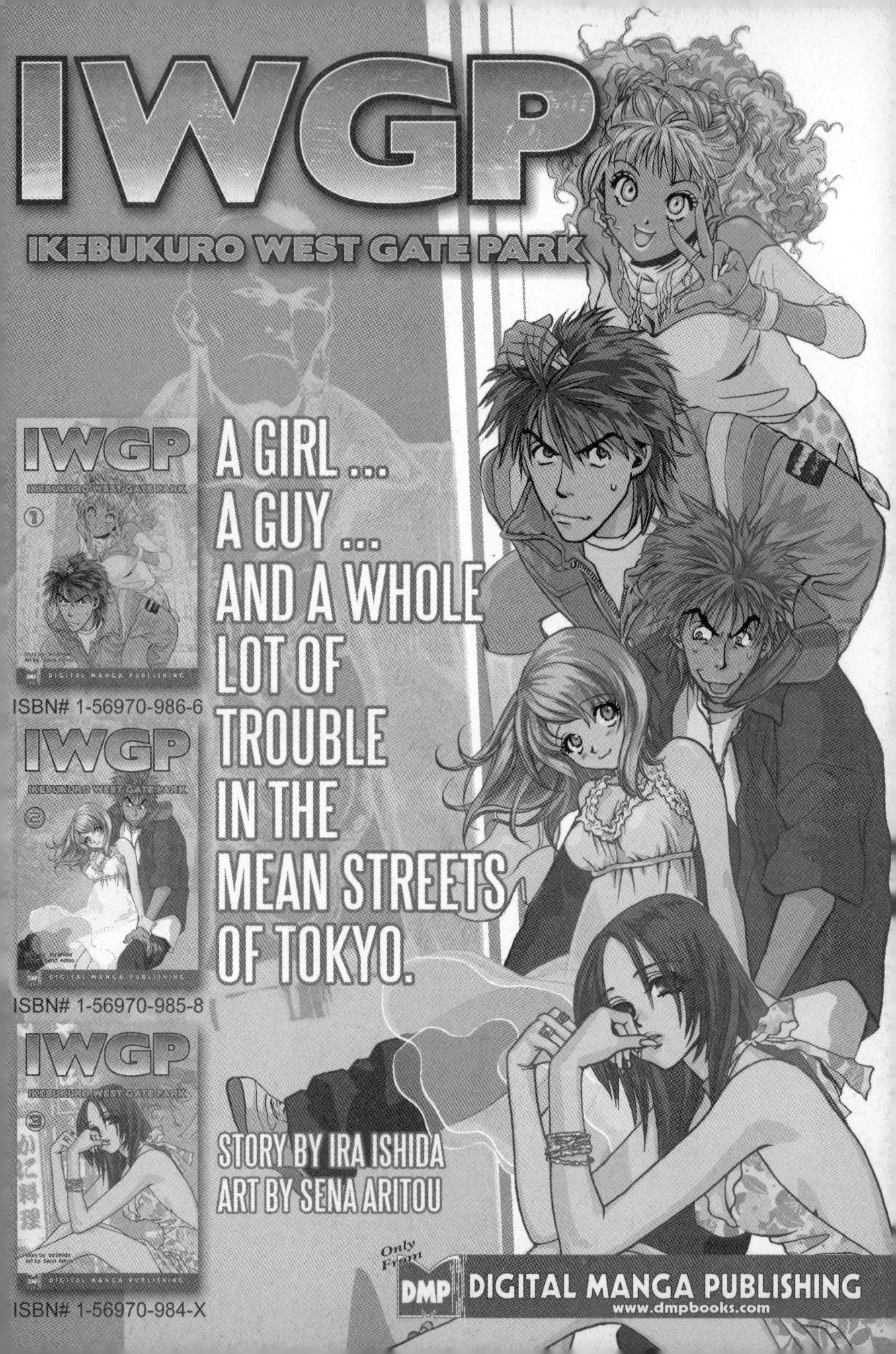
IWGP
IKEBUKURO WEST GATE PARK
A GIRL ...
A GUY ...
AND A WHOLE
LOT OF
TROUBLE
IN THE
MEAN STREETS
OF TOKYO.
ISBN# 1-56970-986-6
ISBN# 1-56970-985-8
ISBN# 1-56970-984-X
STORY BY IRA ISHIDA
ART BY SENA ARITOU
Only From
DMP DIGITAL MANGA PUBLISHING
www.dmpbooks.com

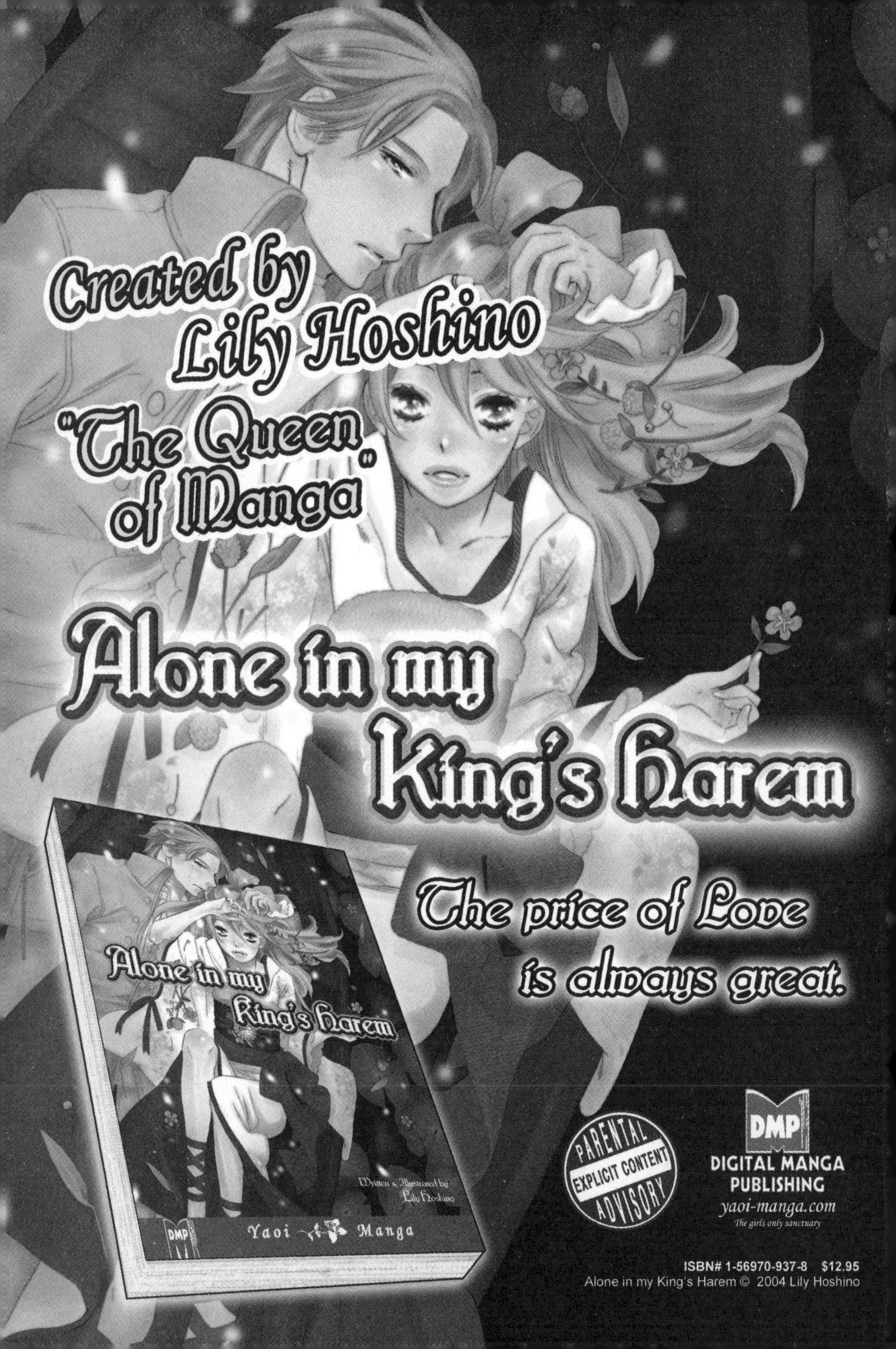

Created by
Lily Hoshino
"The Queen" of Manga
Alone in my
King's Harem
The price of Love
is always great.
Alone in my
King's harem
Written & Illustrated by
Lily Hoshino
DMP
Yaoi Manga
PARENTAL ADVISORY
EXPLICIT CONTENT
DMP
DIGITAL MANGA
PUBLISHING
yaoi-manga.com
The girls only sanctuary
ISBN# 1-56970-937-8 $12.95
Alone in my King's Harem © 2004 Lily Hoshino

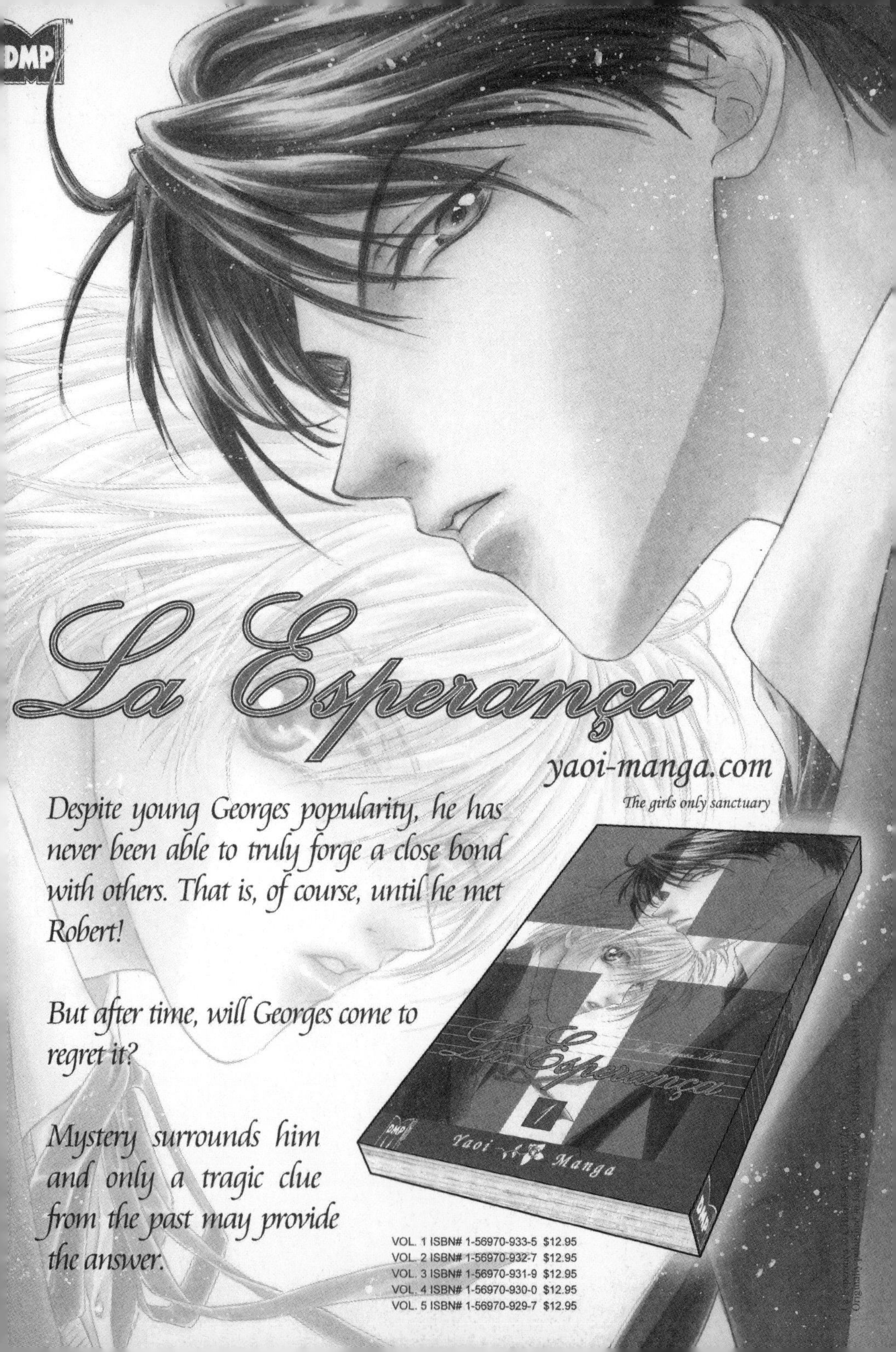

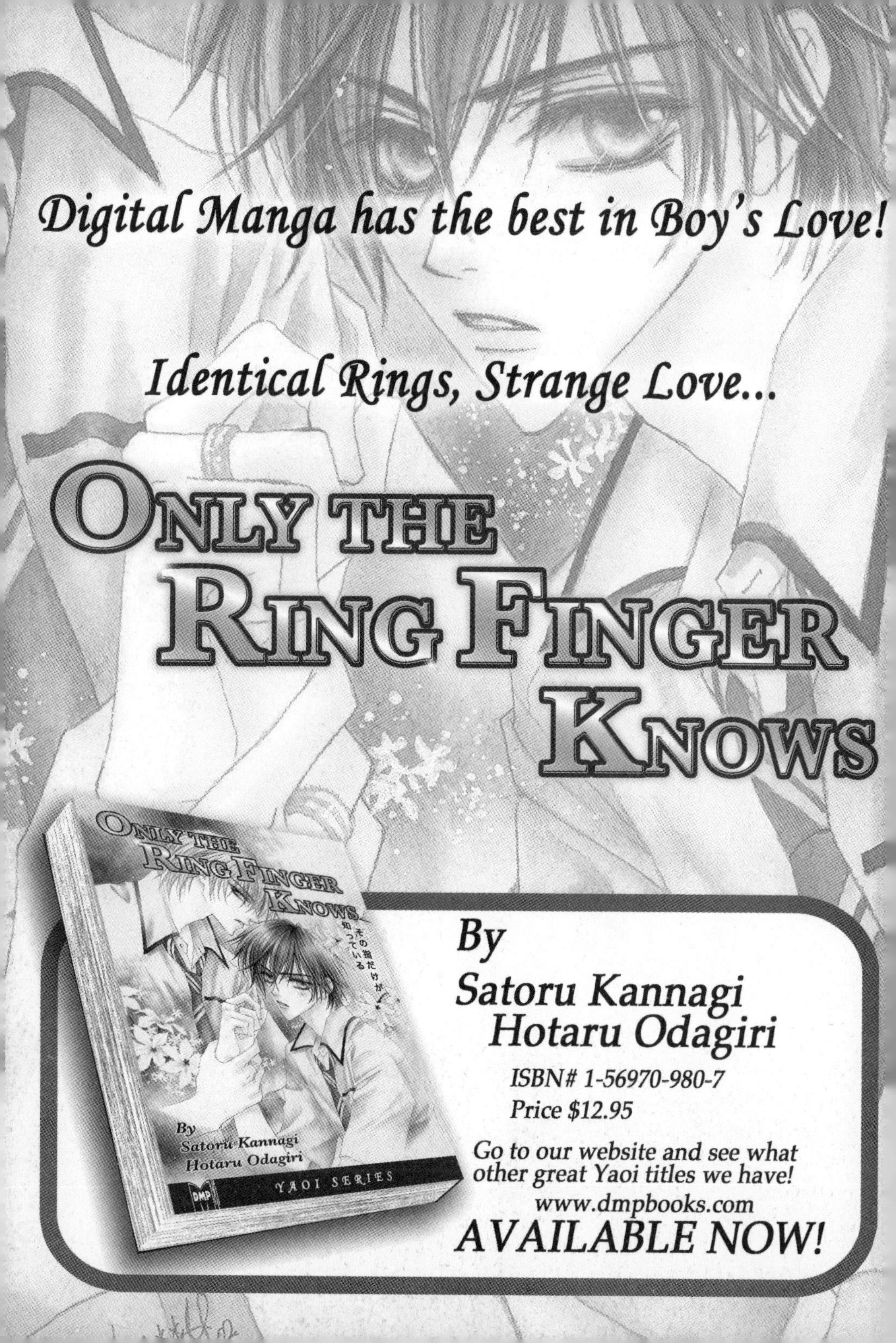
Digital Manga has the best in Boy's Love!
Identical Rings, Strange Love...
ONLY THE RING FINGER KNOWS
ONLY THE RING FINGER KNOWS
その指だけが知っている
By
Satoru Kannagi
Hotaru Odagiri
DMP
YAOI SERIES
By
Satoru Kannagi
Hotaru Odagiri
ISBN# 1-56970-980-7
Price $12.95
Go to our website and see what other great Yaoi titles we have!
www.dmpbooks.com
AVAILABLE NOW!

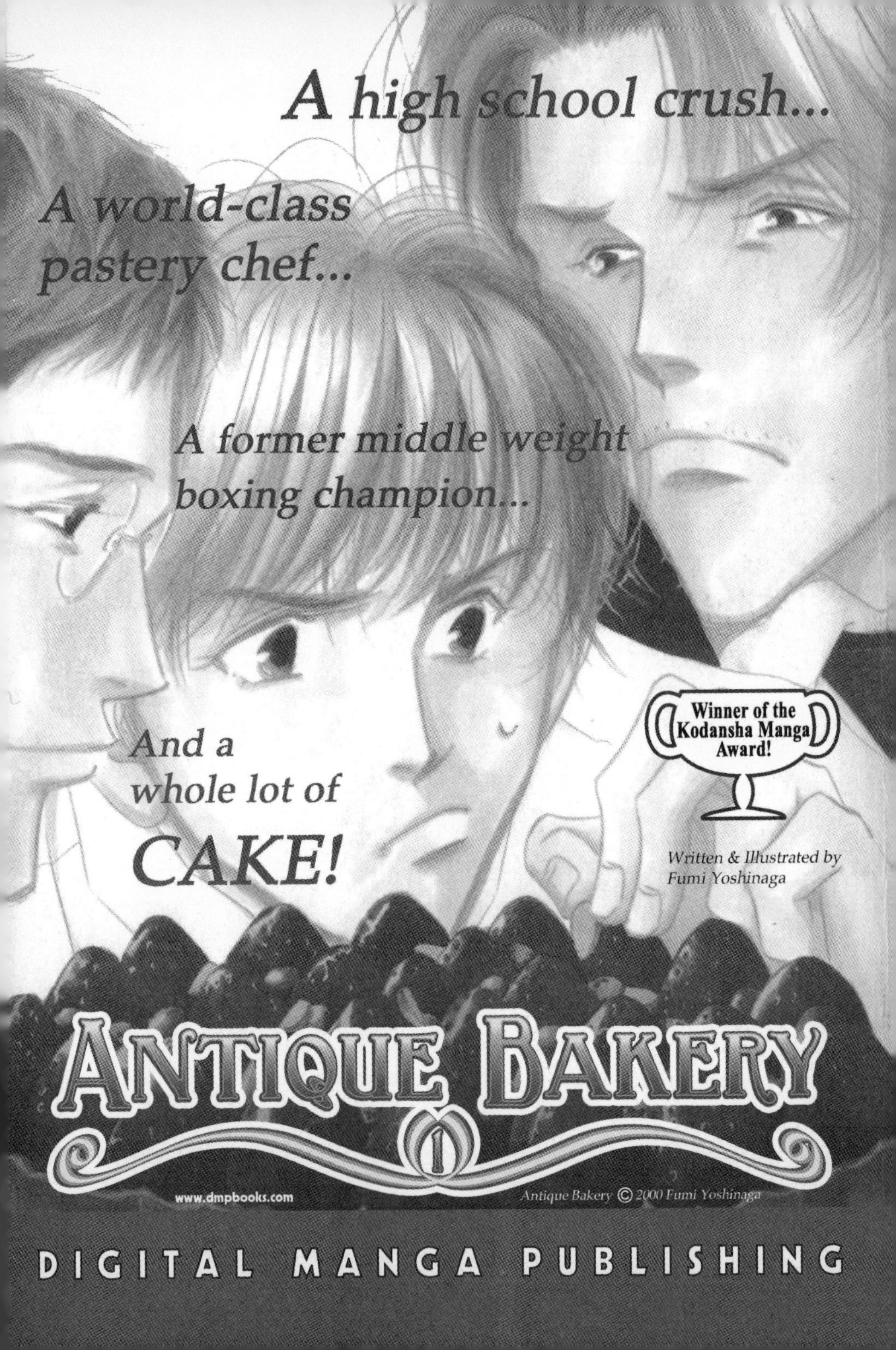
A high school crush...
A world-class pastery chef...
A former middle weight boxing champion...
And a whole lot of CAKE!
Winner of the Kodansha Manga Award!
Written & Illustrated by Fumi Yoshinaga
ANTIQUE BAKERY
1
www.dmpbooks.com
Antique Bakery © 2000 Fumi Yoshinaga
DIGITAL MANGA PUBLISHING

Two's company,
Three's a crowd.
Only one thing can keep them together...

DESIRE

ヤバイ気持ち

yaoi-manga.com
The girls only sanctuary!

PARENTAL ADVISORY
EXPLICIT CONTENT

by Maki Kazumi Yukine Honami
ISBN# 1-56970-979-3 SRP 12.95

Yaoi 🌹 Manga

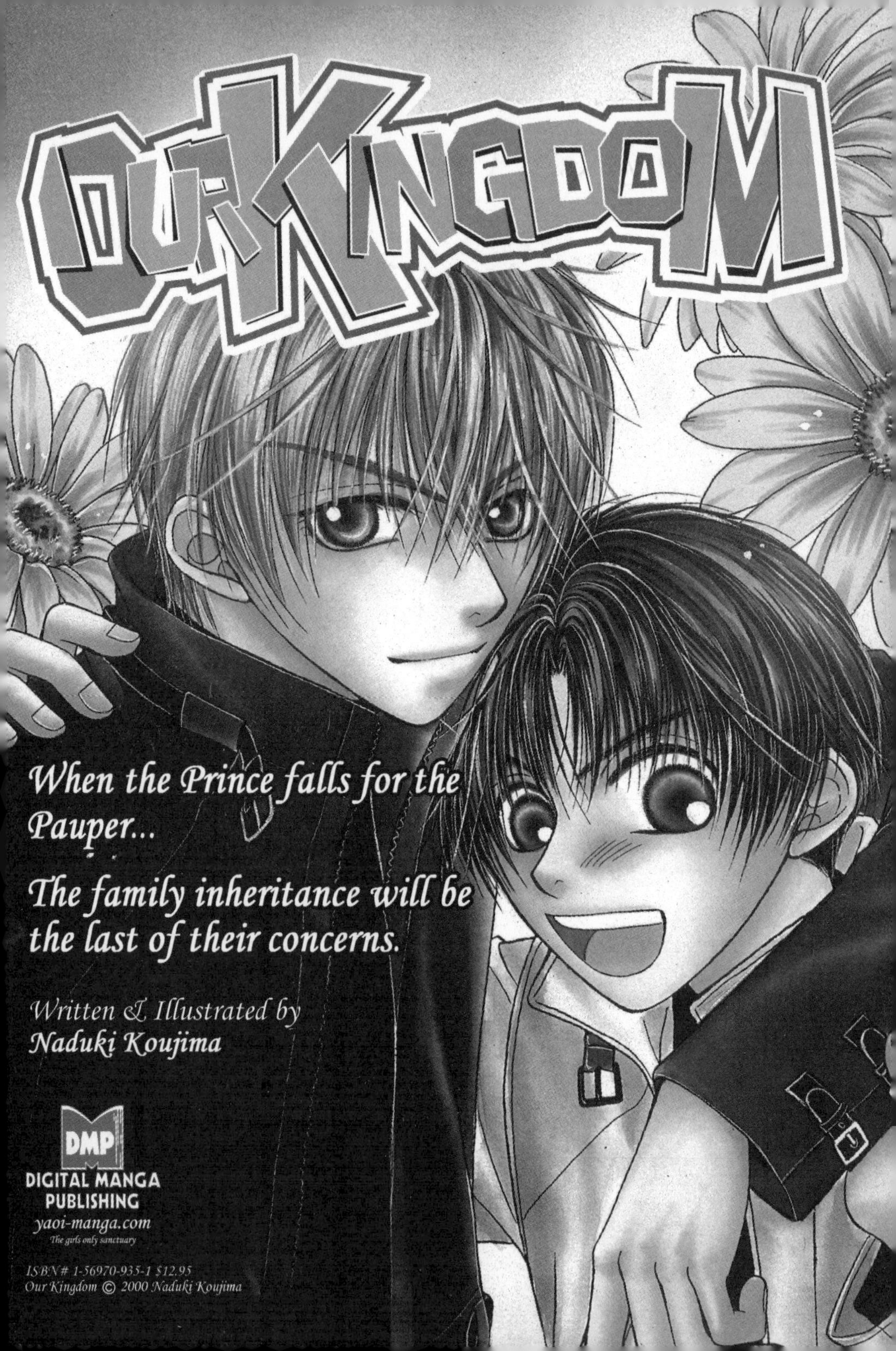
OUR KINGDOM
When the Prince falls for the Pauper...
The family inheritance will be the last of their concerns.
Written & Illustrated by
Naduki Koujima
DMP
DIGITAL MANGA PUBLISHING
yaoi-manga.com
The girls only sanctuary
ISBN# 1-56970-935-1 $12.95
Our Kingdom © 2000 Naduki Koujima

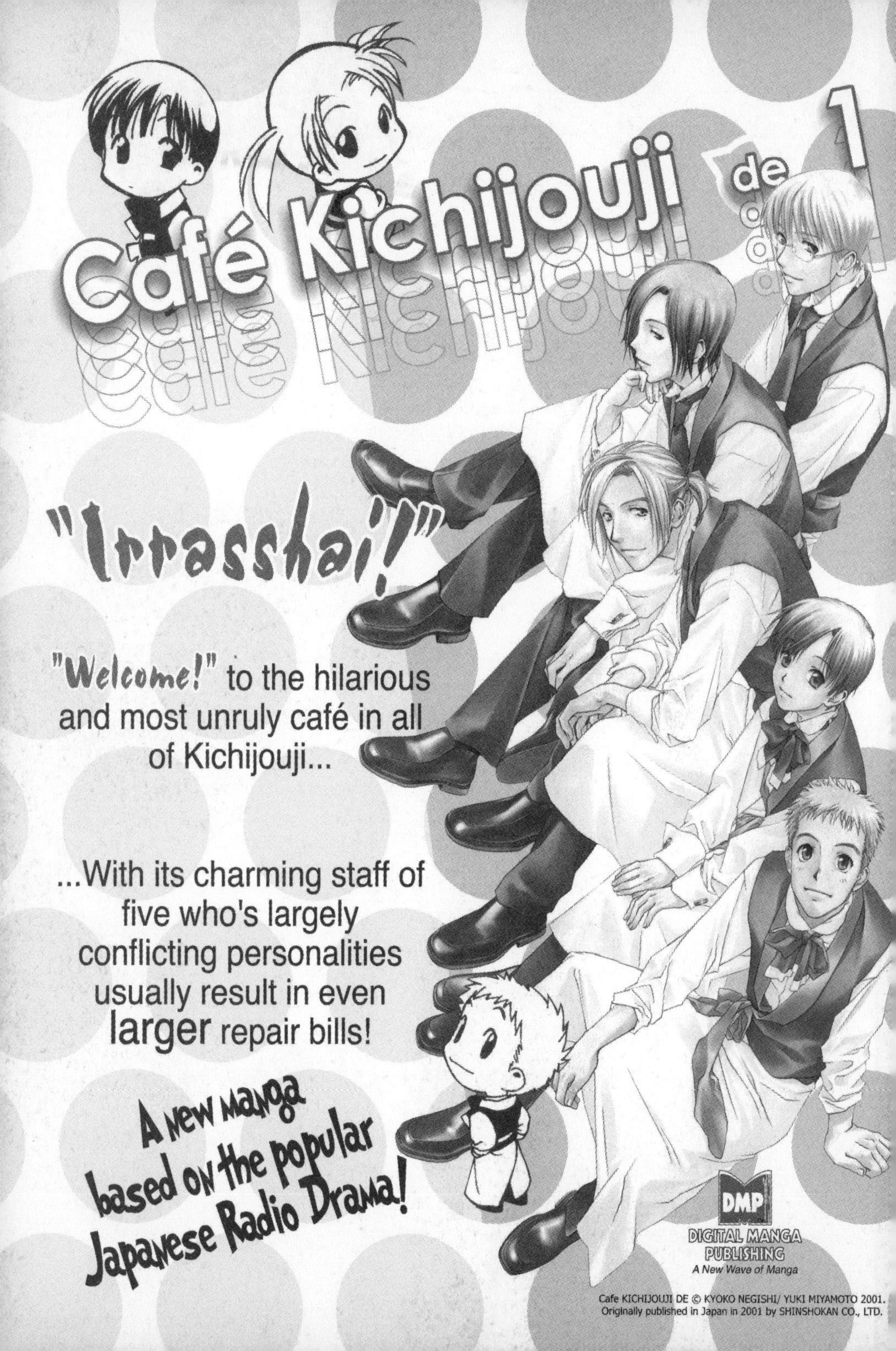
Café Kichijouji de 1
"Irrasshai!"
"Welcome!" to the hilarious and most unruly café in all of Kichijouji...
...With its charming staff of five who's largely conflicting personalities usually result in even larger repair bills!
A new manga based on the popular Japanese Radio Drama!
DMP
DIGITAL MANGA PUBLISHING
A New Wave of Manga
Cafe KICHIJOUJI DE © KYOKO NEGISHI/ YUKI MIYAMOTO 2001.
Originally published in Japan in 2001 by SHINSHOKAN CO., LTD.

STOP

This is the back of the book! Start from the other side.

NATIVE MANGA readers read manga from *right to left*.

1
2
1
3
2
3
5
4
4
6
5
8
7
6

*If you run into our **Native Manga** logo on any of our books... you'll know that this manga is published in it's true original native Japanese right to left reading format, as it was intended. Turn to the other side of the book and start reading from right to left, top to bottom.*

Follow the diagram to see how its done.
Surf's Up!

NATIVE MANGA
READ RIGHT TO LEFT